The Global Challenge of Intellectual Property Rights

A UCONN CIBER SUPPORTED RESEARCH INITIATIVE

CIBER is a program of the US Department of Education. The CIBER program's mandate is to enhance US competitiveness in the global business arena through activities involving US businesses, educators and students.

The Global Challenge of Intellectual Property Rights

Edited by

Robert C. Bird

University of Connecticut, USA

and

Subhash C. Jain

University of Connecticut, USA and Graduate School of Business, Switzerland

Edward Elgar

Cheltenham, UK • Northampton, MA, USA

Published by
Edward Elgar Publishing Limited
The Lypiatts
15 Lansdown Road
Cheltenham
Glos GL50 2JA
UK

Edward Elgar Publishing, Inc.
William Pratt House
9 Dewey Court
Northampton
Massachusetts 01060
USA

A catalogue record for this book
is available from the British Library

Library of Congress Control Number: 2008937105

PEFC
PEFC/16-33-111
CATG-PEFC-052
www.pefc.org

ISBN 978 1 84720 360 1

Printed and bound in Great Britain by MPG Books Ltd, Bodmin, Cornwall

Contents

Figures

Tables

Boxes

Contributors

Robert C. Bird

Robert C. Bird is Assistant Professor of Business Law at the University of Connecticut. Robert received his JD and MBA from Boston University. Robert's research interests include employment law and international intellectual property law, including compulsory licensing and foreign direct investment. Guest lectures include presentations at Indiana University, University of Texas, New York University and the United Nations. In 2004, Robert received the Junior Faculty of the Year award from the Academy of Legal Studies in Business. Robert has published research articles in the *American Business Law Journal*, *Boston University International Law Journal*, *Cincinnati Law Review*, *Journal of Law and Economics*, *Journal of Public Policy and Marketing*, *Kentucky Law Journal*, *Law and Society Review*, and the *Trademark Reporter*.

Daniel R. Cahoy

Dan Cahoy is Associate Professor of Business Law at Pennsylvania State University. He specializes in the teaching and study of intellectual property law, as well as related issues in technology law and general business law concepts. He has published numerous articles in academic law journals on topics such as FDA regulatory policy, the optimal policy for reforming the US patent system, the use of contracts to extend limited intellectual property rights, and the use of experimental economics to improve jury studies. Professor Cahoy has received particular recognition for his work on the impact of government takings (eminent domain power) on private patent rights. Professor Cahoy is a patent attorney, licensed to practice before the United States Patent and Trademark Office, and is admitted to the New York State Bar and several federal courts, including the United States Court of Appeals for the Federal Circuit.

Larry A. DiMatteo

Larry A. DiMatteo is the Huber Hurst Professor of Contract Law & Legal Studies at the Warrington College of Business Administration, University of Florida.

He received his JD from Cornell Law School and his LLM from Harvard Law School. He has a PhD in Business and Commercial Law from Monash University, Victoria, Australia. He is the former Chair of the Department of Management at the University of Florida and Editor-in-Chief of the *American Business Law Journal*. He is the author or co-author of about 50 publications including 7 books and 25 law review articles. His books include *International Law of Sales* (with Dhooge, Greene, Maurer and Pagnattaro) (Cambridge University Press), *Visions of Contract Theory: Rationality, Bargaining, and Interpretation* (with Prentice, Morant and Barnhizer) (Carolina

Academic Press), *International Business Law: A Transactional Approach* (with Dhooge) (West), and *Contract Theory: The Evolution of Contractual Intent* (Michigan State University Press). His articles have appeared in the *Harvard International Law Journal, Yale Journal of International Law, Northwestern Journal of International Law & Business, Vanderbilt Journal of Transnational Law, American Business Law Journal, Hofstra Law Review, University of Pittsburg Law Review, Penn State Law Review, Florida State Law Review, South Carolina Law Review, Michigan State Law Review, Rutgers Computer & Technology Law Journal, Cornell International Law Journal*, and the *Journal of Legal Studies Education*. His awards include the Ray August Master Teacher Award (2005), Ralph J. Bunche Award (2003), and Ralph C. Hoeber Award (2001).

Stephanie M. Greene

Stephanie Greene is an Associate Professor of Business Law at Boston College. She is a graduate of Princeton University, 1980, and Boston College Law School, 1984, where she served as Executive Editor of the *Boston College Law Review*. She is a member of the Massachusetts bar. She has practiced law in the Real Estate Department at Hale & Dorr.

Professor Greene's research interests include employment law and intellectual property issues. Her recent works include: 'Employee threshold on federal antidiscrimination statutes: A matter of the merits', *Kentucky Law Journal* (2007) (with C. O'Brien); 'Who counts? The United States Supreme Court Cites "Control" as the key to distinguishing employers from employees under federal employment antidiscrimination laws' *Columbia Business Law Review* (2003) (with C. O'Brien); 'Partners and shareholders as covered employees under federal antidiscrimination acts' *American Business Law Journal* (2003) (with C. O'Brien); *International Sales Law*, Cambridge University Press (2005) (with L. DiMatteo, G. Maurer and M. Pagnattaro); 'False claims act liability for off-label promotion of pharmaceutical products' *Penn State Law Review* (2005); 'A prescription for change: How the Medicare Act revises Hatch-Waxman to speed market entry of generic drugs' *Journal of Corporation Law* (2005); 'Sorting out "fair use" and "likelihood of confusion" in trademark law' *American Business Law Journal* (2006).

George T. Haley

George T. Haley (PhD, University of Texas at Austin) is tenured Professor of Industrial Marketing and International Business at the University of New Haven where he teaches in graduate and executive programs. He is also the founding Director of the Center for International Industry Competitiveness. His research deals with business strategies in emerging and industrial markets. His expertise includes strategic forecasting, B2B marketing, channels of distribution, branding, new product development, auditing of technology and the management of intellectual property in emerging markets.

Before he joined UNH, he taught at several universities worldwide, including the Instituto Tecnologico y de Estudios Superiores de Monterrey (Mexico), National University of Singapore, Queensland University of Technology (Australia), Thammasat University (Thailand), DePaul University (Chicago), Fordham University

(New York), Baruch College (New York) and Harvard University. He has presented seminars to academics, managers and government policy makers in the USA, Vietnam, Thailand, Finland, India, Singapore, Mexico, Australia, and New Zealand.

Professor Haley is the author of over 100 books, book chapters, articles, research reports and presentations. His books include *The Chinese Tao of Business: The Logic of Successful Business Strategy*, which the *Wall Street Journal* recommended as the only book on Asian business to buy in 2004; and *New Asian Emperors: The Overseas Chinese, their Strategies and Competitive Advantages*, the top-selling book on Asian business strategy worldwide in 1999. He is on the Review and Advisory boards of seven academic journals including *International Marketing Review*, *Industrial Marketing Management*, *Journal of Business & Industrial Marketing*, *Marketing Intelligence & Planning*, and the *Journal of Management Development*. He is the current Editor of *American Business Review*.

He has conducted policy analyses seminars for the National Intelligence Council/CIA on Business in Emerging Economies, and has testified before US Congress in May 2007 on his research on China. His research is regularly profiled in the popular media including the *Economist*, the *Los Angeles Times*, CNN, *Fortune* and the *Wall Street Journal*. He is listed in *Who's Who in America*. Professor Haley also consults with several multinational companies and governments in Asia, Australia, Latin America and the USA. He serves as advisor to the Strategic Planning Board of Rio Tinto, Ltd (Australia), the Export Promotion Board (State of Connecticut), and the Metal Manufacturers' Education and Training Alliance (METAL); and as mentor in DBM Associates' Corporate Global Supply Chain Mentoring Program.

Usha C.V. Haley

Usha Haley is currently a tenured Professor of International Business and Founding Director of the Global Business Center at the University of New Haven. She is also a Research Associate at the Economic Policy Institute in Washington, DC. Previously, she has held full-time faculty positions at the University of Tennessee-Knoxville, New Jersey Institute of Technology/Rutgers, Australian National University, National University of Singapore and ITESM-Monterrey, Mexico and taught classes in her expertise at Harvard University, Purdue University, and New York University, among others. Additionally, she has taught in major corporate, governmental and universities' executive-development programs, for top and middle managers and policy makers, in the United States, Australia, Russia, Mexico, Vietnam, Italy, Finland, India and Singapore. She received her PhD from the Stern School of Business, New York University. She also holds Masters degrees from New York University, the University of Wisconsin-Madison, and the University of Illinois at Urbana-Champaign, and a Bachelors degree from Elphinstone College, Bombay, India.

Dr Haley is author of more than 100 publications and presentations on multinational corporation and international strategic management, especially in Asian and emerging markets. Her books include *The Chinese Tao of Business: The Logic of Successful Business Strategy*; *New Asian Emperors: The Overseas Chinese, their Strategies and Competitive Advantages* and several others. Dr Haley consults on strategic management and foreign direct investment for several companies and governments worldwide, sits on six journal editorial boards, including the *Journal of International Management*, *Journal of Organizational Change Management*, *Management Decision*, *Asia Pacific Business Review*, and *Journal of Business Strategy*, and serves as Regional Editor (Asia Pacific) for two of these journals. Her expertise has been profiled over 100 times in the media and business publications including the *New York Times*, *Wall Street Journal*, *USA Today*, CNN, *Wall Street Journal* (Europe), *Forbes*, the *Economist*, *Barron's*, *Newsweek*, the *San Francisco Chronicle*, PBS's *WideAngle*, and Voice of America.

In 2003 she received a *Life-time Achievement Award* from the Literati Club (UK) and a panel of businesspersons, policy makers, and academics, for her contributions to the understanding of business in the Asia Pacific. She has testified on her research on China to the *US–China Economic and Security Review Commission* and twice before the *Committee on Ways and Means*, including on the pending federal legislation, the *Nonmarket Economy Trade Remedy Act of 2007*. She has also presented on her research to the *National Intelligence Council/CIA*. She is listed in *Who's Who in America*, *Who's Who in The World*, *American Women*, and *Who's Who in Business and Finance*. Additionally, she sits on three corporate and governmental boards of directors.

Subhash C. Jain

Subhash C. Jain PhD is Professor of International Marketing at the School of Business at the University of Connecticut, and has served as Director for the Center for International Business Education and Research (CIBER) since 1995. He is also Director of the GE Global Learning Center (GEGLC) at the University. His teaching, consulting and research activities include marketing strategy and multinational marketing. Dr Jain is the author of more than 100 publications, including articles in *Journal of Marketing Research*, *Journal of Marketing*, *Journal of International Marketing*; *Journal of Economic Abstracts*, *Long Range Planning*, *Journal of Applied Psychology*, and *Columbia Journal of World Business*. He is the author of several books, including *Marketing Planning and Strategy*, 6th edition (South-Western), *International Marketing*, 6th edition (South-Western), *Export Strategy* (Quorum Books), and *Market Evolution in Developing Countries* (Haworth Press).

Dr Jain has served on the Editorial Review Board of the *Journal of Marketing*, *Journal of International Business Studies*, and *Journal of the Academy of Marketing Science*. Currently, he serves on the Editorial Boards of *International Marketing Review*, *Journal of Global Marketing* and *Journal of International Marketing*. He is an active member of a number of professional organizations, including the American Marketing Association and the Academy of International Business.

Dr Jain has presented seminars, both in the United States and in other countries, and has frequently served as a consultant to such organizations as Xerox Corporation, General Electric, Aetna Life & Casualty, GATT (now WTO), United Technologies Corporation, Mead Corporation, General Motors, NCR, Control Data, Pitney Bowes, and Corning Glass. He has advised government agencies in Malaysia, Chile, India, Pakistan, St Lucia, Kenya, and Indonesia on their trade problems.

Dr Jain carried out his graduate work at the University of Oregon, Stanford University, and the University of Rajasthan, India.

Douglas Lippoldt

Douglas Lippoldt is a senior economist and policy analyst with the Organisation for Economic Co-operation and Development in Paris (1992 – present). His current assignment in the OECD Science, Technology and Industry Directorate focuses on innovation, industry and entrepreneurship. In recent years, he has published a number of papers, briefs, and articles on intellectual property and development issues. During the 1990s he managed a number of projects related to economic transition in Russia and Eastern Europe, producing a series of publications on adjustment-related topics. He was also a contributing author for a series of labor market studies of OECD member countries. Prior to coming to the OECD, he worked for ten years for the US Government as an international economist on trade policy, labor market and economic development issues. Currently, he has an academic affiliation with the Groupe d'Economie Mondiale at Sciences Po in Paris.

Willajeanne F. McLean

Willajeanne F. McLean teaches courses in trademarks, European Union law, and torts, as well as a seminar on intellectual property law in the European Union at the University of Connecticut School of Law. A French Literature and European History major at Wellesley, Professor McLean also has a degree in Microbiology from the University of Massachusetts-Amherst. After working in a research lab at Sloan-Kettering Cancer Institute, Professor McLean attended law school at Fordham University. She practiced law at Darby & Darby, an intellectual property firm, where her main work was in the field of trademark law. In addition to her law studies in the United States, Professor McLean attended the Free University of Brussels where she obtained a degree in European Law. Prior to joining the faculty at Connecticut, she was an intern in the Competition Division of the European Commission. More recently, Professor McLean was a Fulbright fellow at Adam Mickiewicz University in Poznan, Poland, where she taught comparative European Union and US intellectual property law, and lectured at the Intellectual Property Law Institute of the Jagiellonian University in Cracow, Poland. Her research interests include the interface of intellectual property and European competition law.

Lynda J. Oswald

Lynda J. Oswald is a Professor of Business Law at the Stephen M. Ross School of Business at the University of Michigan. Her research focuses on intellectual and real property law issues, including environmental liability issues and land use law. She has served as the Louis and Myrtle Moskowitz Research Professor of Law and Business and as a Contributing Editor to the *Real Estate Law Journal*. She is currently the Editor of the *Michigan Real Property Review*. She has taught at the University of Florida Law School, the University of Michigan Law School, China University of Political Science and Law in Beijing and L'viv State University in Ukraine. Professor Oswald has received numerous awards for her research, including the Hoeber Memorial Award and the Holmes-Cardozo Award for Research Excellence from the *American Business Law Journal*. Her work has been cited by numerous courts, including the US Supreme Court in *United States v Bestfoods*. She is the author of a book entitled *The Law of Marketing* (West, 2002). Professor Oswald is also past President of the Academy of Legal Studies in Business.

Marisa Anne Pagnattaro

Marisa Anne Pagnattaro is an Associate Professor of Legal Studies at the Terry College of Business at the University of Georgia, where she teaches courses on business law and international legal transactions. She is a co-author of *International Sales Law: A Critical Analysis of CISG Jurisprudence*, Cambridge University Press (2005) (with L. DiMatteo, L. Dhooge, S. Greene and G. Maurer) and *The Legal and Regulatory Environment of Business* (14th edn). She is also the author of the book *In Defiance of the Law*, as well as numerous articles which have been published in journals such as the *Northwestern Journal of International Law & Business*, *Vanderbilt Journal of Transnational Law*, the University of Pennsylvania *Journal of Labor and Employment Law*, and the *Berkeley Journal of Employment and Labor Law* (forthcoming). Prior to teaching, she was a litigation associate with Kilpatrick & Cody (now known as Kilpatrick Stockton LLP) in Atlanta.

Lucille M. Ponte

Lucille Ponte is an Associate Professor of Law at Florida Coastal School of Law (ABA-approved) in Jacksonville, FL where she teaches cyberlaw and contracts. She previously taught cyberlaw at the University of Central Florida in Orlando, FL and Bentley College and the McCallum Graduate School of Business in Waltham, MA. She has written two books, several manuals, and numerous national and regional law review articles on cyberlaw and alternative/online dispute resolution (ADR/ODR). Her most recent book is *Cyberjustice: Online Dispute Resolution for E-Commerce* (Prentice Hall, 2005) (with Prof. Thomas D. Cavenagh, JD). Her research has also addressed moral rights in the online world, copyright infringement in digital sampling disputes, the use of workplace emails in employment discrimination cases, the need for fair and effective ODR methods and procedures, and the proposed development of the first public virtual courthouse in Michigan. These articles appeared in such national law journals as the *B. U. International Law Journal*, *North Carolina Journal of Law & Technology*, *Ohio State Journal on Dispute Resolution*, *Tulane Journal of Technology and Intellectual Property*, and *Albany Law Journal of Science & Technology*. She has twice received the national Hoeber Memorial Award for excellence in pedagogical research for cyberlaw topics. In addition, she was selected as a national finalist for both the 2005 Holmes-Cardozo Award for scholarship excellence for an article on digital sampling and the 2003 Hewitt Master Teacher Competition. Professor Ponte is an external advisory board member for the Bentley College Global Cyberlaw Center in Massachusetts. A member of the Massachusetts bar, she previously served as in-house counsel for technology firms and governmental agencies.

Donald G. Richards

Donald Richards is Professor of Economics at Indiana State University. He specializes in international and development economics. His current research is on the multilateral trading system and intellectual property rights. Dr Richards earned his PhD from the University of Connecticut in 1983.

Robert E. Thomas

Robert Thomas is Associate Professor of Business Law and Legal Studies, and Huber Hurst Fellow in the Warrington College of Business Department of Management at the University of Florida and Invited Professor at the Institut D'Administration Des Entreprises D'Aix-en-Provence, France. He is an expert in the areas of negotiation, intellectual property and technology law and has published numerous articles in these areas. He teaches business law, intellectual property and technology law, and negotiation courses in the Warrington College graduate programs. His courses are typically among the most popular elective offerings in the Florida MBA curriculum, and he has received awards for excellence in teaching and research. Prior to his University of Florida appointment, Professor Thomas held dual faculty appointments in the University of Michigan Department of Economics and the University of Michigan Business School.

Professor Thomas has lectured throughout the United States and Western Europe. In 1999 he was the Whitney Young Visiting Professorship of Legal Studies at the Wharton School of Business at the University of Pennsylvania. His current research examines factors that influence decision-making in regulatory and legislative bodies, and how interest groups influence the development of copyright and patent laws.

Professor Thomas graduated from Princeton University with honors in economics. He received his JD and PhD in economics from Stanford University.

V.C. Vivekanandan

Professor (Dr) V.C. Vivekanandan is the HRD IP Chair Professor of Law and the Director of NALSAR Proximate Education at the National Academy of Legal Studies and Research University of Hyderabad. He specializes in intellectual property laws, cyber laws, and media laws. He directs the Proximate Education Programs of NALSAR University, offering the Post Graduate Diploma Programs in patents law, cyber laws, media laws, and international humanitarian law.

He received his PhD in 'Impact of TRIPS on IP legal regime in India – with special reference to Patents and Health care' from the National Law School of India University, Bangalore. He has a Master's Degree in Corporate Law and Securities. He also holds a Master's Degree and M. Phil degree in Public Administration from Madras University.

He is a visiting faculty of the Business School of University of Buffalo, SUNY. He is also a visiting faculty for programs at AP Judicial Academy, Administrative Staff College of India, Hyderabad; National Police Academy, Hyderabad; National Academy of Direct Taxes, Nagpur; National Law School of India, Bangalore; MHRD Institute, Hyderabad; National Academy of Agricultural Research and Management, Hyderabad, and the Indian School of Business at Hyderabad.

He also heads NC Banerjee Centre for IP law studies at NALSAR. He serves as the expert committee member of the IPR for the Copyright Division of the Ministry of HRD, Government of India, member of the 'Special Interest Group' of the Association of Biotech-led Enterprises (ABLE) Bangalore. He is also a consultant for the ISTE-ASTE programme for IPR, IPR programs for DSIR, member of bioethics committee of the APIDC Venture capital fund, and founding member and legal advisor to Engineers Without Borders (EWB) (India).

His latest publications include *Patents for Biotechnology* for ISTE-AICTE; *Patents – A Primer* for DSIR; *IP in Agriculture*; *IP in Information Technology*; *IP in Biotechnology and Life Forms*; *Patent Examination – Manual for Patent Controllers and Examiners* for Indo German.

Bernard Yeung

Bernard Yeung is the Dean and Stephen Riady Distinguished Professor of Finance, NUS Business School, National University of Singapore, and the Abraham Krasnoff Professor in Global Business, Professor in Economics and Professor in Management at New York University Stern School of Business. He is also the Director of the NYU China House, the honorary co-chair of the Strategy Department of the Peking University Guanghua School of Management, and Advisory Professor at the East China Normal University.

Professor Yeung's research covers topics in international corporate finance, corporate strategy, foreign direct investment, and the relationship between institutions, economic development, and firm behavior. Over one hundred of his research articles have appeared in top rated journals in Economics, Finance, Strategic Management, International Business, and Accounting. He is currently serving as a Senior Consulting Editor of the *Journal of International Business Studies*, on the Editorial board of the *Academy of Management Review*, and as an associate editor of *Management Science*. Dr Yeung is also an elected AIB fellow.

Dr Yeung received his BA in economics and mathematics from the University of Western Ontario and his MBA and PhD from the Graduate School of Business at the University of Chicago. Dr. Yeung previously taught at the University of Michigan (assistant, associate and full) and the University of Alberta (assistant and associate). Dr Yeung's website is: http://pages.stern.nyu.edu/~byeung/

Peter K. Yu

Peter K. Yu (余家明) is the Kern Family Chair in Intellectual Property Law and the founding director of the Intellectual Property Law Center at Drake University Law School. He is also a Wenlan Scholar Chair Professor at Zhongnan University of Economics and Law in Wuhan, China. In the summer, he served as Visiting Professor of Law at the University of Hong Kong Faculty of Law. Before joining Drake University he founded the nationally-renowned Intellectual Property and Communications Law Program at Michigan State University, at which he held faculty appointments in law, communication arts and sciences, and Asian studies.

Born and raised in Hong Kong, Professor Yu is a leading expert in international intellectual property and communications law. He also writes and lectures extensively on international trade, international and comparative law, and the transition of the legal systems in China and Hong Kong. An editor or co-editor of three books, Professor Yu has spoken at events organized by the ITU, UNCTAD, WIPO and the Chinese, Hong Kong and US governments as well as at leading research institutions from around the world. His lectures and presentations have spanned more than 15 countries on five continents, and he is a frequent commentator in the national and international media. His publications are available on his website at www.peteryu.com.

Minyuan Zhao

Minyuan Zhao is Assistant Professor of Strategy at the Ross School of Business, University of Michigan. She earned her PhD from Stern School of Business, New York University in May 2004. Before joining Michigan, Minyuan was Assistant Professor at the University of Minnesota, where she taught Strategy and International Environment classes to MBA and EMBA students. Minyuan's research interests are in the interaction between firm strategies and external environments in a global context. Her research papers on multinational R&D organization received first place in the 2003 INFORMS Dissertation Proposal Competition, the 2004 BPS Best Paper Award at the Academy of Management, and the 2006 Best Conference Paper Award at the Strategic Management Society. Her recent studies examine how internal linkages among firms' geographically dispersed units allow them to alleviate uncertainties at the local level.

Preface

Intellectual property is a strategic tool for any company. It is imperative, therefore, for firms to have not just a general understanding of the intellectual property issues facing their business and their industry, but to have adequate expertise in dealing with those issues. After all, companies spend millions of dollars to establish patents, trademarks and brand names. If a foreign firm steals one's property-patent, trademark or brand name, the original firm could lose heavily. For the property owner, not only are potential markets lost, but often the company's reputation is hurt if the locally manufactured product is of inferior quality, as is frequently the case.

US companies are particularly susceptible to piracy because of their lead in many technologies and a number of household brand names. The traditional way to protect property outside the home country has been to obtain parallel protection in each host country. This process is cumbersome, expensive and very risky. For example, the patent may not be granted because the standards for patentability in some nations are not compatible with accepted practices in other countries. There are international conventions and agreements that can make it easier to secure property rights. But overall, international arrangements for property protection are insufficient and inadequate.

In recent years, intellectual property has received a lot more attention because ideas and innovations have become the most important resource replacing land, energy and raw materials. It has been estimated that three-quarters of the value of public companies in the US comes from intangible assets, almost twice as much as in the early 1980s.

The economic product of the United States has become predominately conceptual. Intellectual property forms part of those conceptual assets. Considering the importance of protecting the US intellectual properties for its global competitiveness, the University of Connecticut Center for International Business Education and Research (CIBER) planned a by-invitation-only conference in the spring of 2007 to examine various facets of international protection of intellectual properties. Twenty-three scholars from academic and international organizations such as OECD and WTO accepted our invitation to participate in the conference. Many of the participants wrote papers to present at the conference, which are included in this book.

We are grateful to the conference participants for accepting our invitations to attend, engage in creative discussions and write the papers. Without their full cooperation and interest this conference would not have succeeded. Professor Donald Richards from Indiana State University made an excellent presentation in his keynote address and we sincerely thank him for his contribution. We hope this book will encourage other international business scholars to consider intellectual protection of intellectual property rights as a worthwhile theme for future conferences and research.

Subhash C. Jain
Robert C. Bird

PART I

Introduction

1. The continuing challenge of global intellectual property rights

Robert C. Bird* and Subhash C. Jain**

INTRODUCTION

Intellectual property law was traditionally an obscure and highly technical discipline usually dealt with by lawyers (Yu, 2004). In the 1980s, however, international protection of intellectual property became an important trade-related policy issue for the United States. Today, the United States stands as a global leader in its trade in ideas (Spero, 1990), and the result has been sustained high-wage jobs arising from these innovations (Ketels, 2007). Intellectual property has been one important source of American global leadership. In 2003, trade in intellectual property in the United States produced a $28.2 billion surplus, a 5 per cent increase over the previous year (National Science Board, 2006).

US firms have obtained competitive advantages from intellectual property rights by licensing a new technology or generating revenue from a useful patent. Intellectual property rights have also protected brand equity by controlling use of firm tag-lines and symbols. Intellectual property rights have helped implement vertical and horizontal product differentiation, convey information, raise entry barriers, and create power with suppliers who want to associate with a successful brand (Reitzig, 2004).

The United States and other industrialized countries argue that technological superiority is the cornerstone of their competitiveness. Because intellectual property rights foster creativity in high technology, strengthening its protection has been a priority for these nations. Advocates of stronger protection argue that without protection, businesses will not be willing or able to invest adequate resources in the development of new products. Consequently, US competitiveness will decrease (Duvall, 1992). Furthermore, with adequate protection, companies will be willing and able to transfer technology to foreign countries, both developed and developing. This will result in higher economic growth around the world.

There is thus no doubt that the United States government and its allied interests want to sustain strong intellectual property rights for most goods and services sold around the world. Such protection is a lynchpin for defending technological innovation and superiority. This interest in strong intellectual property rights, however, has produced tensions

* Assistant Professor, Department of Marketing, School of Business, University of Connecticut. This chapter is based in part on an article by Subhash C. Jain (1996), 'Problems in international protection of intellectual property rights', *Journal of International Marketing*, **4**(1), 9–32.

** Professor of International Business, Director of the Center for International Business Education and Research (CIBER), and Director of the GE Global Learning Center, School of Business, University of Connecticut.

when trade expansions outpace legal protections. For example, global marketing and international trade remain important tools for the success of the enterprise. Yet a lack of strong intellectual property protection and enforcement can inhibit the effectiveness of trading and marketing by creating barriers and unfair competition. Over time, surmounting these barriers has become increasingly important to multinationals, especially of American and European origin (Bradica, 2002). Questions have been raised concerning whether America's position as a global innovation leader is sustainable (Ketels, 2007).

Despite the importance of international protection of intellectual property rights, it should receive greater emphasis among international business scholars. While it is widely accepted that world intellectual property rights need to be strengthened, questions are raised about exactly what should be protected. In addition, debate continues that arises from the diverse views held by developing countries on the protection of intellectual property rights.

Firms shoulder significant costs arising from the violation of intellectual property rights. One estimate places losses from counterfeit goods, stolen patents and violated copyrights at $250 billion annually. Losses for software companies alone cost these firms $7.3 billion in 2006. One study estimates that for every two dollars' worth of software purchased legally, one dollar's worth was obtained through illicit means. Some commentators have even argued that firms and governments should not even bother trying to enforce intellectual property rights in the digital realm because it has become so easy to copy copyrighted products (Preston, 2007). Efforts to enforce still occur, however, and have met with limited success. Select countries are threatened with retaliatory action if they fail to punish their businesses responsible for the infringements (Bird, 2006). These short-term measures do not go far, and the problem persists.

The purpose of this chapter is to briefly address some basic issues in intellectual property rights protection. This chapter should give the reader an introduction to some of the problems in intellectual property rights. In addition, it should present a background by which subsequent chapters in this book discussing specific topics may be better illuminated. No single book can offer all possible answers to a problem, but we hope this text, beginning with this chapter, can raise some important questions that require further discussion in the academic and mainstream literature.

UNDERSTANDING INTELLECTUAL PROPERTY RIGHTS

Inasmuch as there is an emerging limited international framework that protects intellectual property rights, each country has its own detailed legislative codes that protect and encourage ideas, inventions and creative expressions developed by its people. This legislative framework in the United States consists of patent, trademark, copyright and trade secrets (Searing, 1989).

Patent

A patent is a government grant of certain rights given to an inventor for a limited time in exchange for the disclosure of the invention. Most patents are subject to either the 17-year term from grant or the 20-year term from earliest effective US filing date, whichever is longer. A design patent term lasts 14 years from patent grant. On obtaining a patent through registration, the law provides the company with an exclusive monopoly by protecting ideas, designs and inventions against copying. In order for a patent to be granted in the United States, the invention or design must be new, useful, and non-obvious to a person of average skill in the area.

The underlying purposes of the patent system are to protect the property rights of the inventor of a novel and useful product or process and to encourage a society's inventiveness and technical progress. The differences among the patent systems of different countries can be explained by the emphasis placed on these two purposes. For example, the patent system of the United States places the greatest emphasis on the rights of the inventor (Helfgott, 1990). Japan, on the other hand, stresses the societal benefits of an invention (Kotabe and Cox, 1993; Kotabe, 1991).

Trademark

A trademark is a word, symbol or device that identifies the source of goods and may serve as an index of quality. It is used in trade to differentiate or distinguish a product or service from another. Trademark laws are used to prevent others from making a product with a confusingly similar mark. Similar rights may be acquired in marks used in the sale of services. These are called service marks.

Although filing to obtain a US federal trademark registration is not absolutely necessary, such a filing provides important benefits to the trademark owner. These include constructive notice nationwide of the trademark owner's claim, clear evidence of ownership of the trademark, established basis for obtaining registration in foreign countries, and filing with the US Customs Service to prevent importation of infringing foreign goods. For a trademark registration to remain valid, an Affidavit of Use must be filed: (1) between the fifth and sixth year following registration, and (2) within the year before the end of every ten-year period after the date of registration. Renewals granted on or after 16 November, 1989, last for a ten-year term.

Internationally, trademark laws vary. Some allow service trademarks while others do not. Since there are no deadlines for registering a trademark, a company may face problems if it enters a foreign market late in the life of a product. It may find that its trademark has been registered by someone else. Therefore, a trademark should be registered in every country in which protection is desired.

Copyright

Copyrights are more limited in scope than patents. They protect original works of authorship, not the ideas they contain. In the United States, *original works* include literary, dramatic, musical, artistic and certain other intellectual works. A computer program, for example, is protected by copyright law. A copyright gives its owner the exclusive right to reproduce and distribute the material or perform or display it publicly. However, copyright law does permit limited reproduction of copyrighted works without the owner's permission for 'fair use' such as criticism, teaching and news reporting.

In the United States, notice of copyright ownership has not been required since 1989. If notice is to be given, it should possess the symbol © or the word 'Copyright' or the abbreviation 'Copr.', the year of first publication and the name of the copyright owner. Although formal notice is no longer necessary, it is still desirable. Formal notice prevents an accused infringer of the right to claim innocent infringement, a potential defense in copyright actions. Like notice, registration is no longer required. Registration is recommended, however, because it enables the copyright owner to obtain statutory damages for infringement that would not otherwise be available (Rubin, 2007).

Many countries offer copyright protection without these formalities, while others offer little or no protection for the works of foreign nationals (Hilts, 1992). International agreements fostered in the mid-1990s and later have alleviated this problem somewhat by establishing minimum standards for copyright protection that a signatory nation must follow. Before publishing a work anywhere, it is advisable to investigate the scope of protection available as well as the specific legal requirements for copyright protection in countries where copyright protection is desired.

Trade Secret

A trade secret is another means of protecting intellectual property. It is simply information that an organization keeps from being known to its competitors. A trade secret is different from patent, trademark or copyright since it is not registered. Thus, it is not legally protected. However, it can be protected in the courts if the company can prove that it took all precautions to protect the idea from outsiders and that infringement occurred illegally. The uniqueness of trade secrets is that there is no time limit and no one has public access to the information, which is not so in the case of other forms of intellectual property.

The United States International Trade Commission (ITC) is responsible for regulating trade relations between and among US and foreign competitors. Foreign firms that infringe run a risk of being caught and excluded from US markets, and US firms contemplating the use of the ITC to defend markets strategically from foreign competitors run a risk of losing their patents or being reprimanded. A substantial portion of cases referred to the ITC are being settled through agreements (Thomas, 1989).

INTERNATIONAL INTELLECTUAL PROPERTY TREATIES

One of the most important methods of concretizing intellectual property protection for US firms abroad is the enactment and enforcement of international agreement. These agreements can help standardize protections and provide a global baseline of respect for intellectual property regardless of its origin.

Paris Convention

The primary agreement for the protection of industrial property is the Paris Convention. It covers such properties as patents, trademarks, service marks, trade names, utility models, industrial designs and inventions. Established in 1883, the Paris Convention is the oldest agreement and it secured early participation from most industrialized countries. The United States joined in 1887.

From its inception, the Paris Convention has been based on reciprocity: (a) the people from member states have the same rights that the state grants to its own nationals, and (b) the foreigners have equal access to local courts to pursue infringement remedies. In addition, the convention establishes rights of priority that stipulate that once an application for protection is filed in one member country, the applicant has 12 months to file in any other contracting state, which should consider such an application as if it were filed on the same date as the original application.

Berne Convention

The oldest and most comprehensive international copyright agreement is the Berne Convention. This treaty provides reciprocal copyright protection in each of the signatory countries. Until 1989, the United States was not a member of the Berne Convention. The Berne Convention establishes the principle of national treatment and provides for protection without formalities, independence of protection and certain minimum rights.

TRIPS

The Agreement on Trade-Related Aspects of Intellectual Property Rights, commonly known as TRIPS, is widely considered the most relevant intellectual property treaty. Prior to TRIPS, nations offered different levels of protection based upon domestic, political and cultural preferences. Some nations did not protect whole categories of products, such as pharmaceutical drugs. Signatories to the TRIPS agreement agree to follow previous conventions, such as the Berne Convention and the Paris Convention. Nations that have agreed to implement TRIPS must provide significant protections for patents, copyrights and trademarks through their domestic laws. In short, signatories must treat foreign intellectual property rights holders the same as domestic ones (Harris, 2004). Furthermore, nations must have systems in place to enforce intellectual property rights and prevent export of infringing goods. TRIPS may be enforced by the WTO and includes a settlement mechanism for resolving disputes (WTO, 2006a).

For patents, TRIPS requires signatories to provide patent protection to almost any invention or process regardless of the field of technology. Exceptions for food products, medicines and agriculture once given by developing nations are no longer permitted. The agreement harmonizes the length of patent terms by requiring that nations protect patents for at least 20 years (Harris, 2004).

The TRIPS agreement also addresses trademarks by requiring signatories to have a central place with which to register trademarks. Trademarks much be protected for at least seven years with the possibility of indefinite renewals. A trademark's use can neither be subject to a compulsory license nor unjustifiably burdened with special requirements. The licensing and assignment of a trademark must also be transferable without the business to which the trademark belongs (Weckström, 2007).

For copyrights, signatories of TRIPS must provide protection under the Berne Convention and extend that protection to source and object code of computer programs as well as data compilations. Authors and their successors must have the ability to authorize or prohibit the commercial rental of their works. The term of protection for copyright must be for the life of the author or 50 years from publication or creation of the work (WTO, 2006b).

Other Agreements

Other more focused treaties apply to specific types of intellectual property. For example, the Patent Cooperation Treaty (PCT) presents a unified method for filing patent applications on an international basis (WIPO, 2006a). While not granting an 'international patent', the PCT system allows for a single filing and search with procedures maintained by relevant national authorities. Similarly, the Madrid Protocol allows a trademark owner to file a single application that could potentially protect the mark in multiple countries more expeditiously and cheaply than individual national filings (WIPO, 2006b). The Madrid Protocol became effective in the United States in 2003 (Samuels and Samuels, 2004). Other conventions that deal with different aspects of industrial property protection include: Madrid Agreement, Source of Goods (1891); Madrid Agreement, Registration of Marks (1891); Hague Agreement (1925); Nice Agreement (1957); Lisbon Agreement (1958); International Convention for the Protection of New Varieties of Plants (1961); Locarno Agreement (1968); Trademark Registration Treaty (1973); Budapest Treaty (1977); and Nairobi Treaty (1981). The other major international copyright agreements comprise the Rome Convention (1961), Geneva Convention (1971), Brussels Convention (1974), and Madrid Multilateral Convention (1979). Finally, numerous bilateral and unilateral treaties protect intellectual property rights on a country-by-country basis.

Most agreements, both for the protection of industrial property and copyrights, fall under the jurisdiction of the World Intellectual Property Organization (WIPO). In other words, WIPO facilitates international agreements regulating intellectual property. WIPO was created in 1967, came into force in 1970, and was made a specialized agency of the United Nations in December 1974. WIPO pursues the following objectives: (a) promote the protection of intellectual property rights by encouraging new treaties; (b) assist in the modernization of domestic laws; (c) collect and provide information and technical assistance; and (d) ensure cooperation among member countries through centralizing administration of the agreements. Its membership consists of most European countries, the United States, Japan and other major countries. Overall, 184 countries hold membership in WIPO.

There are a number of conventions relative to industrial property and copyright that have not fallen under the jurisdiction of WIPO. Important among them are the European Patent Convention (1973) for the protection of industrial property, and the Universal Copyright Convention (1952) for copyrights. The former is administered by the European Union offices in Brussels, and the latter by the United Nations Educational, Scientific and Cultural Organization (UNESCO).

In the 1980s, the protection of intellectual property figured prominently in multilateral talks (the Uruguay Round). In the Uruguay Round of GATT negotiations, intellectual property was a new issue deliberated by the nations. When the Uruguay Round talks started in 1986, GATT members were apprehensive about including intellectual property rights as a subject for multilateral trade negotiations. However, at the insistence of the United States, GATT members agreed to a negotiating framework that allowed for conclusion of a comprehensive agreement that ultimately became the TRIPS agreement (Bird, 2006).

The NAFTA agreement devotes considerable attention to intellectual property rights. It ensures adequate protection and enforcement of these rights. For example, Article 1714 of the agreement requires that the laws of each member country provide enforcement procedures and effective action to protect intellectual properties. Finally, The EU has set forth procedures to adequately protect intellectual properties, both internally and externally. In addition, it seeks to harmonize national legislation of member states on intellectual property rights to eliminate trade restrictions among the members.

THE ADEQUACY OF INTELLECTUAL PROPERTY PROTECTION

From the viewpoint of the United States, international protection of intellectual property is far from sufficient. In a study of 52 countries for five core copyright industries, losses were estimated to be $12.5 billion in 2005. Internet piracy has grown rapidly and is contributing an increasing percentage of overall piracy losses. One study by the Business Software Alliance concludes that in 2004 35 per cent of all software used globally was pirated (Horan et al., 2005).

A number of factors may be responsible for these and other intellectual property losses. These include export losses for sales never made, sales lost relative to previous sales, export sales at risk, domestic sales displaced by imports of infringing goods, revenue losses from fees or royalties not paid, reduced profit margins, damage to reputation or trade name, research costs not recovered, research or business forgone, increased product liability costs, weakening of sales with concurrent damage to other product lines, enforced reductions in plant efficiency (for example, those resulting from decreased sales) and intentional reductions in efficiency (for example, use of older technology in overseas plants to safeguard protected technology). By 2008, these losses are estimated to cost the US economy nearly $1 billion in tax receipts, $4.5 billion in wages, and 175 000 jobs (Horan et al., 2005).

Pirated and counterfeit products distort international trade. In 1984, for example, Pharmaceutical Manufacturers Association members with new products protected by patents in countries such as the United States sold $29 million worth of those products in Korea. Patent pirates, on the other hand, sold $70 million in unauthorized copies of these same drugs in Korea. In five countries (Argentina, Brazil, Korea, Mexico, Taiwan), sales of new pharmaceutical products by patent owners in 1984 totaled $162 million, while sales of unauthorized copies of the same products totaled $192 million (Rozek, 1990). Losses due to lack of enforcement as well has ambiguous laws have only increased today (Table 1.1).

In addition, pirates can tarnish valuable trademarks and destroy carefully created images. Pirated goods cheapen the image and dilute the prestige of real products (Richardson, 1988). Furthermore, the product's creator is blamed when a fake breaks or malfunctions and the company refuses to fix it. New technologies are making piracy increasingly easy to carry out (Bush et al., 1989). Inexpensive personal computers, desktop copiers and digital technology have made it simpler to steal hours of creativity

Table 1.1 Estimated 2004 US sales losses due to copyright piracy in 52 selected countries

US Industry	Estimated losses (Millions of dollars)
Business software applications	6 155.0
Sound recordings	2 437.8
Entertainment software	1 743.9
Motion pictures	1 635.5
Books	571.0
Total	12 543.2

Source: Horan et al. (2005).

and research from the innovators. Many pirates work out of basements and garages, moving from location to location. They use relatively portable and inexpensive machinery to sew logos on clothes, silk-screen characters on shirts, copy DVDs and computer software, and duplicate music. Obviously, their mobile, decentralized operations make enforcement difficult. They are also highly efficient. Pirates can copy a design prototype so quickly they sometimes beat the product's creator to market (Alster, 1988).

DEFICIENCIES IN LEGAL REGIMES

The following are the major enforcement inadequacies in the protection of intellectual property rights (Goans, 1986):

a. No preliminary or final injunctive relief;
b. Lack of seizure and impoundment relief;
c. Lack of exclusion of infringing imports;
d. Lack of compulsory court process and/or discovery;
e. Inadequate civil remedies, usually in monetary damages; limits on recoveries preclude deterrent effects;
f. Fine or other criminal penalties inadequate;
g. Unreasonably slow enforcement process during which illegal activity continues;
h. Enforcement officials systematically discriminate against foreigners;
i. Training and resources for enforcement inadequate;
j. Court decisions biased or political; and
k. Corruption.

The types of deficiencies vary by countries. Comparatively speaking, the industrialized countries have a stronger protection regime and workable enforcement arrangements. At the other extreme, the developing countries (with a few exceptions) have a more or less 'acceptable' protection regime but lack sufficient enforcement.

The above deficiencies lead to piracy of intellectual properties, which is harmful for the firms owning these properties. By losing sales, they forgo potential profits. By not knowing the users of pirated goods they also lose opportunities to cross-sell their other products, market new generations of products and capitalize on any suggestions from pirates for improving the products or developing new products (Givon et al., 1995). A frustrating issue for the firms is how to manage the product when there is a significant number of product users they don't know about.

Protection deficiencies may be divided into two major groups: (a) *regime deficiencies – that is*, inadequacies in the protection provision for particular types of intellectual property, and (b) *enforcement inadequacies*. The regime deficiencies vary from one type of property to another. As far as enforcement is concerned, it is one thing to have a law on the books, but it is another thing to have cultural values and views changed in order to accommodate, particularly, the interests of people who are from outside the country or region. For example, Indonesia in 1993 beefed up anti-piracy laws and policies because of pressures by the United States and other countries. The new law did away with the country's previous trademark approval process, under which the first company to file for a trademark received it – even if it was already used by another company.

In spite of laws, businesspeople in certain countries continue to ignore intellectual property laws and do not receive punishment form the judicial system (Woo and Borsuk, 1994). In another example, Brazil is a signatory to the Paris Convention, an intellectual property rights protection agreement. Most of the country's statutes on intellectual property rights are consistent with Western standards. In practice, however, the government often discounts existing statutes and enforcement mechanisms in its quest for rapid economic growth, annual trade surpluses and advanced technology (Turner, 1988). In spite of numerous efforts by the United States and the presence of laws in Chinese statutes, China still does not remain fully committed to the defense of foreign intellectual property protection (Bird, 2006).

DIFFERING VIEWS OF INTELLECTUAL PROPERTY RIGHTS

Developing nations oppose strong intellectual property rights protection for both philosophical and economic reasons. They have traditionally favored shorter patent periods and other measures of weakening protection of intellectual property. Free riding may not necessarily be a forbidden practice, but a necessary precursor to advancement.

Developing countries may argue that intellectual property rights raise prices and profits for one country or company at the expense of the well-being of a developing nation. One example is in the area of pharmaceuticals. By temporarily creating a monopoly on new pharmaceutical products, intellectual property rights create higher prices that profit the industrialized nations. The international community loses the opportunity to benefit from the products because they cannot afford them. In this respect, intellectual property protection restricts the widespread use of new technology (Subramanian, 1991).

Developing nations feel that without free use of technology and information, they will consistently fall behind industrialized nations. Weaker protection of intellectual property rights is seen as a means of increasing access to the information and technology needed for economic growth. They submit that it is in the industrialized nations' best interests to allow free use of information. This way developing nations will need less financial support and can provide a larger market of consumers to MNCs (Higgins and Rubin, 1986).

Regarding technology, the price given by western multinationals may be unjustly expensive. Intellectual property rights give innovators a monopoly on information that is used to exact unreasonably high prices for their knowledge and to impose severe and unwarranted restrictions on its use. These restrictions hinder the efforts of the developing countries to modernize, thereby perpetuating and strengthening the split between them and the developed nations (Feinberg and Rousslang, 1990). Some of these nations maintain that knowledge is the common heritage of mankind and should be made available at low cost. Others argue that third world development is in the interests of all nations and that technological information should be provided readily, at low cost and with a minimum of restrictions on its use.

On balance, economic growth is a common goal pursued by both developed and developing countries. Historically, technology has played the central role in achieving economic growth among all factors of production. Mansfield (1990) refers to a study that found that 90 per cent of the increase in output per capita during the period 1909–1949 was attributable to technological change. Since then, the role of technology as an engine of growth has increased much more rapidly.

The development of technology should be an important aim of a society desirous of economic growth. Public policy should encourage the development of technology through providing incentives for engaging in knowledge generation and in creating innovations. Thus, adequate intellectual property protection is essential. Mansfield (1990) determined that a substantial proportion of innovations would never have taken place if it were not for patent protection. His research showed that 60 per cent of the inventions in pharmaceuticals and 38 per cent in chemicals would not be developed if there were no patent protection. In the same two industries, in the absence of protection, 65 per cent and 30 per cent of inventions, respectively, would not be commercially introduced.

A country has two broad choices regarding intellectual property: allowing free access or providing protection. The free access solution yields short-term benefits at best while it imposes long-term costs. The protection solution enhances the prospects for economic growth to produce long-term benefits in exchange for a grant of monopoly power to the innovator (Blass, 1992). Protecting intellectual property improves the size, quality and efficiency of both the labor force and the capital stock within a country. In other words, strong protection of intellectual property tends to: (1) create jobs in primary industries as well as in supporting industries; (2) create a higher-quality labor force through on-the-job training; (3) shift jobs to higher-productivity areas; (4) increase the capital stock of the country; (5) improve the quality of the capital stock through innovation; (6) improve the allocation of the capital stock; (7) expand those activities subject to economies of scale; (8) improve efficiency through a reduction in local monopoly elements; (9) provide lower-cost methods of production for existing products; and (10) provide new products. Both developed and developing countries agree that innovation is a good thing and that innovators should be rewarded. But the problem is to find the best way to encourage the former and reward the latter (Main, 1989).

CONCLUSION

The efforts to protect intellectual property rights suffer from three major problems: institutional issues, philosophical issues and the incorporation of new technologies. Countries may have laws prohibiting piracy, but enforcing those laws remains problematic in many developing nations. Some governments have little incentive to enforce patent laws against companies who make life-saving pharmaceuticals for their citizens at an affordable price. Other regimes lack the financial will to pursue pirates when other more pressing matters such as hunger, unemployment and social strife remain. A unified set of measures is emerging, but countries still follow a wide variety of protection measures, even those who submitted to TRIPS. The chapters in this book should help address many of the current problems facing intellectual property rights on a global scale.

REFERENCES

Alster, Norm (1988), 'New profits from patents', *Fortune*, 25 April, p. 187.

Bird, Robert C. (2006), 'Defending intellectual property rights in the BRIC economies', *American Business Law Journal*, **43**(2), 317–63.

Blass, Anthony (1992), 'Learning the soft way', *Far Eastern Economic Review*, **17**.

Bradica, Joseph (2002), 'Havana Club rum: One step back for US international trademark policy', *Temple International and Comparative Law Journal*, **16**(Spring), 147–73.

Bush, Ronald F., P.H. Bloch and S. Dawson (1989), 'Remedies for product counterfeiting', *Business Horizons*, **32**, 18–26.

Conner, Kathleen Reavis and R.P. Rumelt (1991), 'Software piracy: An analysis of protection strategies', *Management Science*, **37**, 125–39.

Duvall, Donald K. (1992), 'Import relief or risk? Protection is a double edged sword', *Industry Week*, **48**(2), 46–51.

Feinberg, Robert M., and D.J. Rousslang (1990), 'The economic effects of intellectual property right infringements', *Journal of Business*, **63**(1), 79–90.

Givon, Moshe, V. Mahajan and E. Muller (1995), 'Software piracy: Estimation of lost sales and the impact on software diffusion', *Journal of Marketing*, **59**, 29–37.

Goans, J. Winegar (1986), 'Protecting American intellectual property abroad', *Business America*, 27 October, 2–13.

Harris, Donald P. (2004), ' "TRIPS" rebound: an historical analysis of how the TRIPS agreement can ricochet bach against the United States', *Northwestern Journal of International Law and Business*, **25**(Fall), 99–164.

Helfgott, Samson (1990), 'Cultural differences between US and Japanese patent systems', *Journal of Patent and Trademark Societies*, **72**, 231–38.

Higgins, Richard S. and P.H. Rubin (1986), 'Counterfeit goods', *Journal of Law and Economics*, **29**, 211–30.

Hilts, Paul (1992), 'Through the electronic copyright maze', *Publishers Weekly*, 14 April, 35–7.

Horan, Amanda, Christopher Johnson and Heather Sykes (2005), 'Foreign infringment of intellectual property rights: Implications for selected US industries', No. ID-14, Office of Industries Working Paper: International Trade Commission, pp. 1–52.

Ketels, Christian H.M. (2007), 'Industrial policy in the United States', *Journal of Industry, Competition and Trade*, **7**, 147–67.

Kotabe, Masaaki (1991), 'A comparative study of US and Japanese patent systems', *Journal of International Business Studies*, **23**(1), 147–68.

Kotabe, Masaaki and E.P. Cox III (1993), 'Assessment of shifting global competitiveness: Patent applications and grants in four major trading countries', *Business Horizons*, **36**, 57–64.

Main, Ann (1989), 'Pursuing US goals bilaterally: Intellectual property and "Special301" ', *Business America*, **23**(12), December, 6–8.

Mansfield, Edwin (1990), 'Intellectual property, technology and economic growth', in F.W. Rushing and C.G. Brown (eds), *Intellectual Property Rights in Science, Technology, and Economic Performance*, Boulder, CO: Westview Press, pp. 17–30.

National Science Board (2006), 'Industry, technology, and the global marketplace', *Science and Engineering Indicator 2006*, pp. 6–23. http://www.nsf.gov/statistics/seind06/c6/c6s 4.htm.

Preston, Rob (2007), 'Why our intellectual property is worth protecting', *Information Week*, 7 July, p. 60.
Reitzig, Markus (2004), 'Strategic management of intellectual property', *Sloan Management Review*, **45**(3), 35–40.
Richardson, Michael (1988), 'In old bottles, all-too-new cognac', *International Herald Tribune*, 14 March, 11.
Rozek, Richard P. (1990), 'Protection of intellectual property rights', in F.W. Rushing and C.G. Brown (eds), *Intellectual Property Rights in Science, Technology, and Economic Performance*, Boulder, CO: Westview Press.
Rubin, Leonard E. (2007), 'Basic provisions of US copyright law', *Practising Law Institute*, **901**, 9–22.
Samuels, Jeffrey M. and Linda B. Samuels (2004), 'International trademark protection streamlined: The Madrid protocol comes into force in the United States', *Journal of Intellectual Property Law*, **12**(Fall), 151–60.
Searing, Marjory E. (1989), 'Working for strong intellectual property protection: A US priority', *Business America*, **23**(7), July, 2–4.
Spero, Donald M. (1990), 'Patent protection or piracy: A CEO views Japan', *Harvard Business Review*, **68**, 58–67.
Subramanian, Arrind (1991), 'The international economics of intellectual property right protection: A welfare-theoretic trade policy analysis', *World Development*, **19**, 945–56.
Thomas, Robert J. (1989), 'Patent infringement of innovations by foreign competitors: The role of the international trade commission', *Journal of Marketing*, **53**, 63–75.
Turner, Roger (1988), 'Brazil: A practical guide to intellectual property protection', *Business America*, **22**(4), April, 14.
Weckström, Katja (2007), 'When two giants collide: Article 17 and the scope of trademark protection afforded under the TRIPS Agreement', *Loyola of Los Angeles International and Comparative Law Review*, **29**(Spring), 167–200.
WIPO (2006a), 'International protection of industrial property: Patent Cooperation Treaty', http://www.wipo.int/pct/en/treaty/about.htm.
WIPO (2006b), 'Madrid system for the international registration of marks', http://www.wipo.int/adrid/en/.
Woo, Junda and R. Borsuk (1994), 'Asian trademark litigation continues', *Wall Street Journal*, 23 September, A8.
WTO (2006a), 'Understanding the WTO: Intellectual property: Protection and enforcement', http://www.wto.org/english/thewto_e/whatis_e/tif_e/agrm7_e.htm.
WTO (2006b), 'TRIPS Agreement on Trade-Related Aspects of Intellectual Property Rights: Part II – Standards concerning the availability, scope and use of intellectual property', http://www.wto.org/english/tratop_e/trips_e/t_agm3_e.htm.
Yu, Peter K. (2004), 'Currents and crosscurrents in the international intellectual property regime', *Loyola of Los Angeles Law Review*, **38**(Fall), 323–443.

PART II

Developed nations in a global market

2. Unifying the international law of business method and software patents

Larry A. DiMatteo[1] and Robert E. Thomas[2]

INTRODUCTION

The Trilateral Patent System consists of the world's three major patent law regimes – those in Europe, Japan and the United States. The trilateral system has been remarkably successful in harmonizing the law of the three legal regimes. The history of the trilateral system has been one of convergence. A notable exception has been the recent divergence among the patent law regimes in the area of business method and software patentability. This chapter analyzes the divergence in the patent systems in these areas and reviews the reasons for their continued divergence. It then makes recommendations on how best to harmonize international patent law.

Our analysis concludes that the EU and non-EU European countries are unlikely to adopt the US's expansive recognition of business method patents. Statutory prohibitions against issuing business method and software patents prevent a full-scale adoption of the US approach. The EU has been able, through often-tortured interpretations, to approve a multitude of patents for computer-implemented inventions, but these interpretations have produced a degree of uncertainty and inconsistency. Therefore, a necessary condition for harmonization is for the US to revoke its full recognition of non-computer-implemented business method patents.

The first part of the chapter reviews the state of business method and software patent law in the US, Europe and Japan. The chapter then examines the extent to which the three systems have converged in the area of business method and software patent law. The final part of the chapter recognizes that completely revoking recognition of business method and software patents in the US is likely to be unattainable. It then recommends that the US adopt the stricter European and Japanese inventive step requirement for such patents. Alternatively, should harmonization fail, we recommend creating a *sui generis* category, which would limit the patent period for business method and software patents.

US BUSINESS METHOD AND COMPUTER-IMPLEMENTED PATENT LAW

This part examines the current state of the law on the patentability of business methods and software in the US, the European Union (EU) and Japan. The review of US law includes the United States Patent and Trademark Office (USPTO) response to the Federal

Circuit's recognition of business method patents in *State Street Bank* and a review of the more recent decisions in *Bowman* and *Lundgren*. The EU law analysis includes a review of the failed legislative effort to clarify and expand the patentability of software and business methods. The analysis of Japanese law includes a review of its Guidelines for Computer Software Related Inventions.

United States Patent Law

From a scope of patentability perspective, the US possesses the most liberal patent law among the trilateral partners. Unlike patent law in Europe and Japan, US patent law does not expressly exclude business methods and software from the definition of patentable subject matter.[3] The US openly recognizes the patentability of software and business methods. The recognition of business method patentability in the United States was the logical culmination of a long progression of steps starting from the recognition of patents containing computers and software as components to the recognition of software patents independent of any other patentable element, and finally, to the recognition of business methods independent of computers and software.

Yet, from a policy standpoint, this progression has been problematic. The United States Patent and Trademark Office (USPTO) struggles with the quality of accepted business method applications and has been criticized for issuing questionable business method patents (Shapiro, 2004; Allison and Tiller, 2003; Allison and Hunter, 2006). Governed by the judicial mandate to grant patents to 'anything under the sun made by man',[4] current US patent law stands as an obstacle to a common international treatment of business method and software patents.

The following sections examine developments subsequent to *State Street Bank*'s recognition of the patentability of business methods. The first section reviews the USPTO and Congressional responses to *State Street Bank*. The second section concludes with a review of the decisions in *Bowman*[5] and *Lundgren*.[6]

USPTO and Congressional Responses to the Patentability of Business Methods

The Court of Appeals of the Federal Circuit (CAFC) eliminated the last vestige of a common law physical manifestation patent requirement through a series of decisions. In *State Street Bank*, the CAFC rejected the business method exception to statutory matter and concluded that mathematical algorithms are non-statutory only when they are shown to be abstract ideas devoid of a useful purpose. A year later, the CAFC in *AT&T Corp. v. Excel Communications, Inc.* eliminated the 'machine' requirement altogether. In this later case, the business method claim employed mathematical algorithms without an associated machine or apparatus. Nonetheless, the court held that a method of applying a mathematical algorithm constitutes patentable subject matter, regardless of whether its application requires the use of a machine or computer, as long as it produces a useful, concrete, tangible result.

The proliferation of business method patents created a number of problems. Prior to *State Street Bank*, many companies never thought to patent innovations in business. Thus, companies that continued using business methods that had become subject to patent protection were vulnerable to patent infringement claims by parties who subsequently obtained patents covering these business methods. Congress attempted to remediate this risk by enacting the American Inventor's Protection Act (AIPA), which provided a prior use affirmative defense to business method patent infringement claims.[7] However, Congress did not address other implications of granting such patents.

Following the US courts' recognition of business method patents, the USPTO had difficulty responding to the dramatic increase in patent applications (Wild, 2002). The absence of a database covering prior art for business methods left the USPTO ill-equipped to rule on business method patent claims. These difficulties resulted in it granting patents for claims that many commentators believed did not deserve patent protection. Specifically, the criticism centered upon the issuance of patents for overly broad business methods that did not meet the patentability thresholds of novelty and non-obviousness (Merges, 1999; Gleick, 2000).

The USPTO responded by implementing the 'Business method patent initiative: An action plan' (USPTO, 2000). As a result the number of Class 705 (business method) patents issued dramatically declined. The action plan was merely a process-directed response that made it more likely that such claims met the threshold of a 'useful, concrete, and tangible result'.

Board of Patent Appeal's Responses: Bowman and Lundgren Decisions

The Board of Patent Appeals (BPA) also attempted to rein in patent coverage of business methods. In *Ex parte Bowman*, the BPA reviewed an appeal of an examiner's rejection of a claim for a method for creating a chart and plotting points thereon. In defending his invention, the appellant attempted to tie his claim to the USPTO's guidelines (Bowman, 2001, p. 1671). However, the examiner, and BPA, rejected this effort because nothing in the claims suggested that computers were required to practice the invention. Instead, the BPA concluded that the invention was merely an abstract idea that was not statutory subject matter and was obvious to someone of ordinary skill in the art. While this conclusion would have easily disposed of the immediate appeal, the BPA explained its conclusion by asserting that the reason the claimed invention was non-statutory was because it was not tied to a 'technological art'. They asserted that the term 'technological arts' was a synonym for 'useful arts', the term used in Article I, Section 8 of the US Constitution.

Thus, the BPA created a requirement that business method patent claims be computer-implemented. The decision completely ignored the precedent established by the *Diamond-Alappat-State Street Bank* line of legal rulings, which minimally require that a patent meet only the generic requirements of novelty, non-obviousness and utility, with no additional requirement that the invention advance the technical arts. Some commentators believe this decision was an intentional attempt to rein in the broad mandate of *State Street Bank* and prior court precedents (Squires and Biemer, 2006). The inclusion of the technical arts threshold excluded almost all non-computer-implemented business methods from statutory subject matter. It also served to move US patent law toward harmonization with European and Japanese patent law by focusing on the technical aspects of computer-related business method inventions. Both European and Japanese patent laws require, *inter alia*, computer implementation for patentability and do not consider pure or 'naked' business methods patentable.

The 2005 BPA decision, *Ex parte Lundgren*, rejected the international trend towards requiring a minimal technical advancement or contribution for the patentability of business methods. In reviewing an appeal from the rejection of a claim for a method of determining incentive-based managerial compensation based on performance standards, the BPA addressed the narrow question of whether the claim covered statutory subject matter. Instead of relying on *Bowman*, the *Lundgren* Board looked to Section 101 of the Patent Act for guidance. In reiterating that Section 101 only requires inventions to be new and useful, the BPA noted that the Supreme Court had previously excluded 'nature, physical phenomenon, and abstract ideas' from statutory subject matter (*Diamond v. Diehr* (1981), p. 185). The BPA then affirmed that there were no other exclusions from statutory subject matter and rejected the notion that a patent claimant had to satisfy a technical arts requirement. It reasoned that there was no workable definition of technical or technology. The decision, therefore, rejected the technological arts patentability test promulgated in *Bowman*. The Board determined that the subject matter test for patentability merely requires that a process claim produce a useful, concrete, tangible result without pre-empting other uses of the included mathematical principle, in order to come within the scope of § 101.

The *Lundgren* decision eliminated the potential for the USPTO to place non-Congressionally-mandated limits on the patentability of business methods. In *Lundgren*, the BPA retreated from its *Bowman* decision, realizing that there was no authoritative support for unilaterally reinterpreting the definition of statutory subject matter. Clearly, any effort to harmonize US business method and software patent law with the international trend will not originate inside the USPTO. In the absence of Congressional intent to address this issue, some commentators are holding out hope that the Supreme Court will supply guidance.

The hope would be that the Supreme Court would reject or narrow the decision in *State Street Bank*. It could reiterate the standard it established in its last relevant decision, *Diamond v. Diehr*. The *Diamond v. Diehr* Court required a physical transformation to occur in order for a process to be eligible for patent protection. This requirement implicitly rules out all non-computer-implemented business method inventions. However, following the *Diamond* decision would probably eliminate many software inventions from the definition of statutory subject matter because they often lack a physical change component. It is doubtful that the Supreme Court would take such a radical step.

Alternatively, the Supreme Court could modify the physical transformation requirement to allow some software patents while still removing business methods from statutory subject matter. For example, the Court could replace the physical transformation requirement for patentable subject matter with a transformation perceivable by one of the five senses requirement. Employing this test, software that manipulates images or sounds alarms would be considered statutory subject matter. Finally, it could adopt the technological arts requirement proposed in *Bowman* or the inventive step requirement found in some foreign patent laws.

European Patent Law

A dichotomy between patentability in law versus practical expediency has characterized the response of European countries and the EU to the US recognition of business method and software patents. In substantive law, Europe rejects recognition of business method patentability and significantly limits software patentability. In practice, the European Patent Office (EPO) has followed a much more difficult, perhaps even tortured, path in distinguishing between patentable, innovative computer-implemented inventions and unpatentable software and business methods (Abid, 2005; Guntersdorfer, 2003). However, in neither case is there indication that these countries will duplicate the extremely liberal recognition of business method and software patents that exists in the US.

Previously, we predicted a relatively quick convergence of the three major patent law systems in recognizing the patentability of business method and software inventions (DiMatteo, 2002). We predicted that the US expansion of the scope of patentability would force the EU and Japan to fall in line with the US standard. For one, the benefits of harmonization of intellectual property law are widely accepted (often with formal treaties enacted to expedite harmonization). Added to that, market forces would pressure the Trilateral Patent System to avoid allowing any single member to maintain a competitive advantage due to differences in patent law. With estimates of upwards of 40 000 business method and software patents having already been granted in Europe (Matter of CFPH, 2005), it seemed only a matter of time before Europe completed its convergence to the US system through legislation. However, in 2005 the EU soundly rejected an effort to expand business method and software patent coverage (Ford, 2005). The remainder of this section addresses the question of why European patent law failed to converge to the US approach and prospects for future convergence in Europe.

EU Patent Law and National Patent Laws

There are some notable differences among the patent-granting states in Europe. Two of the strongest patent law traditions are those of Germany and the United Kingdom (UK). Historically, in Germany inventions received patent protection if they included a 'technical effect' (Ford, 2005, pp. 87–8). In the UK, inventions received patent protection if they were novel, useful and subject to an inventive step. This distinction between the two approaches is subtle. Some commentators characterize the distinction to be a one-step evaluation of the nature of invention in the German approach versus the application of multiple measures or requirements in the UK approach (Ford, 2005, p. 88).

In the 1950s and 1960s, proponents of harmonization recognized the futility of trying to completely harmonize patent law throughout Europe, which consisted of the European Economic Community (EEC), the predecessor of the EU, and non-EEC members. The plan eventually adopted included the establishment of the European Patent Office (EPO) pursuant to the Convention on the Grant of European Patents (EPC).[8] Contracting countries consist of EU member states and non-EU European countries. The EPO has patent prosecution responsibility based on rules, procedures and standards adopted by all members of the EPC.

The EPC streamlines the patent prosecution process but does not supplant existing patent laws in contracting countries. Rather, the EPC created an additional layer of bureaucracy that coexists with each member country's existing patent prosecution and review system. A filing with the EPO constitutes a filing in each designated European country. In addition to prosecution of patent applications, the EPO is also responsible for patent opposition proceedings. The outcome of the opposition process can be appealed to the EPO Boards of Appeal.

In the absence of a true European patent, the ad hoc EPO Boards of Appeal occupy a curious position. The Boards of Appeal accept appeals from actions originating from EPO divisions. Since the EPO's primary functions are the review and prosecution of patent applications, the Boards of Appeal decisions deal primarily with procedural issues and questions of patent validity. Decisions of the Boards of Appeal are not precedents and are not binding on contracting states. In the event of a conflict between Boards of Appeal decisions, the EPO can convene an enlarged Board of Appeal to establish uniformity in the application of EPC law. While these decisions are binding on EPO Boards of Appeal, they are merely persuasive but not prescriptive with respect to contracting states. Therefore, there is the potential for conflict between EPO patent decisions and those of contracting states.

European Treatment of Business Method and Software Patents

Conflicts and controversy have surrounded the European treatment of business method and software patents. The EPC states that all inventions 'which are susceptible of industrial application, which are new and which involve an inventive step' shall be granted a European patent. The EPC then excludes certain innovations from the category of patentable subject matter. Many of these exclusions correspond to exceptions recognized under US law such as scientific discoveries and mathematical algorithms.[9] However, the EPC diverges dramatically from US law by explicitly excluding 'schemes, rules and methods for . . . doing business, and programs for computers'.[10] Despite the apparent plain meaning of these exclusions, EPC Article 52(3) introduces ambiguity by limiting the exclusion 'only to the extent to which a European patent application or European patent relates to such subject-matter or activities *as such*'. The 'as such' clause has allowed the EPO to approve patent applications that appear to be excluded as business methods or computer software inventions. While the EPO has successfully employed the EPC's exclusions to avoid patenting most stand-alone business methods they have been able to issue thousands of computer-related business method and software patents (Matter of CFPH, 2005).

While this large estimate of successful patent claims may suggest that Europe is converging to the US standard, a review of EPO Boards of Appeal business method and software patent decisions suggests that the convergence is far from complete. The patent courts initially interpreted the EPC to require that inventions have a technical character or a technical contribution. *VICOM*[11] was one of the first Boards of Appeal cases to consider software patents. The *VICOM* patent application covered a method for digitally processing images stored in a digital format. In this format, images are represented as an information matrix that is subject to mathematical operations. These operations, which are familiar to anyone conversant in image filtering and the application of linear mathematics, are used for smoothing, sharpening and other image processing functions. In its review, the EPO Examining Division rejected several *VICOM* claims because they related to unpatentable mathematical methods. The Examining Division reasoned that these operations, which are mathematical in nature, were not of a technical character because they were essentially mathematical manipulations.

The Board of Appeal, employing a technical contributions test, rejected this conclusion distinguishing between a general 'method for digitally filtering data', which Article 52 would bar, and a *specific application* of the method to, for example, enhancing images.

This method of applying mathematical algorithms to a perceptible object produces an objectively enhanced image. Thus, the application of mathematics to a perceptible object resulting in a perceptibly different object constitutes a technical contribution. Even though the calculations that produced the output could be done by hand or by any standard computer or calculator, the alteration of a physical object was determinative. The Board of Appeal was further comforted by the patent's employment of the mathematical method in a limited application. They reasoned that the specialized use would not preclude others from using the mathematical methods employed in the patent claim in a different application and would be a technical process susceptible of industrial application. Thus, if the incremental contribution to the prior art was technical in nature, the technical character requirement for patentability would be satisfied.

In addition to a perceived or physical transformation, an EPO Board of Appeal found technical contributions when methods were encapsulated in other than generic computer equipment. For example, in *Queueing System*[12] the Board of Appeal had no trouble identifying a technical contribution in a software-based system that assigned priority to customers located at multiple service points. The system not only identified and assigned priority, a data processing function, but it also sent messages to the various service points signaling the availability of the service. The fact that the software was merely a component of a larger electronic system that included a three-dimensional object or apparatus was enough for the claim to escape the Article 52 exclusions. The Board of Appeal emphasized the importance of not conflating the Article 52 patentability requirements with the Article 56 inventive step requirement. For this Board, the inventive step requirement was equivalent to the US Patent Code §103 non-obviousness requirement. The Board of Appeal emphasized that the EPO examiners must first consider whether Article 52 excludes the claim from patent consideration. If not, the claim's subject matter is patentable. The EPO then must consider whether the claim passes the Article 56 non-obviousness test. Applying the second half of this two-part test, the Board of Appeal concluded that the complexity of implementing the queueing system electronically was not obvious to someone skilled in the art. Therefore, the claim survived both the Articles 52 and 56 tests.

The technical contribution requirement, while intuitively satisfying, did not provide a clear delineation between patentable software and non-patentable software. The claim in *VICOM*, while characterized as a physical manipulation, was in reality a data processing method. Its most significant advance over previous methods was speed. Similarly, the major distinction between the disputed claim in *Queueing System* and a pure business method was that the *Queueing System's* invention was inseparable from the included apparatus. The integrated nature of the claim, which utilized input from customers, computer-based analysis and subsequent visual signals directing customers without human intervention, persuaded the court that a technical innovation existed. This process could not be separated from the included apparatus and 'interpreted as a method for doing business as such'. This reasoning raises the question of to what degree must software or a business method be embodied in an electronic apparatus for an invention to pass the Article 52 patentability test.

The lack of a definitively drawn line continued to be a problem for the EPO. In the 2000 *Pension Benefit Systems*[13] decision, an EPO Board of Appeal struggled with the technical character requirement. The case involved a method for calculating pension benefits using a computing apparatus. The EPO rejected the initial application as a business method excluded under Article 52. On appeal, the claimant asserted, among other things, that the pension system was similar to the previously approved *Queueing System* claim in that it employed an apparatus. The *Pension Benefit Systems* Board of Appeal summarily disposed of the appeal by concluding that the claim was for a purely economic innovation. Furthermore, the Board of Appeal maintained that 'methods only involving economic concepts and practices of doing business are not inventions within the meaning of Article 52(1) of the EPC'. Applying a method through the use of a computer or other apparatus does not change the essential nature of the claim nor does it endow a 'purely non-technical purpose' with a technical character.

While the above analysis should have disposed of the matter, the *Pension Benefit System* Board of Appeal opted, instead, to revisit the technical contribution test. They appeared to be troubled by: (1) the absence of a solid definition for technical character and (2) the inescapable logic that a business method or software-based method embodied in a computer or electronic apparatus does indeed have a technical character. In a full retreat from the technical contribution requirement, the Board concluded that Article 52(1) of the EPC does not exclude any concrete apparatus embodying software or a business method.

To escape this quandary, the Board of Appeal took a different approach. Rather than apply the technical contribution test, it opted instead to decide the case based on the Article 56 inventive step requirement. The Board posed the question: What is the prior art to which the claim contributes? In this case, the relevant prior art was all prior pension plans. However, since pension plans fall entirely within the fields of business and economics, there could be no inventive step or contribution of a technical character because such fields are excluded from patentability. Therefore, the Board of Appeal avoided the conundrum of determining when a claim is of technical character by asserting that any claim embodied in a physical computer or apparatus is of a technical character. Instead, the Board relocated the issue of technical contribution to the determination of inventive step. Thus, after *Pension Benefit Systems*, the EPO Boards of Appeal abandoned the technical contribution test in favor of interpreting the inventive step requirement to be satisfied only for inventions with a technical character.

In sum, the reasons behind the technical contribution analysis based on Article 52 and the Boards of Appeal reformulation are different, but in a substantial majority of patent claims the outcome would be identical. The major difference between the tests is the relative clarity of analysis. The original technical contribution test was murky due to its inability to delineate between patentable and non-patentable software innovations. The Boards of Appeal reformulation removed much of the ambiguity by eliminating the technical contribution test and the need to debate the existence of technical character. However, the reformulation is susceptible to criticism by requiring the examiner to subjectively determine whether the claim's contribution to the prior art lies in a technical area or in an area excluded by Article 52.

Subsequent EU Legislative Efforts

The effort to reform perceived shortcomings in the EPO treatment of software and computer-implemented inventions has been intense. In 2002, the EC introduced, under the authority of Article 95 of the Treaty Establishing the European Community (EC Treaty),[14] the proposed EU Directive on the patentability of computer-implemented inventions (Proposed Directive) for review and passage by the European Parliament and European Council (EU, 2002). Proponents and supporters of software patents criticize the EPO's inability to develop a concrete, unambiguous treatment of business method and software patent claims. The European Economic and Social Committee, a group comprised primarily of industry representatives, decried the EPO's approach to software patents as 'the product of legal casuistry' (EESC, 2002). The Proposed Directive criticized the EPO's 'lack of clarity' as 'an important negative influence on the [software] industry' (EU, 2002). The Proposed Directive concluded that software patents had promoted growth of US computer-related industries and that allowing European business method and software patents would aid European producers by creating 'a level playing field'. By contrast, the open source community, committed to open development and free distribution of software, feared that full recognition of software patents would allow large software developers to erect access barriers to huge segments of the software industry (Cane, 2005). With this backdrop, it is not surprising that software patent reform has been a difficult undertaking in Europe.

The stated goal of the Proposed Directive was to tie EU treatment of computer-implemented patent claims closely to the then current EPO treatment of such claims as expressed by the EPO Boards of Appeal decision in *Pension Benefit Systems*. In addition to *Pension Benefit Systems*, the EC claimed that the Proposed Directive was consistent with its *Koch & Sterzel*, T0026/86 (1987), decision (EU, 2002, p. 9). However, it was impossible to be consistent with both cases since the Boards of Appeal in *Pension Benefit Systems* explicitly rejected the technical contribution test followed in the *Koch & Sterzel* case. Therefore, the Proposed Directive's embrace of a technical contribution test was actually a rejection of recent Boards of Appeal case law.

Proposed Directive Article 4(2) states that a necessary condition for the existence of an inventive step is that 'a computer-implemented invention must make a technical contribution'. Proposed Directive Article 4(3) directs member states to determine technical contribution by 'consideration of the difference between the scope of the patent claim considered as a whole, elements of which may comprise both technical and non-technical features, and the state of the art'.

The Proposed Directive Article 4(3) mandate to consider the patent claim as a whole was indeed drawn from similar language in the *Pension Benefit Systems*' approach (EU, 2002, p. 14). However, the relevant reference was a quote of EPO guidelines and came immediately after the EPO Board of Appeal concluded that the technical contribution approach was *not* an appropriate method for determining whether a claim constituted a patentable invention with respect to EPC Article 52 (EU, 2002, p. 16).

The deviation of the Proposed Directive language from the EPO Boards of Appeal approach in *Pension Benefit Systems* would allow an expansion of computer-implemented patent coverage into areas that would not qualify under existing Boards of Appeal analysis. The Proposed Directive would allow patent grants for business methods claims for which 'a non-obvious technical contribution was present'. According to the EC, Proposed Directive Article 4(3) would, however, exclude business method claims that contained no technical contribution whatsoever. Thus, the Proposed Directive would exclude many of the non-technical US-styled business method patents, but not all of them.

Applying Proposed Directive Article 4 to a claim for a new accounting system implemented by a computer-based system in a new and non-obvious way would likely result in a patent grant under both US patent law and the Proposed Directive. Since implementation of the accounting system is new and non-obvious, it would satisfy the 'new' and 'industrial application' requirements of Proposed Directive Article 4(1). In addition, the claim or invention would need to satisfy the Proposed Directive Article 4(2) requirement for an inventive step, which requires the invention to make a technical contribution. In assessing technical contribution, Proposed Directive Article 4(3) requires consideration of the claim as a whole without distinguishing between technical and non-technical elements. Employing this test, the examiner would have to conclude that there is a technical contribution relative to the prior art because, judged as a whole, the invention has a technical character, it is an advance over the prior art and, therefore, makes a technical contribution. Therefore, rather than simply harmonizing European software patent law based on *Pension Benefit Systems*, the Proposed Directive would significantly increase the scope of business method and software patent coverage in the EU beyond prior case law.

The European Parliament, with the support of the open-source software community (*Financial Times*, 2005, p. 18), rejected the Proposed Directive and offered in its place a set of amendments that significantly limited the patentability of computer-implemented inventions (EU, 2003). The Amended Proposed Directive, while leaving much of Proposed Directive Article 4 unchanged, limited the patentability of computer-implemented inventions by allowing patents only for inventions that make contributions in technical fields. Technical fields include 'the use of natural forces to control physical effects beyond the digital representation of information'. Amended Proposed Directive Article 2b explicitly excluded 'the processing, handling, and presentation of information' from technical field consideration. Amended Proposed Directive Article 3a stated that 'data processing is not considered to be a field of technology in the sense of patent law, and that innovations in the field of data processing are not considered to be inventions in the sense of patent law'.[15] Amended Proposed Directive Article 4a made the European Parliament's repudiation of the EC's Proposed Directive clear in stating, 'a computer-implemented invention shall not be regarded as making a technical contribution merely because it involves the use of a computer, network or other programmable apparatus'. Article 4a continued by explicitly excluding claims for 'business, mathematical and other methods' that do not produce any non-computer based physical effects. In July 2005, the European Parliament voted 648 to 14 to reject the Proposed Directive. Critics of the Proposed Directive argue that the actual intent of the proposal was to move the EU towards 'unlimited patentability and patent enforceability' of business methods and software.[16]

Japanese Patent Law

The Japanese Patent Office's (JPO) path to increased recognition of the patentability of business method and software patents has been far less contentious than the European experience. Japanese patent law, based in large part on German patent law, bears a strong resemblance to EU law (Duffy, 2002). However, the evolution of Japanese patent law also drew from the US patent experience. Purportedly, a Japanese delegation visited the US patent office in 1899. The delegates, thoroughly impressed and believing that the greatness of the US was in some part attributable to its patent system, vowed to create a patent system in Japan.[17] Therefore, it is not surprising that the Japanese treatment of business method and software patents is somewhere between the two other patent law traditions. Japan, as a civil law country, has no case law to provide guidance. Therefore, relevant patent law is embodied in statutory law and administrative guidelines. Under Japanese law, patentability requires that an invention be, similar to Europe, 'industrially applicable' (Japan Patent Law, 1999). Japanese patent law refines this definition by requiring an industrially applicable invention to be also a 'highly advanced creation of technical ideas by which a law of nature is utilized'.

In response to the US recognition of business method patents, the Japanese Patent Office (JPO) drafted Guidelines for Computer-Software Related Inventions (Guidelines), which explicitly prohibit granting patents for business methods (Japan Patent Office, 2000). Referring to 'statutory' requirements, the Guidelines state that '[i]f a claimed invention [uses] . . . any laws other than natural laws, such as arbitrary arrangements, mathematical methods or mental activities, or *methods of doing business*, for example, the invention is not considered statutory'. However, a software or computer-implemented business method invention is patentable if it involves 'a creation of *technical ideas* utilizing natural laws'. The JPO at one level has not categorically rejected the patentability of business methods, as EPC Article 52 appears to do. Instead, at the review level, it has adopted the criteria of technical advancement or contribution akin to that found in EU patent law.

The Guidelines list a number of requirements for patentability. They include: (1) Description Requirement; (2) Enablement Requirement; (3) Ministerial Ordinance Requirement; (4) Statutory Invention Requirement; and the (5) Inventive Step Requirement. The first three requirements stated above are more procedural in nature in that they are directed at the content and format of the description of the invention in the patent application. The Description Requirement requires that the claimed invention be described so that it can be identified by a person skilled in the relevant art. The Enablement Requirement requires that the patent application provide a detailed description 'in such a manner sufficiently clear and complete for the invention to be carried out by a person having ordinary skill in the art to which the invention pertains' (Japan Patent Office, 2000a, §1.2.1.).

The Ministerial Ordinance Requirement requires that the description of an invention include a statement of the problem being solved by the invention and its solution. It also provides an exception to this requirement for inventions developed based on an entirely new conception (Japan Patent Office, 2000a, §1.2.2.). However, the Guidelines expressly single out software as not being based on an entirely new conception: 'One could hardly imagine that such kind of inventions are created in the field of software related technology.' The Guidelines conclude that it is therefore imperative that such inventions state the technical field to which the invention pertains and the technical significance of the invention.

The Ministerial Ordinance Requirement is simply the descriptive form for providing the information needed to satisfy the substantive elements of patentability – statutory invention and inventive step or non-obviousness. The statutory invention or subject matter requirement mandates that a patentable invention is one that is a 'creation of technical ideas utilizing natural laws'. In the area of software, business methods, or computer-related inventions this requires more than the 'mere processing of information by a computer' and more than the mere statement of programming language or a program listing

(Japan Patent Office, 2000a, §2.2.3(2) and (3)). The Guidelines assert that solutions to problems relating to a number of computer related problems – including control of hardware, information processing based on the physical or technical properties of an object, and information processing using hardward – are deemed to utilize natural laws, thereby bringing them within the scope of statutory inventions. The Guidelines provide these examples: (1) a computer program for controling the rate of fuel injection for an automobile engine (control of hardware); (2) computer program for image processing (information processing based on physical or technical properties of object); and (3) an apparatus for predicting daily sales of commodities (information processing using hardware) (Japan Patent Office, 2000a, §2.2.1(c)).

The final requirement of patentability is the inventive step requirement. The Guidelines partially define an inventive step in the negative. An innovation is not an inventive step if 'it would have been easy for a person skilled in the art to have made the claimed invention' (Japan Patent Office, 2000a, §2.3). Alternatively stated, a claimed invention is not inventive if it is a product of the exercise of ordinary creative ability expected of a person skilled in the art. The Guidelines then provide discussion of areas where this is often the case. This discussion is most relevant to business method and software even though business method is not expressly mentioned.

Those areas where the inventive step requirement is difficult to prove include: applications to other fields, supplement or replacement by a commonly known means of systemization, implementation by software of functions which are otherwise performed by hardware, and systemization of human transactions (Japan Patent Office, 2000a, §2.3(2)(b)–(e)). Thus, if a known business method in one field, is applied in another field, such application would not be considered an inventive step (Japan Patent Office, 2000a, §2.3(2)(b)). Software-related inventions that integrate hardware and software by supplementing or replacing that integration with a 'commonly known means for systemization' would also not constitute an inventive step.

The exclusion from patentability that has the most bearing on business methods that do not possess a high level of technological advancement is the one pertaining to the systemization of human transactions. The Guidelines exclude from patentability due to a lack of a sufficiently inventive step:

> [Inventions that are] within the exercise of ordinary creative ability expected of a person skilled in the art to systematize existing human transactions in an applied field by means of a computer, if the transactions are such that they can be realized by a routine application of a usual system analysis and system design technologies. (Japan Patent Office, 2000a, §2.3(2)(e))

It is likely that the invention patented in *State Street Bank* would have found difficulty in avoiding this exclusion under Japanese patent law. For example, two Japanese courts held that a support system for managing condominium buildings, a message management apparatus, and an apparatus for an auction center were not patentable because they were 'something at which a person skilled in the art could have easily arrived'.[18] In the area of ordering and marketing, Japanese courts have rejected the patentability of a product selling system,[19] customer management system,[20] and a site control distribution system.[21]

Closely related to the exclusion for the systemization of human transactions is the test recognized under the Guidelines that looks to the effects of the invention to determine if there is a legally recognizable technical (inventive) step. Thus, an invention that allows for quicker processing of data, minimizes errors, or allows for obtaining uniform results would not be patentable because such improvements are considered foreseeable from the existing state of art. Note the different use of the effects of the invention approach compared to US law. Under US law something that produces a tangible, useful result would be patentable. Under Japanese law, such a result may be insufficient to satisfy the inventive step requirement. The requirement of technical advancement is defined as methods involving the use of a high level of a creative technological idea and may include hardware and related computer programs. The JPO states that:

> [T]he purpose of the law is to protect a high level of creativity in technological concepts which use natural laws and rules. Consequently calculation methods or encryption determined by arbitrarily defined rules, for instance for finance and insurance systems or taxation methods, which are not based on natural laws and rules, do not represent a protected subject . . . [T]he created product must be characterized by a high level of technological creativity because a creation characterized by a low technological creativity level cannot be protected.[22]

Elsewhere, the JPO states that an inventive step is to be denied where there is an application of technology from one field to another field, the invention involves the automation of manual tasks, or involves merely the change of a design based on artificial arrangements (Japan Patent Office, 2000b). Despite these exclusions, one thing is clear, like US patent law, computer programs are treated like any other type of product invention (Japan Patent Office, 2002). The EPO's inventive step 'plus' is not required in Japan. Therefore, while Japan's business method patent law is in most cases more restrictive than the corresponding US patent law, it is not as restrictive as European patent law.

Summary

Even though all three major patent law regimes have considered full recognition of business method patents, only the US has accepted the patentability of non-technical and non-computer-implemented business methods. Europe and Japan have emphatically rejected the recognition of abstract, intangible business methods. However, both regimes continue to struggle to draw a line between non-patent-worthy computer-implemented business methods and patentable technically innovative computer-implemented claims.

Europe and Japan have attempted to draw the above distinction through the implementation of the 'inventive step' patentability requirement. In Europe, the EPO deals with the problem by identifying the area of technical contribution. Japan addresses the problem by imposing a 'high level of technological creativity' requirement for patentability. The lack of consistency between the three major patenting regimes continues to produce the potential for commercial conflicts and inter-regime competitive imbalances.

TOWARDS AN INTERNATIONAL LAW OF BUSINESS METHODS AND SOFTWARE PATENTS

The US rejection of a technical aspects requirement guarantees that US recognition of the patentability of business methods will not align with European and Japanese laws in the foreseeable future. Our analysis shows that it is highly unlikely that Europe and Japan will adopt the US treatment of business method and software patents. Furthermore, the present common-law approach in the US is unable to address the economic failures and impracticalities associated with the overly broad protection endemic to business method patents. Congress should revise US patent law to align it more closely with the laws of Europe and Japan. The final sections explore what a policy-driven patent law would look like in the US.

The Need to Reform US Business Method and Software Patent Law

We have previously presented the case against the recognition of business method patents (DiMatteo, 2002). We make the case here that the hope of international harmonization of business method and software patent law rests with a change in the US patent law system. The problem with completely revoking recognition of such patents is that the expansion of patent protection for business methods and software has become accepted practice in the US. As one commentator noted:

> [P]atent policy has now progressed to the point where computer-related inventions no longer are considered a unique class of technology requiring special scrutiny. The fact that [such inventions] rely heavily on mathematical algorithms or implement methods of doing business is not important in appraising their suitability for patent protection. (Burgunder, 2007, pp. 183–4)

This position, unique to the US patent system, stands squarely in the path of the goal of international patent harmonization. The following subsections discuss the policy arguments against the liberal granting of business method and software patents. Based upon this analysis, the article concludes with a discussion of recommended reform options available to Congress.

Social Welfare Losses Outweigh Marginal Patent-associated Benefits

Moving the US patent treatment of business method and software towards the European and Japanese approaches would not only increase harmonization but would enhance social welfare. Recognition of business method and software patents is welfare diminishing (Nordhaus, 1969). The purpose of patent law is to provide inventors with incentives to innovate by providing limited periods of exclusive control over inventions. The exclusive rights associated with a patent provide its holder with a monopoly over the invention (Cahoy, 2003). The deadweight losses that accompany underproduction and non-marginal-cost pricing in monopoly situations are also present in markets in which a patented product is dominant with few or no close substitutes (Kaplow, 1984). The gains in innovation and knowledge creation must be substantial to exceed the losses associated with patent exclusivity. In fact, there is evidence that business method and software patents do not increase innovation. Prior to broad recognition of software patents, innovation was extremely high (Jaffe and Lerner, 2004). Much of the software innovations during the 1970s and 1980s occurred with little reliance on patent law. Rather than enhance innovation, it may be the case that software patents actually impede innovation. In the next section, we explore the implications of patent protection for cumulative and sequential technologies.

The Problem of Patent Scope

The potential harm from continued recognition of business method and software patents is due to the tendency for business method and software patent grants to be overly broad in scope. Although Professor Kitch suggests that broad patent grants may be welfare enhancing (Kitch, 1977), his conjecture is based on specific assumptions that are not likely to apply to software patents because software innovations are cumulative and sequential in nature. Professors Merges and Nelson in their analysis of patent scope provide qualitative evidence rebutting Kitch's conclusion for cumulative innovative technologies (Merges and Nelson, 1990). In such industries, they argue, holders of broad patents covering key technologies tend to slow innovation rates and block others from gaining access to the subject areas of such patents.

Software and business method innovations are subject to the dynamics that Merges and Nelson describe for technologies in which innovation occurs in small incremental steps often advancing the prior art with small but significant refinements. At trial, a jury is often unable to recognize the subtlety and significance of the advance. Therefore, a significant and important improvement may be blocked, or worse, subject to an equivalents claim.[23] In sum, the incremental and sequential nature of software innovation, combined with the absence of clear guidance in determining the relevant art, gives patent holders power to block others from innovating in related fields.

The Problem of Non-disclosure

Patent law requires inventors to publish information that is sufficient to enable one of ordinary skill in the art to make and use the invention. However, evidence suggests that US software and business method patent grants tend to be overly broad. This bias is connected to the CAFC's allowance of such patent claims with limited disclosure. (Cohen and Lemley, 2001). Inventors prefer to limit disclosure for several reasons. First, the inventor may want to conceal a truly clever innovation from competitors. This strategy in essence provides the inventor with trade secret as well as patent protection. Second, in a patent race, an inventor may wish to stake a claim at the earliest possible date in order to lock out potential challengers. Third, limited disclosure also allows the inventor to exaggerate the breadth of his invention. Fourth, limited disclosure allows inventors to hide defects in enablement specifications. The lack of disclosure gives the inventor additional time to correct defects in his invention and continue research in order to expand his patent's coverage while at the same time deterring other potential innovators.

Limited enablement-level disclosure has several additional implications. The first implication is that patent publication does not advance the prior art. The published patent provides little notice as to the boundaries of the patent and fails to provide enough information to facilitate additional research in the field. Without full disclosure, some 'innovations' that are obvious extensions cannot be challenged because the prior art is not available. Limited disclosure also creates ambiguity as to the expanse of prior art. This ambiguity enhances the potential for innovators to inadvertently infringe or for patent trolls to claim infringement (Thomas, 2006).

As discussed above, there is a tendency for business method and software patents to be overly broad due to the lack of enablement-level disclosure and the relatively undeveloped prior-art record. In some cases, the bias towards allowing broad software patents may come close to the level of patenting ideas or, at minimum, protecting unpatentable components of an invention. Without a comprehensive prior-art record and detailed patent disclosure, patent examiners and courts are unlikely to accurately distinguish infringing minor improvements from software innovations that are different and truly significant advances entitled to protection under the reverse doctrine of equivalents.[24] Thus, extending software patent coverage in such instances significantly increases welfare losses without any concomitant social gain.

Reform Recommendations

In light of the preceding section's analysis, the adoption of substantive reforms is needed to address the deficiencies in US business method and software patent law. Business method and software patents may not provide significant innovation incentives, but they do contribute to corporate wealth. The powerful interest groups that benefit from business method and software patents are likely to form a formidable blocking coalition against radical reforms (Thomas, 2006, pp. 724–5). Hence, revocation of the patentability of software and business methods is not politically feasible. Therefore, this section considers less draconian reforms that Congress is more likely to implement given political realities.

The best alternative short of eliminating business method and software patents is for the US to adopt an inventive step requirement akin to the European and Japanese approaches. This approach requires the examiner to identify the field or useful art to which the innovation contributes. Most business methods in areas related to economics, accounting, mathematics or another business-related field, would not satisfy the inventive step requirement. This approach eliminates all non-computer-implemented business method patents and raises the bar for software patents. Therefore, this approach would improve the quality of issued patents. Second, it would largely harmonize the Trilateral Patent System. The EPO already employs this approach and the Japanese approach is not substantially different.

Alternatively, along with adopting the inventive step requirement for patentability, non-computer-related business method inventions could be protected through the creation of a *sui generis* category of protection. This *sui generis* approach would create an independent category of intellectual property protections. These protections would be of a lower order than protections granted under present patent law. Such a new category of intellectual property protections would provide a reduced duration or term of protection. This protection would be similar to the EU protection granted to developers of databases. This protection, like those for databases, would only be available to those who have incurred a substantial investment in developing the invention or innovation.[25] Business method and software that fail the inventive step requirement but otherwise satisfy the requirements for patentability would qualify for *sui generis* protection.

The primary rationale for *sui generis* treatment of business method and software patents is that the social costs of full patent protection are so great relative to their social benefits that these costs need to be contained by limiting the exclusivity term. We do not contest the benefit of valuable business method and software patents to their holders, rather we question whether such benefits exceed the social costs such patents impose. We recommend a *sui generis* exclusivity period of three to five years. Due to the rapid advance of technology and the generally lower investment levels required to create such inventions relative to the amounts required to produce more technology-intensive investments such as semiconductors and pharmaceutical products (Grabowski, 2003), this shorter period would provide inventors enough time to recoup their investments while limiting the innovation-retarding effects on others. At the same time, it provides sufficient time for innovators to recoup their investments in developing business methods and software.

CONCLUSION

US court recognition of business method and software patents created a substantial divide in international patent law. In contrast to the US's full recognition approach, Europe and Japan have attempted to limit the negative social welfare implications of expanding patent recognition by legislatively prohibiting non-computer-implemented business method patents and imposing limitations on the patentability of software.

The broad recognition of the patentability of all types of business methods by US courts, including the recognition of non-technical or non-computer-implemented business methods, is the source of significant social welfare losses in the US. Europe and Japan's attempts to draw a line between high and low quality business method and software innovations better balances the need to stimulate innovation while preventing unnecessary anti-competitive or overly broad patent recognition. Furthermore, the lack of consistency and harmony among members of the Trilateral Patent System, due to the US recognition of business methods, increases the costs of engaging in international business.

After reviewing the current state of business method and software patent law internationally, we conclude that the requirement of an 'inventive step' found in Europe, and to a lesser extent in Japan, is superior to the US approach. The European–Japan approaches do a superior job of distinguishing between innovative and non-innovative computer-implemented inventions. While the European and Japanese approaches are not optimal, they come much closer to achieving optimality than does the US approach. The best possibility for international harmonization of business method and software patent law rests on reforming the US patent system in order to bring it into alignment with European and Japanese patent laws.

If our recommendation for limiting the scope of patentability for business methods and software inventions is rejected, then the creation of *sui generis* protections for non-computer-implemented business methods should be considered. Either alternative would significantly enhance the efficiency of US business method and software patent law while achieving a higher level of international patent law harmonization.

NOTES

1. Huber Hurst Professor of Contract Law & Legal Studies, Warrington College of Business Administration, University of Florida; JD, Cornell Law School; LLM, Harvard Law School; PhD, Monash University. The authors would like it to be noted that an expanded version of this chapter appears in Volume 16 of the *Texas Intellectual Property Law Journal*, 2007, pp. 1–46.
2. Associate Professor, Huber Hurst Fellow, Warrington College of Business Administration, University of Florida; JD, Stanford Law School; PhD, Stanford Business School.

3. *State Street Bank & Trust Co. v. Signature Financial Group, Inc.* (*State Street Bank*), 149 F.3d 1368 (Fed. Cir. 1998) (holding that business software designed to perform financial calculations for an investment fund are patentable). A year later, the CAFC reinforced its support for the patentability of business methods, *AT&T Corp. v. Excel Communications, Inc.*, 172 F.3d 1352, 1357 (Fed. Cir. 1999) ('[T]he scope of [patentable subject matter is] the same regardless of form – machine or process – in which a particular claim is drafted.'). As long as the claim covers an invention that is novel, useful, and non-obvious it is entitled to patent protection under US law, 35 USC 101–103 (2000). See also *Diamond v. Diehr*, 450 US 175, 182 (1981) ('Congress intended statutory subject matter to "include anything under the sun that is made by man" ').
4. *Diamond v. Chakrabarty*, 447 US 303, 309 (1980).
5. *In re Bowman*, 61 USPQ2d 1669 (BPAI June 12, 2001).
6. No. 2003–2088 (Bd. Pat. App. & Int. 2005).
7. First Inventor Defense Act of 1999, Pub. L. No. 106–113, 113 Stat. 1536 (codified as amended at 35 USC 273 (2000)).
8. Convention on the Grant of European Patents, 5 October, 1973, available at http://www.european-patent-office.org/legal/epc/e/ma1.html#CVN.
9. Ibid. at art. 52(2)(a).
10. Ibid. at art. 52(2)(c).
11. Case T-208/84 *VICOM* (EPO board of Appeal, 1986), available at http://legal.european-patent-office.org/dg 3/biblio/t840208ep 1.htm.
12. Case T-1002/92 *Queueing System/Petterson*, (1994), available at http://legal.european-patent-office.org/dg 3/biblio/t921002ex1.htm.
13. Case T-0931/95 Pension Benefit Systems, (2000), available at http://legal.european-patent-office.org/dg 3/biblio/t950931eu1.htm.
14. Treaty Establishing the European Community, 10 November, 1997, 1997 OJ (C 340) 3.
15. Ibid. at art. 3a.
16. Foundation for a Free Information Infrastructure, 'EU Council 2004 Proposal on Software Patents', available at http://swpat.ffii.org/papers/europarl0309/cons 0401.
17. Khan (1995 , pp. 58, 59 n.4).
18. Heisei 15 (Gyo ke) 430 and Heisei 15 (Gyo ke) 300 discussed at 'Major judicial precedents of business method-related inventions', at 1–2, available at http://www.jpo.go.jp.
19. Ibid. at 3–4 (Heisei 14 (Gyo ke) 598).
20. Ibid. at 4–5 (Heisei 17 (Gyo ke) 10084).
21. Ibid. at 4 (Heisei 15 (Gyo ke) 240).
22. Outline of the industrial property right system', at 6 of 7, available at http:www.jpo.go.jp/seido_e/s_gaiyou_e/4houe.htm.
23. When an invention is similar to a prior invention but falls outside its scope it may be infringing under the doctrine of equivalents if the court decides that the differences are not substantive.
24. The reverse doctrine of equivalents provides a defense against infringement when the new invention is a significant improvement over the plaintiff's patent.
25. Council Directive 96/9/EC of the European Parliament and of the Council of 11 March 1996 on the Legal Protection of Databases, 1996 OJ L77, 27 Mar. 1996, 20.

REFERENCES

Abid, J.G. (2005), 'Software patents on both sides of the Atlantic', *John Marshall Journal of Computer and Information Law*, **23**(4), 815–44.

Allison, J.R. and S.D. Hunter (2006), 'On the feasibility of improving patent quality one technology at a time: The case of business methods', *Berkeley Technology Law Journal*, **21**(2), 729–94.

Allison, J.R. and E.H. Tiller (2003), 'The business method patent myth', *Berkeley Technology Law Journal*, **18**(4), 987–1084.

Burgunder, Lee (2007), *Legal Aspects of Managing Technology* (4th edn), Mason, Ohio: Thomson West.

Cahoy, D.R. (2003), 'Changing the rules in the middle of the game: How the prospective application of judicial decisions related to intellectual property can promote economic efficiency', *American Business Law Journal*, **41**(1), 1–66.

Cane, A. (2005), 'Patently an EU tangle', *Financial Times*, 20 April, p. 6.

Cohen, J.E. and M.A. Lemley (2001), 'Patent scope and innovation in the software industry', *California Law Review*, **89**(1), 1–57.
DiMatteo, L.A. (2002), 'International internet transactions and the new "problem" of business method patents', *Rutgers Computer and Technology Law Journal*, **28**(1), 1–45.
Duffy, J.F. (2002), 'Harmony and diversity in global patent law', *Berkeley Technology Law Journal*, **17**(2), 685–726.
EESC (2002), 'Opinion of the Economic and Social Committee on the Proposal for a Directive of the European Parliament and of the Council on the Patentability of Computer-Implemented Inventions', EESC Opinions, INT/145, art 3.1 (19 September 2002), available at http://eescopinions.eesc.europa.eu/EESCopinionDocument.aspx?identifier=ces\int\int145\ces 1031–2002_ac.doc&language=EN.
European Union (2002), 'Commission Proposal for a Directive of the European Parliament and of the Council on the Patentability of Computer-Implemented Inventions' COM(2002) 92 final, 2002/0047(COD) 4 (2002), available at http://europa.eu.int/eur-lex/lex/LexUriServ/site/en/com/2002com2002_0092en01.pdf.
European Union (2003), Europarl 2003-09-24: 'Amended Software Patent Directive, Consolidated version of the amended directive on the patentability of computer-implemented inventions', available at http://swpat.ffii.org/papers/europarl0309/index.en.html.
Financial Times (2005), 'A sorry software saga killing the directive preserves a fragmented system', 7 July, p. 18.
Ford, L.R. (2005), 'Alchemy and patentability: Technology, "useful arts", and the chimerical mind-machine', *California Western Law Review*, **42**(1), 49–119.
Gleick, J. (2000), 'Patently absurd', *New York Times Magazine*, 12 March, p. 44.
Grabowski, H. (2003), 'Pharmaceuticals: Politics policy and availability: Patents and new product development in the pharmaceutical and biotechnology industries', *Georgetown Public Policy Review*, **8**(2), 7–23.
Guntersdorfer, M. (2003), 'Software patent law: United States and Europe compared', *Duke Law and Technology Review*, No. 6, 6–17.
Jaffe, Adam B. and Josh Lerner (2004), *Innovation and its Discontents: How our Broken Patent System is Endangering Innovation and Progress, and what to do about it*, Princeton, New Jersey: Princeton University Press.
Japan Patent Law (1999) No. 121 of 1959 (Apr. 13, 1959) (as amended by Law No. 220 ch. 1 § 2(1) of 1999 translated in World Intellectual Property Organization, Patent Law (22 December).
Japan Patent Office (2000a), 'Draft revised examination guidelines for computer software-related inventions', available at http://www. jpo.go.jp/tetzuki_e/t_tokkyo_e/Guidelines/PartVII-1.pdf.
Japan Patent Office (2000b), 'Policies concerning business method patents', available at http://www.jpo.go.jp/tetuzuki_e/t_tokkyo_e/tt1211–055.htm.
Japan Patent Office (2002), 'Annual Report, Part I: Strengthening of industrial competitiveness and promotion of intellectual property policy', 16, available at http://www.jpo.go.jp.
Kaplow, L. (1984), 'The patent-antitrust intersection: A reappraisal', *Harvard Law Review*, **97**(8), 1813–92.
Khan, B.Z. (1995), 'Property rights and patent litigation in early nineteenth-century America', *Journal of Economic History*, **55**.
Kitch, E.W. (1977), 'The nature and function of the patent system', *Journal of Law and Economics*, **20**(2), 265–90.
Matter of CFPH L.L.C.'s Applications, 2005 EWHC 1589 (Pat) (2005), available at http://www.bailii.org/ew/cases/EWHC/Patents/2005/1589.html.
Merges, R.P. (1999), 'As many as six impossible patents before breakfast: Property rights for business concepts and patent system reform', *Berkeley Technology Law Journal*, **14**(1), 577–615.
Merges, R.P. and R.R. Nelson (1990), 'On the complex economics of patent scope', *Columbia Law Review*, **90**(4), 839–916.
Nordhaus, W. (1969), *Invention, Growth, and Welfare: A Theoretical Treatment of Technological Change*, Cambridge, Mass.: MIT Press.
Shapiro, C. (2004), 'Patent system reform: Economic analysis and critique', *Berkeley Technology Law Journal*, **19**(3), 1017–47.

Squires, J.A. and T.S. Biemer (2006), 'Does a grudging Lundgren panel decision mean that the USPTO is finally getting the statutory subject matter question right?', *IDEA*, **46**(4), 561–86.
Thomas, R.E. (2006), 'Vanquishing copyright pirates and patent trolls: The divergent evolution of copyright and patent laws', *American Business Law Journal*, **43**(4), 689–739.
USPTO (1996), 'Examination guidelines for computer-related inventions', available at http://www.uspto.gov/web/offices/pac/compexam/comguide.htm.
USPTO (2000), 'Business method patent initiative: An action plan', available at http://www.uspto.gov/web/offices/com/sol/actionplan.html.
Wild, J. (2002), 'Europe lags US in business-method patents,' *Euromoney*, March, p. 28.

Main Library 2 self issue receipt

Customer ID: **********3013

Title: The global challenge of intellectual property rights / edited by Robert C. Bird and Subhash C. Jain

ID: 30110007554695

Due: 11-06-12

Total items: 1
02 04 2012
Checked out: 2
Overdue: 0
Hold requests: 0
Ready for pickup: 0

Thank you for using
this self issue machine.

3. Secondary liability for intellectual property law infringement in the international arena: framing the dialogue

Lynda J. Oswald*

Secondary liability is liability that is imposed upon a defendant who did not directly commit the wrongdoing at issue, but who the law nonetheless holds responsible for the injuries caused (Bartholomew and Tehranian, 2006, p. 1366). Imposition of secondary liability has been justified both on efficiency grounds (that is, as a mechanism to shift costs to those in the best position to prevent future harm), and on moral grounds (that is, those who intend to bring about a harm should be held liable even if another party was the direct cause of the harm incurred by the plaintiff) (Bartholomew and Tehranian, 2006, p. 1366).

International treaties currently generally do not address issues of secondary liability for infringement of intellectual property rights, and international consensus on this topic is limited at best, even among the major industrialized nations. Legal protection of intellectual property rights is inherently territorial in reach (Holbrook, 2004, p. 758), absurd as that might seem in a world of increasing intertwined global activity.

Absent a governing international agreement imposing specific obligations and fostering global harmonization, each nation is free to create its own rules and levels of legal protection regarding intellectual property rights, and innovators must seek protection of their copyrights, patents, trademarks or trade secrets within the confines of the legal regimes of the jurisdictions in which they operate (Thomas, 2005, p. CRS-5). National laws vary considerably regarding the availability and extent of secondary liability, with the United States tending to be more liberal with the imposition of such liability than most of its major trading partners. This lack of uniformity in secondary liability rules in the international arena makes the evaluation of infringement liability in that setting uncertain and makes it difficult for businesses to plan international intellectual property strategies effectively.

The United States Supreme Court's recent decision in *MGM v. Grokster*, which has implications for the extent and scope of secondary liability for both the patent and copyright law fields under US law (Oswald, 2006), highlights the uncertainty over international standards for secondary liability. The role of secondary liability for copyright infringement in the international arena was debated in the amici briefs in *Grokster* (IRO Amici Brief, 2005; Sharman Amicus Brief, 2005), and has been a topic of some interest among US commentators post-*Grokster* as well. However, the discussion, both domestically and internationally, seems to have shifted in focus and narrowed considerably in scope. Instead of discussing the full panoply of situations in which secondary liability for intellectual property infringement can occur and the range of considerations that might affect imposition of such liability, such as notions of respondeat superior, intent, authorization, and control, the debate has settled on the imposition of secondary liability in the digital arena and, more particularly, on secondary liability for peer-to-peer file-swapping. While *Grokster* itself was a file-swapping case, the Supreme Court's decision had broader implications for imposition of secondary liability for intellectual property infringement generally (Oswald, 2006); consideration of those broader implications is seemingly being ignored in present discourse.

At some level, it is understandable why the current dialogue on secondary liability for intellectual property infringement focuses on the digital environment. As Marybeth Peters, the US Register of Copyrights, recently noted, the advent of and rapid growth in digital technologies over the past ten years has now made it possible for a single individual to make and distribute millions of infringing copies over the Internet with little effort or investment (Peters, 2006). Peer-to-peer file-sharing raises the stakes even further, allowing millions of consumers to link in a network and engage in copyright infringement on an unprecedented scale (Peters, 2006).

As Peters noted, it is difficult for copyright holders to enforce their rights in this peer-to-peer setting, in part because of the difficulty of identifying, locating and suing each individual infringer, and in part because the individual users are often judgment-proof and lack the financial resources to compensate for their infringement (Peters, 2006). In the United States, copyright holders turn to secondary liability in such instances, seeking to hold the companies that facilitate these networks liable for their end users' infringement. The solution is imperfect – imposition of secondary liability for intellectual property infringement is problematic under US law and the rules can be uncertain – but nonetheless, secondary liability is clearly recognized and embraced by the US legal system, and offers some degree of protection for intellectual property rights holders.

The picture is less clear at the international level. As discussed below, some foreign jurisdictions do recognize secondary liability for intellectual property infringement. Indeed, secondary liability can be of critical importance in this setting for intellectual property holders seeking to protect their intellectual property rights. For example, if the foreign jurisdiction's laws do not provide for exclusive distribution or importation rights, secondary liability may be used to bring distributors, importers and retailers within the purview of the copyright laws, or to provide necessary relief to copyright holders where the direct infringer is not within the court's jurisdiction (Goldstein, 2001, p. 270). There is, however, as Peters noted, 'very little uniformity among national laws as to secondary liability, whether it be liability for a company that uses peer-to-peer technology to encourage infringement, or . . . an Internet service provider that provides facilities used by others to infringe' (Peters, 2006). For example, as discussed below, foreign jurisdictions may regard as direct infringement behavior that US law would classify as indirect infringement instead, or may not classify as infringement at all behavior that would clearly be actionable under US or other countries' laws. The net result is an inevitable degree of inconsistency in legal rules around the world, which creates uncertainty for intellectual property rights holders, business and other global actors.

Given the global nature of modern business generally and the inherent worldwide reach of Internet-based business activities in particular, the time has come to open serious dialogue on the advisability of creating uniform international standards for secondary liability for intellectual property law infringement. Before we can evaluate the wisdom or necessity of international standards for secondary liability for intellectual property infringement, however, we need to understand the current playing field. Currently, we have a mish-mash of national rules regarding secondary liability, with United States law being considerably more likely to contemplate imposition of secondary liability than the laws of many other nations. This is not to say that the American system should necessarily serve as the paradigm for global standards, but the considerable diversity in global thought on the issue of secondary liability for intellectual property infringement highlights the important fact that not all participants in discussion of this topic start from the same place in terms of legal theory and practice.

In addition, we need to carefully consider the parameters of potential international harmonization of secondary liability rules. The current debate focuses on a subset of copyright law, even though secondary liability has application in other areas of intellectual property law, such as patent and trademark as well. On the other hand, it is logical that the discussion of secondary liability in the international context should begin with and center on copyright law, because modern technology makes illegal copying and, hence, copyright infringement, easier to achieve, because ease of distribution of digital copies in particular means that territoriality notions break down more quickly in this arena, and because copyright law is already the subject of substantial efforts to achieve international harmonization.

It is unfortunate, however, that the debate has already been artificially constrained and, in effect, tainted by focusing primarily on peer-to-peer file-swapping activities, which pose idiosyncratic and difficult issues of copyright protection and infringement, complex questions regarding culpability and lawful versus unlawful uses, and more emotional reactions to the nature of the suits being brought. As the Canadian Supreme Court noted, the Internet poses unique problems for copyright law:

> The capacity of the Internet to disseminate 'works of the arts and intellect' is one of the great innovations of the information age. Its use should be facilitated rather than discouraged, but this should not be done unfairly at the expense of those who created the works of arts and intellect in the first place.
>
> The issue of the proper balance in matters of copyright plays out against the much larger conundrum of trying to apply national laws to a fast-evolving technology that in essence respects no national boundaries. (*SOCAN*, 2004, paras 40–41)

Intellectual property holders in this arena have a choice between suing individual users (often impecunious and thus judgment-proof college students or parents who were unaware of their minor children's downloading activities)[1] or suing the service providers who indirectly made the infringement possible by providing a service that typically can be used for both lawful and unlawful purposes.

Because of both the negative publicity and the logistical difficulties associated with suing the multitude of direct infringers, secondary liability often appears an appealing strategy for intellectual property rights holders in the file-swapping arena. The net result, however, is that the debate over secondary liability in the international context is beginning in the often factually-murky and emotionally-charged environment of peer-to-peer file-swapping. If we could remove the debate from this highly-charged sphere, and back it out into a more macro discussion of secondary liability generally – the pros and cons of imposing such liability, the situations in which such liability makes sense, and the manner in which we balance the rights of the public and goals of free trade and markets against the need to encourage innovation by protecting the rights of the innovators – the debate would proceed more easily and would be less cluttered by the complex baggage of the digital environment.

SECONDARY LIABILTY FOR INFRINGMENT OF INTELLECTUAL PROPERTY RIGHTS UNDER US LAW: *GROKSTER* AND ITS ANTECEDENTS

Theory of Secondary Liability Under US Law

In American law, secondary liability in general originates in tort law, as a mechanism for holding liable a defendant who did not directly cause the harm at issue but who should nonetheless be held liable for it (Bartholomew and Tehranian, 2006, pp. 1366–69; *A & M Records*, 2001, pp. 1019–24). Under traditional tort law, secondary liability took one of two forms: vicarious liability or contributory liability. Vicarious liability seeks to hold the defendant liable because of his or her relationship with the direct wrongdoer (for example, a master–servant relationship), and does not require that the defendant 'know' of the wrongdoing. Rather, the focus is on whether the indirect wrongdoer controls or has the right to control the direct wrongdoer (Bartholomew and Tehranian, 2006, p. 1366). Generally, vicarious infringement requires a showing of: (1) direct infringement by a primary wrongdoer; (2) a direct financial benefit to the secondary wrongdoer from the direct infringement; and (3) a right and ability on the part of the secondary wrongdoer to control and supervise the actions of the primary wrongdoer (Pessach, 2007, p. 91 n.6).

Contributory infringement, on the other hand, requires a showing of: (1) direct infringement by the primary wrongdoer; (2) knowledge of the direct infringement by the secondary wrongdoer; and (3) a material contribution by the secondary wrongdoer to the direct infringement (Pessach, 2007, p. 91 n.7; Bartholomew and Tehranian, 2006, p. 1367). Contributory infringement thus does have a knowledge requirement in the sense that the defendant must have deliberately and purposefully assisted or encouraged the direct wrongdoer, and must have recognized the wrongful nature of the underlying act of direct infringement (Bartholomew and Tehranian, 2006, p. 1366; *A & M Records*, 2001, p. 1020).

There are both pragmatic and philosophical reasons proffered for imposing secondary liability. In practical terms, secondary liability provides a means of affording intellectual property rights holders relief in situations where suing the direct infringer is impracticable (for example, because the direct infringer is financially incapable of compensating fully for the damages, or is a customer of the intellectual property rights holder), or where the actual infringement by each direct infringer is so small that the costs of litigation would greatly exceed the recovery, even though the aggregate damages caused by the direct infringement might be very large (Chisum, 2007, [5], § 17.04[4](f); Lemley, 2005, p. 228; *Aimster*, 2003, p. 645; Groennings, 2005).[2] As one commentator put it, 'chasing individual consumers is time consuming and is a teaspoon solution to an ocean problem' (Picker, 2002, p. 442). In these instances, it may be more practical to sue the indirect infringers who, in many instances, may well be more morally culpable for the infringement than the direct infringer anyway. As the United States Supreme Court noted in *Grokster*:

> When a widely shared service or product is used to commit infringement, it may be impossible to enforce rights in the protected work effectively against all direct infringers, the only practical alternative being to go against the distributor of the copying device for secondary liability on a theory of contributory or vicarious infringement. (*Grokster*, 2005, p. 930)

In more theoretical terms, secondary liability can be justified on either efficiency or moral grounds as well: 'First, secondary liability serves a fundamentally economic purpose by shifting risks from direct to indirect infringers. Second, secondary liability law serves a moral end by placing fault on a party deserving of punishment even though that party did not commit the underlying infringing act' (Bartholomew and Tehranian, 2006, p. 1419).

However, counterbalancing American law's broad view of secondary liability is the notion that secondary liability ought not be imposed on inappropriate parties or in a manner that would impede the stream of lawful commerce (Lemley, 2005, p. 228; Lichtman and Landes, 2003, pp. 409–10). The US Supreme Court has expressly recognized the need to 'strike a balance between a copyright holder's legitimate demand for effective – not merely symbolic – protection of the statutory monopoly, and the rights of others freely to engage in substantially unrelated areas of commerce' (*Sony*, 1984, p. 422). This inherent tension between protection of intellectual property holders' rights and the promotion of free commerce and open markets has important implications for the development of American legal doctrine relating to secondary liability.

General Development of Secondary Liability Under US Law

Secondary liability for patent and copyright infringement has had a rather muddled legislative and judicial history in the United States. Notions of secondary liability developed initially in the patent law area, first as common law, and then as statutory law, and were subsequently imported to the copyright area as a form of common law. US copyright law lacks a statutory basis for secondary liability even today, making the basis and rules for secondary liability for intellectual property infringement under US law rather unclear.

The first US patent act, enacted in 1790, embraced the notion of liability for direct infringement of a patent. Indirect patent infringement liability, on the other hand, developed initially as a form of common law. Over a century ago, the courts, recognizing that imposing only liability for direct infringement might well allow parties whose culpability in the infringing actions is even greater than that of the direct infringer to escape liability, developed a doctrine of contributory liability for patent infringement. Initially, contributory liability was applied to those who did not directly infringe another's patent, yet who nonetheless helped others to infringe by supplying a component part specially adapted to infringement (Adams, 2006, pp. 371–2). A second line of cases also emerged, addressing those situations where the component had non-infringing uses but was used for infringing purposes (Oswald, 2005, pp. 227–8). While the courts were reluctant to automatically hold liable a defendant who sold a component that had both infringing and non-infringing uses, they did hold defendants liable where the evidence indicated that those defendants were actually encouraging infringement by the end users (that is, the direct infringers) (Chisum, 2007, [5], § 17.02(1); Oswald, 2006, pp. 227–8).

These notions of direct and secondary liability were codified in the Patent Act of 1952, in Section 271. Section 271(a) of the Patent Act addresses direct infringement, providing that one who practices the patented invention shall be liable for infringement. Direct infringement is in effect a strict liability provision (*Jurgens*, 1996, p. 1770 n.2); lack of intent to infringe or lack of bad faith may mitigate the availability of enhanced damages for infringement, but does not obviate liability itself (Oswald, 2006, p. 229). The Patent Act separates the common law's original notion of a single type of secondary liability into two distinct causes of action: inducement of infringement (codified in Section 271(b)) and contributory infringement (codified in Section 271(c)). Under the Patent Act, secondary liability of either type is inextricably linked to direct infringement, and neither contributory infringement liability nor liability for inducement to infringe can attach unless another party is first found to have directly infringed (Oswald, 2006, pp. 228–9).

Unlike the Patent Act, the Copyright Act has no express language creating secondary liability for infringement. Nonetheless, the United States Supreme Court has long held that secondary liability for copyright infringement is actionable under US law. The Court has stated:

> The absence of such express language in the copyright statute does not preclude the imposition of liability for copyright infringement on certain parties who have not themselves engaged in the infringing activity. For vicarious liability is imposed in virtually all areas of the law, and the concept of contributory infringement is merely a species of the broader problem of identifying the circumstances in which it is just to hold one individual accountable for the actions of another. (*Sony*, 1984, p. 435)

A leading treatise identifies three theories of secondary liability under copyright law: (1) respondeat superior, in which the master is held liable for the infringement of the agent; (2) vicarious liability, which exists when the defendant (a) has 'the right and ability to supervise the infringing conduct', and (b) has 'an obvious and direct financial interest in the exploitation of copyrighted materials'; and (3) contributory liability, which takes the form of either (a) personal conduct that results in participation in or furthering of the infringement, or (b) 'contribution of machinery or goods that provide the means to infringe' (Nimmer, 2007, [3], § 12.04[A]).

MGM v. Grokster

It was against this convoluted background that the dispute in *MGM v. Grokster* emerged. *Grokster* was not the United States Supreme Court's first foray into secondary liability for copyright infringement. Two decades earlier, in *Sony Corp. of America v. Universal City Studios, Inc.*, the Supreme Court had held that the manufacturer of a VCR could not be held liable for contributory copyright infringement, even if some (or many) of the consumers used the product to infringe copyrights, because the VCR was capable of commercially significant non-infringing uses (such as time-shifting for personal viewing). The advent of the Internet and the evolution of digital technology, however, raised the stakes in the secondary liability struggle considerably beyond those found in the much simpler VCR context, as the advances in technology allowed infringing copies to now be made very rapidly and inexpensively, as opposed to the comparatively slow and cumbersome mechanism for copying provided by VCRs.

Defendants Grokster Ltd and StreamCast Networks, Inc. distributed free software that allowed computer users to share electronic files through peer-to-peer networks, thus avoiding the central service system and mediated file transfers between users of the ill-fated Napster system. Because Grokster and StreamCast did not have central servers, they contended that they had no knowledge of which files users were copying or when, and had little or no control over the users' behavior, and thus could not be held secondarily liable for any direct infringement engaged in by their end users (Oswald, 2006, p. 233).

The plaintiffs consisted of the major movie studios and record companies and various music publishers and songwriters. They argued that the defendants should be held secondarily liable for the direct infringement of their copyrighted works by the end users because the defendants' software enabled the unauthorized transfer of copyrighted works and because the defendants intended, promoted and profited from these acts of infringement (Oswald, 2006, p. 233–4).

The defendants' technology could facilitate the transfer of any type of electronic file, both infringing and non-infringing. However, the plaintiffs produced evidence that the software was used primarily to distribute copyrighted works in violation of the copyright owners' rights and without the payment of royalties, and that the defendants had taken active steps to encourage this extensive direct infringement by end users. In addition, the plaintiffs demonstrated that the defendants' business models were financially dependent upon this infringement. While the lower courts ruled for the defendants, the US Supreme Court disagreed, holding instead that: 'one who distributes a device with the object of promoting its use to infringe copyright, as shown by clear expression or other affirmative steps taken to foster infringement, is liable for the resulting acts of infringement by third parties' (*Grokster*, 2005, p. 919). In effect, the *Grokster* Court stated that it was not knowledge that leads to contributory infringement, but rather intent. According to the Court: 'One infringes contributorily by intentionally inducing or encouraging direct infringement . . .' (*Grokster*, 2005, p. 930). Moreover, the necessary intent must be shown 'by clear expression or other affirmative steps taken to foster infringement' (*Grokster*, 2005, p. 919).

The *Grokster* Court also recast *Sony* in terms of intent, not knowledge, stating: '*Sony* barred secondary liability based on presuming or imputing intent to cause infringement solely from the design or distribution of a product capable of substantial lawful use, which the distributor knows is in fact used for infringement' (*Grokster*, 2005, p. 933). According to the *Grokster* Court, the *Sony* rule 'limits imputing culpable intent as a matter of law from the characteristics or uses of a distributed product' (*Grokster*, 2005, p. 934). This, the *Grokster* Court stated, was true even though Sony knew its product could be used for infringing purposes; the key was that '[t]here was no evidence that Sony had expressed an object of' encouraging the product to be used in an infringing manner, nor had it 'taken active steps to increase its profits from' such infringing activities (*Grokster*, 2005, p. 931).

Although a full analysis of *Grokster* is beyond the scope of this chapter, it is fair to say that the *Grokster* Court's treatment of secondary liability in the copyright arena was unclear and is difficult to mesh with its earlier decision in *Sony*. The *Grokster* Court acknowledged the *Sony* Court's borrowing of the Patent Act's contributory infringement language for copyright law, and then went on to import the inducement rule from section 271(b) of the Patent Act as well. The Court explicitly recognized 'the need to keep from trenching on regular commerce or discouraging the development of technologies with lawful and unlawful potential' (*Grokster*, 2005, p. 937), and so qualified its holding by stating:

> [M]ere knowledge of infringing potential or of actual infringing uses would not be enough here to subject a distributor to liability. Nor would ordinary acts incident to product distribution . . . support liability in themselves. The inducement rule, instead, premises liability on purposeful, culpable expression and conduct, and thus does nothing to compromise legitimate commerce or discourage innovation having a lawful promise. (*Grokster*, 2005, p. 937)

In the international context, it is this message of *Grokster* that is most enduring: the need to balance the aims of legitimate commerce against the need to promote innovation by protecting the rights of intellectual property rights holders. To this end, we should consider whether secondary liability holds 'a' (though almost certainly not 'the') key to creating meaningful international standards for global protection of intellectual property rights.

SECONDARY LIABILITY IN THE INTERNATIONAL ARENA

There are numerous international treaties concerning the protection of intellectual property (Geller, 2000, para. 3[3](b)), including the Berne Convention for the Protection of Literary and Artistic Works; the Paris Convention; the World Trade Organization (WTO) Agreement on Trade-Related Aspects of Intellectual Property Rights (TRIPS, 1994); the World Intellectual Property Organization (WIPO) 'Internet Treaties'; the Universal Copyright Convention; and the Geneva Phonograms Convention. However, these treaties primarily focus on enforcement and procedural issues, not on substantive obligations. With very limited exception, these treaties do not deal, directly or indirectly, with the notion of secondary liability for infringement.

The most significant of current international agreements on intellectual property rights is TRIPS, which requires 'each WTO member state to provide minimum substantive standards of intellectual property protection and enforcement' (Thomas, 2005, p. CRS-6). TRIPS also provides a unique exception to the rule that international agreements generally do not address secondary liability issues. Article 39 of TRIPS provides for the protection of undisclosed secret information (that is, trade secrets). Footnote 10 defines 'in a manner contrary to honest commercial practices' for purposes of Article 39 as 'at least practices such as a breach of contract, breach of confidence and inducement to breach . . .' (TRIPS, Art. 39, fn. 10), thus providing a limited exception to the rule that international agreements do not address secondary liability. During the TRIPS negotiations, the United States proposed language protecting confidential business information as a trade secret; this proposal was opposed by many negotiating parties, who did not recognize such information as intellectual property. The final language was the result of compromise.

There is no clear international norm demanding imposition of secondary liability for intellectual property infringement, even among the major western nations (Peters, 2006). Nonetheless, secondary liability is recognized as a basis for intellectual property infringement liability around the world in many countries, though it may take different forms and bear different labels. There is, therefore, at least some, though perhaps minimal, common ground on which the dialogue for international standards can begin.

International Implications of Secondary Liability for Intellectual Property Infringement: The Grokster Amici Briefs

It is helpful to start the analysis of the role, existing or potential, that secondary liability for intellectual property law infringement plays in the international arena by looking first at the amici briefs filed in *Grokster*, for two of these briefs focused specifically on the issue of whether the international treaty obligations of the United States dictated an outcome in that case. Do existing treaty obligations mandate imposition of secondary liability for copyright infringement at the national level?

A group which labeled itself as 'International Rights Owners' (IRO) and which was self-described as 'trade associations and professional associations based outside the United States, representing hundreds of thousands of owners of copyrights and related rights all over the world' (IRO Amici Brief, 2005, p. 1), filed a brief in support of the petitioners, the plaintiff members of the entertainment industry. IRO's argument to the Supreme Court was largely a policy-based one, and was grounded in its assertion that international treaty obligations compelled US law to impose secondary liability for copyright infringement. IRO argued that the Ninth Circuit's decision in *Grokster* had a 'potentially devastating impact . . . on the international property landscape', and had 'an equally harmful potential disruptive effect on the harmonization of intellectual property law and the development and maintenance of uniform protection of intellectual property rights in the international arena' (IRO Amici Brief, 2005, p. 1). IRO characterized *Grokster* as being 'primarily about ensuring that the United States does not falter in its responsibilities under various international agreements and norms, by permitting a safe haven for entities to set up businesses deliberately designed to enable copyright infringement on a massive scale' (IRO Amici Brief, 2005, p. 2).

IRO argued that international agreements to which the United States was a party obligated it to provide intellectual property rights owners (and especially foreign rights owners) 'adequate and effective means of enforcing such rights' (IRO Amici Brief, 2005, p. 5). Their argument had two components. First, IRO argued that the Ninth Circuit's opinion would subject international rights owners to infringement on a 'massive and unprecedented scale' because the decision would prevent such rights holders from effectively enforcing against infringement occurring on peer-to-peer networks (IRO Amici Brief, 2005, p. 5). This, IRO argued, threatened 'to place the United States in breach of its international obligations and responsibilities' (IRO Amici Brief, 2005, p. 5). Instead, IRO argued, the US Supreme Court should ensure that rights holders had the 'important enforcement mechanism' of secondary (that is, vicarious or contributory) liability available to them (IRO Amici Brief, 2005, p. 13).

Second, IRO argued that if the Ninth Circuit's decision were to stand, there could a 'potential spill-over effect' on enforcement of intellectual property rights outside the United States, especially where the infringing material emanated from the United States. As characterized by IRO:

> Rights owners have always faced the problem of pursuing counterfeit or infringing copies produced in countries with lax copyright enforcement practices, that cross borders and infiltrate markets in other countries. If United States law is now perceived to allow businesses like defendants' to function without restraint, or is perceived as inconsistent and unreliable, this spillover problem will be global, massive and impossible to reverse. (IRO Amici Brief, 2005, p. 6)

In effect, IRO's argument was that a failure of the *Grokster* Court to find secondary liability available for copyright right infringement under US law would send the global legal system irretrievably down a slippery slope leading to an erosion of intellectual property rights around the world.

On the other side of the coin was an amicus brief filed by Sharman Networks, Ltd, in support of the respondents, Grokster and Streamcast. (Sharman was a defendant in the original action in *Grokster*, but was not a party to the appeal.) Like Grokster, Sharman licensed the protocols that enabled peer-to-peer communications over the Internet. Sharman took issue with IRO's arguments, contending instead that nothing in the relevant international treaties would impose an obligation on the United States to adopt secondary liability of any type, much less the specific type that IRO asserted (Sharman Amicus Brief, 2005, p. 4). In fact, Sharman argued, 'by any measure of international norms, the United States not only provides foreign interests with effective enforcement procedures and mechanisms, but gives them significant advantages in this respect over American copyright owners' (Sharman Amicus Brief, 2005, p. 5).

Perhaps the most compelling argument raised by Sharman, however, was its point that IRO was presenting its arguments to the wrong branch of government. As eloquently stated by Sharman:

> The IRO's belief that [the United States Supreme] Court should concern itself with trade policy, diplomacy, the raising of international norms in America's interest, and the setting of precedents for foreign jurisprudence not only goes well beyond the mandate of even this Court, it usurps the role of Congress and has no constitutional underpinnings. (Sharman Amicus Brief, 2005, p. 5)

As the US Supreme Court itself noted in *Sony*:

> The judiciary's reluctance to expand the protections afforded by the copyright without explicit legislative guidance is a recurring theme. Sound policy, as well as history, supports our consistent deference to Congress when major technological innovations alter the market for copyrighted materials. Congress has the constitutional authority and the institutional ability to accommodate fully the varied permutations of competing interests that are inevitably implicated by such new technology. (*Sony*, 1984, p. 432)

Ultimately, the argument between the two amici was over whether international treaty obligations do or do not require imposition of secondary liability for copyright infringement. However, it is clear that no such treaty obligations exist, and IRO's argument in this respect was a non-starter. The more interesting and relevant questions are: (1) what forms of secondary liability do foreign jurisdictions already provide; and (2) should international agreements require or encourage the imposition of secondary liability for intellectual property infringement, and if so, what form should those standards take? As Sharman correctly pointed out, however, these are issues of trade policy and diplomacy to be handled via international policy and agreement, and not imposed unilaterally by the courts.

Secondary Liability for Copyright Infringement in Foreign Jurisdictions

Examination of available sources of laws of other countries regarding liability for infringement of intellectual property rights reveals a somewhat checkered pattern.[3] The easy case is where the defendant has committed the infringing act himself or herself, of course: this is direct infringement and imposition of liability is straightforward.

Complexities start to arise when the infringement is more indirect. Countries characterize the underlying wrongdoing in manners or terms that are often unfamiliar to American lawyers or businesses. For example, as noted by amicus Sharman in *Grokster*, US law treats as direct infringement much behavior that is viewed as 'secondary infringement' elsewhere in the world. Sharman pointed specifically to infringement of the right of distribution, which is a form of direct infringement under US law, but under Canadian law is treated as 'secondary infringement' requiring the showing of knowledge and acts 'to such an extent as to affect prejudicially the owner of the copyright' (Canadian Copyright Act, 1985, ch. C-42, s. 27(2)(b)). In addition, in most jurisdictions, a defendant is generally liable for 'consciously bringing about or assisting in the bringing about' of infringements by third parties (Garnett et al., 1999, p. 471), that is for somehow contributing to the infringing acts of a third party (Sterling, 2003, p. 511). Knowledge of the infringement is often, but not always, an element of such liability. Under United Kingdom law, for example, the defendant's lack of knowledge of the plaintiff's copyright will relieve the defendant of liability for damages (UK Copyright, Designs and Patent Act, 1988, § 97).

The converse is also true – foreign jurisdictions may treat as direct infringement activities that would be viewed as secondary infringement in the United States. For example, many countries address copyright infringement in terms of 'authorization'. Some countries find infringement where the defendant has authorized a third party to undertake an action that actually is within the purview of the copyright holder (Sterling, 2003, p. 511). Other countries (for example, the United Kingdom) provide that authorizing someone else to commit an infringing act is itself direct copyright infringement[4] (UK Copyright, Designs and Patent Act, 1988, § 16(2)). The US, by contrast, would treat authorization as a form of either contributory or vicarious infringement, both a form of secondary liability. UK law, on the other hand, identifies, among other things, as forms of secondary infringement importing an infringing copy of a copyrighted work (UK Copyrights, Designs and Patent Act, 1988, § 22), possessing or dealing with an infringing copy (UK Copyrights, Designs and Patent Act, 1988, § 23) or providing the means for making an infringing copy (UK Copyrights, Designs and Patent Act, 1988, § 24).

Under UK law, authorization

> can only come from someone having or purporting to have authority, and an act is not authorised by someone who merely enables or possibly assists or even encourages another to do that act, but does not purport to have any authority which he can grant to justify the doing of the act. (*Ames Records and Tapes*, 1982, p. 106)

According to a leading UK treatise:

> A person does not necessarily authorize an act to be done merely because he intentionally puts into another's hands the means by which the infringing act can be done if those means can also be used for a perfectly legitimate purpose, even where it is known that they will in fact inevitably be used for an infringing purpose. This will be particularly so if the supplier has no control over how the means will be used, since it is the essence of a grant or purported grant that the grantor has some degree of actual or apparent right to control the relevant actions of the grantee. (Garnett et al., 1999, p. 471)

Jurisdictions may reach very different results, even in cases with similar facts, depending upon how they view the role of 'control'. For example, an early precursor to the current spate of peer-to-peer file-swapping cases was a series of copying machine cases around the world. Courts in Australia, France and Germany found various defendants secondarily liable for providing the copying machines on which others committed copyright infringement of one type or another (Sterling, 2003, pp. 512–14). However, Canadian and United Kingdom courts reached a very different result.

In the United Kingdom, *CBS Songs v. Amstrad* centered on a lawsuit against a manufacturer of a dual cassette player/recorder. The House of Lords declined to impose liability upon the manufacturer, noting that the manufacturer did not control the actions of its customers. Similarly, in an earlier case, *CBS v. Ames Records and Tapes Ltd*, the court had refused to hold the operator of the shop that rented sound recordings and blank tapes liable for infringement even though the operator knew its customers were probably committing infringement. The court stated: 'The proper approach, consistent with all the United Kingdom cases, is that there is no authorisation where, as in the present case, the defendant is in no position to control the conduct of the person alleged to have been authorized' (*Ames Records and Tapes*, 1982, p. 106).

Control is thus a key factor under UK law. Commentators recently summarized the status of United Kingdom law as follows:

> The relevant concept in UK copyright is *authorisation of infringement*. The copyright in a work is infringed by any person who, without the license of the copyright owner, authorises another person to do any of the restricted acts . . . . However, the concept has been applied in a relatively restricted way, by employing a test of the degree of authority, or control, which the defender had over those who actually carried out the infringement.
>
> . . . Leading cases [*Ames* and *Amstrad*] have held the providers of certain facilities . . . not liable despite the fact that their services and products rendered infringement easy and probable, the crucial factors in each case being that lawful activity was possible with the facilities provided, that the defendants had given express warnings to customers against use for infringing copying, and that they lacked the necessary control over what their customers did with the facilities provided.
>
> Where however one or more of these factors is lacking, then liability for authorisation is more likely. (MacQueen and Waelde, 2006, p. 9)

Similarly, the Supreme Court of Canada has focused on the element of 'control' in determining whether copyright infringement exists. In *CCH Canadian Ltd. v. Law Society of Upper Canada*, the Canadian Supreme Court held that a law library that provided self-service photocopiers was not liable for infringing copying by its patrons, stating that: 'a person does not authorize copyright infringement by authoring the mere use of equipment (such as photocopiers) that could be used to infringe copyright. In fact, courts should presume that a person who authorizes an activity does so only so far as it is in accordance with the law' (*CCH*, 2004, paras 38, 43–45). The *CCH* Court expressly rejected a 1976 Australian High Court opinion, *Moorhouse v. University of New South Wales*, which had imposed copyright liability on a university library that provided self-service photocopiers to its patrons, stating that the Australian court's decision 'shifts the balance in copyright too far in favor of the owner's rights and unnecessarily interferes with the proper use of copyrighted works for the good of society as a whole' (*CCH*, 2004, para. 41). Thus, the Canadian Supreme Court seemed concerned with the same balance between the public good and the rights of the innovator that the US Supreme Court addressed in *Sony*.

Shortly after the *CCH* decision, the Canadian Supreme Court ruled that an ISP that functioned merely as a 'conduit' of content was not liable for infringement, stating: 'The knowledge that someone *might* be using neutral technology to violate copyright (as with the photocopier in the *CCH* case) is not necessarily sufficient to constitute authorization, which requires a demonstration that the defendant did "[g]ive approval to; sanction; permit; favor; encourage"' the infringement by the end user (*SOCAN*, 2004, paras 122, 127).

Other countries address issues of secondary liability for intellectual property infringement in still different ways. For example, under the German civil code, secondary liability for copyright infringement arises from code provisions that impose joint and vicarious liability upon tortfeasors (German Civil Code, §§ 830 and 831). German courts have found secondary liability appropriate where the defendant has engaged in activities such as 'promoting a concert at which copyrighted works are performed without authority, operating a restaurant or dance hall where music is performed by live bands or jukebox, and manufacturing or selling copying equipment, at least if the equipment lacks any substantial noninfringing use' (Goldstein, 2001, p. 272).

By contrast, some countries recognize the notion of 'inciting' others to commit copyright infringement. Article 1382 of the French Civil Code, for example, provides: 'Any act whatever of man, which causes damage to another, obliges the one by whose fault it occurred, to compensate it.' This section provides the basis under French law for imposing liability not only for authorizing another to commit an infringing act, but for inciting the infringement of another as well (Sterling, 2003, pp. 511–12).

The most recent push on secondary liability for intellectual property infringement is coming from the European Union and takes the form of criminal, as opposed to civil, sanctions.[5] The European Parliament's Legal Affairs Committee met in March 2007 to vote on the proposed EU Directive on Criminal Measures Aimed at Ensuring the Enforcement of Intellectual Property Rights. This directive would criminalize and create a new basis for secondary liability for intellectual property infringements (excluding patents) not currently found in most European nations – that of 'inciting' infringement. Article 3 of the proposed Directive states: 'Member States shall ensure that all intentional infringements of an intellectual property right on a commercial scale, and attempting, aiding or abetting and inciting such infringements, are treated as criminal offenses.' The directive had its first reading before the plenary session of the European Parliament in April 2007, but was amended to exclude patent infringement, and to reject criminal sanctions for copyright infringement in the private, non-profit arena. During the parliamentary debate, several members emphasized that the directive was not meant to target young peer-to-peer file sharers (European Parliament, 20 March, 2007).

Post-Grokster Secondary Liability in the International Arena for Peer-to-peer File Swapping

Within months of the *Grokster* decision, courts in several other countries also faced the issue of secondary liability in the context of peer-to-peer networks. The decision of the Federal Court of Australia in *Universal Music Australia Pty Ltd v. Sharman License*

Holdings Ltd is discussed separately, and first, because of its similarities to *Grokster*, and then measures taken in other countries are described.

Australia: *Universal Music Australia Pty Ltd v. Sharman License Holdings Ltd*

Direct infringement occurs under Australian law when a person, without the license or permission of the copyright holder, does or authorizes the doing in Australia of an act properly within the purview of the copyright holder (Australian Copyright Act, 1968, §§ 36, 101). Direct infringement does not require any knowledge or intent on the part of the infringer (*Francis Day & Hunter Ltd*, 1963). 'Authorization' occurs when a person 'sanctions, approves or countenances' (*Nationwide News Pty Ltd*, 1996) another's doing of an act that would consist of direct infringement. Thus, direct infringement through authorization in Australia is akin to the notion of secondary liability in the United States. Indirect infringement under Australian law, by contrast, consists of importing into Australia or distributing within Australia infringing copies for a commercial purpose without the permission of the copyright holder (Australian Copyright Act, 1968, §§ 37, 38, 102, 103). There is a mens rea requirement for indirect infringement, but '[i]t is sufficient that there be actual or constructive knowledge that intellectual property rights would be infringed, without knowledge of the precise nature of those rights' (Gilchrist and Nott, 1997, p. 14).

Section 101(1) of the Australian Copyright Act of 1968 imposes liability upon someone who 'authorizes' a direct act of infringement by another. In addition, the Copyright Amendment (Digital Agenda) of 2000 provides that, in determining whether an unlawful 'authorization' has occurred, the court must consider:

> (a) the extent (if any) of the person's power to prevent the doing of the act concerned; (b) the nature of any relationship existing between the person and the person who did the act concerned; (c) whether the person took any other reasonable steps to prevent or avoid the doing of the act, including whether the person complied with any relevant industry codes of practice.

Justice Wilcox of the Federal Court of Australia addressed secondary liability in the file-swapping area in 2005 in *Universal Music Australia Pty Ltd v. Sharman License Holdings Ltd*, reaching an outcome very similar to that of the United States Supreme Court in *Grokster*, though on different grounds. Under Australian law, secondary liability for copyright is primarily statutory in origin, as opposed to the common-law origins of United States secondary liability for copyright infringement; the difference in underlying authority creates a substantial difference in analysis as well.

According to the *Sharman* court, '[k]knowledge, or lack of knowledge, is an important factor in determining whether a person has authorized an infringement' (*Sharman*, 2005, para. 370). Authorization, the court noted, need not arise from 'express or formal permission or sanction', but rather encompasses as well 'inactivity or indifference . . . from which an authorization or permission may be inferred' (*Sharman*, 2005, paras 366–7).The *Sharman* court noted that Sharman qualified for the statutory safe harbor of Section 112E of the Copyright Act, which provides that:

> A person . . . who provides facilities for making, or facilitating the making of, a communication is not taken to have authorized any infringement of copyright in an audio-visual item merely because another person uses the facilities so provided to do something the right to do which is included in the copyright. (Australian Copyright Act, 1968, § 112E)

In this sense, *Sharman* and *Grokster* are similar in that both declined to find that secondary liability attaches merely because a defendant provides facilities that are used by others to engage in direct infringement.

However, the *Sharman* court went on to state, neither does Section 112E 'confer general immunity against a finding of authorization' (*Sharman*, 2005, para. 399). The court found additional evidence indicating Sharman had authorized infringement by its end users, including limited efforts to prevent its users from engaging in copyright infringement and evidence that Sharman had the 'power' to prevent or limit such infringement, but failed to do so (*Sharman*, 2005, para. 411). In this sense, both *Sharman* and *Grokster* were looking for additional behavior that would support imposition of secondary liability. In *Sharman*, the additional behavior was advertising on Sharman's website that 'would have conveyed the idea that was "cool" to defy the record companies and their stuffy reliance on their copyrights' (*Sharman*, 2005, para. 405); in *Grokster*, it was the targeted advertisements and solicitations that induced end users to infringe (*Grokster*, 2005, pp. 937–8).

Ultimately, the *Sharman* court issued an injunction in favor of the copyright holders, but provided an opportunity for the relevant respondents to modify the Kazaa system in a targeted way, so as to protect the applicants' copyright interests (as far as possible) but without unnecessarily intruding on others' freedom of speech and communication' (*Sharman*, 2005, para. 520).[6] Thus, the *Sharman* court, like the *Grokster* court, recognized the need to balance the protection of copyright through imposition secondary liability with the need to protect free speech and commercial activity.

Other countries' responses to peer-to-peer file-swapping activities

In the months following *Grokster*, courts in several nations had the opportunity to address assertions of secondary liability in the peer-to-peer file-swapping context.[7] In some instances (for example, Hong Kong, Spain and Taiwan), criminal sanctions were issued against the defendants. For example, in October 2005, a Hong Kong court criminally convicted an individual of using BitTorrent technology to illegally distribute copyrighted movies via a peer-to-peer network (MPAA, 2005). On 31 May, 2005, Weblisten, a Spain-based website that offered songs for downloading and streaming, admitted to criminal copyright infringement, and the site was shut down (IFPI, 2005). And in June, 2006, the Spanish Congress passed intellectual property legislation that banned unauthorized peer-to-peer file-sharing in Spain, making it a civil offense to download even for personal use and making it a criminal offense for ISPs to facilitate unauthorized downloading (TMCNET, 2006).

The Taiwanese Copyright Act of 2003 also provides for criminal penalties and civil liability of violators of the law. The first Taiwanese file-sharing case, which involved both a criminal and a civil action, was brought against Weber Wu, president of ezPeer, a for-fee peer-to-peer file-swapping service. The criminal action failed. The Shihlin District Court ruled on 30 June, 2005 that Wu was not guilty of infringing intellectual property rights (Ho, 2005) because Taiwanese laws did not subject a distributor of peer-to-peer file-sharing software to criminal liability (Kuo and Li, 2006). The court also found that ezPeer was not directly liable for copyright infringement and that the defendants were not secondarily liable for copyright infringement occurring as a result of the use of ezPeer services by third parties (Kuo and Li, 2006). The court stated that the copyright law did not impose an independent duty on software developers or distributors to monitor or curb infringement by end users and rejected the notion that foreign courts' decisions upholding contributory liability of distributors, such as *Napster* in the United States or *Soribada* in Korea, were relevant as those cases involved civil liability, not criminal prosecution (Kuo and Li, 2006).

However, the Taiwan International Federation of the Phonographic Industry (IFPI) had brought a simultaneous civil suit proceeding against ezPeer, and the result there was very different. In July 2006, the parties announced that they had settled their dispute by entering into a cooperative agreement in which ezPeer would become Ezpeer+, 'the world's first legal P2P music-download Web site' (MyEGov, 2006).

Just three months after the ezPeer ruling, two directors and the president of the Taiwanese peer-to-peer file-sharing network, KURO, were criminally convicted of copyright infringement in September 2005 by the Taipei District Court. Although KURO operates in a manner similar to ezPeer, the *KURO* court found that KURO was aware that users were using its product to infringe copyrights, had failed to act to prevent such infringement, and had in fact intentionally advertised and distributed its software to enable users to download works illegally (Kuo and Li, 2006). Thus, the court found that KURO had knowingly facilitated copyright infringement and was just as criminally liable as the end users. The president received a jail term of two years; the two directors (both sons of the president) received jail terms of three years. Each of the three was also fined US $91 000 as well (Fang, 2005). At the same time, one of the subscribers was sentenced to four months in jail and three years' probation (Kuo and Li, 2006). To settle a simultaneous civil suit brought by the IFPI, KURO paid approximately US $9 million in damages to the record companies and agreed to shut down its operations (Taiwan Intellectual Property Office, 2006).

In a purely civil suit, South Korea's largest on-line music service, Soribada, was shut down in November 2005 by the Seoul Central District Court. The suit had been filed by the Korean Association of Phonogram Producers, the Korean equivalent of RIAA (Smith, 2005). Within months of the decision, Soribada announced plans to convert to a paid subscription service (Rosenblatt, 2006).

WHERE TO GO FROM HERE: SECONDARY LIABILITY IN THE INTERNATIONAL ARENA

It is easy to focus on peer-to-peer networks when looking at secondary liability issues for intellectual property right infringement; the prevalence of such networks, the ease with which copying and distribution can occur in the digital environment, their substantial impact on the market for lawful copies of the copyrighted works, and the vigilance of the entertainment industry in seeking out and suing the providers of such networks all provide ample fodder for analysis.

There are without question problems with imposing secondary liability in the file-swapping arena. Two leading commentators have pointed out several of these problems, including: (1) the likelihood that secondary liability rules will ban lawful as well as unlawful conduct; (2) the potential that imposition of secondary liability would discourage creation of peer-to-peer networks, which are powerful, socially-beneficial tools for dissemination of information when used appropriately; (3) the inappropriateness of asking facilitators to police in what is essentially a gray area of the law; (4) the agency cost problems engendered by the fact that facilitators do not have correct incentives to distinguish lawful from unlawful conduct, and so may unnecessarily take down lawful content, thus giving intellectual property rights holders too much power; and (5) unintended negative consequences on innovation occasioned by cutting short development of technology that might be currently used for primarily unlawful purposes, but which could evolve into lawful technology that creates new and unexpected markets for the rights holders (such as the VCR) (Lemley and Reese, 2004, pp. 1379–90).

The answer to this dilemma, however, is that the current dialogue on secondary liability for intellectual property infringement in the international arena is focusing on the wrong question – or at least, not upon the fundamental questions that should underpin the initial discussion. Even though the Internet may bring indirect infringement activities to new highs (or lows, depending upon your view), secondary liability issues are prominent in the bricks-and-mortar world as well. Indirect infringement is not just a phenomenon created by the evolution of digital technology, and analysis of this subject should not be artificially restricted by focusing on this narrow application. However, the current state of technology does make transnational copyright infringement much easier than it was in the pre-digital, pre-Internet era. It also highlights the need to create international norms for secondary liability that make it easier for business to operate in a global marketplace by making it easier for actors to predict outcomes and easier for intellectual property rights holders to structure their activities in a way that enables them to adequately protect their resources or minimize their liabilities (depending upon which side of the dispute they occupy).

Ultimately, creation of international standards for secondary liability for copyright infringement in particular (or intellectual property rights infringement in general) would require consensus at the international level that such a standard should exist (as memorialized in an international agreement), followed by implementing legislation at the national level in all signatory nations. It might well be easier to consider international responses to secondary liability for copyright infringement in the peer-to-peer file-swapping context if we had a clearer sense of the convergence or divergence of international norms on secondary liability for copyright infringement generally.

So, the bottom-line solution is that we pull away from the current dialogue about peer-to-peer file-swapping and commence the discussion instead at the less refined and perhaps less charged level of traditional applications of secondary liability outside the digital context. When does it make sense to hold another liable for the direct infringement of another party? What is the significance of identifying certain behavior as direct infringement in some countries and indirect infringement in others? Current national standards define secondary liability based upon a number of different factors, including: (1) financial benefit; (2) actual control; (3) the right to control (even though unexercised); (4) knowledge; (5) contribution; (6) intent; (7) inducement; and (8) incitement. Which of these factors makes most sense in the international context, and is there a way of synthesizing them down to a few, widely-acceptable factors? Or is there some other, as yet unarticulated standard that should be considered instead?

The Supreme Courts of both Canada and the United States have emphasized the need to balance the goals of commerce and free markets with the protection and encouragement of innovation. These concerns are worthy of substantial debate and consideration at the international level, and should underlie any debate on imposition of secondary liability.

NOTES

* Copyright 2007 Lynda J. Oswald.

1. On 18 July 2007, the RIAA sent its latest round of pre-litigation letters to 408 users at 23 universities. RIAA activities are described in press releases found at http://www.riaa.com/news-room.php.
2. As explained in Oswald (2006, pp. 235–6):

> *Grokster* is, in fact, the prototypical inducement case: many small, individual infringers, each inflicting a small injury and each relatively judgment-proof, and one or a few alleged inducers, each possessing significantly deeper pockets. The direct infringers in *Grokster* are the multitude of individual users of the peer-to-peer networks, who use the networks to illegally download copyrighted materials. Identifying and taking action against these individual users is cumbersome, expensive, and offensive to those whom the copyright holders would like to have become lawful, paying consumers of the copyrighted materials. The courts (followed in the patent arena by the legislature) have recognized that in instances such as these, it is not only the direct infringers who should be held liable but those who encourage and enable such direct infringement as well. While the injury inflicted by each individual direct infringer may well be very small, the aggregated injury made possible by the machinations of the inducer of that direct infringement may be crushingly large.

3. For a general survey of individual countries' intellectual property laws, see McDonald et al. (2006).
4. Authorization is a separate act of infringement from the act itself which is authorized. See *Ash v. Hutchinson & Co. (Publishers) Ltd*, [1936] Ch. 489; *ABKCO Music v. Music Collection Int'l Ltd*, [1995] RPC 657.
5. Existing directives on intellectual property infringement include Directive 2001/29/Ec of the European Parliament and of the Council of 22 May 2001 on the Harmonization of Certain Aspects of Copyright and Related Rights in the Information Society; Directive 2004/48/Ec of the European Parliament and of the Council of 29 April 2004 on the Enforcement of Intellectual Property Rights L 195/16 EN Official Journal of the European Union 2.6.2004. Civil sanctions were covered in the later directive, which is available at http://eur-lex.europa.eu/LexUriServ/LexUriServ/LexUriSer.do?uri=CELEX:22004l0048R(01):EN:NOT.
6. An appeal was taken in the case to the full Australian federal court, but the parties settled the case in November 2006 before a decision was handed down. Reportedly, the settlement required Kazaa to implement filtering technology to prevent its users from distributing infringing copies of files, and Sharman Networks agreed to pay over $100 million to certain global record labels. See Caroline McCarty, 'With settlement, Kazaa casts off its pirate garb', available at http://news.com.com/Kazaa+settles+suits+with+more+than+100+million/2100–1027_3–6099064.html.
7. For a general analysis of secondary liability in the international peer-to-per file-sharing context, see Pessach (2007). In addition to the actions described in this subsection, there have been peer-to-peer file-sharing suits brought in Japan and China.

REFERENCES

A & M Records v. Napster, 239 F.3d 1004 (9th Cir. 2001) (cited as *A & M Records*).

Adams, Charles W. (2006), 'A brief history of indirect liability for patent infringement', *Santa Clara Computer & High Technology Law Review*, **22**, 369–98.

Aimster (2003), In re Aimster Copyright Litig., 334 F.3d 643 (7th Cir. 2003).

Ames Records and Tapes (1982), *CBS v. Ames Records and Tapes Ltd*, [1982] Ch. 91.

Australian Copyright Act, 1968, (Australia)

Bartholomew, Mark and John Tehranian (2006), 'The secret life of legal doctrine: The divergent evolution of secondary liability in trademark and copyright law', *Berkeley Technology Law Journal*, **21**, 1363–419.

Berne Convention for the Protection of Literary and Artistic Works (1971), 24 July, 1979, US Senate Treaty Doc. 99–27, KAV 2245, 1 BDIEL 715, 17 USC § 104, available at http://wipo.int/treaties/en/index.jsp

Canadian Copyright Act (1985), Copyright Act, R.S.C. 1985, as amended, ch. C-42.
CBS Songs v. Amstrad, [1988] AC 1013.
CCH (2004), *CCH Canadian Ltd. v. Law Society of Upper Canada*, 2004 SCC 12.
Chisum, Donald S. (2007), *Chisum on Patents*, USA: Matthew Bender & Co.
Convention for the Protection of Producers of Phonograms Against Unauthorized Duplication of Their Phonograms (1971), Oct. 29, 1971, 25 UST 309, TIAS 7808, 888 UNTS 67, Geneva, reprinted at http://www.wipo.int/clea/docs/en/wo/wo023en.htm.
EU Directive on Criminal Measures Aimed at Ensuring the Enforcement of Intellectual Property Rights (proposed), available at http://europa.eu.int/eur-lex/lex/LexUriServ/site/en/com/2006/com2006_0168en01.pdf.
European Parliament (2007), 'Intellectual property rights: Criminal sanctions to fight piracy and counterfeiting', 20 March, available at http://www.europarl.europa.eu/news/expert/infopress_page/057–4356-078-03-12-909-20070319IPR04284-19-03-2007-2007-false/default_en.htm.
Fang, Rita (2005), 'District court delivers guilty verdict in peer-to-peer file-swapping case', 27 September, available at http://www.gio.gov.tw/taiwan-website/4-oa/20050927/2005092701.html.
Fonovisa, Inc. v. Cherry Auction, Inc., 76 F.3d 256 (9th Cir. 1999).
Francis Day & Hunter Ltd. v. Bron, [1963] Ch. 587.
French Civil Code, art. 1382, English translation available at: http://www.legifrance.gouv.fr/html/codes_traduits/code_civil_textA.htm#CHAPTER%20II%20%20OF%20INTENTIONAL%20AND.
Garnett, Kevin, Gillian Davies and Gwilym Harbottle (eds) (1999), *Copinger and Skone James on Copyright*, Andover, UK: Sweet & Maxwell.
Geller, Paul (2000), *International Copyright Law and Practice*, USA: Matthew Bender & Co.
German Civil Code §§ 830 and 831, available at http://www.law.ed.ac.uk/file_download/courses/handouts/LLM/119/1730_germancivilcode.pdf.
Gilchrist, Simon and Fiona Nott (1997), 'Australia', in Susan Cotter (ed.), *Copyright Infringement: Comparative Law Yearbook of International Business, Special Issue 1997*, Kluwer Law International.
Ginsburg, Jane C. and Sam Ricketson (2006), 'Inducers and authorisers: A comparison of the US Supreme Court's Grokster decision and the Australian Federal Court's KaZaa ruling', *Media and Arts Law Review*, **11**(1).
Goldstein, Paul (2001), *International Copyright: Principles, Law, and Practice*, USA: Oxford University Press.
Grokster (2005), *MGM v. Grokster, Ltd*, 545 US 913 (2005).
Groennings, Kristina (2005), 'Costs and benefits of the recording industry's litigation against individuals', *Berkeley Technology Law Journal*, **20**, 511–601.
Heise online, (2007), 'EU Parliament restricts criminal-law sanctions for IP violations', 26 April, available at http://www.heise.de/english/newsticker/news/88908.
Ho, Jessie (2005), 'Ezpeer found not guilty in landmark copyright verdict', *Taipei Times*, 1 July, available at http://www.taipeitimes.com/News/front/archives/2005/07/01/2003261705.
Holbrook, Timothy (2004), 'Territoriality waning? Patent infringement for offering in the United States to sell an invention abroad', *University of California at Davis Law Review*, **37**, 701–59.
IFPI (2005), 'International recording industry weclomes closure of weblisten', 1 June, available at http://www.ifpi.org/content/section_news/20050601.html.
IRO Amici Brief (2005), Brief of Amici Curiae International Rights Owners Supporting Petitioners, in *MGM v. Grokster*, 545 US 913 (2005).
Jurgens (1996), *Jurgens v. CBK, Ltd*, 80 F.3d 1566 (Fed. Cir. 1996).
Kuo, Yu-law and Hsien-Chen Li (2006), 'Changes in the IP enforcement regime', available at http://www.buildingipvalue.com/06AP/345_348 .htm.
Lemley, Mark A. (2005), 'Inducing patent infringement', *University of California at Davis Law Review*, **39**, 225–46.
Lemley, Mark A. and R. Anthony Reese (2004), 'Reducing digital copyright infringement without restricting innovation', *Stanford Law Review*, **56**, 1345–434.
Lichtman, Douglas and William Landes (2003), 'Indirect liability for copyright infringement: An economic perspective', *Harvard Journal of Law and Technology*, **16**, 395–410.

MacQueen, Hector and Charlotte Waelde (2006), 'UK copyright law in the digital environment', *Electronic Journal of Comparative Law*, **10**(3), available at http://www.ejcl.org/103/art103–10.pdf.
McDonald, Morag, Uma Suthersanen and Christina Garigues (eds) (2006), *Copyright: World Law and Practice*, London: Sweet & Maxwell.
Moorhouse v. University of New South Wales, [1976] RPC 151.
MPAA (2005), 'P2P movie pirate convicted in Hong Kong in first criminal case against BitTorrent user', 24 October, available at http://www.mpaa.org/press_releases/2005_10_24.pdf.
MyEGov (2006), 'ezPeer, IFPI reach IP-infringement case settlement', Taiwan Headlines, 7 July, available at http://english.www.gov.tw/TaiwanHeadlines/index.jsp?categid=9&recordid=96724.
Nationwide News Pty Ltd v. Copyright Agency Ltd, [1996] 34 IPR 53.
Nimmer, David (2007), *Nimmer on Copyright*, USA: Matthew Bender & Co.
Oswald, Lynda J. (2006), 'The intent element of "inducement to infringe" under patent law: reflections on *Grokster*', *Michigan Telecommunications and Technology Law Review*, **13**(Fall), 225–46.
Paris Convention for the Protection of Industrial Property, 20 March, 1883, 13 UST 1.
Patent Act of 1790, ch. 7, 1 Stat. 109–12, § 4.
Pessach, Guy (2007), 'An international-comparative perspective on peer-to-peer file-sharing and third party liability in copyright law: Framing the past, present, and next generations' questions', *Vanderbilt Journal of Transnational Law*, **40**, 87–133.
Peters, Marybeth (2006), 'The challenge of copyright in the digital age', posted January, available at http://usinfo.state.gov/products/pubs/intelprp/challenge.htm.
Picker, Randal C. (2002), 'Copyright as entry policy: The case of digital distribution', *Antitrust Bulletin*, **47**, 423–64.
Rosenblatt, Bill (2006), 'Soribada to charge differently for DRM and non-DRM music tracks', 20 March, available at http://www.drmwatch.com/ocr/article.php/3595426.
Sharman Amicus Brief (2005), Brief of Amicus Curiae Sharman Networks Ltd., in *MGM v. Grokster*, 545 US 913 (2005).
Sharman (2005), *Universal Music Australia Pty Ltd v. Sharman License Holdings Ltd*, [2005] FCA 1242.
Smith, Tony (2005), 'South Korean P2P service powers down', available at http://www.theregister.co.uk/2005/11/08/korean_p2per_down/.
SOCAN (2004), *Society of Composers, Authors and Music Publishers of Canada v. Canadian Ass'n of Internet Providers*, 2004 SCC 45.
Sony (1984), *Sony Corp. of America v. Universal City Studios, Inc.*, 464 US 417, 422 (1984).
Sterling, J.A.L. (2003), *World Copyright Law*, 2nd edn, London, UK: Sweet & Maxwell.
Taiwan Intellectual Property Office (2006), 'KURO and IFPI Taiwan legal action and settlement', 22 September, available at http://www.tipo.gov.tw/eng/press/ne20060922_1.asp.
Thomas, John R. (2005), 'Intellectual property and the Free Trade Agreements: Innovation policy issues', CRS Report for Congress, 21 December, available at http://www.opencrs.com/rpts/RL33205_20051221.pdf.
TMCNet (2006), 'Spain outlaws P2P filesharing', 27 June, http://www.tmcnet.com/usubmit/2006/06/27/1696993.htm.
TRIPS (1994), Agreement on Trade Related Aspects of Intellectual Property Rights, Marrakesh Agreement Establishing the World Trade Organization, Annex 1C, Apr. 15, 1994, 869 UNTS 299, 33 ILM 1125, 1197, available at http://www.wto.org/english/docs_e/legal_e/27-trips.pdf.
UK Copyright, Designs and Patent Act (1988), available at http://www.opsi.gov.uk/acts/acts1988/Ukpga_19880048_en_1.htm
Universal Copyright Convention (1971), July 24, 1971, 25 UST 1341, TIAS 7868, 1 BDIEL 813, Paris text, reprinted at http://www.unesco.org/culture/laws/copyright.html_eng/page1.shtml.
World Intellectual Property Organization (1997), Copyright Treaty, S. Treaty Doc. No. 105–17, at 1, 36 ILM 65 (Geneva, 1997), available at http://www.wipo.int/treaties/en/index.jsp; WIPO Performances and Phonograms Treaty, S. Treaty Doc. No. 105–17, at 18, 36 ILM 76 (Geneva, 1997), at 18, 36 ILM 76 (Geneva, 1997), available at http://www.wipo.int/treaties/en/index/jsp.

4. Coming attractions: opportunities and challenges in thwarting global movie piracy

Lucille M. Ponte[1]

INTRODUCTION

Disaster films have long been a staple of the movie industry, reaping huge revenues by scaring moviegoers with the familiar formula of catastrophes threatening to destroy the world as we know it (Rabinowitz, 1997). Theater patrons have thrilled to man-made disasters such as burning skyscrapers in *Towering Inferno* and mad scientist cloning in *Jurassic Park* to natural disasters such as 'Sensurround' seismic calamities for *Earthquake* or flying cows and gas tankers in *Twister* to doomsday scenarios involving errant asteroids in *Armageddon*, invading aliens in *War of the Worlds*, or instantaneous global warming in *The Day After Tomorrow*. In recent years, the movie industry seems to be producing its own disaster film, *Global Movie Piracy*, starring menacing theater cammers, devious downloaders and corrupt optical disc manufacturers. The Motion Picture Association of America (MPAA) claims that the industry lost $18 billion in potential revenues in 2005 alone due to global film piracy (MPAA, 2005c); resulting in approximately 141 030 job losses and $837 million in lost US tax revenues (MPAA, 2006b). The industry asserts that international movie piracy endangers its teetering business model in which only one in ten films recovers its initial investments (Taylor, 2005).

Since Hollywood finds comfort in following a safe formula, the MPAA along with its global arm, the Motion Picture Association (MPA), have shadowed the actions of the Recording Industry Association of America (RIAA) in its battle against music piracy, using courtroom, legislative and technological strategies. The film industry has sued movie consumers and open content sites like YouTube, for copyright violations (Liedtke, 2006; Veiga, 2006; Williams, 2007) and won legal actions against companies offering file-sharing (*MGM Studios, Inc. v. Grokster, Ltd*, 2005; see MPAA, 2005c) and DVD duplication software for videos (*321 Studios v. MGM Studios, Inc.*; see Borland, 2004a). The industry has also successfully lobbied Congress and the legislative bodies of foreign nations to increase the breadth and severity of criminal copyright infringement (Daly, 2007; Morea, 2006; MPAA, 2005c) and prodded international law enforcement to utilize public resources to investigate and prosecute infringers to vindicate their private economic rights (see Clark, 2006; MPAA, 2005c; Nasheri, 2004). Furthermore, these film organizations have also spearheaded global educational programs to inculcate in the public consciousness the importance of respecting intellectual property rights and the civil and criminal penalties for failing to do so (MPAA, 2005c; see WIPO, n.d.b).

From a technological standpoint, the film industry rushed to develop digital rights management (DRM) tools that seek to deter illegal copying (Gardiner, 2006; Taylor, 2005), which often end up being more successful in frustrating average consumers who wish simply to view or make back-up copies of digital media they have lawfully purchased for use on a wide range of home technology devices (Daly, 2007; Gardiner, 2006; Taylor, 2005). While legitimate purchasers are confounded by DRM protections, pirates have consistently hacked these systems and made circumvention tools, such as DeCSS and mod chips, readily available to dishonest users. Many commentators have questioned continuing efforts to shore up DRM tools in light of easy access of circumvention tools and the failure of DRM to halt movie piracy (EFF, 2006; Haber et al., 2003).

Some experts have criticized these approaches as unfairly penalizing honest consumer behavior (Clark, 2006; Fitzdam, 2005) and improperly utilizing limited public law enforcement resources to enforce private economic rights (Clark, 2006; Nasheri, 2004; Yang and Hoffstadt, 2006). Furthermore, First Amendment advocates are concerned that the further criminalization of copyright violations places a chilling effect on free speech and continues to seek to dismantle fair use principles in this march toward zero tolerance against movie copyright violations (EFF, 2007; Heneghan, 2002; Jesdanun, 2007). Additionally, some industry experts have challenged the validity of the film industry's piracy statistics as gross exaggerations of the claimed disaster of film revenue losses (Lyman, 2004), particularly in light of 2006's highest box office revenues in global movie industry history ($28.5 billion) (*MPAA Box Office Press Release*, 2006e) and the continuing profitability of DVD sales (EFF, 2006).

While the film industry has focused almost exclusively on the doomsday scenario of movie piracy, other movie executives are trying to learn some lessons from the motivations for piracy in order to improve their economic prospects. Speaking at the 2006 MIPCOM, the global audio-visual content industry conference, Anne Sweeney, president of Disney-ABC, jolted the audience with her assertion that '[p]iracy is a business model . . . [i]t exists to serve a need in the market . . . [a]nd piracy competes for consumers, the same way we do: through quality, price, and availability' (Daly, 2007; Kiss, 2006). She added that the industry doesn't 'like the model but we realize it's competitive enough to make it a major competitor going forward' (Kiss, 2006).

Ms Sweeney hit upon the key error of many others in her industry – the failure to recognize that piracy serves customer interests in ways that the industry has long ignored. In addition, the ability of pirates to consistently defeat technological efforts to protect copyrighted materials suggests that the time has come to try to compete, rather than defeat, piracy's business model (Haber et al., 2003). There are numerous self-help remedies that the movie business could implement, but has not chosen to do so, which would reduce movie piracy without further aggravating honest consumers or draining precious law enforcement resources.

This chapter considers the three main forms of global movie piracy; camcorder piracy, optical disc piracy and Internet piracy, and discusses some of the typical players and distribution channels for pirated films. In response to these forms of piracy, the industry's efforts to lobby for tougher criminal sanctions and greater protections for DRM in the US and worldwide are considered, as well as their negative impact on consumer fair use rights. The failure of national laws and DRM to stymie movie piracy illustrates the need for the industry to consider new strategies that involve competing with the 'business model' of piracy (see Haber et al., 2003). Through key lessons from piracy, this chapter makes recommendations on self-help remedies that the film industry can implement to reshape its own business model in a manner that deters global movie piracy without alienating its customer base or straining already limited international law enforcement resources.

MAIN FORMS OF MOVIE PIRACY

Movie piracy involves instances of either illegal copying or bootlegged materials. Illegal copying is derived from illicit copies made of an authentic DVD, VHS tape or Video CD, either legally or illegally obtained. Individuals might make copies of a movie they purchased or received illegally from third party copies of authentic goods. For example, a film critic providing copies of an authentic film to friends and family before its wide public release would be an example of illegal copying. Typically, bootlegging deals with illicit recording of a live performance in the theater from which illegal copies are subsequently made and distributed (MPAA, 2005c). Bootlegging in the film business is primarily as a result of individuals secretly using camcorders in a theater who pass on the video to third parties for illegal duplication and quick distribution.

There are three main forms of movie piracy; 1) camcorder piracy, 2) optical disc piracy, and 3) Internet piracy. Each form of piracy provides a channel for illegal copying and distribution of films, often hours after the film has premiered, and in some instances, before the film is released in theaters worldwide (MPAA, 2005b; Nasheri, 2004; Department of Justice, 2007). Camcorder piracy concerns the illegal recording of a movie at its release by a theater patron or cinema employee (MPAA, 2005b; MPAA, 2005c). This bricks-and-mortar practice is the main source of illicit film copies, about 90 per cent of all pirated films, which end up in the illegal stream of goods on the Internet and in hard goods piracy in the real world (MPAA, 2005c). However, the visual quality of camcorded films is certainly less than authentic copies or copies reproduced in digital formats.

Optical disc piracy concerns bricks-and-mortar factories often operated by organized crime gangs, often readily found in Russia and Asia (Nasheri, 2004; Department of Justice, 2007). These optical disc factories can generate hundreds of thousands of counterfeit discs from illegal and/or bootleg copies of movies in a range of digital formats for quick distribution and sale in the real world (Bennett and Gershuny, 2006; MPAA, 2005a; MPAA, 2005c). It is estimated that Russian optical disc factories generate anywhere from 50 to 80 million counterfeit DVDs annually for global exports (MPA Europe, 2005). Unlike camcorder piracy, the illegal copies made in these factories tend to be high quality since they utilize the same technology and equipment used in legitimate replication factories (Bennett and Gershuny, 2006). In turn, the revenues from these counterfeit film sales may help fund the gang's other criminal activities and can seriously damage the legitimate market for these movies (Bennett and Gershuny, 2006; Nasheri, 2004; Department of Justice, 2007). In 2005, global law enforcement in collaboration with the MPAA confiscated more than 81 million illegal optical discs (MPAA, 2005a). In April 2007, the US filed complaints against China with the World Trade Organization (WTO) for its failure to crack down on piracy of copyrighted goods, especially the production and sales of counterfeit DVDs (Reuters, 2007; The Age Company Ltd, 2007; see Bloomberg News, 2007; Drajem, 2007).

Internet piracy deals with hacking vulnerable websites to steal movies or defeating DRM tools on authentic films, and then posting the materials on the Web for illegal file-sharing (MPAA, 2005c). Secretive and loosely-affiliated groups, known as 'warez traders' or 'warez release groups', specialize in hacking anti-theft protections on films and then transmitting their pirated films or 'moviez' over the Internet (Granade, n.d.; Department of Justice, 2007). They may view and exchange their illegal moviez with other top warez groups or simply collect them to try to impress others with their technical abilities and the breadth of their warez (Goldman, 2003; Granade, n.d.). Warez traders are seldom motivated by profit (National Institute of Justice (NIJ), 2004), but their hacked goods often end up on other websites with more entrepreneurial and criminal aims (Sag, 2006).

Although one hears a great deal about illegal file-sharing, more than 90 per cent of all initial releases of pirated movies come from illegal camcording, not from P2P sites. In addition, hard goods piracy of films sold both online (for example, auction sites) and in the bricks-and-mortar world (for example, street vendors or flea markets) is estimated to cost over $2.9 billion globally compared to Internet piracy from illegal downloading, projected to be $1.85 billion in losses. Similarly, in the US, hard goods movie piracy outpaces illegal file-sharing of films, with about $864 million in predicted losses compared to $447 million for illegal file-sharing (MPAA, 2005c). Industry analysts have also indicated that movie downloaders are the industry's core customers for whom downloading has little impact on their attendance at movie theaters; 43 per cent attended the movies at the same rate as in the past and 41 per cent attended more often. In fact, downloaders tend to be the movie industry's biggest fans, who enjoy watching the same movies, multiple times, in the theater and on a wide range of home and mobile devices (Lyman, 2004).

Regardless of the method of piracy, each form needs someone or some group to supply new movies to feed the production and distribution chains. At the beginning of the chain are 'brokers' who recruit other individuals or groups to become 'suppliers' who undertake the illicit copying activities (Department of Justice, 2006b; Department of Justice, 2007). 'Cammers' are the main suppliers of bootleg films, rushing to the cinema with their camcorders to illegally record a film at its opening. Cammers may be secretly filming the movie as a theater patron, but may also work in concert with theater employees, gaining access to the projectionist booth to record movies while avoiding detection. Cammers are key suppliers, but other industry insiders, such as movie critics and theater projectionists, are often involved in providing illegal copies of legitimate films to third parties (Department of Justice, 2006b; MPAA, 2005(c)).

'Couriers' gather the ill-gotten video from their suppliers, delivering their bootlegged or illegally copied products to 'replicators' who make hard goods copies for distribution, typically at optical disc factories. Couriers may also hand over illegal copies with DRM controls to release groups whose 'crackers' will break the DRM controls. The cracker will then test the movie, stripped of its DRM protections, to make sure it still plays correctly. The cracker then breaks the newly cracked film into smaller file packets and sends it to clusters of high speed and high storage 'top sites' for distribution over the Internet for illicit file-sharing or replication at remote optical disc factories (MPAA, 2005c; see Department of Justice, 2006b; Department of Justice, 2007; 'US Customs Dismantles', 2002).

'Facilitators', such as P2P movie sites, then provide the tools, including search engines, directories and P2P software, to aid file-sharers in locating and exchanging materials. Once on the Internet, the film can be illegally uploaded and downloaded by millions of individuals on their computers across the globe, sometimes within hours of its public release (MPAA, 2005c; see Department of Justice, 2006b; Department of Justice, 2007).

INDUSTRY LOBBYING FOR TOUGHER CRIMINAL SANCTIONS

The movie industry, along with others in digital media and entertainment industries, lobbied Congress to broaden the reach of copyright laws and to toughen the civil and criminal penalties for piracy. Although the civil courts may be the appropriate venue for copyright violations (Clark, 2006; Nasheri, 2004), three major revisions to US copyright laws made it easier for the film industry to push for more criminal investigations and prosecutions of movie piracy. First, the No Electronic Theft Act of 1997 (NET Act) specifically targeted warez release groups (Clark, 2006; Goldman and Gladstone, 2003; Goldman, 2003; Morea, 2006), expanding the definition of economic gain to include benefits derived from file-sharing of pirated goods (NET Act, 1997; see Andrews, 2005; Goldman, 2003). In the file-sharing environment, the Act amended the criminal copyright laws to permit prosecutions in cases in which there is no profit or economic motives (NET Act, 1997; see Clark, 2006; Goldman, 2003; Goldman and Gladstone, 2003; Morea, 2006).

Subsequently, Congress enacted the Digital Millennium Copyright Act (DMCA) in 1998, which, in part, made it a felony to try to circumvent or to manufacture, offer, or seek to provide devices that would circumvent DRM tools on copyrighted works (17 USC 1201; see Ferrera et al., 2004; Fitzdam, 2005; Morea, 2006; Erekosima and Koosed, 2004). Although the provisions of the DMCA specifically exempt fair use (17 USC §1201(c) (3)) from its reach, fair use has suffered significantly under the Act in practice. In the Copyright Office's triennial review of the law, persistent complaints about fair use encroachments and harms to consumer rights have been routinely rejected as 'mere inconveniences' with no DRM exemptions being granted under the law in 2000 and 2003 (EFF, 2005; Sweeting, 2003).

The US has been lobbying other nations to enact similar anti-circumvention provisions in their national laws through international trade agreements (Arnotts Lawyers, n.d.; Doctorow et al., 2005; WIPO, n.d.b) as well as through US support for the WIPO Internet treaties (WIPO, n.d.b). These treaties, the WIPO Copyright Treaty (WCT) and WIPO Performances and Phonogram Treaty (WPPT) call on member nations to provide adequate protection for DRM measures and effective legal remedies to enforce them (WCT, art. 11, 1997; WPPT, art. 18, 1997).

In the wake of the DMCA, the EU subsequently adopted the controversial European Union's Copyright Directive (EUCD) in 2001. The EUCD requires member nations to offer sufficient legal protections of DRM and to enforce appropriate anti-circumvention remedies (Goodman, 2005; Gasser and Girsberger, 2004; Grassmuck, 2004). Since its passage, EU member nations have struggled with harmonizing national consumer protection laws and the Directive's DRM mandates. Conforming national laws have been challenged in court and criticized as contradictory to established EU consumer rights and notions of fair use (Goodman, 2005; Grassmuck, 2004).

Under the DRM umbrella, the movie industry tossed in a number of add-ons, such as regional coding or locks on DVDs, barriers to the creation of back-up copies of DVDs for personal use, and tethering DVDs to specific proprietary platforms. These claimed DRM measures have no relationship to protecting legitimate copyright concerns and unfairly limit fair use options for consumers worldwide (CDT, 2006; EFF, 2005; Grassmuck, 2004; IP Justice, 2002). Few consumers are aware of these hidden DRM limitations because there are no clear disclosure obligations placed on industry regarding DRM limitations (see CDT, 2006; Grassmuck, 2004).

Most recently in 2005, Congress enacted the Family Entertainment and Copyright Act (FECA) (18 USC Appx §2B5.3). The Act made illegal camcording in the movie theater a felony under federal criminal law. Further, FECA enhanced the penalties for those who post online pre-release copies of copyrighted materials, such as movies (18 USC Appx §2B5.3(b)(2); see MPAA, 2005b; MPAA, 2005c). Besides federal statutes in the US, most states have long had criminal statutes against the use of recording devices in movie theaters (MPAA, 2005b).

With these key changes to copyright law, the movie industry has pressed for more criminal investigations and prosecutions of movie piracy, both domestically and globally (Daly, 2007; see MPA Asia Pacific, 2005; MPA-Europe, 2005; MPAA, 2005c). With the prodding of the movie association, US federal and international law enforcement agencies have collaborated in copyright infringement investigations and prosecutions, involving simultaneous search warrants in more than a dozen nations under various law enforcement operations in an effort to deter film piracy (US Fed News, 2006; see 'Internet Piracy Sweep', 2005). The MPAA reports that global law enforcement undertook 43 000 raids, resulting in 31 000 criminal cases, and the seizure of millions of illegal discs (MPAA, 2005c).

Pressure has been put on other nations to step up their prosecutions of movie piracy. For example, one of the recent US filings with the WTO contended that China was not doing enough to prosecute movie piracy within its borders (Drajem, 2007; Bloomberg News, 2007). Under the shadow of the pending WTO complaints, China announced that the possession of 500 or more pirated CDs or DVDs would now be sufficient to permit prosecution, compared to the previous threshold of 1000 illegal discs (Bloomberg News, 2007).

Yet law enforcement seldom receives plaudits or support from the public or their elected government representatives for their efforts (Nasheri, 2004). Recently, after much MPA prodding, Swedish law enforcement raided the offices of Pirate Bay, a well-known movie file-sharing site. After the raid, over 1000 Swedish citizens participated in rallies in favor of Pirate Bay in two major cities, Stockholm and Gothenburg, with mainstream politicians decrying the heavy-handed tactics (Daly, 2007). Similarly, surveys in the US show that most Americans do not view movie piracy as a major societal issue that deserves serious criminal sanctions or as worthy of a high priority within the law enforcement agenda (Morea, 2006; Nasheri, 2004).

In addition, many other nations question the ethics and legal bases for current copyright laws (Piquero and Piquero, 2006). Other cultures may view the enforcement of copyright as merely another chance for rich developed nations to force their values on poor developing countries (Doctorow, 2005; Piquero and Piquero, 2006) and to preserve the assets of wealthy elites (Piquero and Piquero, 2006). In the DVD distribution chain, if poorer nations even receive a film, they are the last countries to obtain the goods and only 'after all possible revenue has been wrung from the rich countries' (Doctorow, 2005).

Further, some cultures may simply eschew the Western legalistic approach to copyright and will focus on the morality of their conduct based upon an assessment of its impact on their social and familial networks (Piquero and Piquero, 2006). In one survey, Singaporean students were significantly more aware of the legal mandates of copyright than their North American counterparts, but viewed the ethics of their copying in a positive light as something beneficial to their family, friends and themselves (Piquero and Piquero, 2006). Indifference to intellectual property rights may also arise from growing consumer expectations about receiving information and entertainment on demand and customized to their tastes and interests (Goldman and Gladstone, 2003; Morea, 2006; Sohn, 2006; see Grassmuck, 2004).

However, some commentators have questioned the use of finite law enforcement resources to vindicate private economic interests, especially in light of more serious criminal activities that threaten public safety, such as drug trafficking and terrorism (Nasheri, 2004; Yang and Hoffstadt, 2006). Experts suggest that the highly profitable entertainment industry should focus on civil lawsuits using their own funds, rather than drawing on public resources, to vindicate their copyright interests (Clark, 2006; Nasheri, 2004). Legal commentators have also noted that most people want criminal laws to attack truly serious risks to public safety and that criminalizing copyright is not appropriate due to the absence of the potential for substantial physical harm to others (Morea, 2006). Reflecting public sentiment, Professor Joel Feinberg contends that copyright violations should only be subject to criminal sanctions if there are no other alternatives to curbing such conduct (Morea, 2006).

Since the film industry claims that movie piracy is rampant, then national laws and DRM technologies have been largely ineffective. Perhaps the time has come for the industry to consider other strategies in their battle against movie piracy. If the industry listened to Ms Sweeney and considered the 'business model' of piracy, they might easily find several self-help remedies that would improve customer satisfaction and deter piracy without draining public law enforcement resources.

LEARNING KEY LESSONS FROM PIRACY'S 'BUSINESS MODEL' – SELF-HELP REMEDIES

Pirates have no Trouble Finding Reliable Suppliers of New or Pre-release Films

Like any successful business model, pirates must be able to rely on dependable suppliers of films who can deliver illicit or bootlegged copies within hours of movie premieres and, in some cases, before general film release. Regardless of the criminal provisions of FECA or state laws against camming and online postings of pre-release films, pirates appear to have little difficulty finding willing suppliers primarily working within the motion picture and theater industries. As previously noted, cammers in the bricks-and-mortar world provide about 90 per cent of all pirated films. Since most films premiere in the US, this figure indicates that most piracy occurs on the business premises of US movie theaters either under the noses of or in collaboration with theater employees and other industry insiders. The MPAA and the National Association of Theater Owners (NATO) organization must take more proactive steps to cut off or decrease the supply of copyrighted materials, rather than drawing upon strained public law enforcement resources to prevent movie piracy.

Despite claims of devastating piracy losses, the MPAA and NATO seem to have had little success from a security perspective in deterring illegal camcorder conduct in the movie theater. The MPAA states that it is 'spending substantial amounts of money to upgrade movie print security across the country', including bag searches at selected pre-screening events, the use of night-vision monoculars, and warning signs about illegal camcording (MPAA, 2005b). Yet most moviegoers do not have to contend with any additional security measures at the theater, and if anything, there is less staff presence in the viewing audience than in the old days of ushers patrolling with flashlights. With cammers being the overwhelming source for pirated films, the industry's security measuresss are clearly inadequate. If the MPAA and NATO were more vigilant about security inside US cinemas, there would be less worry about piracy losses outside the multiplex.

However, in a competitive entertainment market, it seems unlikely that theater owners would want to inconvenience theater patrons further with additional security measures that may turn moviegoers off the theater experience (Mohl, 2007). Also, theater owners may not be willing to invest more money on print security when 90 per cent of the ticket revenues for opening weeks go to the movie studios while selling concessions accounts for 46 per cent of all cinema profits (Mohl, 2007). Ian M. Judge, the director of operations at FEI theaters, indicated that in today's movie world, a cinema operator may not consider itself to be 'a theater, but a restaurant that shows movies' (Mohl, 2007), which may result in less concern about film piracy.

In contrast to their willingness to use limited public law enforcement resources to fight piracy, the MPAA and NATO have focused largely on low or no cost tactics to prevent camming when the expenses come out of their own funds (see MPAA, 2006a). A review of the MPAA and NATO-sponsored guide, *Best Practices to Prevent Film Theft*, illustrates a generally superficial low-budget approach, such as suggestions to theater employees to 'look for glowing lights' or 'look for coats in summer' and posting signs that camcording is not allowed in the theater (MPAA, 2006a). In addition, the guide suggests such basic film print security behavior as locking or alarming projection booth doors, not handing film prints over to unauthorized persons, making regular entries into print movement logs, and being vigilant about friends of staff in the projection booth (MPAA, 2006a). Clearly mindful of expenses, the guide mildly suggests that cinema owners 'consider hiring private security' primarily on major opening weekends for blockbuster films (MPAA, 2006a).

The movie industry also proclaims that NATO employees 'are the first line of defense against this growing criminal enterprise'. Clearly, this defense is seriously flawed because cammers continue to be successful as consistent providers of illicit copies of first-run films to pirates. At present, the MPAA and NATO offer very weak training and incentive programs for theater employees to watch for and stop camming activities within the cinema. In 2005, the MPAA created Fightfilmtheft.org, a rudimentary website that offers a brief online tutorial and quiz (with a $300.00 prize draw) to theater employees who visit the site (MPAA, 2006c).

In addition, their 'Take Action' Reward Program offers employees the paltry sum of $500.00 under very limited circumstances for preventing camming activities in the cinema. The theater employee must meet five initial requirements to be eligible for the reward:

detect the individual using a camcorder in the cinema; immediately contact law enforcement; halt the recording before the film reaches its end; complete a police report; and then contact the MPAA within 24 hours of the occurrence (MPAA Reward Program, 2006). The theater employee is also warned not to endanger theater patrons when trying to stop camming (Training Guide, 2006), but it is unclear how the employee is supposed to recognize or prevent this potential threat. If they meet these mandates, they must then complete an application for the reward which can still be denied in the sole discretion of the MPAA and NATO (MPAA, 2006d).

Even though there are nearly 38 000 movie screens in the US (NATO, 2005) with multiple showings of films every day, the reward program has only distributed rewards to 84 recipients since May 2004 (E. Kaltman, E-Mail Communication, 24 April, 2007). Considering the supposed losses due to camming, the small reward and associated limitations on receiving it are unlikely to encourage employees to make the extra, and perhaps dangerous, effort to stop this illegal conduct. These organizations need to undertake more proactive training of their employees, emphasizing the importance of protecting copyrighted films to sustain company revenues and employee job security. Theaters and film companies should also better supervise employees to ensure compliance with their legal and fiduciary duties regarding copyrighted movies. By improving theater security, strengthening employee training and supervision, and providing better reward incentives, the industry could help prevent camming in US theaters and root out the main source of supply of pirated films.

Besides camming, pirates also often find helpful suppliers amongst other industry insiders, such as film critics, video store employees, and movie projectionists with pre- or early release access to films (MPAA, 2005c; Department of Justice, 2006b). For example, two film critics were indicted in Operation Copycat for selling advance copies of films online, one claiming to have sold more than 31 films and the other more than 100 advance copies (Department of Justice, 2006a; Department of Justice, 2006b). Film critics and movie projectionists could be required to sign additional confidentiality agreements that spell out stiff civil sanctions for selling or disclosing copyrighted films to third parties as well as the potential for discharges or loss of any applicable licenses for offending employees.

The theater and movie industries could also limit camming as well as the theft or illegal disclosure of film prints through the use of digital projection and distribution technology (Captain, 2006; Lyman, 2005). Digital projection systems replace physical copies of films with digital ones that contain imperceptible 'forensic trackers' (Captain, 2006). With digital cinema, physical prints need not be moved between theaters (The Big Screen Cinema Guide, n.d.), avoiding opportunities for theft or disclosure. Although digital projection does not prevent camming, investigators can examine the illicit copies for forensic markers, such as audio tones outside of human hearing or additional video frames unseen by the human eye, but captured on the camcorder, which indicate the date, time and location of the cammed movie (ibid.). The identifying information can be used to determine the source of the camming (Captain, 2006) and may aid in efforts to improve film protection and security at that theater. Also inserting additional frames imperceptible to the audience, but picked up by the camcorder, helps to degrade the quality of illegal copies (ibid.).

This technological option already exists, but the cost of transitioning to the new digital equipment has led many theater owners to balk at this opportunity (Lyman, 2005). In

2005, cinema giants AMC Entertainment, Cinemark USA and Regal Entertainment agreed to work together to volume purchase some of the devices to reduce costs and to create finance options to spread the costs of this new equipment (ibid.). It is expected that by 2007, 4000 digital cinema systems will be installed in the US, a tiny influx against piracy in light of the nearly 38 000 movie screens in the US (NATO, 2005) and another 100 000 movie screens worldwide (Lyman, 2005). But ultimately the MPAA and NATO will have to work together to speed up this transition globally by sharing the costs for these innovations (ibid.) to help combat illegal camming and reduce chances for film print theft.

Pirates give you Quick and Easy Access to a Great Selection of Movies at a Cheap Price

Pirates and illegal downloading sites owe much of their success to their ability to meet consumer demand for greater choice as well as faster and cheaper access to a wide selection of materials. Although civil litigation and criminal prosecution helped to decrease some illegal file-sharing of music, the development of legal file-sharing sites is widely viewed as the main reason for the downturn in illegal downloading (see Groennings, 2005; Morea, 2006). Most industry experts contend that the availability of cheap and fast access to digital products is essential to deter illegal file-sharing (Groennings, 2005; Morea, 2006; Pew Internet, 2004).

While the music industry has improved its fortunes by embracing legal digital downloading, the movie industry has been more resistant to change and has stumbled in its attempts to take advantage of this technological shift (Daly, 2007). Legal movie downloading sites have been roundly criticized for offering limited selections and film downloads priced at nearly the same level as physical media. Also unappealing technical restrictions have harmed the viability of these movie sites by requiring consumers to buy new kinds of DVD media, software and burners, locking users into certain proprietary platforms to play the downloaded movie, and/or requiring users to view films within 24 hours to avoid self-deletion (Daly, 2007).

In addition, new movie downloads on legitimate sites are normally delayed by the industry's standard cycle of permitting films to first complete their theatrical runs before they move into other outlets, such as cable, pay-per-view and DVD release (see MPAA, 2005c). Over the past few years, the window between theatrical and DVD release has remained largely unchanged, about 4½ months (Thompson, 2006). Unlike the industry, pirates manage to offer films within hours of a movie theatrical premiere and sometimes before a film has been formally debuted, at low or no cost.

One way to beat the pirates at their own game would be to experiment with options that allow fast, easy and cheap public access to films. A controversial strategy is to release a film on DVD and cable television on the same day as the theatrical release of a film. This approach, called 'day and date' release, may blunt some piracy by allowing the general public to view or download films immediately in a variety of ways (Gentile, 2006). The 'day and date' release strategy has been roundly criticized by traditional movie distributors who see it as endangering their revenues.

Award-winning director Steven Soderbergh of *Traffic* and *Ocean's Eleven* fame, teamed up with Magnolia Pictures, Landmark Theaters and HDNet Movies, a cable TV channel, to propose making six films that would use the 'day and date' strategy. Their first effort at day and date release was the experimental digital film *Bubble*, a mystery using amateur actors released in January 2006 (Gentile, 2006; Thompson, 2006). The major theater chains boycotted the film, so *Bubble* only opened in 32 theaters, including 19 Landmark theater screens, grossing only $200 000 in box office revenues. However, the quirky film had some success in its revenues from HDNet, foreign presales and DVD sales, which were in excess of 100 000 units, more DVD sales than would be expected for this type of film under the standard distribution window. Undeterred by the mixed results, Magnolia and Soderburgh are planning to experiment with this approach on some future films (Thompson, 2006).

Google Video has also undertaken some experimental film releases. In January 2006, Google provided online streaming of an independent filmmaker's digital thriller *Waterborne* for free for 2½ weeks as a marketing device. The service then opened the film up for free movie trailer downloads as well as film downloads in different formats; $3.99 for HD and 99 cents for low-definition versions. The DVD release followed six weeks later, rather than the standard of more than four months. Although the initial revenues were disappointing, the experiment was considered an important first step for independent film-makers seeking alternative channels for distribution as well as for consumers seeking quick and inexpensive access to content (Thompson, 2006). Subsequently, the Independent Film Channel announced that it would work with Comcast On-Demand to offer some independent films using the day and date release approach, permitting on-demand viewing at the same time as the theatrical release (Bylund, 2006).

The movie industry needs to undertake more experimentation to provide consumers with quick and cost-effective access to a broad selection of films. As consumer demand for content continues to evolve and as consumer expectations for on-demand viewing increase, the development of creative and legal access to films will help benefit both the movie industry and consumers, and deter movie piracy.

Pirates let you Watch (or Not Watch) your DVD Anywhere you Want to in the World

Any good business recognizes that customer satisfaction is a key foundation for business success. Unlike the movie industry, pirates recognize that the customer is always right and that routinely irritating your customers is bad for business. Pirated copies of films involve stripping away a broad range of DRM protections built into DVDs that are bundled into the content scrambling system (CSS) (Carroll, 2002; Grassmuck, 2004; Sarah, 2005a). The movie industry indicates that CSS is critical to protect copyrighted films from piracy and national laws, such as the DMCA, and international treaties criminalize tools that block or strip away CSS (see EFF, 2005; EFF, 2006). While the film-makers have a right to protect their creative works, copyright laws and the WIPO Internet treaties recognize the need for a balance between public access to creative materials and the protection of the rights of copyright owners (IP Justice, 2002; Sarah, 2005a). In the industry's zeal for DRM, its actions have unfairly tipped this delicate balance in favor of copyright owners in a manner that harms public access to legally-acquired DVDs (IP Justice, 2002; Sarah, 2005a) and pushes honest consumers towards piracy (Gardiner, 2006). Consumer advocates are calling for greater transparency on the breadth of DRM limitations (CDT, 2006; Grassmuck, 2004).

Region codes or locks on DVDs are a good example of commercial abuse of DRM under the CSS regime that has little to do with copyright protection and much to do with anti-competitive economic protectionism and unfair limits on customer fair use rights (Carroll, 2002; Doctorow, 2004; Grassmuck, 2004; IP Justice, 2002; Silva, n.d.; Sarah, 2005a). In 1996, the movie industry and DVD device manufacturers divided the globe into eight regions, with the US being region 1 (Silva, n.d.; Sarah, 2005a). These industries collaborated to create the DVD Copy Control Association which will only license the patent to CSS, the gateway to DVD technology, to companies that agree to use CSS on their devices, including region locks (Carroll, 2002; Doctorow, 2004; Grassmuck, 2004; IP Justice, 2002; Sarah, 2005a). Under this organization's mandates, the regional code embedded in the DVD must match the region code residing on the DVD device or else it will not play the DVD (Carroll, 2002; Doctorow, 2004; IP Justice, 2002; Sarah, 2005a). Therefore, region locks prevent consumers in one region of the world from playing back DVDs they legally purchased in another region of the world (Carroll, 2002; Doctorow, 2004; IP Justice, 2002; Sarah, 2005a; Silva, n.d). In 2005, the Blu-Ray Disc Association followed suit and adopted region codes for High Definition (HD) film releases, continuing these restrictive measures into the next generation of products (CDRinfo, 2005).

Most consumers have no idea about region locks until after they have made an ill-fated purchase. Therefore, an individual who purchases an Australian film on vacation will not be able to play it on their DVD player in the US because each country is in a separate, artificially-created DVD region (see Doctorow, 2004; Sarah, 2005a). Similarly, researchers, educators and students who may wish to explore another culture through film (Carroll, 2002) or individuals who want to keep cultural ties with their native countries (Doctorow, et al., 2005) are prevented from viewing items that they legally acquired because of region codes. Norwegian teenager Jon Johansen's desire to watch French DVDs by breaking these region locks, led him and friends to post DeCSS code that circumvents DRM tools, making him a marked man in the US but resulting in two acquittals in Norway (Doctorow, 2004; Doctorow et al., 2005; Sarah, 2005b). In addition, many developing nations rely on donated or low-cost used goods to gain access to instructional and creative works which are blocked by region-coding measures (Doctorow, 2004).

Prior to the development of DVDs, VHS tapes were not subject to DRM controls, and therefore contained no region locks. One could buy a VHS tape and play it on any VCR player anywhere. With the advent of DVDs, consumers have seen a marked decrease in their access to legally-obtained films through the use of region locks. While consumers have the right to watch legitimate DVDs from another region, the DMCA and other similar national laws criminalize consumer efforts to circumvent region locks on their own DVD player as well as others who might provide tools to help consumers avoid them (Doctorow, 2004).

With most films now only released on DVD, and VCR players becoming obsolete, it is becoming virtually impossible for consumers to make effective use of the prior alternative of region-free VHS tapes (Carroll, 2002; EFF, 2005). Unlike copyrighted books, vinyl records, CDs or VHS tapes which can be purchased and enjoyed anywhere, the consumer may not use their legally purchased DVD anywhere they wish, unfairly damaging the public access to creative works under copyright law (CDT, 2006; Doctorow, 2004; Grassmuck, 2004). Although one can buy DVDs from across the globe, consumers cannot play them without having regionally-matched DVD players. In essence, law-abiding consumers end up with less access to their legally acquired materials than pirates and those who trade or buy their illicit copies.

The consumer has few options to avoid region codes. Some consumers have altered their DVD players with mod chips that disable regional locks, which are illegal in the US under the DMCA and of questionable legality in other nations (see Gasser and Girsberger, 2004; Sarah, 2005b; Silva, n.d.). Secondly, DVD viewers could import expensive region-free DVD players with disabled region locks (Carroll, 2002; IP Justice, 2002; Silva, n.d.). However, the film industry recently introduced Regional Coding Enhancement (RCE) to ensure that certain region 1 DVDs will not even play on region-free DVD players (Gasser and Girsberger, 2004; Silva, n.d.). Therefore, the consumer might be forced to buy multiple DVD players for each region represented in their DVD collection or multiple copies of the same DVD (if they can find it) to match the region code on their current DVD device (Carroll, 2002; EFF, 2006; IP Justice, 2002). The Copyright Office recognized that viewing non-region DVDs is a non-infringing activity, yet concluded that any additional costs to consumers were a 'mere inconvenience' and rejected the request for an exemption from region locks under the DMCA (EFF, 2005; EFF, 2006).

Recognizing the consumer's dilemma, some savvy DVD device makers, outside of the CSS licensing scheme, have found that DVDs may be coded for use in two separate regions that may share a common language and the same television format, such as the UK (Region 2) and Australia (Region 4), and have begun to offer combination DVD players coded for both regions that utilize the PAL television format (Sarah, 2005b). For the technically astute, some DVD players permit limited switching between regions, but remain stuck on one region once the maximum number of changes (usually 4 or 5) is reached, preventing further out-of-region movie screening (Carroll, 2002). Faced with having to shell out even more money to buy redundant equipment to view legally purchased films (Carroll, 2002; EFF, 2006), it is no surprise that pirates with their region-free DVDs are so successful.

The movie industry itself recognizes that frustrated consumers will pirate content (Gardiner, 2006), and its persistent use of region codes promotes a market for pirated films without DRM controls. Experts contend that region codes are technically distinct from other DRM tools and could easily be removed without hampering other anti-theft controls (Carroll, 2002). The industry could follow the pirate's business model and offer region-free films, helping to reduce the demand for pirated films, but so far has chosen not to do so. Although the licensing mandates of CSS only bind DVD device makers, the film industry prefers to retain region locks purely for commercial and anti-competitive reasons, such as segmenting markets for film advertising and distribution purposes (CDT, 2006; Sarah, 2005a), protecting theatrical revenues as movies are released over time globally (Carroll, 2002; Silva, n.d.; Sarah, 2005a), and keeping out parallel imports of DVDs. The region locks also allow the movie industry to engage in global price discrimination for the same titles (IP Justice, 2002; Silva, n.d.; Sarah, 2005a), to distribute poorer quality DVD options to non-Region 1 countries (Sarah, 2005b), and to lock consumers into film collections and DVD devices solely from one artificially-created region (IP Justice, 2002; Sarah, 2005a).

The industry's own failure to step away from this anti-competitive and anti-consumer approach is only further fueling the already healthy market for pirated films. To help decrease the piracy incentive, the industry need only remove region locks from its own products and allow the DVD Copy Control Association to release CSS licensees from the region lock requirement (see Doctorow, 2005). By ignoring this self-help remedy, the movie industry is forcing honest consumers to seek out pirated movies.

While region codes block honest consumers from viewing DVDs, the film industry conversely often forces viewers to watch certain DVD materials under the DRM regime. Typically, one cannot fast-forward past copyright declarations and warning about illegal copying and distribution of films. In addition, under the guise of DRM, the film industry stops legitimate consumers from skipping past previews and other promotional materials at the start of a legally obtained DVD (CDT, 2006; EFF, 2005; IP Justice, 2002). In some instances, parents may wish to skip over trailers for films or promotional ads they believe are inappropriate for their children's viewing (IP Justice, 2002). Although copyright warnings are relevant to DRM and copyright protections, slipping in mandatory advertising materials about an upcoming film or DVD release under the DRM regime is absurd. While a reader can skip ahead in a book or a listener might fast-forward through a song, DVD viewers do not have the same control over their private movie experience (IP Justice, 2002).

Consumer advocates have pressed the Copyright Office for an exemption to access controls under the DMCA to allow purchasers to skip over promotional materials. However, the Copyright Office determined that 'being forced to play (not necessarily watch) the promotional material constituted no more than a mere inconvenience for users' and refused to grant the exemption under the DMCA (EFF, 2005). Unlike legitimate purchasers, those who purchase bootleg or illicit copies of DVDs are not required to play promotional materials. Clearly, pirates are smart enough to recognize that inconveniencing their users is bad for business. One wonders why the film industry has not similarly recognized the importance of customer satisfaction and the importance of allowing consumers to shape their own DVD viewing experiences. As part of DRM, mandatory promotional materials are not relevant to copyright protection and the industry should stop forcing legitimate buyers to view their promotional materials.

Pirates Let you Make Personal Copies of your Purchases

Consumers who legitimately purchase DVDs may wish to copy all or part of a DVD under the provisions of fair use. Some users may make non-commercial back-up copies for personal use in case the original be lost or damaged. In other cases, the consumer may wish to space-shift the DVD to different devices, such as other DVD players or computers in the home, at work, or on the road. For example, an individual may wish to make a personal copy of a DVD for viewing on an airplane flight or by passengers on a long car ride. In addition, educators and students may wish to copy portions of a DVD as part of a compilation of materials for critical review or educational comparison in classroom presentations (CDT, 2006; EFF, 2005; Grassmuck, 2004).

Although the Copyright Office has rejected the consumer's fair use right to make DVD copies as actionable infringements, courts have taken a different view, finding that CSS may indeed block some fair uses of DVD materials, such as personal back-up copies. While recognizing consumer rights to make copies in certain fair use instances, the court have determined that access to tools they would need to circumvent CSS in order to make copies, such as DeCSS or DVD copying programs, are illegal under the DMCA (*Universal City Studios v. Corley*, 2001; *Universal City Studios v. Reimerdes*, 2000; *321 Studios v.*

MGM Studios, Inc., 2004). Therefore, fair use is acknowledged, but the tools for consumers to take advantage of fair use are banned. In *Reimerdes*, the court recognized this obvious dilemma.

> The use of technological means of controlling access to a copyrighted work may affect the ability to make fair uses of the work. Focusing specifically on the facts of this case, the application of CSS to encrypt a copyrighted motion picture requires the use of a compliant DVD player to view or listen to the movie. Perhaps more significantly, it prevents exact copying of either the video or the audio portion of all or any part of the film. This latter point means that certain uses that might qualify as 'fair' for purposes of copyright infringement – for example, the preparation by a film studies professor of a single CD-ROM or tape containing two scenes from different movies in order to illustrate a point in a lecture on cinematography, as opposed to showing relevant parts of two different DVDs – would be difficult or impossible absent circumvention of the CSS encryption. [footnotes omitted] (*Universal City Studios v. Reimerdes*, 2000, p. 322)

Outside the US, private copying exceptions have long been recognized under copyright in such nations as Austria, Canada, France, Germany, Italy and the Netherlands (Gasser and Girsberger, 2004; Goodman, 2005; Grassmuck, 2004; May, 2006; NIJ, 2004). Consumer and legal advocates have challenged the ability of DRM to supersede national laws that permit private copying of legitimately purchased copyrighted materials (Goodman, 2005; Grassmuck, 2004; May, 2006). EU nations have had difficulty trying to reconcile national laws on private copying with the EUCD's protections of DRM, and it is unclear how these different approaches will be harmonized (Gasser and Girsberger, 2004). Italy left its private copy law in tact, while Germany and Austria tightened up the breadth of private copying while legalizing only certain kinds of DRM systems. Similar to the US, the UK determined that a case-by-case approach would work best in handling such fair use conflicts (May, 2006). However, recent court decisions in France, Belgium and Germany illustrate a growing trend away from allowing private copying in the digital environment (Gasser and Girsberger, 2004).

In the absence of disclosure obligations on DVDs, most consumers have no idea that they cannot make back-up copies until they try to do it (see CDT, 2006; Grassmuck, 2004). Individuals who share or buy illicit DVDs do not have to contend with DRM and therefore can make unlimited copies, for themselves or anyone they wish. Meanwhile, honest consumers are once again punished when they buy legitimate DVDs because of undisclosed DRM restrictions. Disclosure of these limitations is one option, but it is important to recognize that DRM is a software issue that could also be reprogrammed to allow one or two private copies.

Critics of DRM have argued that with piracy rampant in society, the film industry should be looking for alternative business models and creative compensation schemes rather than propping up outdated ones through tighter DRM controls (CDT, 2006; Grassmuck, 2004; Haber et al., 2003). Rather than limiting use through DRM, media industries should focus on developing new business models and tracking mechanisms to ensure payment, such as royalty funds, peer referral groups, and secure viewing groups (CDT, 2006; Gardiner, 2006; NIJ, 2004).

For example, in Canada, copyrighted materials may be downloaded from file-sharing sites if limited to private use (NIJ, 2004). To compensate artists, the Canadian government taxes blank CDs, DVDs and other recording products that provide revenues for a royalty fund that compensates artists (NIJ, 2004). Other countries have private copying taxes that allow some copying for non-commercial purposes by placing levies on the copying tools and accessories to fund royalties for copyright holders (Morea, 2006).

With a peer referral system, individuals recommend video playlists to others who receive a limited number of free plays. If after their free plays, they decide to purchase the item, then the referring member receives a commission on the legitimate purchase (CDT, 2006).

Under secure viewing groups, a purchaser or subscriber would be allowed to make copies and use media within a registered network of televisions, computers and cell phones. In this environment, consumers can make personal copies of legally obtained materials for viewing amongst a variety of devices (CDT, 2006; Gardiner, 2006). Currently, TiVo offers TiVoToGo to its DVR subscribers as a way of allowing them access to materials between various registered devices (CDT, 2006). By reshaping DRM to emphasize payment tracking and new compensation schemes, rather than broadly restricting use, the movie industry would provide legitimate purchasers with copying opportunities that pirates already offer to their customers.

Pirates Don't Care about Proprietary DRM Formats

Despite the record-breaking box office revenues in 2006, the film industry still makes most of its money from home video entertainment (47.1 per cent) and not from theater revenues (15.7 per cent) (Bangeman, 2006). In addition, the MPAA has found that their most avid moviegoers either own or subscribe to four or more home-based technologies (MPAA, 2006f). As devices for viewing content proliferate, legitimate file-sharers and consumers are discovering on their own that different media distributors are using different DRM formats. While users may have a variety of hardware for viewing content, they may find that content they legitimately downloaded or purchased may only play on certain complementary device platforms (CDT, 2006; Doctorow, 2004; Grassmuck, 2004; IP Justice, 2002). For example, films purchased at the iTunes Store may only operate on Apple devices, while a film purchased as a DVD cannot be easily transferred for viewing on a video iPod (Bangeman, 2006; CDT, 2006; IP Justice, 2002). In November 2006, the MPAA sued Load 'N Go services under the DMCA for ripping and re-encoding consumers' legally-obtained DVDs for viewing on their iPods (Bangeman, 2006).

Since DRM is focused on restricting use, consumers find themselves in the position of trying to determine which DRM format will provide them with the broadest range of devices for viewing, sometimes referred to as a 'DRM ecosystem' (Doctorow, 2004). Ultimately, consumers once again are locked into one set of devices with little opportunity to change platforms without considerable expense (Bangeman, 2006; IP Justice, 2002; see Grassmuck, 2004). Furthermore, consumers have to deal with software or product updates that may make their prior content purchases obsolete or inoperable (Doctorow, 2004). The industry itself has recognized that the lack of DRM interoperability between home devices has also pushed many legitimate consumers to piracy (Gardiner, 2006).

The movie business is calling for the establishment of an interoperable DRM solution that will maximize the consumer's ability to play content on multiple devices (Gardiner, 2006). The establishment of DRM standards or protocols is one way to improve interoperability and make it easier for consumers to use legally obtained movies on a variety of devices without sacrificing the protection of copyright (CDT, 2006). However, concerns have been raised that dominant media players will attempt to skew any protocols to maximize benefits for their own platforms (Grassmuck, 2004). Unfortunately, with three separate organizations working on different DRM interoperability standards or protocols for home networks, it is unlikely that a uniform solution will emerge any time soon (Bangeman, 2006).

While some battle over the proper DRM standards for increased interoperability, others contend that the real problem is the unwillingness of companies to step away from proprietary formats to open source formats, such as OGG formats. Open source formats could be licensed for use on a broad range of platforms, dramatically reducing DRM interoperability obstacles (Bangeman, 2006; CDT, 2006). Open source advocates contend that OGG formats will spur unprecedented innovation and creativity in video devices which has long been dormant under the control of the DVD Copy Control Association, as well as promote consumer choice as to device platforms (Grassmuck, 2004; Xiph.org, 1999; see Veitch, 2007).

Despite calls for improved DRM interoperability, the continuing problem works to the benefit of the film business so there is no real urgency from the industry's perspective.

> It's perfect for the movie studios. . . . [T]hey get to sell you the same content multiple times for multiple devices. Say you purchased a copy of *The Hitchhiker's Guide to the Galaxy* when it came out on DVD. If you want a version to play on your iPod, you have no legal way of getting one other than spending $9.99 for an iPod friendly copy at the iTunes Store. It's a great scheme for the movie studios, but really bad news for consumers. (Bangeman, 2006)

Although the movie industry cries crocodile tears over DRM interoperability, pirates do not make their customers worry about such concerns. Pirates are not wedded to any proprietary DRM format so they just strip out DRM controls, making it easier for their customers to use or customize their purchases for use on different devices. Once again the honest consumer remains disadvantaged, largely because the movie industry cannot or is not motivated to solve the DRM interoperability problem it helped to create.

CONCLUSION

It is obvious that the enactment of tougher criminal laws and the tightening of DRM controls has done little to blunt movie piracy worldwide and has pushed many honest consumers to seek out pirated films and DRM circumvention tools. In order to compete with the piracy model, the movie and theater industries need to undertake a serious review of numerous self-help remedies that will aid efforts to thwart piracy without alienating their customer base and straining limited public law enforcement resources. First, the supply of pirated films, coming primarily from industry insiders, can be severely limited through improved theater security, strengthened employee training and supervision, greater reward incentives against camming, and serious civil sanctions and workplace consequences for offending insiders. In addition, the movie makers and theater owners should collaborate to accelerate the transition to digital cinema systems that offer greater protections from illegal camming and help decrease opportunities for the theft or improper disclosure of film prints.

Second, the film business should experiment creatively with ways to offer the public faster and cheaper access to a broad selection of films. Movie file-sharing sites need to provide better and more cost-effective film downloading options and be revamped to decrease onerous and expensive technical requirements and to improve the breadth of site offerings. Also the industry should continue to experiment with new release strategies aimed at speeding up public access to films.

Third, the film industry should seriously reevaluate the benefits and burdens of DRM. Unnecessary DRM controls, such as region locks and required promotional materials, should be immediately removed. Future programming of DRM controls on DVDs could be coded to allow legitimate purchasers to make at least one personal copy of their legally-obtained films. Rather than focusing on limiting consumer use through restrictive DRM measures, the movie industry should also develop and implement new business models focusing on tracking payment and usage, such as royalty funds, peer referral systems, and secure viewing groups. Lastly, the movie industry should be driving hard to resolve the DRM interoperability problem it helped to foster, so that consumers can fairly use their purchased works on a wide range of devices without being locked into certain proprietary device platforms. Although unified efforts to establish DRM standards and protocols may be one path, open source formats may better serve the long-term needs of consumers while invigorating innovation in the movie device manufacturing sector.

Despite these numerous self-help remedies, the movie industry will be likely to opt to continue on the same path of demanding tougher criminal sanctions and prosecutions while maintaining DRM measures that are certain to irritate their legitimate customers and promote the consumer demand for pirated films. At most, the industry may grudgingly offer to disclose the impact of DRM controls on consumers in the fine print that pirates would not bother their customers with in this competitive environment. Unfortunately, the film industry seems to be moving slower than a dinosaur in *Jurassic Park* to learn the customer satisfaction lessons of the business model of piracy ensuring that their disaster movie, *Global Movie Piracy*, will have a long and successful run worldwide.

NOTE

1. Associate Professor of Law, Florida Coastal School of Law (ABA-approved), Jacksonville, FL. The author wishes to acknowledge and thank Joseph Ferrandino, Masters in Criminal Justice, and PhD candidate in Public Affairs, University of Central Florida, for his research assistance on aspects of criminal copyright infringement for this article.

REFERENCES

321 Studios v. MGM Studios, Inc., 307 F. Supp. 2d 1085 (N.D. Cal. 2004).

Age Company Ltd, The (2007), 'US files WTO piracy case against China', April, from http://www.theage.com.au.

Andrews, Robin (2005), 'Copyright infringement and the Internet: An economic analysis of crime', *Boston University Journal of Science & Technology Law*, **11** Summer, 256–82.
Arnotts Lawyers (n.d.), 'Chipping at the mod chip case', http://www.arnotts.net.au/mod-chip-case.html.
Bangeman, Eric (2006), 'MPAA sues over DVD-to-iPod service', *Ars Technica*, November, http://arstechnica.com/news.ars/post/20061117-8241.html.
Bennett, Gwenda and Pamela Gershuny (2006), 'Ahoy music pirates! Navigating the past, present, and future of preemption defenses to state and federal criminal laws', *Proceedings of the ALSB 2006 Annual Conference & Meeting*, St Petersburg, FL, http://www.alsb.org/proceedings/copyright/Pirates_Gwenda_Bennett_Pamela_Gershuny.pdf.
Big Screen Cinema Guide, The (n.d.), 'What is digital cinema projection?', http://www.bigscreen.com/about/help.php?id=36.
Bloomberg News (2007), 'US plans WTO charge on China piracy goods', *The Boston Globe*, (April), http://www.boston.com.
Borland, John (2004a), 'Judge: DVD-copying software is illegal', *CNet News.Com*, February, http://www.news.com.com.
Borland, John (2004b), 'DVD-copying trailblazer shuts its doors', *CNet News.Com*, August, http://www.news.com.com.
Bylund, Anders (2006), 'IFC, Comcast starts day-and-date distribution service', *Ars Technica*, March, http://arstechnica.com/news.ars/post/20060301-6294.html.
Captain, Séan (2006), 'Will digital cinema can pirates?', *Wired*, January, http://www.wired.com/print/science/discoveries/news/2006/01/6992.
Carroll, David B. (2002), 'Proposal for a specific exemption from prohibition on circumvention of technological measures that control access to a certain class of copyrighted works', December, http://www.copyright.gov/1201/2003/*COMMENTS/036.PDF*.
CDRinfo (2005), 'Blu-Ray proposes region codes for future HD titles', *CDRinfo*, December, http://www.cdrinfo.com/Sections/News/Details.aspx?NewsId=15856.
Center for Democracy & Technology (CDT) (2006), 'Evaluating DRM: Building a marketplace for the convergent world', September, http://www.cdt.org/copyright/20060907drm.pdf.
Clark (2006), 'Copyright law and the digital millennium copyright act: Do the penalties fit the crime?', *New England Journal on Criminal and Civil Confinement*, **32**, Summer, 379–403.
Daly, Steven (2007), 'Pirates of the multiplex', *Vanity Fair*, March, 278, 280–82, 284, 286, 288.
Department of Justice (2006a), Press Release, US Departmant of Justice, 'Four men sentenced and another film critic pleads guilty in Operation Copycat', August 1, http://www.usdoj.gov/criminal/cybercrime/jacobsonplea.htm.
Department of Justice (2006b), Press Release, US Department of Justice, 'Thirtieth copyright conviction as part of Operation Copycat', June 20, http://sanfrancisco.fbi.gov/dojpressrel/2006/sfo62006.htm.
Department of Justice (2007), 'Operation Buccaneer', http://www.usdoj.gov/criminal/cybercrime/ob/OBMain.htm (last visited December 14, 2007).
Department of Justice (n.d.), 'Illegal "warez" organizations and Internet piracy', http://www.usdoj.gov/criminal/cybercrime/ob/OBorg&pr.htm.
Digital Millennium Copyright Act (DMCA) of 1998, 17 USC §§512(h–i), 1201 (2005).
Doctorow, Cory (2004), 'Microsoft research DRM talk', June, http://www.dashes.com/anil/stuff/doctorow-drm-ms.html.
Doctorow, Cory, Electronic Frontier Foundation, Union for the Public Domain, Open Knowledge Forum, IP Justice, Alternative Law Forum, World Blind Union, European Digital Rights Initiative, Electronic Frontier Finland, Foundation for Information Policy Research, Free Government Information and Vereniging Open Source Nederland (2005), 'Digital Rights Management (DRM): A failure in the developed world, a danger to the developing world. A paper for the International Telecommunications Union, ITU-R Working Party 6M Report on Content Protection Technologies', *Proceedings ITU-R Working Party 6M Report on Content Protection Technologies*, Geneva (Switzerland), pp. 1–28.
Drajem, Mark (2007), 'US plans WTO case against China on movies, books', *Bloomberg.com*, April, from http://www.bloomberg.com.

Electronic Frontier Foundation (EFF) (2005), 'DMCA triennial rulemaking: Failing the digital consumer', December, pp. 1–8, http://www.eff.org/IP/DMCA/copyrightoffice/DMCA_rulemaking_broken.pdf.

Electronic Frontier Foundation (EFF) (2006), 'Reply comment of the Electronic Frontier Foundation before the Copyright Office Library of Congress in the matter of exemption to the prohibition of circumvention of copyright protection systems for access control technologies', http://www.eff.org/ 2006_ DMCA_RM_EFF_reply_comments[1].pdf.

Electronic Frontier Foundation (EFF) (2007), 'Free speech battle over online parody of "Colbert Report" ', *EFF Press Release*, March, http://www.eff.org/news/.

Erekosima, Onimi and Brian Koosed (2004), 'Intellectual property crimes', *American Criminal Law Review*, **41**, Spring, 809–63.

Family Entertainment and Copyright Act (FECA), 18 USC Appx §2B5.3 (2006).

Ferrera, Gerald R., Stephen D. Lichtenstein, Margot E.K. Reder, Robert C. Bird and William T. Schiano (2004), *Cyber Law: Text and Cases* (2nd edn), Ohio, US: West Legal Studies in Business.

Fitzdam, Justin D. (2005), 'Private enforcement of the Digital Millennium Copyright Act: Effective without government intervention', *Cornell Law Review*, **90**, May, 1085–117.

Gardiner, Bryan (2006), 'MPAA: Frustrated consumers will pirate', *PCMag.Com*, October, http://www.pcmag.com/print_article2/0,1217,a= 191502, 00.asp.

Gasser, Urs and Michael Girsberger (2004), 'Transposing the copyright directive: Legal protection of technological measures in EU-member states, a genie stuck in the bottle?', Berkman Pub. Series No. 2004-10, November, pp. 1–31, http://cyber.law.harvard.edu/publications.

Gentile, Gary (2006), ' "Bubble" hits theaters, TV, DVD on same day', *USA Today*, January, http://www.usatoday.com/tech/news/2006-01-18-bubble-theater-threat_x.htm.

Goldman, Eric (2003), 'A road to no warez: The No Electronic Theft Act and criminal copyright infringement', *Oregon Law Review*, **82**, Summer, 369–432.

Goldman, Eric and Julia Alpert Gladstone (2003), ' "No Electronic Theft Act" proves a partial success', *National Law Journal*, March, p. B9, http://ericgoldman.org/Articles/nljnet.htm.

Gonsalves, Antone (2006), 'Analyst firm predicts YouTube is "Goin Down" ', *InformationWeek*, October, http://www.informationweek.com/newshowArticle.jhtml?articleID=193101661&subSection=All+Stories.

Goodman, J. David (2005), 'Consumers fight copy protection', *International Herald Tribune*, November, http://www.iht.com/articles/2005/11/11/ business/ptcopy12.php.

Granade, Stephen (n.d.), 'Warez, abandonware and the software industry', http://brasslantern.org/community/companies/warez-b.html.

Grassmuck, Volker (2004), 'Putting users at the centre – achieving an "information society for all" ', Comments in response to the Informal Consultation of the Final Report of the High Level Group on DRM, September, pp. 1–13, http://privatkopie.net/files/privatkopie-bof_on-DRM.pdf.

Groennings, Kristina (2005), 'Costs and benefits of the recording industry's litigation against individuals', *Berkeley Technology Law Journal*, **20**, 571–601.

Haber, Stuart, Bill Horne, Joe Pato, Tomas Sander and Roberto Endre Tarjan (2003), 'If piracy is the problem, is DRM the answer?', HPL-2003-110, May, pp. 1–11, http://www.hpl.hp.com/techreports/2003/HPL-2003-110.pdf.

Heneghan, Brian P. (2002), 'The NET Act, fair use, and willfulness – Is Congress making a scarecrow of the law?', *Journal of High Technology Law*, **1**, pp. 27–46, http://www.jhtl.org/docs/pdf/BHENEGHANV1N1N.pdf.

IP Justice (2002), 'Comments of IP Justice to US Copyright Office Rulemaking proceeding pursuant to Section 1201 of the Digital Millennium Copyright Act', (December), http://www.ipjustice.org/IPJ_1201_Comments.shtml.

Jesdanun, Anick (2007), 'Viacom sued over YouTube parody removal', *The Boston Globe*, March, http://www.boston.com.

'Justice Department conducts international Internet piracy sweep' (2005), *The Computer & Internet Lawyer*, **22**, September, 34, LexisNexis Academic Universe.

Kiss, Jemima (2006), '@MIPCOM: Piracy is a business model, says Disney co-Chair Anne Sweeney', *PaidContent.org.*, October, http://www.paidcontent.org/entry/mipcom-piracy-is-a-business-model-says-disney-co-chair-anne-sweeney.

Liedtke, Michael (2006), 'Google video suit could signal YouTube trouble ahead', *USA Today*, November, http://www.usatoday.com/tech/news/2006-11-08-google-sued_x.htm.

Lyman, Jay (2004), 'Analysts question MPAA's findings on film piracy', *CRMBuyer*, July, http://www.crmbuyer.com/story/news/35036.html.

Lyman, Jay (2005), 'Theater companies join to speed digital cinema', *TechNewsWorld*, December, http://www.technewsworld.com/story/47882.html.

May, Benjamin (2006), 'Private copies: one (triple) test to rule them all', *Know IP Newsletter*, May, http://www.economag.com.

MGM Studios, Inc. v. Grokster, Ltd, 545 US 913, 125 S. Ct. 2764 (2005).

Mohl, Bruce (2007), 'Now showing: epic cost of cinema snacks', *The Boston Globe*, March, http://www.boston.com.

Morea, Lori A. (2006), 'The future of music in a digital age: The ongoing conflict between copyright law and peer-to-peer technology', *Campbell Law Review*, **28**, Spring, 195–250.

Motion Picture Association of America (MPAA) (2005a), 'Fighting optical disc piracy around the World', http://www.mpaa.org/piracy_ OptDisk.asp.

Motion Picture Association of America (MPAA) (2005b), 'Theatrical camcorder piracy', http://www.mpaa.org/piracy_theatrical_cam.asp.

Motion Picture Association of America (MPAA) (2005c), '2005 US piracy fact sheet', http://www.mpaa.org/USpiracyfactsheet.pdf.

Motion Picture Association of America (MPAA) (2006a), 'Best practices to prevent film theft', March, http://www.fightfilmtheft.org/pdfs/BP_US_ English.pdf.

Motion Picture Association of America (MPAA) (2006b), 'Motion picture piracy costs US economy thousands of jobs, billions in lost wages', *MPAA Press Release*, September, htpp://www.mpaa.org.ipirelease_9_29_06.pdf.

Motion Picture Association of America (MPAA) (2006c), 'NATO theater employee camcorder training guide', http://www.fightfilmtheft.org/en.

Motion Picture Association of America (MPAA) (2006d), '"Take action" reward program', http://www.fightfilmtheft.org/en/reward.asp.

Motion Picture Association of America (MPAA) (2006e), '2006 box office rebounds', *MPAA Press Release*, September, http://www.mpaa.org/press_releases/2006 market stats release final.pdf.

Motion Picture Association of America (MPAA) (2006f), 'US theatrical market statistics, worldwide 19', http://www.mpaa.org/2006-us-Theatrical-Market-Statistics-Report.pdf.

Motion Picture Association (MPA) Asia Pacific (2005), 'MPA Asia Pacific', http://www.mpaa.org/inter_asia.asp.

Motion Picture Association (MPA) Europe (2005), 'MPA Europe – Europe, Middle East and Africa', http://www.mpaa.org/inter_ europe.asp.

Nasheri, Hedi (2004), 'Addressing global scope of intellectual property law', National Institute of Justice, The International Center Department of Justice, Document No. 208384 (November), pp. 1–93, htpp://www.ncjrs.gov/pdffiles 1/nij/grants/208384.pdf.

National Association of Theatre Owners (NATO) (2005), 'Number of US movie screens', http://www.natoonline.org/statisticsscreens.htm.

National Institute of Justice (NIJ) (2004), 'Intellectual property and white-collar crime: Report of issues, trends, and problems for future research', Document No. 208135, May, pp. 1–45, htpp://www.ncjrs.gov/pdffiles 1/nij/grants/208135.pdf.

Pew Internet and American Life Project and Comscore (2004), Media Metriz Data Memo, 3 January, http://www.pewinternet.org/pdfs/PIP_File_Swapping_Memo_0104.pdf.

Piquero, Nicole Leeper and Alex R. Piquero (2006), 'Democracy and intellectual property: Examining trajectories of software piracy', *Annals*, **605**, May, 104–27.

Rabinowitz, Howard (1997), 'The end is near! Why disaster movies make sense in the '90s – and dollars', *Washington Monthly*, April, htttp://findarticles.com/p/articles/mi_m1316/ is_n4_v29/ai_19279949.

Reuters (2007), 'Washington files WTO piracy cases against China', (April), http://www.reuters.com/articlePrint?articleID=USL1031680320070410.
Sag, M. (2006), 'Piracy: twelve year-olds, grandmothers, and other good targets for the recording industry's file sharing litigation', *Northwestern Journal of Technology & Intellectual Property*, **4**, Spring, 133–55.
Sarah (2005a), 'Blog: What is region coding? (Part 1)', *Lawfont.com*, December, http://www.lawfont.com/2005/12/22/what-is-region-coding/.
Sarah (2005b), 'Blog: What is region coding? (Part 2)', *Lawfont.com*, December, http://www.lawfont.com/2005/12/31/what-is-region-coding-2/.
Silva, Robert (n.d.), 'DVD region codes – what you need to know', http://www.hometheater.about.com/cs/dvdlaserdisc/a/aaregioncodesa.htm.
Sohn, Gigi B. (2006), 'Don't mess with success: government technology mandates and the marketplace for online content', *S.J. Telecomm and High Tech*, L. 73, 74–5.
States News Service (2006a), 'Four men sentenced and another film critic pleads guilty in Operation Copycat', *States News Service*, August, LexisNexis Academic Universe.
States News Service (2006b), 'Thirtieth copyright conviction as part of Operation Copycat', *States News Service*, June, LexisNexis Academic Universe.
Sweeting, Paul (2003), 'Copyright office shoots down DMCA exemptions', *Video Business*, October, http://www.videobusiness.com/index.asp? layout=articlePrint&articleID= CA615549.
Taylor, Richard (2005), 'Piracy on campus: An overview of the problem and a look at emerging practices to reduce online theft of copyrighted works', presentation to the Subcommittee on Courts, the Internet, and Intellectual Property, http://www.mpaa.org/MPAAtestimonyfor9.22.05hearing.pdf.
Thompson, Anne (2006), 'Distributors hold firm against day-and-date', *The Hollywood Reporter*, March, http://www.hollywoodreporter.com/hr/search/article_display.jsp?vnu_content_id=1002198452.
'US Customs Dismantles Sophisticated Internet Piracy Network' (2002), *The Computer & Internet Lawyer*, **19** (February), p. 18, LexisNexis Academic Universe.
Universal City Studios v. Corley, 273 F.3d 429 (2d Cir. 2001).
Universal City Studios v. Reimerdes, 111 F. Supp. 2d 294 (S.D.N.Y. 2000).
US Fed News (2006), 'Five additional defendants charged in crackdown against worldwide Internet piracy groups', *US Fed News*, April, LexisNexis Academic Universe.
Veiga, Alex (2006), 'Morris: YouTube, MySpace abuse copyright', *ABCNews*, September, http://abcnews.go.com/Technology/wireStory?id=2447506.
Veitch, Nick (2007), 'Music of politics', *Linux Format*, April, p. 5.
Williams, Martyn (2007), 'YouTube tackles copyright', *PC World*, September, http://www.pcworld.com/article/id,128743/article.html.
World Intellectual Property Organization (WIPO) (n.d.a), 'Copyright FAQs – How are copyright and related rights protected on the Internet?', http://www.wipo.int/copyright/en/faq/faqs.htm#P21_3830.
World Intellectual Property Organization (WIPO) (n.d.b), 'Program activities: Campaigns', http://www.wipo.int/ip-development/en/creative_ industry/campaigns.html.
World Intellectual Property Organization (WIPO) (1997a), 'WIPO Copyright Treaty (WCT)', http://www.wipo.int/treaties/en/ip/wct/ trtdocs_wo033.html.
World Intellectual Property Organization (WIPO) (1997b), 'WIPO Performances and Phonogram Treaty (WPPT)', http://www.wipo.int/treaties/en/ip/wppt/index.html.
Xiph.org (1999), 'About Xiph', May, http://xiph.org/about/.
Yang, Debra Wong and Brian M. Hoffstadt (2006), 'Countering the cyber-crime threat', *American Criminal Law Review*, **43**, Spring, 201–15.

PART III

India and China

5. Protecting well known marks in China: challenges for foreign mark holders

Stephanie M. Greene

INTRODUCTION

China has made substantial progress in terms of complying with its World Trade Organization (WTO) obligations and bringing its intellectual property laws into conformity with the Agreement on Trade Related Aspects of Intellectual Property (TRIPS). In the 2007 Special 301 Report, the United States Trade Representative (USTR) recognized the continued progress China has made in improving intellectual property (IP) protection. Nevertheless, China was listed on the Priority Watch List again and the United States sought WTO consultation on several discrete issues involving China's inadequate protection of intellectual property rights (IPR). The problems that persist with protecting IPR in China stem primarily from an inability or unwillingness to enforce the laws and to deter illegal activity. Inadequate enforcement of IP laws may be attributed to a lack of political will, an unwieldy bureaucracy, cultural intransigence and local protectionism. It seems impossible to detect the extent to which these various factors influence the continued escalation of IP infringement in a country that is developing economically and socially at an unprecedented pace. China's professed commitment and determination to fulfil its international obligations and plan for its long-term interests is compromised by conflict with the immediate demands and concerns of local enterprises and populations (Chow, 2006). Consequently, although China continues to emphasize improvements in IPR protection, multinational enterprises (MNEs) that have entered the market in China face challenges in protecting IPR.

As a member of the WTO, China is required to have national laws and regulations that conform to the requirements of the TRIPS Agreement. Giving special recognition to well known trademarks is a requirement of TRIPS. The special legal protection accorded to well known marks is particularly appropriate in China where the temptations and incentives to free ride on the goodwill of well known marks usually outweigh the risks of violating the laws (Chow, 2006). In the area of counterfeiting, owners of well known marks continue to face serious challenges related to enforcement and deterrence. In the area of infringement, however, there are indications that foreign well known marks may receive proper recognition and protection through the administrative and judicial systems. Trademark protection in China has had considerably more success than patent or copyright protection (Mertha, 2005, p. 173). Nevertheless, challenges persist for foreign mark holders as the administrative system is overburdened and the court system is opaque. The extent to which either system acts independently of the Chinese Communist Party (Party) is speculative. Moreover, there are few official decisions translated into English or other foreign languages. Still, the few published decisions involving well known marks and unofficial translations of court decisions indicate that courts are willing and able to apply the laws in a manner consistent with international expectations. MNEs that have the determination and financial wherewithal to litigate to protect their well known marks may conclude that the courts are a viable avenue of recourse in China, and, in pursuing such recourse, may advance the protection of IPR. Other decisions by the Chinese courts signal that MNEs need to employ native speakers well versed in the relevant market in planning their branding strategy in order to avoid potential confusion with similar marks.

This chapter provides a brief summary of the current status of the protection of well known marks in China. The history of China's trademark law and its recognition of well known marks have been detailed by several authors (Zhou, 2002; Shao, 2005; Cahan, 2004; Lehman et al., 2003). Several scholars and business professionals have offered advice on implementing business strategies that assist MNEs in protecting their well known marks while garnering the important 'guanxi' or goodwill of government officials as well as communities in China (Wall, 2006, pp. 401–11; Yu, 2006, pp. 960–66; Zhou, 2002, pp. 437–42). The Quality Brand Protection Committee (QBPC), a quasi-governmental agency, promotes dialogue between industry and the Chinese government. Devising business strategies and promoting cooperation through the QBPC may be the best course for advancing the interests of foreign mark holders.[1] Nevertheless, these options work in conjunction with the methods in place for protecting well known marks through the administrative and judicial systems.

After summarizing both the administrative and judicial processes of recognizing well known marks, this chapter considers concerns about China's weak enforcement and insufficient measures for deterring trademark infringement, as well as China's response to such criticisms. The chapter explores the impact that the courts have had on protecting foreign well known marks in China. Several decisions, including both successful and unsuccessful outcomes for foreign mark holders, are discussed with a view to discerning how foreign mark holders can protect their marks.

LAWS AND REGULATIONS AFFECTING WELL KNOWN MARKS IN CHINA

International protection for well known trademarks stems from the Paris Convention for the Protection of Industrial Property (Paris Convention) and the TRIPS Agreement. Neither treaty, however, defines the term 'well known'.[2] Despite the vagueness of the term, gaining recognition of well known status allows the trademark holder greater protection than a trademark that is not well known.[3] In China, gaining well known recognition serves several important purposes. Because China has a first to file registration system, it does not, in general, recognize unregistered marks. Pursuant to the Paris Convention and TRIPS, however, China is obligated to recognize unregistered well known marks. Well known status in China also allows the rightful mark owner to seek cancellation of a mark unlawfully registered by a competitor or opportunist.

Protecting well known marks in China involves issues related to trademark infringement, counterfeiting and customs control. This chapter is primarily concerned with cases involving infringement of well known marks. Nevertheless, by gaining recognition and protection of well known marks, foreign mark holders should have greater leverage in enforcement actions against counterfeiters and exporters of counterfeited goods. The following subsections summarize the laws and regulations that impact the recognition and protection of well known marks in China. After summarizing China's Trademark and Unfair Competition Law, this section introduces the regulations that govern administrative recognition and protection of well known marks as well as judicial recognition of well known trademarks.

A Brief Introduction to Trademark Law in China

Prior to WTO accession, China was required to protect well known marks, even those not registered in China, due to its obligations under the Paris Convention, which it joined in 1985. Thus, in 1987, the Chinese Trademark Office (CTMO) recognized Pizza Hut as its first well known trademark. In 1996, China's State Administration for Industry and Commerce (SAIC) issued Provisional Regulations Concerning the Certification and Management of Well Known Trademarks (Provisional Regulations). From 1996 to 1999, no foreign well known marks were registered under the Provisional Regulations. During the same period, SAIC recognized 87 domestic marks as well known (Cahan, 2004, p. 226).

In preparation for joining the WTO and in response to changes in its economy and market structure, China made numerous changes to its intellectual property laws (Yu, 2006). The 2001 Trademark Law of the People's Republic of China (2001 Trademark Law) and its Implementing Regulations brought China's domestic law into substantial compliance with the TRIPS Agreement and international norms. In addition to broadening the array of marks protected, the new trademark laws improved enforcement options for plaintiffs claiming infringement by allowing courts to issue preliminary injunctions and allowing statutory damages up to RMB 500 000, or approximately US $60 000.

Articles 13 and 14 of the 2001 Trademark Law specifically address well known marks. Article 13 protects both registered and unregistered well known marks. Unregistered marks, however, are protected only when a third party uses the same or similar mark in connection with identical or similar goods or services. Registered marks receive greater protection, as non-similar goods and services are protected if use of the third party's mark would 'easily misguide the public' and damage the interests of the well known mark holder.

Article 14 lists the following factors for determining whether a trademark is well known:

1. the reputation of the mark to the relevant public;
2. the duration of continued use of the mark;
3. the extent and geographical area of advertisement of the mark;
4. records of the protection of the mark as a well known mark; and
5. any other factors relevant to the reputation of the mark.

The criteria outlined in Article 14 incorporates the criteria suggested in 1999 by a Joint Commission of the Paris Union for the Protection of Intellectual Property and the World

Intellectual Property Organization in its Joint Recommendation Concerning Provisions on the Protection of Well-Known Marks.

The 2001 Trademark Law is used in conjunction with China's Unfair Competition Law in the protection of well known marks. Article 5 of the Unfair Competition Law prohibits passing off the registered trademark of another person; using the name, packaging or decoration of well known goods without authorization; using the business name or personal name of another; and forging or falsely using another's symbols of quality. The Unfair Competition Law is also used in civil disputes regarding the registration of domain names.

Administrative Recognition of Well Known Marks

The 2001 Trademark Laws state that well known marks may be recognized either by administrative agencies or by judicial decisions. The Provisions on the Determination and Protection of Well Known Marks (2003 Provisions), implemented in June 2003, empower the SAIC to recognize and publish lists of marks it recognizes as having gained well known status. The recognition may be conferred if a holder prevails in a trademark dispute involving opposition, cancellation or infringement. The Chinese Trademark Office (CTMO) and the Trademark Review and Adjudication Board (TRAB) are departments within SAIC that oversee such trademark disputes. In considering whether a mark is well known, the CTMO and TRAB are required to consider all of the factors listed in Article 14, but the mark does not have to satisfy all of the factors.

Article 3 of the 2003 Provisions lists the types of evidence that may prove that a mark is well known. The list includes documents that provide evidence of any of the factors listed in Article 14 of the 2001 Trademark Law, as well as 'other evidences certifying that the mark is well known, including, in the past three years, the outputs, sales volumes, sales incomes, profits and taxes and sales regions etc. of the principal goods to which the mark applies'.

Local divisions of the State Administration of Industry and Commerce (AICs) play an important role in the protection of well known marks. The AIC is a government authority in charge of administering enterprises and trademarks. It enforces the Unfair Competition Law, the Advertising Law, and laws protecting consumers' rights. Every province, town, county and city has an AIC and each is controlled by its directly higher level (Mertha, 2005, p. 176). AICs cannot officially recognize marks as well known, but they may be instrumental in procuring well known status in several ways. Implementing Regulations to the 2001 Trademark Law allow the owner of a well known mark to complain to a local AIC to prevent further use of the mark. The administrator may seize and destroy representations of the well known trademark. AICs are also required to protect well known marks by reporting cases of suspected criminal counterfeiting to competent authorities. The 2003 Provisions allow a local AIC investigating a case of trademark infringement to transfer the case to the CTMO if it believes the requirements of Article 13 are met and the trademark holder requests recognition of well known status.

Enterprise names may cause difficulty for holders of well known marks. Recognizing that local businesses are likely to register well known marks as enterprise names, Article 53 of the Implementing Regulations and Article 14 of the 2003 Provisions provide that the owner of a well known trademark may seek cancellation through a local AIC of an enterprise name used by a third party if use of the name is likely to deceive or mislead consumers.

A local AIC may also protect well known marks, including those that are not officially recognized, by taking action to prevent the sale and distribution of counterfeits of well known marks. For example, in 2004 and 2005, the Beijing AIC recognized well known brands such as Burberry, Louis Vuitton, Prada, Chanel, Gucci and the North Face and posted notices banning the sale of items bearing these marks from markets notorious for selling counterfeit goods (Managing Intellectual Property, 2005). Nevertheless, because AICs operate at the local level and income from trademark registration is at the national SAIC level, AICs may bow to local pressures and incentives that take priority over trademark enforcement (Mertha, 2005, p. 178).

Judicial Recognition of Well Known Marks

The 2001 Trademark Law allows courts to recognize well known marks as part of a trademark dispute. A court will recognize a mark as well known as part of a dispute only if doing so is required to resolve the case. Disputes involving trademarks, as well as those involving domain names, are civil disputes. Such cases are litigated in the Intermediate or Higher People's Courts. The court's determination confers well known status on the trademark, a determination that may be disputed by a third party in a subsequent case only if the third party can introduce evidence that the mark is not well known. The 2001 Trademark Law also allows for judicial review of administrative rulings regarding trademark registration and cancellation proceedings. If a party is dissatisfied with the decision of the TRAB, it may appeal that decision to a court.

Seeking judicial recognition of well known foreign marks has advantages and disadvantages. Administrative enforcement of well known marks may be less expensive, quicker, more flexible and less antagonistic than litigation. Nevertheless, administrative protection is fraught with bureaucratic inefficiency and may be hampered by overriding local concerns. Because IP cases involving foreign marks begin in the Intermediate and Higher People's courts, local protectionism and influence on the courts are less pronounced, at least in the more visible courts such as those in Beijing and Shanghai (Yong-shun, 1998).

CONTROVERSIES CONCERNING CHINA'S PROTECTION OF WELL KNOWN MARKS

In a 2005 report entitled 'New progress in China's protection of IP rights', the State Council of the People's Republic of China emphasized the progress China has made since it resumed trademark protection in 1979. According to the report, applications for trademark registration in China have soared from a mere 20 000 in 1980 to over 2 million by the end of 2004. Applications for the registration of foreign trademarks increased from 1565 in 1982 to 403 000 in 2004. More recently, China notes that in 2006, SAIC certified and offered protection to 189 well known marks in proceedings before the CTMO or TRAB; about two dozen of the marks recognized were brand names of foreign enterprises (Lam and Wong, 2007).

The improvements that China proclaims, however, fall short according to US reports. In its 2007 Trade Summary and in the 2007 Special 301 Report, the USTR maintains that

China needs to promote additional awareness about IPR protection, improve the court system, and increase transparency in both the administrative and judicial systems. The 2007 Special 301 Report raises China's lack of compliance with TRIPS in enforcing and deterring IP infringement as one of the most serious issues. In response to deficiencies in these areas, the US proposes specific reforms in China's criminal law. The US also recognizes serious problems with the coordination between administrative and criminal authorities. The following subsections summarize ongoing criticism of China's compliance with the TRIPS Agreement, the need for reform in enforcement and deterrence regarding IP infringement, and China's response to such criticism.

TRIPS Compliance

Although China has made substantial progress in fulfilling its TRIPS obligations through laws, amendments, regulations and judicial interpretations, enforcement and deterrence remain problematic. The resounding consensus is that the laws are in place, but that China is unable to effectively enforce them (Yu, 2006).

Whether China's enforcement problems warrant resolution through the WTO is the subject of debate. Arguably, China has violated several provisions of the TRIPS Agreement. Article 41 of TRIPS requires WTO members to ensure 'effective action' against infringement of intellectual property rights; Article 46 requires judicial authorities to 'create an effective deterrent to infringement'; and Article 61 requires members to provide 'imprisonment and/or monetary fines sufficient to provide a deterrent' in cases involving willful trademark counterfeiting or copyright piracy. From the US perspective, China has violated these provisions of TRIPS by not doing enough to enforce its IP laws or to deter infringement. The US maintains that China must do more to effectuate its TRIPS obligations and provide remedies that prevent and deter infringement (USTR, 2007a).

Despite this evidence of failure to comply with TRIPS, some scholars maintain that China has a colorable defense for its lack of enforcement (Yu, 2006; Kanji, 2006). Article 41(5) of the TRIPS Agreement states that a WTO member is not required to devote more resources to IP enforcement than to other areas of law enforcement. Using this argument, China could prevail before the WTO by showing that its enforcement problems with piracy and counterfeiting are no more extensive than its problems with other areas of law enforcement (Yu, 2006).

Vague Criminal Laws and Lack of Enforcement

As a means of addressing China's lack of enforcement and deterrence in protecting IP, the United States proposes that China reform its criminal laws. Specifically, the United States seeks the elimination of thresholds for criminal prosecution that provide a legal safe harbor for many commercial infringers (USTR, 2007a). The language in China's criminal law regarding prosecution of IP violations is, according to the United States, unacceptably vague. For example, Article 213 of China's Criminal Law imposes a maximum prison sentence of not more than three years for crimes of serious circumstances involving counterfeiting. A prison term of three to seven years is imposed in especially severe cases. Article 214 imposes up to three years in prison for 'relatively large sales' of counterfeit trademarks and three to seven years is required for 'huge' sales.

The US is also critical of the manner in which China calculates damages in criminal cases. China uses an infringer's profits, rather than the value of the goods, as the basis for criminal liability. Article 56 of the 2001 Trademark Law states that the infringer's profit is used to calculate damages, thereby leaving the investment in infringing infrastructure untouched. In 2004, China established new thresholds, indicating that profit thresholds of RMB 50 000 to 250 000 (approximately US $6200 to $31 000) are actionable but that cases involving illegal business under the RMB 50 000 threshold are not actionable (Supreme People's Court, 2004). Quantitative thresholds for criminal prosecution of trademark counterfeiting and copyright piracy are an issue that the United States is raising in WTO dispute settlement consultation.

In addition to vague laws, local protectionism and corruption, the US complains that there is a lack of coordination between administrative and criminal authorities, a lack of training in enforcement, insufficient allocation of resources for effective deterrence, and a lack of transparency in the enforcement process and its outcomes (USTR, 2007b, p. 110). For example, Article 54 of the 2001 Trademark Law requires that local AICs report cases of infringement and counterfeiting to criminal authorities, but the standards for initiating criminal investigations are not clear. When AICs do take action in counterfeiting raids or infringement actions, the consequences for the violators are negligible. Counterfeiters currently view administrative fines as merely a cost of doing business. According to the US, administrative fines must be increased to serve as an effective deterrent (USTR, 2007b, p. 110).

The ineffectiveness of enforcement efforts is evident in the inability of authorities to close markets notorious for dealing in infringing goods. Despite court victories by several rights holders against vendors in Beijing's Silk Street Market, the market continues to flourish with counterfeit goods in many categories ranging from 80 to 100 per cent (USTR, 2007a, p. 7).

The disposal of IPR infringing goods is another topic raised by the US in its request for WTO dispute settlement consultations. The US and foreign mark holders have long been critical of China's laws regarding the destruction of confiscated goods that infringe on trademarks. Although Article 53 of the 2001 Trademark Law provides that infringing goods shall be confiscated and destroyed, the SAIC has interpreted the term 'destroy' loosely. According to the SAIC, if an infringing trademark can be separated from the commodity and the commodity has 'useful value', it may be 'disposed of by ways other than' destruction (SAIC, 2002).

The United States has also expressed concern over emerging policies in China that might favor domestic well known marks over foreign interests (USTR, 2007a, p. 22). With the intent of encouraging the sale and export of local brands, China's Ministry of Foreign Trade and Economic Cooperation (MOFCOM) pledged RMB 700 million (US $86 million) in 2006 to support local Chinese brands (Wall, 2006). MOFCOM has published a catalogue of China's most competitive brands and hopes to strengthen the value of Chinese brands by according them a special status. Chinese goods that satisfy certain standards, including reputation, quality, innovation and sustainable development, will be given a special title and sign that may be used in promotional activities (Lam and Wong, 2007).

China's Response to Criticism about Infringement

In addition to citing the increased number of foreign marks that have been recognized as well known in China, officials maintain that China has taken numerous steps to improve protection of trademarks. For example, beginning in 2004, China instituted special campaigns targeting trademark infringement and the protection of well known marks. The Ministry of Public Service instituted the Hawk Action and, subsequently, Operations Mountain Eagle I and II. According to a website maintained by the Chinese government, 'IP Protection in China', www.ipr.gov.cn, these campaigns resulted in a substantial increase in criminal arrests. The campaigns are also credited with raising public awareness of IPR and with improving the coordination of administrative and criminal enforcement (IP Protection in China, 2007).

China also defends its efforts to protect IP by pointing out that since August 2006, intellectual property complaint centers have been set up in 50 cities where infringement and counterfeiting are prevalent. Complaints may be filed in these centers by rights holders as well as citizens.

China appears to be well aware of the shortcomings of its IPR regime. In April 2007, China's 2007 Action Plan on IPR Protection appeared on the official government website (Action Plan, 2007). The ambitious Plan proposes 276 measures to be taken in ten areas. In the area of protecting well known marks, the 2007 Plan makes some notable commitments, but is vague in terms of how proposals to solve problems identified will be implemented. For example, legislative initiatives include revising laws and regulations on trademark protection and unfair competition. The 2007 Plan proposes to 'speed up revision to the "Provisions for Identification and Protection of Well-Known Trademarks" and to study the Judicial Interpretations of well-known marks'. In the area of enforcement, the 2007 Plan requires campaigns to protect Olympic logos better, to conduct actions against major cases of unfair competition and to severely penalize copycats of product names, packaging, designs or business logos of well-known brands. The Plan also calls for day-to-day enforcement to 'step up efforts in the recognition and protection of well-known trademarks and to rigorously combat violations of proprietary well-known trademarks'. By working from 'big and critical cases', the Plan calls for investigation and severe punishment of counterfeiters 'especially of well-known domestic and foreign brands' (Action Plan, 2007).

Several sections in the Plan address needed improvements in the judicial system. The Plan states that courts should impose harsher penalties for IP violations and that a case guidance system should be implemented to establish common standards for judicial review. In an effort to increase transparency, the Plan proposes that trials on IP issues be open to the public, that cases and verdict information be published on a regular basis in public journals, and that such information be published 'to the outside world in the English language if conditions permit'. The Plan also calls for higher caliber Chinese lawyers specialized in IP, and more training sessions for judges at the National Judges College.

The Olympic Opportunity

The 2008 Olympics, to be held in Beijing, offer a unique opportunity for China to showcase its new economy and to demonstrate that it can, in fact, implement and enforce protection of IPR (Yu, 2006, pp. 992–9; Wall, 2006, p. 345). The excitement generated by the Olympics also allows China an opportunity to test its ability to inform and educate the public about protecting Olympic symbols in particular and IP in general. The importance of the Olympic experience to China is evident by the fact that the 2008 Beijing Olympic Games Organizing Committee (BOCOG) set up a legal affairs department specifically to address IP protection of Olympic marks.

The Regulations on the Protection of Olympic Symbols became effective on 1 April, 2002. The Regulations are more stringent than the 2001 Trademark Law and the Unfair Competition Law. The Regulations prohibit unauthorized use of Olympic symbols and outline the use of Olympic symbols for business purposes pursuant to licensing contracts with the International Olympic Committee as well as the Chinese Olympic Committee (*China Daily*, 2007).

The Regulations are remarkable in that they provide higher punishments than other IP laws, impose fines even when no illegal income is seized, and calculate damages based on the original Olympic item's licensing fee, instead of the price of the infringing product (Kanji, 2006, p. 1284; State Council of the People's Republic of China, 2002). AICs reportedly have been vigilant in investigating illegal use of Olympic symbols and have destroyed the manufacturing sites of fake products (Xinhua News Agency, 2007a). In addition to enforcement by AICs, BOCOG has hired and trained enforcement staff to supervise the market. BOCOG has launched publicity campaigns about the need to protect Olympic symbols and reminds consumers that franchised outlets are the only sources allowed to sell Olympic souvenirs and that souvenirs sold in other outlets are counterfeit.

Reportedly, China has been effective in minimizing piracy for sales of Beijing 2008 Olympic merchandise (Fowler, 2005). Hopefully, the efforts of BOCOG and the spotlight on the Beijing Olympics will provide a blueprint for improving IP protection on a wider scale. Both the harsher methods in dealing with infringement and counterfeiting and the administrative organization implemented for the Beijing Olympics should instruct the Chinese government on how to improve the overall administrative system regarding trademark infringement.

THE JUDICIAL IMPACT ON PROTECTION OF WELL KNOWN MARKS

Just as China continues to promise improvements in IP protection through its laws and enforcement mechanisms, so it continues to emphasize improvements in the transparency and independence of the judicial system. The following subsections explain that China has taken steps to improve the court system and judicial determination of well known marks. Several court decisions are discussed in an effort to discern when MNEs are likely to be successful in gaining well known status through the judicial process.

The Court System

Writing in 1998, Justice Cheng Yong-Shun of the Supreme People's Court, China's highest court, wrote about the need to improve the quality of the legal profession in

China, as well as the need to establish the independence of the judicial system from Party influence (Yong-Shun, 1998). Nearly ten years later, concerns about the lack of legal training and the lack of judicial independence persist (Halverson, 2004, pp. 358–9). In 1999, China announced a Five Year People's Court Reform Plan. The Plan sought to improve China's court system by improving the expertise of judges, enforcing anti-corruption regulations; allowing some discovery; and improving the efficiency and enforcement of judgments (Chua, 2006, pp. 136–8). The Plan required judges to hold university degrees and to pass a national judicial examination (Zhou, 2002, pp. 431–2). In 2005, the SPC announced a new five year reform plan, again emphasizing the need to establish a more independent judiciary and freedom from Party influence.

Although it is difficult to determine whether the court system is becoming more independent, China seeks guidance from the US and Europe for ways to improve its court system, while it also implements change at the local and city level (Nicholas, 2006). In Shanghai, for example, courts have increased the respect of judges and the court system by raising the salaries of judges. A Beijing court took the initiative to issue a new standard that requires the court to inform parties that they may raise any questions related to the judgment, including questions about the law on which the judgment was based. In cases involving foreign parties, the litigants have 30 days to raise such questions on any type of case (Standard for Answering Queries of Parties, 2006). Although this initiative applies only to the Beijing Court, it represents an encouraging step in raising the transparency and understanding of cases.

The Supreme People's Court (SPC), which operates in both a supervisory and tribunal capacity, has taken initiative in the IP area. In 2005, the SPC designated nearly 150 intermediate and primary courts to handle specific types of IP cases (Burr, 2006, p. 52). The SPC also set up an Intellectual Property Rights Working Office to supervise lower judicial bodies on IP cases (Zhou, 2002, pp. 431–2). The SPC recently issued a notice to lower courts regarding the recognition of well known marks. In November of 2006, the SPC created a central database containing all of the marks that have been recognized as well known in court decisions. The SPC has notified all courts to report both past and future decisions regarding recognition of well known marks to the SPC ('China's Database of Well Known Marks', 2006). The new recording system is expected to promote consistency and transparency in the protection and recognition of well known marks. Of course, such centralization could also signal Party interest in controlling the outcome of lower court decisions.

IKEA and Starbucks Prevail in Infringement Suits

Holders of well known marks, such as IKEA and Starbucks, have prevailed against imitators in cases involving both domain names and enterprise or trade names. These cases illustrate that Chinese courts are capable of applying the law in a manner consistent with international expectations. Neither the IKEA case nor the Starbucks case appears as an official translation in English. The translated versions relied on are unofficial.

In 1999, Inter IKEA Systems (IKEA), the home furnishing provider based in the Netherlands, prevailed in a suit for trademark infringement and unfair competition (Inter IKEA Systems, 1999). The case was China's first involving cybersquatting. Although the 2001 Trademark Law and several implementing regulations and SPC interpretations were not effective at the time of the decision, the IKEA case was an auspicious start to judicial recognition and protection of foreign well known marks. Preparing for WTO accession at the time this case was decided, China demonstrated that its courts could apply its domestic law and international IP treatises to decide cases involving foreign IPR fairly.

The defendant, Beijing CINET Information Company (CINET), one of the first Internet service providers in China, was using 'IKEA' as part of its domain name, 'Ikea.com.cn' (Sun, 2000a).[4] The No. 2 Beijing Intermediate People's Court found for IKEA, ordering that the registration of the domain name be revoked and that the defendant pay the court costs. According to the court, the defendant violated the Provisional Administrative Measures for Registration of Domain Names on the Internet in China as well as the spirit of the Paris Convention and fundamental principles of China's Unfair Competition Law. Although the court's conclusion does not provide an analysis of how these specific laws and treatises were violated, it does offer some basis for its conclusions. The court cited Article 5 (2) of the Unfair Competition Law, Article 6bis of the Paris Convention and the World Intellectual Property Organization's Final Report on Domain Name Process (Inter IKEA Systems, 1999).

In addressing issues of trademark infringement and unfair competition, the Beijing Intermediate People's Court noted that domain names and trademarks are related and that the 'relationship between domain name and trade mark has continuously been more and more tense'. Registration of the well known mark 'IKEA', the court held, would lead to consumer confusion about ownership or sponsorship of the mark. Consequently, the court held that CINET had 'infringed the owner's exclusive right' to its well known trademark (Inter IKEA Systems, 1999).

Without articulating a precise list of criteria, the court considered whether 'IKEA' was a well known mark. The Beijing court noted the continuous use of the mark; the fact that IKEA is one of the largest furnishing retailers in the world; the large amount of money IKEA spends on advertising; the familiarity with the mark of trade groups and consumers in China; and the high commercial goodwill the mark had among consumers (Inter IKEA Systems, 1999).

The court's decision emphasizes the mark holder's international renown rather than its status in China. It is doubtful that the mark 'IKEA' was well known in China in 1997, when the defendant registered the mark. IKEA did not open shops in Beijing and Shanghai until 1998. Nevertheless, the court noted that the Chinese character version of IKEA's mark had become famous to a certain extent in Chinese-speaking countries including Hong Kong and Taiwan. In the final analysis, IKEA's international prominence at the time the defendant registered the mark was enough to convince the court of its well known status. Moreover, the court's decision indicates awareness that opportunists seek to take advantage of the reputation and goodwill of a mark that is well known internationally before it becomes well known in a developing market, such as China.

This awareness of opportunistic behavior is captured in the court's emphasis on the defendant's bad faith in registering the mark. The court was clearly influenced by the fact that the defendant had registered several domain names, using well known trademarks, including Amex, Bacardi, Boss, DuPont, Hertz, Lancôme, Polo and Rolex. The court stated that registering a great number of domain names with the intent of selling them indicates bad faith conduct and 'a kind of unfair competition' (Inter IKEA Systems, 1999).

Although the outcome of the IKEA case would be expected in countries with established laws in trademark dilution, the case had important implications for China's dual system of recognizing well known trademarks. Significantly, the court's decision does not respond to the defendant's argument that any dispute regarding the mark should be settled in an administrative proceeding because the China Internet Network Information Center (CNNIC) had granted the defendant authority to use the domain name. The defendant also argued that SAIC had not recognized 'IKEA' as a well known mark. In deciding the case, the court did not give any deference to the administrative history of the defendant's registration of the mark. The court stated that IKEA's requests to protect its IP rights had 'nothing to do with the agency providing registration service' (Inter IKEA Systems, 1999). This statement is particularly significant given that the defendant, CINET, which had registered more than 2000 domain names, was CNNIC's largest client at the time the case was decided.

The IKEA case set the stage for several MNEs to reclaim their domain names through litigation (Hong, 2004, pp. 8–9). For example, in a case similar to IKEA, the Beijing No. 1 Intermediate Court recognized Dupont as a well known trademark. The court ordered the defendant to withdraw its registration of the domain name www.dupont.com.cn, finding that the defendant's use of Dupont's well known mark violated the Paris Convention and China's Unfair Competition Law (Sun, 2000b).

The 2001 Trademark Law, subsequent Implementing Regulations, and interpretations by the SPC incorporated much of the court's decision in IKEA. For example, the SPC issued a Judicial Interpretation on Application of the Trademark Law stating that registering a domain name that is identical or similar to another's registered trademark and the act of using the domain name in commerce for related goods in a manner that misleads the public constitutes infringement of the exclusive right to use the registered trademark under Article 52(2) of the 2001 Trademark Law.

The IKEA case indicates the importance of statistical evidence of well known status. MNEs should maintain and update records that support well known status including sales figures and advertising expenditures. Such information can be used as evidence in proceedings to oppose the registration of a similar, infringing mark or in a civil suit or arbitration proceeding involving infringement or unfair competition.

Two cases involving Starbucks also indicate that Chinese courts are willing to recognize marks as well known in cases involving foreign mark holders. Starbucks successfully sued two Chinese coffee shops, one in Qingdao and one in Shanghai, for infringing its trademarks and its Chinese name, 'Xingbake'. 'Xingbake' is a combination of translation and transliteration. 'Xing' is a translation of 'star', 'ba ke' is a transliteration of 'bucks' (Miller, 2007). The three characters used to represent 'Xingbake' have no connection or connotation with coffee or food. Starbucks had registered several trademarks related to its products in China in 1996, including the name 'Xingbake', and began doing business in China in 1999.[5]

Starbucks sued the owner of a café in Qingdao, an eastern port city, for trademark infringement. The defendant coffee shop, which opened in 2003, used the name 'Xingbake' on its sign outside the door; used the English name 'Qingdao Star Sbuck Coffee' on its napkins; used several Starbucks trademarks such as 'frappuccino' and 'Yukon blend'; sold coffee beans clearly labeled as Starbucks Coffee in bags identical to those used by Starbucks; and employed a green and white color scheme similar to Starbucks'.[6]

The defendant challenged Starbucks' use of the name 'Xingbake'. The defendant argued that it was justified in using 'Xingbake' as an enterprise name. According to the defendant, use as an enterprise name was distinct from trademark use because Article 13 of China's 2001 Trademark Law prohibits only the Chinese translation of foreign well known trademarks that have been registered or used in China. Thus, the defendant argued that its registered enterprise name, 'Xingbake', was not properly a target for trademark infringement. The defendant also argued that although Starbucks had registered 'Xingbake', it had never used the trademark in China. Finally, the defendant argued that Starbucks was not a well known mark in China.

The court found that the defendant had deliberately copied Starbucks' entire trademark system and that the defendant was not using 'Xingbake' as an enterprise name but as a trademark to identify its business as a coffee shop through signage and logos both inside and outside the shop. The trademark use by the Qingdao coffee shop, the court stated, was likely to confuse consumers. The court also found that Starbucks had, in fact, used the Chinese term 'Xingbake' in identifying its business in China and that Starbucks had been referred to as 'Xingbake' in Taiwan since 1998 (Miller, 2007). The court ordered the defendant to remove the term 'Xingbake' from its legal name; to cease using any Starbucks trademarks; and to cease using the green circle logo. The court stated that 'the defendant was clearly "free riding", an intentional violation of the principle of good faith and recognized business ethics' (Miller, 2007). The defendant was also ordered to pay economic damages to Starbucks in the amount of RMB 500 000 (US $62 000), the maximum amount of statutory damages allowed under Chinese law. In the course of its decision, the court cited provisions of its 2001 Trademark Law, the Unfair Competition Law, the General Principles of Civil Law, as well as the Paris Convention and TRIPS (Miller, 2007).

A second Chinese court found for Starbucks in another suit alleging infringement of its well known mark. In a 2005 ruling, the Shanghai No. 2 People's Court recognized Starbucks as a well known trademark and ordered Shanghai Xingbake Coffee Shop Ltd to pay Starbucks RMB 500 000 (US $62 000). In its decision, the judge ruled that use of the Chinese translation 'Xingbake' constituted trademark infringement. The judge found Starbucks and its green and white logo to be well known trademarks. In December of 2006, the Shanghai People's High Court upheld the decision (Xinhua News Agency, 2007b).

Challenges in Choosing a Chinese Name for Well Known Marks

IKEA and Starbucks were successful in having their marks recognized by the courts as well known. Other foreign companies doing business in China have had more difficulty in gaining well known status. The difficulty may be due to lack of evidence that the mark is well known in China; to poor choice of a Chinese mark; to insufficient monitoring for infringing marks; or, perhaps in some cases, to Party influence.

Article 8 of the Implementing Regulations of the 2001 Trademark Law requires foreign mark holders to register trademarks in Chinese. Consequently, foreign companies must make choices about how to translate their names into Chinese and which marks they are going to use to promote their brand in China. Companies are not required to use the Chinese name they register, but they must be aware that competitors may take advantage of the Chinese or English name by using translations, transliterations, or employing Chinese characters that are pronounced similarly or identically to those of the registered mark. Failure to consult with native speakers who understand the specific market involved in choosing a name can cause difficult trademark issues. Chinese courts may be unsympathetic to a foreign mark holder who does not grasp the subtleties of the Chinese language.

Both Dell and Bloomberg alleged that Chinese competitors registered marks that infringed on their Chinese names. In both cases, however, the courts saw distinctions that eluded the foreign mark holders. Neither Dell nor Bloomberg was successful in seeking well known status for marks they registered in China. Consequently, they were unable to effect cancellation of similar marks registered by competitors.

In 2001, Dell sought cancellation of a mark consisting of Chinese characters which Dell believed infringed its trademarked Chinese character name. The characters Dell registered are pronounced 'dai er'. The name has no particular meaning in Chinese. A Chinese competitor registered characters pronounced 'de er'. The first characters of Dell and the competitor's registered trademarks are written differently and have different meanings, the second characters are written the same. Dell applied to TRAB for cancellation of the competitor's mark, maintaining that it violated China's 2001 Trademark Law as a translation of its registered well known mark. TRAB rejected Dell's request for cancellation, stating that Dell had not proved its mark was well known in 1997. On appeal, the No. 1 Beijing Intermediate Court upheld TRAB's decision (China IP Express, 2006; Minter Ellison, 2007).

Bloomberg, one of the most influential global companies in the field of financial software and information, had a trademark issue similar to that encountered by Dell. Bloomberg registered and used the Chinese name 'Peng Bo' which has a phonetic similarity to Bloomberg and translates as 'wide coverage', an apt name for the global financial news service (China IP Law Blog, 2005). Bloomberg sued defendants, Shanghai Pobo Finance and Economic Information Company and Shanghai Pobo Network Information Consulting Company. The defendant companies, like Bloomberg, provide financial data and news services. The defendants use the domain names 'pobo.com.cn' and 'pobo.net.cn' (IP Protection in China, 2006). The characters used in 'pobo' are identical to those used by Bloomberg in 'Peng Bo' and thus, have the same pronunciation and meaning. The court ruled that Bloomberg was entitled to damages in the amount of RMB 300 000 (US $37 500) and an apology on Pobo's website. But the court did not grant Bloomberg's request to recognize its trademark as well known. Most importantly, because it did not consider Bloomberg's trademark to be well known in China, the court did not require the defendant to change its name. Unfortunately, there are no official decisions reported of the Dell or Bloomberg cases. Thus, it is difficult to understand the basis of the court's reasoning in denying well known status. The issue of bad faith, however, was apparently not addressed by the courts.

Sony Ericsson has also run into difficulty with its Chinese trademarked name. Sony Ericsson chose a Chinese trademark that sounded phonetically like its name 'Sony Ericsson'. Each syllable was represented by a character. Consumers, however, shortened the name to two characters – the first part of Sony, 'Suo', and the first part of Ericsson, 'Ai'. A third party, Suo Ai Digital Technology Company, registered the mark 'Sui Ai'. Sony Ericsson has tried to purchase the shortened form of its name for RMB 20 to 30 million ($US 3 to 4 million) without success (Shi, 2007). Based on the Dell and Bloomberg decisions Sony Ericsson would be unlikely to prevail in a trademark infringement suit against Suo Ai Digital.

As the Dell, Bloomberg and Sony cases suggest, MNEs should consult with local experts in choosing a Chinese name. Due to the tonal system of the Chinese language, the phonetic catalogue is more complex than in many languages. Furthermore, numerous characters may represent the same phonetic sound. Finally, differences in pronunciation between Cantonese, which is spoken in Hong Kong and southern China, and Mandarin, spoken throughout most of mainland China, can sometimes be substantial. To further complicate the issue, Hong Kong and Taiwan use complex or traditional characters, while mainland China uses simplified characters. Distinctive translations that incorporate both sound and meaning are probably most successful. For example, Coca Cola's Chinese name is 'ke kou ke le', which translates loosely as 'making the mouth happy' (Coyler, 2005). Although it is impossible for a foreign company to anticipate the myriad possibilities of Chinese names that might bear some resemblance to one's own, the Chinese courts have indicated an unwillingness to accommodate holders of well known marks when issues involving peculiarities in the language are involved.

CONCLUSION

MNEs seeking to gain well known status for trademarks in China face a variety of challenges. The administrative system may fail when local authorities bow to local pressures. The judicial system offers hope in the form of decisions based on internationally accepted IP principles, but the court system continues to lack transparency, as few decisions are translated and the premise on which a case is based is often not divulged.

China seems well aware of the challenges MNEs face. The government simultaneously defends its effort to protect well known marks, pointing to a variety of campaigns and programs aimed at enforcing its IP laws, while simultaneously conceding that large-scale improvements are needed. China's 2007 Action Plan is a testament to the tension between China's repeated commitments to improving IP protection and its inability to implement and execute meaningful reforms. Nevertheless, China's recognition of its own shortcomings in protecting IP, together with pressure from the US and other countries, should continue to move the system in the right direction.

NOTES

1. The QBPC is registered under the China Association of Enterprises with Foreign Investment. In 2007, the QBPC listed 165 multinational companies in its membership. More information about the organization and its objectives can be found at www.qbpc.org.cn.
2. Article 6bis of the Paris Convention provides that a country may refuse to register or prohibit the use of a trademark that is 'well known'. The Paris Convention protected well known marks only when the infringing use involved identical or similar goods. TRIPS broadens the protection of well known marks to include service marks as well as to infringing uses involving dissimilar goods and services.
3. In the United States, famous marks are protected from dilution by the Federal Trademark Dilution Act of 1995. The difference between well known and famous marks is, apparently, one of degree. In his book, *Famous and Well-Known Marks*, Frederick W. Mostert explains that a well known mark is known to a

substantial segment of the public, whereas a famous mark 'is that which has been able to achieve a secondary function distinct from its first and natural function (i.e., that of distinguishing the products which it distinguishes by means of their origin). This second function involves the exercise of a power of attraction . . . totally independent of the products or their origin' (Mostert, 1997, p. 270).
4. CINET was established in 1995. The Internet provider was backed by the Chinese government departments of the Ministry of Post and Telecommunications, the Information Office of the State Council and the China Institute of Science and Technology Net Center.
5. As of 2 October, 2006, Starbucks operated more than 430 stores in Greater China, including more than 190 stores in 19 cities on Mainland China. One of the most controversial locations is that in the Forbidden City.
6. Despite the use of Starbucks' trademarks and some aspects of its trade dress, anecdotal evidence suggests that no one would confuse the Qingdao coffee shop for Starbucks. A visitor to the Qingdao Xingbake described the outlet as a typical Chinese coffee shop with a 'do it all' approach. Customers in the shop were served tea, beer, fruit and ice cream (Dickinson, 2006). The poor service and shabby decor of the shop were obviously damaging to Starbucks' image and brand identity.

REFERENCES

Action Plan (2007), 'Action Plan on IPR Protection for 2007', GOV.cn (6 April, 2007) http://english.gov.cn/2007-04/06/content_574197_6.htm.
Burr, Michael (2006), 'China's IP protections are improving, but enforcement remedies remain weak', The China Report, *InsideCounsel*, November, pp. 52–3.
Cahan, Alisa (2004), 'China's protection of famous and well-known marks: The impact of China's latest trademark law reform on infringement and remedies', *Cardozo Journal of International & Comparative Law*, **12**, 219–49.
China Daily (2007), 'Infringers on Olympic emblem should bear legal liability', http://english.ipr.gov.en.info/Article.jsp?a_no48490&col_no=893&dir=200701.
China IP Express (2006), 'Dell's trade mark/trade name infringement and false advertising lawsuit reaches a conclusion', *China IP Express*, no. 279, www.iprights.com.
China IP Law Blog (2005), 'Why Bloomberg sued two Chinese companies over the mark "pengbo"', 22 November, http://chinaip.wordpress.com/2005/11/22/why-bloomberg-sued-two-chinese-companies-over-the-mark-%&29.80%9cpengbo%2%80%9d.
Chow, Daniel C.K. (2006), 'Why China does not take commercial piracy seriously', *Ohio Northern University Law Review*, **32**, 203–25.
Chua, Eu Jin (2006), 'The laws of the People's Republic of China: An introduction for international investors', *Chicago Journal of International Law*, **7**, 133–68.
Coyler, Edward (2005), 'Branding with Chinese characters', 17 January, www.brandchannel.com.
Dickinson, Steve (2006), 'Qingdao court rules in favor of Starbucks in landmark Chinese trademark case (Part II)', *China Law Blog* (www.chinalawblog.com), 10 April.
Fowler, Geoffrey (2005), 'China's logo crackdown', *Wall Street Journal*, B1, 4 November.
Halverson, Karen (2004), 'China's WTO accession: Economic, legal, and political implications', *Boston College International & Comparative Law Review*, **27**, 319–70.
Hong, Xue (2004), 'Domain name dispute resolution in China: A comprehensive review', *Temple International & Comparative Law Journal*, **18**, 1–50.
Inter IKEA Systems B.V. v. Beijing CINET Information Co., Ltd No. 86 (1999), Intellectual Chamber of Beijing No. 2 Intermediate People's Court (Wei Shuangjuan, unofficial trans.).
IP Protection in China (2006), 'Collection of IPR-related cases (06-11-27) Bloomberg suit', *IP Protection in China*, 27 November, www.ipr.gov.cn.
IP Protection in China (2007), 'Mountain Eagle campaign II shows effect', *IP Protection in China*, 16 March, www.ipr.gov.cn.
Kanji, Omario (2006), 'Paper dragon: Inadequate protection of intellectual property rights in China', *Michigan Journal of International Law*, **27**, 1261–86.
Lam, Cedric and Janet Wong (2007), 'China's latest push on well-known marks', China IP Focus 2007, 5th edn, *Managing Intellectual Property*, www.managingip.com.

Lehman, Edward Eugene, Camilla Ojansivu and Stan Abrams (2003), 'Well-known trademark protection in the People's Republic of China – Evolution of the system', *Fordham International Law Journal*, **26**, 257–72.
Managing Intellectual Property (2005), 'More famous marks win protection', May, http://www.managingip.com/Article.aspx?ArticleID=1255039.
Managing Intellectual Property (2006–2007), 'China's databases of well-known marks', (January–December), www.managingip.com.
Mertha, Andrew C. (2005), *The Politics of Piracy*, Ithaca, USA and London, UK: Cornell University Press.
Miller, Michelle M. (2007), *Starbucks v. Qingdao Xingbake* (translation on file with author).
Minter Ellison (2007), 'Legal update – Dell's appeal against registered Chinese translation dismissed', www.minterellison.com, 10 November.
Mostert, Frederick W. (1997), *Famous and Well-Known Marks*, London: Butterworths.
Nicholas, Adele (2006), 'Legal reform: China takes a slow path to an independent and impartial judiciary', The China Report, *Inside Counsel* (November), at 50, http://devinsidecounsel.com/assets/article/China.pdf.
Safro, Bella I. and Thomas S. Keaty (2004), 'What's in a name? Protection of well-known trademarks under international and national law', *Tulane Journal of Technology & Intellectual Property*, **6**, 33–61.
SAIC (2002), 'The Reply of the State Administration for Industry and Commerce on How to Understand the Relevant Requirement in Article 53 of the Trademark Law', 21 October, http://www.lawinfochina.com/law/display.asp?db=1&id=2887.
Shao, Ke (2005), 'Look at my sign! – Trademarks in China from antiquity to the early modern times', *Journal of the Patent & Trademark Office Society*, **87**, 654–82.
Shi, Kim (2007), 'Sony Ericsson fails to buy Chinese trademark', Pacific Epoch, www.pacificepoch.com, 6 April.
Standard for Answering Queries of Parties after Adjudication (2006), 'Beijing court more accountable to litigants', *Managing Intellectual Property*, December 2005–January 2006.
State Council of the People's Republic of China (2002), 'Regulations on the protection of Olympic symbols'.
Sun, Andy Y. (ed.) (2000a), 'IKEA scored a major victory in first name dispute in China', *Asia Pacific Legal Institute*, www.apli.org.
Sun, Andy Y. (ed.) (2000b), 'Beijing first intermediate court conducted trial on domain name dispute over Dupont', *Asia Pacific Legal Institute*, www.apli.org.
Supreme People's Court (2004), 'Interpretation of the concrete application of the law in handling criminal cases of intellectual property infringement', translated at http://english.people.com.cn/data/laws/detail.php?id=4.
USTR (United States Trade Representative) (2007a), '2007 Special 301Review'.
USTR, (United States Trade Representative) (2007b), '2007 Trade Summary (China)', pp. 105–12.
Wall, Anne M. (2006), 'Intellectual property protection in China: Enforcing trademark rights', *Marquette Sports Law Review*, **17**, 341–426.
Xinhua News Agency (2007a), 'Olympic IPR strengthened in Beijing', 13 March.
Xinhua News Agency (2007b), 'Starbucks China copycat punished', 5 January.
Yong-shun, Justice Chen (1998), 'Juridical protection of intellectual property in China', *Duke Journal of Comparative & International Law*, **9**, 267–73.
Yu, Peter K. (2006), 'From pirates to partners (Episode II): Protecting intellectual property in post-WTO China', *American University Law Review*, **55**, 901–1000.
Zhou, Jessica Jiong (2002), 'Trademark law & enforcement in China: A transnational perspective', *Wisconsin International Law Journal*, **20**, 415–44.

6. India: a study in patent-law effects

George T. Haley and Usha C.V. Haley*

INTRODUCTION

For the past two decades, the pharmaceutical industry in Western industrialized economies has perceived India as both a benefit and a cost. As a source of high-quality, low-cost bulk drugs, India provides a benefit by permitting Western companies to cut their production costs. However, as India did not recognize product patents, but only process patents, its backwards engineering of new, extremely high-cost pharmaceutical drugs associated with HIV/AIDS, aging, heart disease, cancer and numerous other medical conditions, posed a significant cost.

Until 31 December 2004, India's process-patenting regime limited patent protection to providing exclusive rights only to the process through which a product was produced, rather than to the product itself. This regime thereby allowed India's innovative, high-quality and low-cost pharmaceutical industry to develop and to produce low-cost Indian versions of high-cost Western pharmaceuticals for sale in developing nations without infringing on the original patent holders' patents. The Indian companies had the legal rights to produce and sell the drugs if their processes to produce the drugs differed sufficiently from the original patent holders' processes to satisfy Indian law.

Unlike many other Asian countries, India has a long legal history for both its legal system and patent law, as it inherited both from the British. India adopted its first patent law in 1856 (Zacharias and Farias, 2003). Unlike other Asian former British colonies, upon India's independence in 1947, it decided to adopt, and has maintained, a democratic political system. Other countries with recent histories of both rule of law and patent law have also recently switched from process-patent to product-patent regimes. Yet, unlike India, these other countries, such as Poland, had communist governments which did not recognize Western patents; and, unlike India, their governments controlled and directed pharmaceutical research, production and distribution. Hence, India provides a close to ideal legal jurisdiction to test so far untested claims that pharmaceutical product-patent regimes result in greater rates of innovation, which in turn improve social health and contribute to greater social returns.

First, we discuss the evolution of India's patent laws. Next, we review existing research on the effects of product-patent-law regimes. In the following sections, we focus on India's pharmaceutical industry, covering its domestic characteristics and its place in the global pharmaceutical industry. We contrast the data on pre-reform patents (prior to 2005) with the preliminary data on post-reform patents (after 2005). We conclude with implications for the Indian pharmaceutical industry and highlight the need for future empirical research to establish the social returns from product-patent regimes.

Table 6.1 A timeline for India's patent law

1856	First Indian patent laws
1859	First major revision of patent laws
1872	Patents & Designs Protection Act
1888	Inventions & Designs Act
1911	Indian Patents & Designs Act
1911–1970	Myriad minor amendments
1970	The Patents Act
	Signatory of 1883 Paris Convention
	Patent Cooperation Agreement
1994	GATT Agreement & TRIPS
2005	TRIPS requirements met

THE EVOLUTION OF INDIA'S PATENT REGIME

India adopted its first patent laws in 1856 (Zacharias and Farias, 2003). The first major revisions came in 1859 and in 1872 with the Patents and Designs Act. Table 6.1 provides a timeline of India's patent regimes.

As Table 6.1 shows, many changes and amendments have occurred in India's patent laws over the years. For our study, the most important new legislation and agreements came in the 1970 enactment of the Indian Patents Act; and, in the 1994 signings of the Uruguay Round of General Agreement of Tariffs and Trade (GATT) and the Trade Related Aspects of Intellectual Property Rights Agreement (TRIPS). The 1970 Patents Act established the process-patent regime in India's pharmaceutical and agro-chemical sectors; the 1994 signings accepted the eventual change to a full product-patent regime in all Indian economic sectors, including pharmaceuticals and agro-chemicals.

The Indian Patent Act of 1970 replaced a product-patent regime which severely constrained the Indian pharmaceutical industry's participation in its own home market (Pharmaceutical & Drug Manufacturers, 2007). The Indian Patent Act contradicted the TRIPS agreement policies favored by the industrialized economies' pharmaceutical industry. It provided seven-year process patents from the application times, or five-year process patents from the sealing times with attendant requirements that the patent holders license the processes at reasonable fees to individuals or companies seeking these technologies. After three years, if the Indian patent holders appeared to demand unreasonable licensing fees, the Indian Patent Office could stipulate what it viewed as fair fees and require the patent holders to grant the licenses.

Since the Patent Act's passage in 1970, the Indian pharmaceutical industry soared. Table 6.2 presents the growth in the number of companies in the industry over the latter part of the twentieth century when the process-patent regime was in effect. The number of Indian pharmaceutical companies burgeoned from 2257 in 1970 to over 23 000 in 2004/05. Similar growth occurred among pharmaceutical preparations developed and made in India and in bulk drugs (used in preparing pharmaceutical compounds and medications) made in India for domestic and export purposes. This growth

Table 6.2 Number of companies in the Indian pharmaceutical industry

Year	Number of companies
1970	2 257
1980	5 156
1990	16 000
2000	20 053

Source: Pharmaceutical & Drug Manufacturers (2007).

appears to contradict the argument that product-patent regimes constitute necessary conditions for innovation, volume and prosperity in national pharmaceutical industries.

The year 1994 proved a watershed year for the Indian pharmaceutical industry when the Indian government signed agreements that would lead to planned changes, in January 2005, to its then product-patent regime. The ten-year lag between the signing of the TRIPS agreement and the change-over complied with the maximum time allowed by TRIPS. Though the new product-patent regime provides for 20-year patents, the Western pharmaceutical industry has highlighted several negative characteristics. Specifically, India's new patent laws:

- define products narrowly as 'new chemical entities';
- fail to guarantee data protection;
- continue to provide for compulsory licensing if the Controller of patents determines that public interest is not being served.

India also passed patent-reform amendments to the 1970 Patent Act, providing for a mailbox system of patent applications and a system of Exclusive Marketing Rights (EMR) for products developed after 1 January 1995. The mailbox system conformed to global standards and provided pharmaceutical or agro-chemical companies with the abilities to file for patents for approval upon implementation of the 2005 product-patent regime. In March 2006, India granted the first product patent under the new product-patent regime for the Roche drug Pegasys. Roche filed for the patent through a 1997 mailbox application, introduced the drug to the Indian market in 2003, and the Indian patent for the drug ran through to 15 May 2007 (Datta, 2006). The EMR amendment that was passed in 1999 was retroactive to 1995. The EMR addressed pharmaceutical companies that had developed products after 1 January 1995, had obtained patents for the products from Patent Convention member nations, and had also obtained rights to market the products in the patent-granting nation. The EMR granted these companies the exclusive right to market the products in India for either five years or until the Indian patent office granted or rejected the companies' patents, whichever came earlier. Consideration of companies' Indian product-patent applications would not begin until after 31 December 2004 (Indian Patent Office 2007).

The next section reviews theories on the relative benefits of process vs. product-patent regimes.

THEORETICAL VIEWS ON PRODUCT-PATENT BENEFITS

The concept of patents derives from John Locke's economic philosophy. In his *Second Treatise of Government* (1764), Locke argued that just as people own their bodies, they also own the 'fruits of their labor'. Since Locke, several theorists, philosophers and policy makers have attempted to define 'the fruits of labor'. If fruits of labor referred to the technologies developed to produce products, it covered process patents; if the phrase referred to the products that resulted from the technologies, it covered product patents. Usually, nations have recognized and enforced patents when they coincide with their economic interests. Today, the USA serves as the most adamant champion of Intellectual Property Rights (IPR); yet, at its founding in 1776, the USA became the only nation in history to establish the theft of foreign intellectual property as an official government policy (Haley, 2000, 2007; *Report on the Subject of Manufactures 1791*, in Hamilton, 2001).

Since these early days, researchers have continued to debate the effectiveness of patents vis-à-vis other mechanisms (such as secrecy) to protect technologies and the effects of patents on innovations. Mansfield et al. (1981) found that 60 per cent of patented products are imitated within four years. In addition Mansfield (1986) and Co et al. (2004) found that patents are most highly valued in industries where imitation is relatively easy, but that the majority of patentable products are not patented. Mansfield (1986) also found that the strengthening of patents had, at best, mixed effects on foreign direct investment (FDI). In a subsequent study Lee and Mansfield (1996) found that strengthening patents in developing economies had the desired effect of increasing inward FDI. However, Pfister and Defains (2005) concluded that French companies tended to reduce investment in countries that strengthened their patent protection and that have high GDP or low research intensity. Lee and Mansfield (1996) and Pfister and Defains (2005) appear to contradict one another, but form logical complements. High GDP countries generally have developed, not developing, economies, hence no conflict exists between the two studies' findings. Thumm (2004, p. 536) summarized the findings on effective patenting policy when he stated:

> The provision of intellectual property rights is a matter of finding the right balance between an innovation spurring effect and a certain limitation to the diffusion of technological knowledge. For practical policy making it is hard to find the adequate level of protection in order to arrive at maximum wealth creation.

Jensen and Webster (2004) arrived at a similar conclusion.

Even with strong patent-protection regimes, secrecy plays an important role in IPR protection. Anton and Yao (2004) found that the more important an innovation, the more likely that the developing company emphasizes secrecy over patenting as the major form of IPR protection. Cohen, Nelson and Walsh (2000) concluded that companies viewed secrecy as more important than patents in protecting IPR.

Other researchers have studied the benefits of patents through effects on industries. For example, Co et al. (2004) found that strengthening patent protection in industries such as pharmaceuticals and chemicals tended to have a greater effect on inward FDI than strengthening it in industries where imitation becomes more difficult. Lanjouw (2003) focused on enhancing patent protections within the pharmaceutical industry. He concluded that innovations and patent protection should have different characteristics based upon their therapeutic markets. He also argued that insufficient research existed on diseases endemic to poor and middle-income countries; hence pharmaceutical companies should receive worldwide patents for these drugs to promote research in these areas. His research made a case against limiting access through patents to treatment for diseases that strike both prosperous and poor or middle-income countries. Lanjouw (2003) concluded that in the latter case, pharmaceutical companies should receive patent protection in the wealthier countries, but medications should be free of patent protection when their projected sales in poorer countries consist of less than 2 per cent of total world sales.

The next section describes the salient characteristics of India's pharmaceutical industry.

INDIA'S PHARMACEUTICAL INDUSTRY

India has the fourth-largest pharmaceutical industry in the world by volume but only the thirteenth largest in sales. Despite these statistics, India's pharmaceutical industry has enjoyed enormous sales growth. In 2006, India's pharmaceutical companies supplied 95 per cent of its total domestic pharmaceutical market, whereas in 1970 they supplied only about 20 per cent. Simultaneously, in 2006, Indian companies supplied 75 per cent of the medicinal market. Over the past decade the Indian pharmaceutical industry has enjoyed a compounded annual growth rate of 22.7 per cent. Since 1970, it has transformed itself from primarily a producer of bulk pharmaceuticals used for formulations, to an industry comprised of about 45 per cent bulk pharmaceuticals and 55 per cent formulations.

The Indian pharmaceutical industry remains fragmented, with over 23 000 companies. Despite industry fragmentation, Indian pharmaceutical companies have become highly competitive globally and export over 40 per cent of total production. Concentration occurs at the top end of the industry: the ten largest Indian pharmaceutical companies control 36 per cent of the market. The industry provides direct employment for about 5 000 000 Indians and indirect employment for 24 000 000. Table 6.3 summarizes the industry's characteristics. Tables 6.4 and 6.5 present the ten largest Indian pharmaceutical companies by capitalization and sales, respectively.

Table 6.6 highlights the Indian pharmaceutical industry's strength at the market's low end, in price-sensitive generic drugs; it also describes some of the Indian pharmaceutical industry's important opportunities and advantages. Analysts expect Indian companies to capture 30 per cent market share of the drugs losing their US and European patent protection. Not surprisingly, emerging-market pharmaceutical industries emerging from process-patent regimes possess advantages in generics. India too has excelled at the production of bulk, generic chemicals, as in this sector, India's production costs approximate 50 per cent of the USA's and the European Union's (EU's) production costs.

Table 6.6 also reveals that, surprisingly, the USA's and other industrialized countries' advantages in high value-added products and innovation seem to have withered in the pharmaceutical industry. India has excelled at the higher value-added medicinal preparations market. In 1970, India imported virtually all medicinal preparations; today India's domestic pharmaceuticals supply over 75 per cent of its home market (KPMG International, 2006). Some estimates have placed the figure at over 85 per cent. These results contradict researchers and policy makers who argue that process-patent regimes discourage the development of significant research functions.

Table 6.3 Characteristics of the Indian pharmaceutical industry

Exports:
40% of total production
22.7% compounded annual growth
55% formulations/45% bulk
Domestic markets:
Supplies 95% of market today vs. < 20% in 1970
Supplies over 75% of medicinal market
4th largest globally by volume
13th largest globally by value
23 000 + companies
10 largest control 36% of market
Capital investment:
US$1.16 billion
14.8% annual growth
150% tax benefits for capital goods imported
Employment:
Direct: 5 000 000
Indirect: 24 000 000

Sources: Intec.net (2004); Third World Network (2003).

Table 6.4 India's ten largest pharmaceutical companies by market capitalization in 2004

Company	Market capitalization (bn Rs)
Ranbaxy Labs	78.2
Cipla	37.9
Dr Reddy's Labs	27.6
Glaxo	24.1
Wockhardt	13.1
Sun Pharma	12.9
Nicholas Piramal	8.9
Pfizer	7.4
Novartis	6.9
Aventis Pharma	6.3

Source: Sagar (2005).

REASONS FOR INDIA'S R&D SUCCESS

In part, the Indian pharmaceutical industry's success stems from reverse engineering. Indian researchers have not tried to develop new drugs, but rather to develop new processes to produce already established drugs. Reverse engineering, even of pharmaceuticals, becomes cheaper than developing new drugs from scratch. Though they conducted their research on a diverse group of industries rather than solely on the pharmaceutical

Table 6.5 India's ten largest pharmaceutical companies by sales in 2004

Company	Market sales (million US$)
Ranbaxy Labs	841.25
Cipla	452.75
Dr Reddy's Labs	366.29
Aurobindo Pharma	294.73
Nicholas Piramal	278.9
Lupin Labs	270.9
Glaxo	261.89
Cadila Healthcare	257.63
Sun Pharma	205.43
Wockhardt	168.31
Total market share for ten largest companies = 36%	

Source: Sagar (2005).

Table 6.6 Strengths and opportunities for the Indian pharmaceutical industry

Opportunities
Production costs: 50% lower than USA & European Union (EU)
R&D & Associated Services: US$48 billion potential in 2007 –
India's costs advantage for equivalent research:
• 1/10 of USA's & EU's costs for clinical research
• 1/8 of USA's & EU's costs for research overall
• 1/3 of EU's costs for basic research
• 1.6% of sales goes to R&D vs. 15% for West's Pharma
Generics: 2007/08 – US$65 billion in drugs lose patent protection in USA & EU – India's estimated share = 30%

Source: KPMG International (2006).

industry, Mansfield et al. (1981) found that in 85.7 per cent of cases, companies that reverse engineered innovations also developed their products at lower costs than the original innovations' developers.

Relative costs for R&D provide important factors for India's success at the product market's higher value-added end. For basic research, the highest value-added activity, India's costs fall to roughly one third of the USA's or EU's. For clinical research trials, India's cost advantages loom even higher and approximate one-eighth of the USA's or EU's. Consequently, even though the Indian pharmaceutical industry spends only 1.6 per cent of its sales on R&D, as compared to 15 per cent in the West, the Indian companies enjoy significant cost advantages in R&D and reap much greater returns for every dollar they invest.

Factors other than costs also contribute to the Indian pharmaceutical industry's success in R&D. These factors include India's technically-skilled workforce with its fluency in English generated by its English language education system. India's workforce

Table 6.7 India's top-ten pharmaceutical companies' R&D expenditures

Statistic	Percentage
Indian pharmas average R&D as % of sales	1.6
Western pharmas average R&D as % of sales	15.0
India's top 10 pharma companies' average R&D as % of sales	5.7
India's top 5 pharma companies' R&D expenditure growth in 2004/05	47.0
Dr Reddy's R&D as % of sales in 2005	14.7

Source: Sagar (2005).

contributes to an environment conducive to joint-venture projects with, and contract research for, Western companies. Its researchers also have greater access to English-language research reports and papers, thereby contributing to free-flowing communication that promotes innovation. Simultaneously, foreign executives and researchers enjoy high comfort levels in India's English language environments. Combined with the Indian market's very high growth potential, their executives' comfort levels promote a willingness among foreign companies to invest in Indian research. Favorable manufacturing environments enhance favorable research environments in India. With 75 US FDA approved facilities, India has more than any other foreign nation. India's manufacturing environments contribute especially to its edge in clinical-trial research as cost efficiencies derive from both production and research, and companies can manufacture medications for clinical trials on site. The reasons for India's R&D success are as follows (source: KPMG international, 2006; Sagar, 2005):

- Population's research capabilities;
- Research and testing activities' lower costs;
- Manufacturing's lower costs;
- Domestic market's rate of growth;
- Increased FDI;
- International alliances and JVs with foreign MNCs;
- Contract manufacturing for foreign MNCs;
- Contract research for foreign MNCs.

India's competitive advantages in R&D, outlined above, also compensate in part for the Indian pharmaceutical industry's fragmentation. R&D investments in this Indian industry approximate 1.6 per cent, but most small and micro-sized pharmaceutical companies engage in almost no basic research. Many of the small and micro-sized pharmaceutical companies focus instead on producing India's traditional folk and Ayurvedic medications. Table 6.7 presents more appropriate figures for global comparisons by concentrating on India's largest companies. The percentages of sales that the Indian companies allocate to R&D remains about one third of the industrialized countries' pharmaceutical companies. Yet, companies in India spend about three times less for comparable research activities than companies spend in the West. Due to the Indian pharmaceutical companies' smaller sizes, they also spend substantially less on total R&D than their counterparts in the West.

We conclude our discussion of India's pharmaceutical industry on a cautionary note as Indian patent reforms do not include issues of data security. Many analysts have argued that this failure vis-à-vis Chinese patent law will hurt India's pharmaceutical industry as its research becomes increasingly valuable. The next section examines measures of success in R&D.

MEASURING R&D SUCCESS

Several methods exist to measure R&D success. Indeed, in a study of the chemicals, computer, steel and specialty metals industries, Haley (1989) found that no single measure of success was used by more than 10 per cent of the companies surveyed. Patents generally provide the most widely accepted measure of success (Economist Intelligence Unit (EIU), 2007), as patents:

- provide objective measures;
- do not depend on self reports;
- clearly indicate research value;
- correlate strongly with other measures such as research publications and a UNO national ratio of medium- and high-technology products to exports.

Yet patents also have their weaknesses. Patents differ greatly in the patented technologies' importance as well as their applications to families of products versus single products. Companies and researchers also have difficulties determining ahead of time if patented technologies represent major breakthroughs (Haley, 1989; EIU, 2007). For instance, almost no one predicted that shipping containers, simple metal boxes, would revolutionize their industry. Some researchers have suggested that shipping containers, along with the container ships and ports that they spawned, facilitated globalization through their enhanced logistical efficiencies. Patents also lag innovation, especially in first-to-invent jurisdictions such as in the USA, where applicants file numerous patents. By law, the patent offices examine the applications to determine the true developers of the technologies, not just the first filers of the patent applications.

To correct for some of the above-mentioned flaws in raw patents, the Organisation for Economic Co-operation and Development (OECD) developed the measure of triadic patents or patents filed in each of the triad economies, the EU, Japan and the USA. By focusing solely on patents filed in all three jurisdictions, the OECD sought to ensure the use of patents of the greatest and most comparable values. The OECD reasoned that companies or individuals will only patent separately, and in all three jurisdictions, technologies that they view as most valuable – despite the Paris Convention's required recognition of patents filed in any Convention member's country. Though the OECD did not differentiate patents by industry, its national data demonstrate increased general R&D performance across various countries.

Figure 6.1 presents the OECD's triadic data. India enjoys a 21.9 per cent rate of growth in triadic patents, the fourth highest in the world, and substantially above the average growth rate of 12.2 per cent for all nations. These data corroborate India's exemplary general R&D performance. The next section focuses on India's pharmaceutical patents.

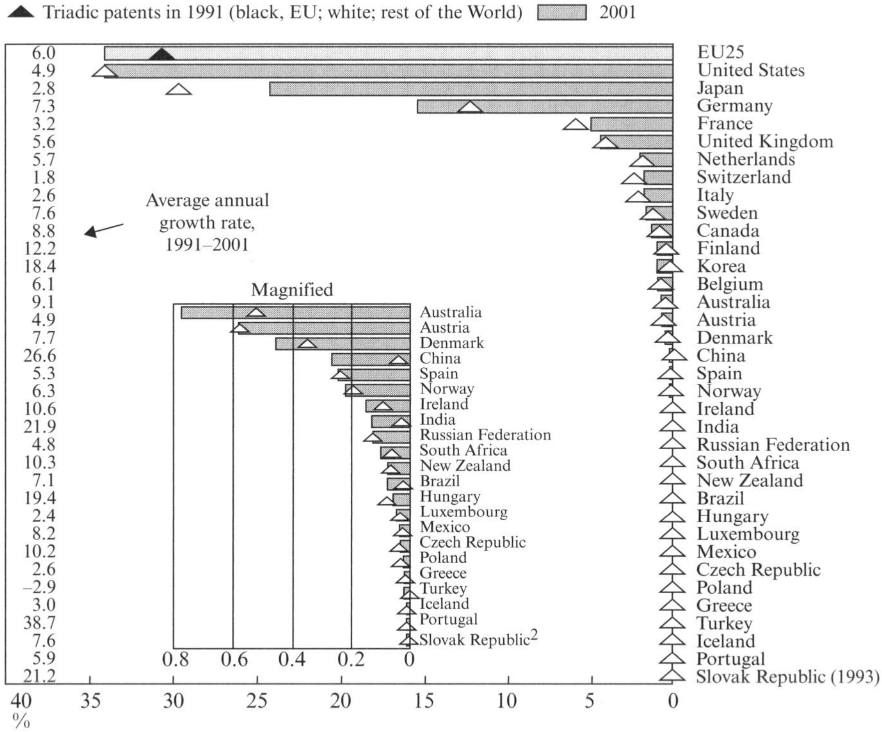

Source: OECD Science, Technology and Industry Scoreboard (2005), www.sourceoeed.org/scoreboard.

Figure 6.1 Share of countries in triadic patent families in 2001

INDIA'S PHARMACEUTICAL PATENTS

Table 6.8 presents available Indian pharmaceutical patent data prior to 2005. Significant growth in patents occurred between 2001 and 2004, despite a substantial decline in patents from the Government's primary research labs, the Council for Science and Industrial Research (CSIR), between 2003 and 2004. Ranbaxy's patent productivity over the same two-year period helped to offset CSIR's decline. Table 6.8 also shows that despite its ranking among India's five largest pharmaceutical companies, Cipla had the lowest percentage of sales invested in R&D.

Table 6.9 presents a partial list of India's pharmaceutical patents from 2005, the start of the new product-patent regime, to 2007. The new patent regime aimed to foster innovation and to increase patents, yet the number of patents fell. Patents for 2006 fell to 259 from 443 in 2005. Though the patenting rate seems to have risen in 2007, it remains substantially below the rate in 2005.

The number of all-India patents for 2004 that we reported in Table 6.8 does not allow a comparison with the data in Table 6.9. Therefore, Table 6.10 presents those companies that can be compared across the years. The overall total number of patents across all companies dropped. After a significant drop between 2004 and 2005, Ranbaxy held constant,

Table 6.8 India's domestic patent growth

Organization	Number of patents			
	2001	2002	2003	2004
All India	295			784
Ranbaxy		66	121	
CSIR	124	69		
Cipla*				32
Jubilant Oraganosys			16	
Vaman Technologies			12	
Matrix Labs			12	
Hetero Drugs				10
Wockhardt**				10

Notes:
* Cipla invested < 5% of sales on R&D, the lowest among India's top 5.
** Especially significant because of its Biotech operations.

Source: Indian Patent Office (2007); Independent research.

Table 6.9 Indian post-reform pharmaceutical patents

Company	2005	2006	2007 (Partial)
Ranbaxy	65	67	43
Cipla	48	23	8
Dr Reddy's	149	12	4
Nicholas Piramal	20	18	4
Aurobindo	6	20	13
Lupin	19	27	8
Cadila	39	34	12
Sun Pharma	61	14	28
Wockhardt	8	13	4
Jubilant Oraganosys	2	8	2
Vaman Technologies	9	2	1
Matrix Labs	2	15	2
Hetero Drugs	15	6	
Totals	443	259	129

Source: India Big Patents Database (2007); Independent research.

but India's second largest pharmaceutical company, Cipla, dropped in number of patents in each of the three years. Matrix Labs and Wockhardt bucked this downward trend by following differing routes to success. Wockhardt moved strongly into bio-genetics, through both purchase and research; conversely, Matrix emphasized generics and process research. These differing strategies seem to indicate that product-patent regimes by themselves do not provide magical routes to increased innovation. In the next section, we examine some of the problems that attend patent metrics in India.

Table 6.10 Pre- and post-reform patents for Indian pharmaceutical companies

Company	2003	2004	2005	2006
Ranbaxy	66	121	65	67
Cipla		69	48	23
Jubilant Organosys		16	2	8
Vaman Technologies		12	9	2
Matrix Labs		12	2	15
Wockhardt		10	8	13
Hetero Drugs		10	15	6
Total		250	149	134

Source: India Big Patents Database (2007); Independent research.

DISCUSSION OF PATENT METRICS IN INDIA

Patents take time to go from research to filing to being granted, and to building momentum for success. Process-patent and product-patent regimes differ in the kinds of research they support. For example, process-patent regimes encourage more investment and effort into reverse-engineering known products; conversely, product-patent regimes encourage investments and efforts into creating new products. Yet product-development research also occurs under process-patent regimes, and process-development research also occurs under product-patent regimes. The number of patents often lags behind changes in research focus. Consequently, Indian patent statistics may provide inappropriate indicators of incipient increases in innovativeness.

As we discussed in a previous section, not all patents denote equal value and some patents reflect greater innovation than others. Citation analysis provides one indicator of value by identifying heavily-cited, and therefore valuable, patents. However, citation analysis also requires sufficient time for patents to build citation records. India has had fewer than three years under the new product-patent regime, and so we cannot engage in legitimate citation comparisons. Though not looking specifically at the pharmaceutical industry, research has found that process innovations generate greater returns on investment for companies than product innovations (EIU, 2007).

As Table 6.11 shows, the Indian pharmaceutical industry does appear to be moving towards greater emphasis on product-patent research, although some individual companies are not. Table 6.11 also shows a significant downward trend in the percentage of process-oriented patents filed by the largest Indian pharmaceutical companies, and especially so by the two companies at the forefront of Indian pharmaceutical research, Ranbaxy and Wockhardt. Sun Pharma's and Cadila's process patents, and most importantly the overall total percentage, have also fallen. The Indian pharmaceutical industry's research appears in transition from a process to a product orientation.

Figure 6.2 highlights the reduction in the percentage of process versus product patents over the first three years of the new product patent regime. The final sections indicate some limitations of the data, and make suggestions for future research.

Table 6.11 Percentage of process-oriented patents in India's pharmaceutical companies

Company	2005	2006	2007
Ranbaxy	72.3	46.3	30.2
Cipla	27.1	34.8	37.5
Dr Reddy's	56.4	41.7	50.0
N. Piramal	15.0	0.0	50.0
Aurobindo	66.7	85.0	61.5
Lupin	50.0	51.9	75.0
Cadila	71.8	64.7	50.0
Sun Pharma	55.7	50.0	7.1
Wockhardt	75.0	61.5	0.0
Totals	55.2	49.1	34.1

Source: India Big Patents Database (2007) Independent research.

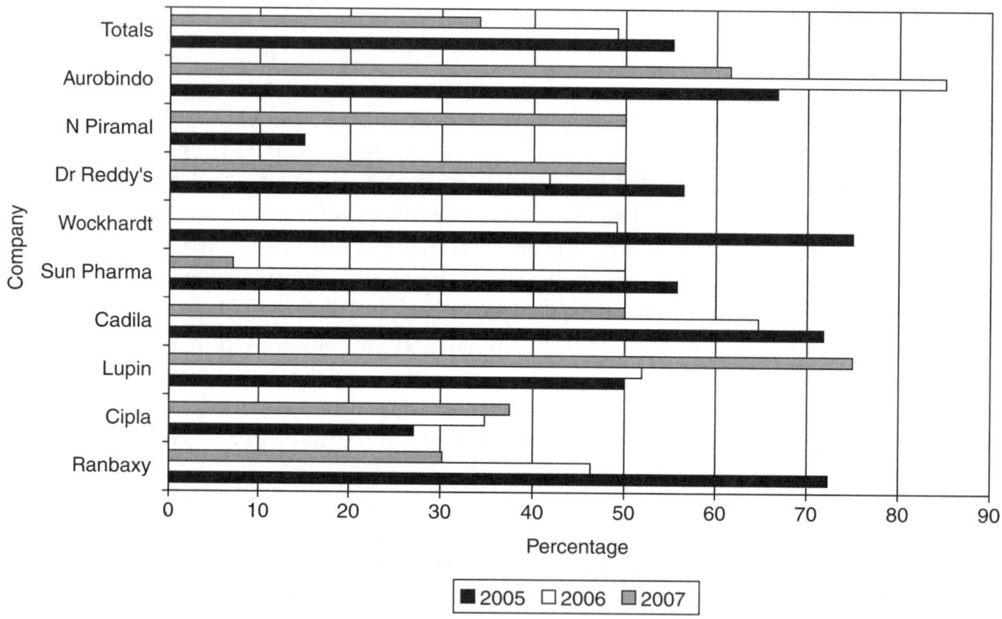

Source: India Big Patents Database (2007); Independent research.

Figure 6.2 Percentage of process-oriented patents

CONCLUSIONS AND IMPLICATIONS

As Table 6.11 showed, generally, Indian pharmaceutical companies are switching their research focus from process to product innovation. Additionally, Table 6.6 described how Indian pharmaceuticals have a significant cost advantage in R&D over their Western competitors, and the cost advantage helps to offset the smaller expenditures in R&D. These factors, combined with information in Table 6.7 on the growth of investment in R&D, indicate that the Indian pharmaceutical industry, especially among its largest companies, has been refocusing its research to product innovation and intends to continue competing in the global pharmaceutical markets. This strategy has not had sufficient time to prove its success.

India's pharmaceutical companies are also leveraging their cost advantage to become major developers of intellectual property for themselves and for Western pharmaceuticals through contract research. As contract researchers, the Indian pharmaceutical companies will not hold title to the products developed, but will retain rights to use the technologies in their domestic market, one of the world's fastest growing. In addition, as contract researchers, the Indian pharmaceutical companies obtain foreign funds to build their own product-research cultures and competitive capabilities. The sharing of risk in conducting research provides additional benefits that Indian companies share with their Western counterparts through contract R&D agreements.

Though contract research provides the Indian pharmaceutical industry with substantial immediate benefits, it may also cause difficulties in the medium to long term. Though Indian developers of medication retain the rights to produce and sell the products in India, they surrender these rights in foreign markets. Consequently, Indian companies may expend some of their best research talent on drugs that generate limited benefits. Indian patent law defines patentable, new pharmaceutical products as entirely new products and does not recognize modifications and enhancements of existing products as patentable. Consequently, foreign companies will be in stronger positions to protect their intellectual property (IP) in India than the Indian companies within their home markets where they can use the products. The Indian Patent Office also retains the rights to intercede in the markets and require the licensing of products if it judges that the public interest is not being served. Consequently, Indian pharmaceutical companies may have limited abilities to protect domestic rights and limited research capacities to develop the drugs they need to retain future competitiveness and to compete abroad as India's domestic markets mature.

The major regulatory caveat for a successful transition from process to product innovation remains data security, which India's patent laws presently do not provide. As Chinese patent laws provide for greater data security, some companies are choosing China over India as a research locale for pharmaceuticals. The next section suggests avenues for further research.

FUTURE RESEARCH

This exploratory study suggests several avenues for future research on the economic and innovative effects of product patents. No conclusive evidence indicates that product-patent regimes provide requirements for success in the pharmaceutical industry, or in any other. Indeed, Mansfield et al. (1981) found that 60 per cent of innovations have been imitated within four years, casting doubt on the protection that product patents provide.

Conversely, besides effective IPR protection, several alternative reasons exist to invest in markets, including rapid growth, as China has proven (see Haley et al., 2004). India, and in particular the Indian pharmaceutical market, fits this description. Given the size and growth of the Indian pharmaceutical market and the rate of India's economic growth, investment in the pharmaceutical industry in India may have occurred regardless of the type of patent regime. Further research could enquire into the important characteristics that prompt domestic and foreign investment including innovativeness, rapid growth and patent regimes. Future research could also look at the influence of data security and protection of IP on investment in pharmaceuticals.

Other possible factors influencing investments in pharmaceuticals include the local population's skills and the cost advantages of doing research in economies. India has a large, well-trained research community to engage in pharmaceutical research and significant cost advantages exist to do research in India. Future research could enquire into the relative weights of these factors as compared to patent regimes.

Finally, research could explore whether product-patent regimes hurt the economic development of emerging markets as Indira Gandhi, India's erstwhile Prime Minister, had stated. As previously mentioned, in the late eighteenth and early nineteenth centuries, the USA made the theft of foreign technology an official government policy. In their early periods of development, other emerging markets that have begun the move to near industrialization or to full industrialization have engaged in IP theft, just as China has. Future research could then shed light on the questions raised by emerging markets' policy makers on the effects of product-patent regimes on India and her society, and to the other emerging and less developed markets that presently depend on India's booming pharmaceutical industry.

NOTE

* An earlier version of this chapter was presented at the 'Global challenge of intellectual property rights', a CIBER conference, University of Connecticut at Storrs, May 2007. The authors thank Jayashree Watal and other participants for their comments.

REFERENCES

Anton, J.J. and D.A. Yao (2004), 'Little patents and big secrets: Managing intellectual property', *Rand Journal of Economics*, **35**(1), 1–22.

Co, C.Y., J.A. List and L.D. Qui (2004), 'Intellectual property rights, environmental regulations, and foreign direct investment', *Land Economics*, **80**(2), 153–73.

Cohen, W.N., R.R. Nelson and J.P. Walsh (2000), 'Protecting their intellectual assets: appropriability conditions and why US manufacturing firms patent (or not)', NBER Working Paper No. 7552.

Datta, P.T.J. (2006), 'Roche gets product patent on Hepatitis C', *The Hindu Online*, posted 3 March.

Economist Intelligence Unit (EIU) (2007), *Innovation: Transforming the Way Business Creates*, London: EIU Publications.

Haley, G.T. (1989), 'New product decision making in major American firms: A study of the chemical, computer and metals industries', University of Texas at Austin, USA, dissertation.

Haley, G.T. (2000), 'Intellectual property rights and foreign direct investment in emerging markets', *Marketing Intelligence and Planning*, Special Issue on 'Strategic Marketing in Emerging Economies', **18**(5), 273–80.

Haley, G.T. (2007), 'The extent of the government's control of China's economy, and implications for the United States', testimony before the United States–China Economic and Security Review Committee of the US Congress, 25 May.

Haley, G.T., U.C.V. Haley and C.T. Tan (2004), *The Chinese Tao of Business: The Logic of Successful Business Strategy*, New York & Singapore: John Wiley & Sons.

Hamilton, A. (2001), *Writings*, New York: Literary Classics of the United States, Inc.

India Big Patents Database (2007), http://india.bigpatents.org, accessed 13–15 March.
Indian Patent Office (2007), 'Exclusive marketing rights', http://www.patentoffice.nic.in/ipr/patent/emr.htm, accessed 16 March.
Intec.net (2004), 'Indian pharmaceutical industry', Berlin: Intec.net Online.
Jensen, P.A. and E. Webster (2004), 'Achieving the optimal power of property rights', *The Australian Economic Review*, **37**(4), 419–26.
KPMG International (2006), 'The Indian pharmaceutical industry: Collaboration for growth, Zurich: KPMG International.
Lanjouw, J.O. (2003), 'Intellectual property and the availability of pharmaceuticals in poor countries', *NBER Innovation Policy and the Economy*, **3**(1), 91–129.
Lee, J.Y. and E. Mansfield (1996), 'Intellectual property protection and US foreign direct investment', *The Review of Economics and Statistics*, **78**(2), 181–6.
Locke, J. (1764/1980), *Second Treatise of Government*, Indianapolis, IN: Hackett Publishing Company.
Mansfield, E. (1986), 'Patents and innovation: an empirical study', *Management Science*, **78**(2), 181–6.
Mansfield, E., M. Shwartz and S. Wagner (1981), 'Imitation costs and patents: an empirical study', *The Economic Journal*, **91**, 907–18.
OECD Statistics Portal (2005), 'OECD science, technology and industry scoreboard, 2005 – towards a knowledge-based economy', www.sourceoecd.org/scoreboard.
Organisation for Economic Co-operation and Development (2006), *OECD Science, Technology and Industry Outlook, 2006*, Paris: OECD Publishing.
Office of the Controller of Patents (2007), 'Exclusive marketing rights', downloaded 13 March, http://www.patentoffice.nic.in/ipr/patent/emr.htm.
Pfister, E. and B. Defains (2005), 'Patent protection, strategic FDI and location choices: Empirical evidence from French subsidiaries' location choices in emerging economies', *International Journal of the Economics of Business*, **12**(3), 329–46.
Pharmaceutical & Drug Manufacturers (2007), 'India pharmaceutical industry: An overview', http://www.pharmaceutical-drug-manufacturers.com/pharmaceutical-industry, downloaded 2 April.
Sagar, D. (2005), 'Indian pharmaceutical industry', *Spandan*, The College Magazine, Mauzana Azad Medical College, New Delhi.
Third World Network (2003), 'How WTO/TRIPS threatens the Indian pharmaceutical industry', http://www.twnside.org.sg/title/twr120h.htm.
Thumm, N. (2004), 'Strategic patenting in biotechnology', *Technology Analysis & Strategic Management*, **16**(4), 529–38.
Zacharias, N. and S. Farias (2003), 'Patents and the Indian pharmaceutical industry', in *Business Briefing Pharmagenerics 2003*, London: Business Briefings, Ltd.

7. Employee disclosures of trade secrets in China: prevention strategies

Marisa Anne Pagnattaro[1]

Spies are a key element
In warfare.
On them depends
An army's
Every move.
(Sun-Tzu, 2002)

INTRODUCTION

In the heated competition between companies doing business in China, protection of trade secrets is a daunting challenge (US–China Business Council, 2006). Economic espionage causes US companies enormous losses in their global operations (Office of the National Counterintelligence Executive, 2006). China is well known for aggressive targeting of US technology and has one of the highest rates of infringement of intellectual property rights in the world (Congressional-Executive Commission on China, 2006). This reality was egregiously evident when General Motors Corporation discovered that the Chinese automaker Chery Automobile Co. Ltd was marketing the 'QQ', a nearly identical copy of GM's Chevrolet 'Spark'. The only substantial difference between the cars was QQ's sticker price: $3600 – a third less than Spark's (Forney, 2005; Buckley, 2005). As US Commerce Secretary Donald Evans stated, '[t]his incident defies an innocent explanation. The QQ and the Spark are twins because both cars were built from the same DNA – the proprietary mathematical data and formulas – that were stolen from GM Daewoo and used to build the QQ' (Evans, 2005). GM brought a lawsuit against Chery in a Shanghai court; soon thereafter the parties entered into a confidential settlement (Roberts, 2005). Just a little over two years later, Chery announced its plans to raise its annual output to one million vehicles by 2010 (Ministry of Commerce, 2007a). Most recently, Chery entered into a low-cost production venture with Chrysler Group, which includes the goal of exporting cars from China to the United States (*International Herald Tribune*, 2007). Although it is unclear how much of an advantage Chery initially gained through misappropriation of trade secrets, this example is particularly troubling because Chery is partially owned by the local Chinese government.[2] When the government participates in the theft of trade secrets, it undermines confidence in the integrity of the law.

How then can US companies doing business in China avoid this kind of loss of trade or business secrets? China's 'strong imitative capacity' (Yu, 2007, p. 8) makes protection of employee disclosures of trade secrets especially important. One way to stop former employees from divulging trade secrets is to require employees with access to confidential information to agree to be bound by specific 'restrictive covenants' outlined in detailed employment agreements. Both covenants not to compete or 'non-compete agreements' and confidentiality provisions lay the groundwork for protection (Porter and Griffaton, 2002; Fisk, 2001). This chapter addresses concerns of US corporations doing business in China by both explaining relevant Chinese law and making best practices suggestions for protection of trade secrets. The first section begins with an explanation of the development of modern Chinese law to establish the context for current laws enacted to protect trade secrets (Mertha, 2005; Yu, 2006). This section then details Chinese statutory law applicable to situations in which employers want to restrict employees from working from competitors and divulging trade secrets, including the requirements of China's new Contract Labor Law.[3] In the second section, Chinese cases involving former employees who divulged secrets and engaged in unfair competition are analyzed. Although these cases demonstrate that former employees may be held liable for unfair competition, the damages awarded are often not substantial.

Looking to Chinese courts or the government to enforce intellectual property rights is one way to address the problem.[4] Despite all of the legal changes to protect IPR, however, China is still lagging in enforcement of this legal regime (United States Trade Representative, 2006c). Although some enforcement difficulties may be due to differing perceptions about IPR (Alford, 1995; Chow, 2006), this lack of protection is of great concern to companies doing business in China. Thus, because it may be desirable for US companies to avoid litigation in Chinese courts, the third section discusses the use of arbitration under the China International Economic and Trade Arbitration Commission (CIETAC) as an alternative. Features of a CIETAC arbitration, such as neutrality, flexibility, finality, confidentiality and enforceability of judgments, make this an attractive alternative to litigation in China. Lastly, the fourth section makes practical recommendations for protecting trade secrets and for drafting employment contracts with non-compete clauses and confidentiality provisions to protect themselves from disclosures of trade secrets by former employees working in China. Although there is no way for employers to completely protect against unauthorized disclosures, carefully crafted provisions consistent with current trends in Chinese law are more likely to result in judicial enforcement and the protection of trade secrets (Clarke, 2003, pp. 107–8). Ultimately, the goal of this chapter is to suggest best practices for firms to protect themselves from the disclosure of trade secrets and other proprietary information by employees in China.

CHINESE STATUTORY LAW GOVERNING NON-COMPETE AGREEMENTS AND THE PROTECTION OF TRADE SECRETS

Chinese laws protecting intellectual property, including trade secrets, are modern imports (Jones, 2003). Historically, Confucian codes of conduct greatly influenced Chinese law, which is significant, because the teachings stated that individuals should be guided by *li*, virtue or propriety, as opposed to *fa*, the law (Zimmerman, 2005; Orts, 2001; Zhang, 1987). The general idea was that virtuous conduct had to come from the individual with an understanding that one should act under duty and obligation to others, not because of some legal compulsion.

The development of modern intellectual property law in China was precipitated by China's desire to engage in global trade, attract foreign investment, and to join the World Trade Organization (WTO). Parallel with other reforms undertaken after Chairman Mao's death in 1986, China requested resumption of its contracting party status with the WTO and, in 1987, a working party on China's membership to GATT was established (Halverson, 2004). From 1995 to 2001, China submitted detailed information to the WTO, including its revision and enforcement of laws – with particular emphasis on intellectual property rights (IPR) – to comply with WTO requirements under its Agreement on Trade-Related Aspects of Intellectual Property Rights (TRIPS) (Yongtu, 2000; Weinstein and Fernandez, 2004; Maskus, 2002). The United States trade relationship also prompted China to enact IPR laws (Bird, 2006). In 1979, for example, when the United States extended non-discriminatory treatment to China, China explicitly agreed to ensure effective protection of patents, trademarks and copyrights, as well as to restrict unfair competition involving unfair use of those rights (Agreement on Trade Relations, 1979). By the time China joined the WTO in 2001, it had completed major reforms to its IPR laws so that it was in compliance with TRIPS (Agreement on Trade-Related Aspects of Intellectual Property Rights, 1994). In addition to providing protection for copyrights, patents and trademarks, TRIPS requires member nations to protect 'undisclosed information' or trade secrets. Underscoring its commitment to developing a transparent legal system, the 1999 Constitution of the People's Republic of China specifically states that China 'exercises the rule of law, building a socialist country governed according to law' (Constitution of the People's Republic of China, 1999). This commitment to the rule of law has been reemphasized by China's President, Hu Jintao (Zimmerman, 2005).[5]

A crucial aspect of this commitment is the Chinese legal framework developed for the protection of such trade secrets, including the control of misappropriation by employees. The focus of this section is Chinese legal protection for the loss of intellectual property and trade secrets when employees with valuable information leave and join a competitor firm (Chow, 2002). To that end, Chinese laws governing the use of employment contracts containing non-compete provisions and those pertaining to trade secrets are detailed.

For over a year, the Standing Committee of the National People's Congress (SCNPC) reviewed various drafts of the Labor Contract Law. On 29 June 2007, the SCNPC passed the Labor Contract Law, to take effect on 1 January 2008.[6] Existing labor contracts are grandfathered by the new law. Thus, employers do not need to require existing employees to sign new contracts. China's 1995 Labor Law required all employers to execute labor contracts with their employees to establish the labor relationship and to specify the 'rights, interests and obligations of each party' (Labor Law, 1994). The Labor Law specified that a written labor contract must contain provisions addressing: 1) the time limit of the contract; 2) the content of the work; 3) labor protection and labor conditions; 4) labor remunerations; 5) labor disciplines (for example work hours, rest periods, rest days, vacation time and holidays); 6) conditions for the termination of the agreement; and 7) liabilities for violations of the agreement. The labor contract may also include provisions 'concerning the keeping of the commercial secrets of the employer'. This provision is important because it affords employers a formal mechanism to prevent employees from divulging trade secrets.[7] These contracts, including confidentiality provisions, are still valid for existing employees.

All employees who commence employment on or after 1 January 2008, however, have the benefit of the new Labor Contract Law, which is designed to protect their legal rights and to promote harmonious and stable employment relationships. The Labor Contract Law requires the employment relationship to be based on a written employment contract. Employment contracts are divided into three types: fixed-term employment contracts, open-ended contracts and contracts for the completion of a certain project. As a disincentive to employers who might be tempted to fail to secure a written contract with an employee, the law provides clear penalties. If an employer fails to secure a written labor contract with the employee for more than one month, but less than one year following the employee's first day of employment, the employer is required to pay double the employee's monthly salary for each month of employment without a labor contract in place. Moreover, if an employer fails to secure an employment contract within the first year of employment, the employee is automatically deemed to have an open-ended employment contract. Similar to the 1995 Labor Law, the Labor Contract Law requires that employment contracts shall specify: 1) the name, domicile and legal representative or main person in charge of the employer; 2) the name, domicile and number of the resident ID card or other valid identity document of the worker; 3) the term of the employment contract; 4) the job description and the place of work; 5) working hours, rest and leave; 6) labor compensation; 7) social insurance; 8) labor protection, working conditions and protection against hazards; and 9) other matters which laws and statutes require to be included in employment contracts.

Additionally, the employer and worker may stipulate other matters, such as confidentiality of trade secrets and intellectual property. If a worker has a confidentiality obligation, the worker and employer may agree on competition restriction provisions in the contract. Such provisions obligate the employer to pay financial compensation to the worker on a monthly basis during the term of the competition restriction after the termination or ending of the employment contract. If the worker violates the non-competition restrictions, he or she is required to pay liquidated damages to the employer, as stipulated under the contract. The Contract Labor Law specifically states that only senior management, senior technicians and those bound to keep information confidential may be held to non-competition agreements. The terms of the non-competes, the geographic limits and the cap on liquidated damages are all subject to mutual agreement between the employer and employee. Importantly, however, the Contract Labor Law specifies that the maximum term of a non-compete clause is two years. Overall, the Contract Labor Law is clear that an employee can be contractually prohibited from working for a competing employer that produces the same type of products or is engaged in the same type of business as the current employer, as well as prohibited from establishing his or her own business to produce the same type of products or engage in the same type of business.

Thus, the 1995 Labor Law and Contract Labor Law in China are designed to help employers protect their trade secrets. This invariably prompts the question: what information is considered to be a trade secret in China and how is it protected? The protection of a company's trade secrets is relatively new in China. Inasmuch as the Chinese economy was centrally planned, trade secrets and technical knowledge were a matter of 'state secrets' and breach could result in severe punishment (Feng, 2003). The economic reforms leading to privatization and market economy changed this perspective, creating the need for private owners to protect their interests. This change was formally made when the State Council issued the Provisional Regulations on Technology Transfer (Provisional Regulations) in 1985. The text of the Provisional Regulations states that it was formulated to 'arouse the enthusiasm, initiative and creativity of staff and workers, in particular scientific and technical personnel, to bring about the rapid application of scientific and technical research results and know-how to material production and to effectively implement the policies of economic construction reliant on science and technology'. Section 1 of the Provisional Regulations creates a new right for the transfer of 'any technology which assists the development of new products, which raises product quality, reduces product cost, improves operational management or leads to increased economic benefit.'

The Provisional Regulations did not change the rules prohibiting the transfer of any technology which violates state law, policy or regulations and the handling of technology involving national security. Thus, the distinction was made between confidential technology 'know-how' and state secrets. The concept of know-how refers to trade secrets or business secrets. There are apparently at least six different Chinese terms used for referring to know-how, which began to appear in the lexicon in the 1960s (Cheng, 1996). During this time, the Chinese government began to take steps to protect commercial and business secrets.

A few months after the Provisional Regulations went into effect, protection of technical know-how or confidential proprietary information was formalized by the State Council when it promulgated the Regulations on Administration of Technology Acquisition Contracts ('Technology Acquisition Regulations'). Pursuant to the Technology Acquisition Regulations, certain technology imported from any corporation, enterprise, organization or individual outside the territory of China is protected by law. Later in 1988, the Ministry of Foreign Economic Relations promulgated detailed rules, which elaborated on the basic provisions of the Technology Acquisition Regulations. Specifically, they addressed:

1. Contracts for transferring or licensing of industrial property rights;
2. Contracts for licensing of technical know-how, including certain technical knowledge which has not been made public and is used for manufacturing a certain product, or applying a certain technology, as well as a product design, a technical process, a formula, quality control and management skills and such technical knowledge that has not yet obtained the legal protection of industrial property rights;
3. Contracts for technical services;
4. Contracts for co-production and co-design that contain any one of the contents as transferring or licensing of industrial property rights, licensing of technical know-how or technical services;
5. Contracts for importing a complete set of equipment, production line and key equipment that contain any one of the contents as transferring or licensing of industrial property rights, licensing of technical know-how or technical services; and
6. Other technology import contracts which need to go through the procedure of examination and approval in the view of the competent authority.

Although this system provided a step towards legal protection of proprietary information, it has shortcomings. All of these rules and regulations are contract based and, accordingly, are not binding on third parties. Additionally, no legal penalties were specified; the only remedy was for breach of the agreement, which was limited at that time.

The most significant development for the protection of trade secrets in China was promulgation of the Law of the People's Republic of China Against Unfair Competition ('Unfair Competition Law'), which became effective in 1993. Enacted in response to the needs of the changing economy in China, as well as to an agreement with the United States, the Chinese government agreed through this law to prevent the disclosure of trade secrets, including disclosure by third parties. As more enterprises in China were becoming privately owned and there was an increasing interest in foreign investment, there was growing pressure to protect technical and commercial secrets. The Unfair Competition Law was promulgated to safeguard the 'healthy development of the socialist market economy', encourage and protect fair competition, prevent acts of unfair competition, and defend the lawful rights and interests of operators and consumers.

A critical aspect of the Unfair Competition Law is the definition of 'business secret' (which is used interchangeably with 'trade secret') as 'technical information and operational information which is not known to the public, which is capable of bringing economic benefits to the owner of rights, which has practical applicability and which the owner of rights has taken measures to keep secret.'[8] The law restricts the acts of an 'operator', which is defined as 'a legal person or other economic organization or individual engaging in the trading of goods or profit-making services'. Specifically, an operator may not adopt any of the following means to infringe on business secrets:

1. obtaining business secrets from the owners of rights by stealing, promising gain, resorting to coercion or other improper means;
2. disclosing, using, or allowing others to use business secrets of the owners of rights obtained by the means mentioned in the preceding item;
3. disclosing, using or allowing others to use business secrets that he has obtained by breaking an engagement or disregarding the requirement of the owners of the rights to maintain the business secrets in confidence.

Inasmuch as the Unfair Competition Law allows for courts to exercise a high degree of subjectivity, the Supreme People's Court recently issued an Interpretation on Several Issues Concerning Law Implementation in Hearing Civil Cases in Respect of Unfair Competition (the 'Interpretation'). The Interpretation also lists specific factors for courts to use to determine if the owner of the trade secrets has undertaken confidentiality measures: 1) restricting disclosure to relevant people; 2) 'locking' or encrypting confidential information; 3) marking the information 'confidential'; 4) using passwords or codes on the confidential information; 5) entering into confidentiality agreements; 6) restricting access/visits to machines or sites with confidential information; and 7) other reasonable measures.

Importantly, the Interpretation also addresses what is or is not a trade secret under the Unfair Competition Law. It clearly states that 'trade secret' information obtained through one's own research and development or reverse engineering does *not* constitute infringing action under the Unfair Competition Law.[9] With regard to customer lists, the Interpretation does recognize this information to be a trade secret if the lists contain special customer information that is not publicly available, such as names, addresses, deal details and contact methods. If, however, a customer conducts business with a company based on the trust of a certain individual employee and the customer voluntarily continues to do business with the former employee at his new employer, this will not constitute a violation of the Unfair Competition Law. Moreover, the Interpretation also clarifies the burden of proof on a plaintiff claiming a violation of the Unfair Competition Law. To make a case successfully, the plaintiff must prove 1) compliance with the statutory requirements (for example the media, detailed content and commercial value of the trade secret and specific confidentiality measures taken); 2) the information is identical or materially identical to its trade secret; and 3) the opposing party's improper means of obtaining the information.

If a plaintiff has a prima facie case under the Unfair Competition Law, staff members or workers who divulge or use business secrets of their employer in breach of contractual stipulations or contrary to confidentiality requirements can be held liable. Article 10 of the Unfair Competition Law imposes liability on any third party who 'obtains, uses or discloses the business secrets of others when he obviously has or should have full awareness of the illegal acts' and the law also provides for legal responsibility for any operator who causes damages to another. Injured parties may institute proceedings before a People's Court (Yang, 2003) or seek administrative enforcement of the law with the offices of the Administration for Industry and Commerce (AIC).[10] Pursuant to the Unfair Competition Law, the injured party is to be compensated for the damages and, where the losses suffered are difficult to calculate, the amount of damages is the profits gained by the infringer during the period of infringement. Additionally, the infringer bears the responsibility of paying all reasonable costs paid by the injured operator in investigating the acts of unfair competition. Operators infringing on another's business secrets may be ordered to desist from the illegal act and the relevant supervising authority may impose a fine between 10 000 and 200 000 Yuan (RMB). Effective 1 February 2007, however, the method for determining damages for unfair competition is to be based on the method for calculating damages for infringing patent rights or trademark infringement, depending on the act of unfair competition. Additionally, where any infringing act causes trade secrets to be known to the public, the damages shall be determined in accordance with the commercial value of the secrets, including such factors as research and development costs, benefits from implementing trade secrets, prospective interests and the time during which competitive advantages can be maintained. Overall, the Interpretation helps to clarify and create more detailed guidelines for the protection of trade secrets in China.

In addition to the Unfair Competition Act, the Criminal Law of the People's Republic of China imposes criminal liability for theft of business secrets. The infringing party who causes 'heavy losses' can face imprisonment or detention for a term of three years or less and/or a fine; however, if the consequences are especially serious, the infringer could be imprisoned for between three and seven years and be fined. Infringing criminal behavior is:

1. obtaining an obligee's business secrets by stealing, luring, coercion or any other illegitimate means;
2. disclosing, using or allowing another to use the business secrets obtained from the obligee by the means mentioned in the preceding paragraph; or
3. in violation of the agreement on or against the obligee's demand for keeping business secrets, disclosing, using or allowing another person to use the business secrets he/she has.[11]

Anyone who obtains, uses or discloses another's business secrets, which they clearly know or ought to know falls under the categories of the enumerated acts, is deemed an offender who infringes on business secrets. Similar to the Unfair Competition Act, 'business secrets' refers to technology information or business information which is unknown to the public, can bring about economic benefits to the owner of the business secrets, is of practical use and with regard to which the owner has adopted secret-keeping measures.

These national laws in China are also supplemented by regional laws (Riley, 2002). For example, in Shanghai, to explicitly bind an employee to confidentiality, an agreement must be signed by each employee, including part-time employees if they are also required to keep commercial secrets confidential. Under the Shanghai regulations, the parties involved may agree upon confidential clauses in a labor contract or make a separate confidentiality agreement. For the employee who has the obligation to keep commercial secrets of the employing unit, the parties involved shall agree upon the advance notification period of revoking the labor contract or confidentiality agreement, but the advance notification period shall not exceed six months. During the notification period, the employer can take measures to keep the employee away from the commercial secrets; however, where the commercial secrets are made public, the confidentiality clauses or confidentiality agreement are automatically invalidated. If an employee breaks the contract, by failing to keep the commercial secrets, the regulations state that fair and reasonable compensation should be paid. Shanghai also has regulations governing against unfair competition that are very similar to the Unfair Competition Law.

Similar to the laws of Shanghai, other local laws also help to regulate labor contracts, trade secrets and non-compete provisions. For example, the Guangdong Regulations on Technology Secret Protection circumscribe the scope of the non-compete, allowing restriction only on matters central to the employer's business. The Shenzhen Measures on the Protection of Technical Secrets in Enterprises in the Special Economic Zone, allow an employer to restrict employment, but require a high degree of consideration in exchange for the non-compete agreement: at least two-thirds of the employee's salary for the previous year must be paid. Similar to the Shanghai Regulations, if the employer's secrets become publicly known, the term of the non-compete is cancelled. Taken together, these national and local laws governing employment contracts and trade secrets can help employers to prevent employees from 'jumping ship', capitalizing on valuable information for personal gain and giving competitors an illegal edge. Despite the development of Chinese law toward greater protection of intellectual property, including trade secrets, China is viewed as having a poor enforcement record (United States Trade Representative, 2006a). In fact, in a 2006 Special Report, the United States Trade Representative stated that because China 'does not provide American copyright materials, inventions, brands and trade secrets the intellectual property protection and enforcement to which they are entitled', China will remain on the Priority Watch List, subject to monitoring (United States Trade Representative, 2006b).

One major reason for poor enforcement cited by the United States Trade Representative is China's 'chronic underutilization' of criminal remedies, which can be effective deterrents (2006 Compliance Report). Instead of tough criminal penalties, China's enforcement authorities rely on 'toothless administrative enforcement', resulting primarily in small fines, administrative injunctions and other 'minor inconveniences' for infringers. Attempting to address this criticism, China issued an action plan on intellectual property rights protection, in which it undertakes to increase protection, including revising laws and regulations on the Law Against Unfair Competition and formulating and issuing the interpretation of the Supreme People's Court on Issues Concerning Application of Law in Dealing with Civil cases of Unfair Competition (Ministry of Commerce, 2007b). Inasmuch as self-innovation and training talent, coupled with reforms in science and education, are prominent aspects of China's most recent Five-Year Guidelines (Key Points of the 11th Five-Year Guidelines, 2006), it would behoove China to continue to increase the protection of trade secrets to protect its own industries, as well as to allay concerns of US investors.

ANALYSIS OF CHINESE CASE LAW: UNFAIR COMPETITION BY FORMER EMPLOYEES

The statutes discussed in the previous section establish the 'law on paper' for labor contracts and for the protection of trade secrets in China; however, it is equally important to note that despite this apparatus, it is impossible to predict just how a case will be resolved by Chinese courts. Judicial decisions do not have binding precedential value under China's civil law system, and the lack of a comprehensive national reporting system makes it difficult to know how the law is being interpreted in different provinces. Even so, it is helpful to analyze a sample of cases to understand the application of the law. This is especially significant in light of the importance that 'tradition' plays in Chinese culture and history. Because tradition can influence outcomes in the legal system, merely concentrating on the letter of the law could result in wrong conclusions or be misleading. The following series of cases illustrates how various courts have responded to trade secret infringement cases involving former employees.[12]

Just a few months after the Unfair Competition law became effective in 1993, an action was brought for trade secret infringement in *Xiamen Metal Powder Melting Factory v. Xiamen Hen Zhu Metal Manufacturing Factory, Chen Kun Xi and Chen Men Zong*. The Xiamen Intermediate People's Court determined that the plaintiff, Xiamen Metal Powder Melting Factory (Powder Melting Factory) used 'know-how' introduced from abroad by the factory, which gave it a competitive advantage and constituted a trade secret. Former employees Chen Kun Xi (Kun) and Chen Men Zong (Men) set up a joint venture, defendant Xiamen Hen Zhu Metal Manufacturing Factory (Hen Zhu Factory), where they utilized Powder Melting Factory's trade secrets. At trial, several experts testified that the know-how achieved by the Powder Melting Factory was unique and advanced technology within China. The experts also identified similarities between the technologies used by Powder Melting Factory and Hen Zhu Factory. The court ordered the defendants to stop using the technology and to pay Powder Melting Factory compensation in the amount of RMB 13 200.50 for economic loss. Powder Melting Factory appealed the judgment, asserting that the compensation was not sufficient. Although the Xiamen Intermediate People's Court found that the infringement lasted over four years, the compensation was much less than the actual loss.

On appeal to the Superior Court in Fujan Province, Powder Melting Factory sought compensation of a much more significant amount, RMB 450 000. The defendants argued that there was no trade secret problem, because Powder Melting Factory sold its old models to recycling stations and provided the model design to other processing factories. The Fujan Superior Court determined that Kun and Men both engaged in technical or management jobs in Powder Melting Factory's production workshop using the know-how gained in the technology-transfer agreement with the foreign company. As a technical employee, Kun signed a labor contract with Powder Melting Factory, which stipulated that he could not 'take advantage of anything from the factory' for the private benefit of himself and he could not 'infringe on the technical rights and economic rights of the factory'. The appeals court determined that Hen Zhu Factory's profits from manufacturing products using the technology were estimated to be RMB 178 418.5. The Fujan Superior Court also determined that Powder Melting Company did not make the know-how at issue public, that it had adopted proper secrecy measurements, and limited access to the technology to a few staff.

Based on Article 10, clause 2 of the Unfair Competition Law, the Fujan Superior Court held that the technology is protected by law as a trade secret. The court concluded that under Article 6 of the Chinese General Principles of Civil Law, which provides that '[c]ivil activities must be in compliance with the law', Kun and Men could be held liable. Additionally, pursuant to Article 20, clause 1 of the Unfair Competition Law, the court found that Kun, Men and Hen Zhu Factory should bear joint and several liability. The court agreed with Powder Melting Factory that the original judgment was too low, and awarded RMB 178 418.5 to compensate Powder Melting Factory for its losses. With regard to the litigation fee of RMB 9260, the court assessed liability for this amount as follows: 4000 from Powder Melting Factory, 2000 each from Kun and Men, and 1260 from Hen Zhu Factory.

Tianjin Nutrexpa Food Co., Ltd v. Li Shaochang also involves a violation of a secrecy agreement in the context of a technology secret infringement dispute. Defendant Li Shaochang (Li) was employed by Tianjin Nutrexpa Food Co., Ltd (Nutrexpa) as a director and assistant general manager. He signed a labor contract on 1 June 1990. Subsequently, when Nutrexpa learned that Li was going to resign, Li signed a notarized secrecy agreement on 18 January 1991. The main clause of the agreement states: 'Li should not divulge the company secrets during his employment period. In addition, Li cannot take on a competing job, like operating similar products or competing products, in two years upon his resignation.' On 28 November 1991, Li was released from his labor contract and Nutrexpa paid Li a salary of RMB 2580. The next month, Li became employed by Fast Food Company as executive deputy manager. The issue in the case arose in April 1992, after Fast Food Company began marketing a chocolate drink with a package design and content similar to that of Nutrexpa's 'Colacao' drink.

Nutrexpa brought a lawsuit in the Tianjin People's Court, claiming that Li violated his agreement by using its know-how to produce a similar drink for his new employer. Li defended against the action by asserting that he never managed technology material on the formula of 'Colacao' during his employment with Nutrexpa. Furthermore Li argued that the two drinks are actually different: one is a chocolate drink, whereas the other one is a malt and milk product. Lastly, Li claimed that the secrecy agreement violated the Chinese Constitution, because it exploited his right to work. The court found that the secrecy agreement was a way for Nutrexpa to protect its legitimate interests and that the two-year limitation did not violate Li's right to work. This is important, because the court upheld the legal validity of the agreement. In a twist due to timing, however, the court held that Li was no longer bound by the agreement because the two-year limitation of the secrecy agreement was already terminated when Nutrexpa brought its case. Additionally, the court held that because Nutrexpa failed to submit information to the court about the similarity between the two drinks in a timely manner, its claim was not supported. Accordingly, the court dismissed the claim, and the RMB 800 costs of the litigation were assessed to Nutrexpa. It is unclear whether the court would have awarded damages if the plaintiff had proffered proof in a timely manner. Moreover, it appears that the court is constructing a statute of limitations, requiring all litigation to be commenced before the term of a secrecy agreement concludes. Naturally, this seems a bit contrary to reason and a fairer approach would obviously have been for the court to award damages based on any injury occurring while the secrecy agreement was in force.

The case *Fuo Tao Group Ltd Pottery Research Institute v. Jin Chang Pottery Factory* also involved the disclosure of technology to a competitor by former employees. In 1984, the Guangdong Science Technology Committee assigned cold treatment and static pressure technology for pottery to the Fuo Tao Group Ltd Pottery Research Group (the Institute). After several years' work, the Institute mastered the technology, which was assessed to be national-level secret technology. Ou Yongchao (Ou) was a technical employee of the Institute, before becoming the factory director of Jin Chang Pottery Factory (Jin Chang Factory). After Jin Chang Factory experienced quality problems with its products, Ou contacted and hired Wu Guoxiong, who also worked for the Institute in technical procedures. In 1992, the Institute learned that Jin Chang Factory used the same mechanical equipment and technological process to produce its products, as well as that Ou and Wu revealed this technology to the defendant. The Institute asked the court for an order requiring Jin Chang Factory to stop infringement, compensate the Institute for its economic loss and make apologies. In its defense, Jin Chang Factory argued that the technology was made public in an article in *Pottery* magazine and that it did not use any unlawful means to obtain the technology.

The Intermediate People's Court of Guangdong Province determined that the Institute adopted various protection measures to keep the information secret by establishing a specific team to keep it secret and by setting up secrecy rules specifying that anyone who intentionally or negligently discloses the technology secrets would be held to legal responsibility. The court also found that Jin Chang Factory employed Ou and Wu (with attractive rewards) and utilized the technology disclosed by them without authorization from the Institute. Because Jin Chang was unable to produce evidence that it developed its own technology, the court held that the defendant engaged in unfair competition under Article 10 of the Unfair Competition Law. Based on Article 20 of the Unfair Competition Law and Article 118 of the Chinese General Principles of Civil Law, the court ordered Jin Chang Factory: to stop its infringement immediately; to pay the Institute RMB 264 019 for economic loss; to issue a newspaper apology within ten days of the judgment; to assume secrecy liability for the Institute's secret technology; and to bear the RMB 30 530 costs of the litigation. In this case, neither Ou nor Wu signed secrecy or non-compete agreements with the Institute. If they had signed such agreements, they would probably have been named as defendants for breach of contract. Moreover, if the Institute had a policy or internal regulations on maintaining confidentiality by its employees, it may also have been able to bring an action against the former employees for violation of the Unfair Competition Law.

In the very similar case of *Beijing Kexing New Materials Research Institute v. Beijing Zhitong Technology-Industry-Trade Company,* the Beijing Haidian District Court found that the plaintiff's internal regulations on maintaining confidentiality by its employees had binding force and, accordingly, held the former employees liable for infringement of trade secrets under the Unfair Competition Law. The court then ordered the competitor and former employee to cease their acts of infringement, and to compensate the plaintiff jointly in the amount of RMB 416 690.

In yet another case of unfair competition, *Beijing Shiweige-Tide Electronic Engineering Company v. Beijing Yin Lan Technology Company, et al.*, former employees went to work for a competitor, where they allegedly divulged trade secrets. In this case, six former employees of Beijing Shiweige-Tide Electronic Engineering Company (STEE Co.) and their new employer, Beijing Yin Lan Technology Company (YLT Co.), were sued in the Beijing Han Dian People's Court regarding a non-compete dispute. STEE Co. claimed that the former employees took advantage of its technology information and worked with YLT Co. to unfairly compete, which caused an obvious drop in STEE Co.'s sales, great economic loss and loss of reputation. YLT Co. argued that the technology at issue was never kept secret, that STEE Co. did not adopt policies to keep it secret, that it did not ask their clients to keep it secret. In sum, YLT Co. maintained that the technology was public.

The central issue for the court to determine was whether the technology at issue was a legally protected 'business secret'. In reaching its decision, the court stated that to be protected under China's non-compete law, a business secret must satisfy four important conditions: 1) it is not known to the public or an unspecified group; 2) it has economic value; 3) it has realizable utility (as opposed to theoretical utility); 4) and the right holder takes certain protection methods. The court found that although STEE Co. did not patent the technology, there was still a business secret entitled to legal protection because the company required employees to sign a secrecy-maintaining contract and strengthened internal management to protect the secrecy. Based on Chapter 1, Article 10 of the Unfair Competition Law, the court ordered the economic loss to be calculated as the defendants' actual profit during the period of infringement, or RMB 136 450. The court also ordered the defendants to issue a public apology in a national newspaper, to stop using the technology, and to bear the cost of litigation in the amount of RMB 20 000.

The final case involves allegations of trade secret infringement, regarding a technology licensed to a Chinese firm by Siemens Germany. In *Xuji Electronic Company, Ltd v. Zheng Xueshen and Aite Electronic Equipment Company*, plaintiff Xuji Electronic Co., Ltd (Xuji) signed a license and secrecy agreement with Siemens Germany. Zheng Xueshen (Zheng) was one of the Xuji employees responsible for starting the development work on the technology. As a project manager, Zheng participated in research and development, which led to the creation of machine technology approved by the Chinese Energy Department and Electromechanical Department. The technology was implemented for mass production that resulted in substantial profits for Xuji. When Zheng joined Xuji, he signed an 11-year labor contract, stipulating that he would obey all rules of the company. Later, when Zheng took a position as an engineer, he signed a five-year labor contract, promising to obey each rule and regulation of the company and to be responsible for secrecy work. Four years later, Zheng left Xuji and started Aite Electronic Equipment Company (Aite Co.) without the approval of Xuji.

Xuji claimed that Zheng mastered its technology, then violated his labor contract and secrecy agreement when he started a competing company and helped Aite Co. develop machines by infringing on Xuji's technology. The Intermediate People's Court of Hebei Province found that the technology was a trade secret entitled to protection under the Unfair Competition Law because Xuji adopted a series of secrecy measures, never transferred the technology to a third party, and never made the information public. The court held that Zheng violated his secrecy agreement with Xuji and that Aite Co. illegally applied the technology, fully knowing that it belonged to Xuji. The court ordered the defendants to stop their infringement immediately and to pay RMB 213 450 in compensatory damages for Xuji's economic losses.

Zheng then appealed to the Superior People's Court of Henan Province, arguing that the technology at issue was already well known and could not be protected as a trade secret. The court rejected Zheng's argument and determined that the technology was truly Xuji's trade secret. The court held that the judgment in the first instance was correct in ordering the defendants to stop their infringement, but it recalculated the damages. The court reversed the judgment on damages, because Xuji Co. failed to support all of the damages claimed. Accordingly, the court reduced the award owed by Zheng and Aite Co. to RMB 62 160.

Taken together, these cases create some sense that Chinese courts will uphold non-competition and secrecy agreements. The cases underscore the importance of documenting steps to keep proprietary information secret. At a minimum, all employees with access to trade secrets should be required to sign agreements. The cases also signal a willingness to hold competitors liable under the Unfair Competition Law. Moreover, it is clear that any litigation should be promptly commenced to avoid enforceability issues due to delay. Lastly, it should always be remembered that even if a judgment is awarded, it may be difficult to collect from the defendant who may lack assets or be elusive (Greene, 2004). Thus, although these cases are not binding on litigants other than the parties, they illustrate the willingness of Chinese courts to enforce non-compete agreements and to hold both former employees and competitors liable if they engage in unfair competition through misappropriation of business secrets.

ARBITRATION AS AN ALTERNATIVE: CIETAC

There are many considerations when deciding what is the best way to enforce an employment contract or other agreements related to the protection of trade secrets. As is the case in any jurisdiction, a key consideration is the enforceability of the resulting judgment. In China, foreign civil judgments can be difficult to enforce, and judgments by domestic courts may also be difficult to enforce. An alternative is to agree to arbitrate any disputes using the Chinese International Economic and Trade Arbitration Commission (CIETAC), the main international arbitration body in China. There are many reasons US companies may favor CIETAC arbitration over litigation in China, including neutrality, flexibility, finality, confidentiality and enforceability of judgments.

In 2005, CIETAC amended its rules, making this an even more attractive alternative for dispute resolution. The jurisdiction of CIETAC extends to cases involving international or foreign-related disputes; disputes related to Hong Kong, Taiwan or Macao; and domestic disputes. An important feature of a CIETAC arbitration is the ability of the parties to agree to the number of arbitrators – typically one or three – and to select the arbitrator from a Panel of Arbitrators provided by CIETAC. Arbitrators are charged with the duty of independence from the parties and are required to disclose in writing any facts or circumstances likely to give rise to justifiable doubts as to impartiality or independence. The parties may also select the place of the arbitration, including a location outside of China and the language of the arbitration. If, however, no language is specified, the Chinese language is deemed to be the official language of the proceedings. Another key feature is the confidentiality of the proceedings, which are held 'in camera', unless the parties request an open hearing. If the parties desire an open hearing, then the tribunal shall decide this request. For most cases, matters will be heard outside of the public. Here, the parties, their representatives, witnesses, interpreters, arbitrators, experts, appraisers and CIETAC staff members will appear and will be bound not to disclose to outsiders any substantive or procedural matters of the case. In the hearing, the parties have the burden of proving the facts relied upon to support their claims, defenses and counterclaims. One somewhat unusual feature to be aware of, however, is that the arbitral tribunal may, on its own initiative, undertake investigations and collect evidence it considers necessary. In so doing, the arbitral tribunal is required to notify the parties promptly and allow them to be present if the parties so desire.

The arbitral tribunal is required to render its award within six months from the date the tribunal is formed, with the possibility of extensions if truly justified. The awards are to include a statement of the claims, the facts of the dispute, the reasons on which the award is based, the result of the award, the allocation of arbitration costs and the date and place at which the award is made. The arbitral award is final and binding on the parties; neither party may bring an action before a court of law or make a request to any organization for revising the award. This lack of judicial or other review of the awards removes the element of uncertainty from the process. Moreover, the parties must fully comply with the terms of the award within the time specified in the award. If one party fails to comply, the other party may apply to a Chinese court (the Intermediate People's Court) for enforcement pursuant to China's Civil Procedure Law or apply to a competent court for enforcement pursuant to the 1958 United Nations Convention on Recognition and Enforcement of Foreign Arbitral Awards or other international treaties that China has concluded or acceded to, such as the New York Convention on the Recognition and Enforcement of Foreign Arbitral Awards.

Because of the confidentiality of many of the proceedings and lack of a public system to track arbitral decisions, at this point it is difficult to assess the content of the awards.

BEST PRACTICE RECOMMENDATIONS

Especially within China where it may be difficult to bring an action for breach of contract and unfair competition, it is important for companies to implement prevention measures that are specific to Chinese operations to safeguard against disclosure. This is also important because violations may be perpetrated by elusive defendants who may be undercapitalized and can easily close a small business, move and reopen elsewhere.

The following recommendations are designed to be consistent with Chinese statutory and case law to help corporations manage trade secret disclosure risk, as well as to prepare for the potential of trade secret litigation in China. The recommendations are divided into two general categories: drafting elements in employment contracts and protecting trade secrets in the workplace.

Key Elements in Non-competition and Secrecy Agreements

Non-competition and secrecy agreements must be carefully drafted for consistency with Chinese law. First, the duration of the non-competition agreement should be limited and must be consistent with local law. Under the new Contract Labor Law, effective 1 January 2008, the maximum length of a non-compete clause is two years. Overall, the governing rule is that the duration of the non-competition agreement should be limited to an amount of time that is just long enough to protect the employer. The longer the time period, the more evidence will be needed to prove that the period is reasonable and necessary to protect against unfair competition and is not an undue restraint on the employee's right to work. Second, remember that only senior management, senior technicians and those bound to keep information confidential may be held to non-competition agreements pursuant to the Contract Labor Law. Third, the scope of the information covered by the non-competition agreement should also be limited to those activities central to the employer's business. Corporations should carefully identify employees who may have access to confidential information; if the employee has no access, then Chinese courts are not likely to uphold a non-compete agreement. Only activities related to legitimate business interests should be limited. Local law in the province should also be consulted on this point. For example, the Guangdong Regulations on Technology Secret Protection limit the scope of protection to subsequent employment at a company that manufactures a similar product that directly competes with a product of the former employer. It is also advisable that the non-competition clause expressly state that it is designed to preserve business secrets, thereby tying the agreement to a legitimate business reason, and undermining any defense that the agreement is an unfair restriction on labor or creates undue hardship on the employee. The employee should be able to work elsewhere as long as there is no direct competition and no legitimate business secrets are divulged.

Fourth, the general rule is that the geographic scope of the non-compete agreement should be no broader than is necessary to protect legitimate business interests. Because the substantive law governing non-compete agreements varies greatly by jurisdiction in China, it is difficult to ascertain how broad the geographic restriction can be. Depending on the circumstances, this could mean that a global scope could be enforced – preventing the employee from working for any competitor in the world (*Business Intell. Svcs., Inc. v. Hudson*, 1984; *Continental Group, Inc. v. Kinsley*, 1976) – or, at the other extreme, a court may uphold a restriction consisting of only a limited number of miles from the original employer. Obviously, for a non-compete agreement to have a global or 'worldwide' scope, the company would need to have global business interests sufficient to justify the agreement. If the agreement reaches beyond any legitimate protectable interest, it is in jeopardy of being invalidated by a court, especially in China (*Prod. Action Int'l., Inc. v. Mero*, 2003).

Fifth, compensation should be provided in exchange for the non-compete agreement. Although it is unclear how much compensation should be given to the employee in exchange for the non-compete agreement, the agreement should specify the amount and method appropriate for the industry. If the agreement is signed at the commencement of employment, the mere employment may be enough. However, if the agreement is signed in connection with a promotion or new job duties, the agreement should make it clear that there was a bargained-for exchange between the employer and the employee.

Lastly, in addition to addressing existing trade secrets of a company, the confidentiality agreement signed by the employee should also incorporate a provision addressing business secrets or 'know-how' developed by the employee. The employer may be well advised to explicitly state that trade secrets developed in the course of an employee's employment belong to the employer and are prohibited from being disclosed to a third party.

Active Protection of Trade Secrets in the Workplace

In addition to careful drafting, companies should take reasonable steps to protect their business secrets; the law may not be enforced if a company does not endeavor to protect itself. The first and most fundamental duty of a company is to limit access to the trade secret information. Only employees with actual access to trade secret information should be signing non-compete agreements with confidentiality provisions. If an employee does not have access to business secrets, a non-compete agreement is not likely to be enforced. The employee signing the agreement should also understand exactly what is considered to be a business secret. Regular review of employees with access to business secrets should be conducted and these employees should also be reminded of their obligations to keep the information strictly confidential. Physical access to documents and equipment, such as computers, containing trade secret information should also be restricted. Files and other places containing trade secrets should be labeled (for example 'Classified' or 'Restricted'), to prevent inadvertent disclosures. Moreover, employees should be instructed to restrict communication of proprietary information over email. To the extent that confidential information needs to be transmitted electronically, security measures should be taken, such as password protection and user identification information. Of course, only information that is truly a legitimate business secret should be restricted.

Second, the company must ensure that the information claimed to be a trade secret has economic value and practical applicability to be protected in China. If a claim of unfair competition through infringement on business secrets is made, the complaining company will be required to prove that the information at issue has economic value. As was illustrated in the cases discussed in the previous section, this is often done by showing products made using the know-how and the ensuing profits to the company. Also in accordance with Chinese law, the information claimed to be a business secret must have practical usefulness. This is sometimes referred to as realizable utility; the bottom line is that the business secret must not be just a theoretical idea.

Third, active steps should be taken to protect the business secret. At the most basic level, companies should adopt and consistently enforce written policies on confidential information. All employees should be required to sign a copy of the policy and sign a statement acknowledging that they understand the policy and will comply. The policy should clearly define what information constitutes a business secret and how such information should be handled by employees. By training all employees and making sure that they have access to and understand the policies, there is a better chance that a court will uphold the policy. Additionally, companies should keep records of employees in attendance at all meetings in which business secrets are discussed or confidential information is distributed in electronic or hard-copy form. Such records could later be used at trial as proof of access to information that is allegedly later being misappropriated. The policy should also include penalties for improper use or disclosure of the information and enforcement of the penalties. Moreover, any non-compete and trade secret agreement signed by an employee can stipulate damages to be paid by the employee if the confidentiality is breached.

Fourth, once an employee resigns or gives notice, that employee's access to business secrets should be limited or removed altogether. All company-owned equipment, especially computers and other electronic equipment that might contain information, should be collected from the employee. The employer should also conduct an exit interview of all employees bound to non-compete agreements, reminding such employees of their ongoing obligation to keep the information secret. Fifth, after a key employee leaves, the employer may want to follow up on where he goes, to protect against breaches of the non-compete agreement, as well as the development of any competitive practices that infringe on business secrets to which the former employee was privy. The former employer can then notify the new employer of ongoing contractual obligations of the former employee. Any such notification should have confirmation of delivery/receipt to put the new employer on notice that the employee had access to trade secrets and the liability that can result from disclosure. Under Chinese law, third parties who obtain or use business secrets of others that they are aware (or ought to be aware) infringe on the methods of another can be held liable. Lastly, the importance of undertaking a thorough investigation before raising allegations of misappropriation of trade secrets should not be underestimated. Unlike litigation in the United States, the legal system in China does not provide for a traditional discovery process, so it can be very difficult, if not impossible, to obtain evidence once a law suit is filed.

Although there is no iron-clad way to prevent the misappropriation of trade secrets in China, all of these best practice recommendations are intended to help stem the unlawful flow of proprietary information. Ultimately, the more preemptive measures that are taken, the more likely it will be for a court or other adjudication body to find in favor of the plaintiff. Moreover, this chapter is written from the perspective of US companies doing business in China; it is also important to note that Chinese firms also have a vested interest in the protection of their trade secrets. As Chinese companies invest more and more in research and development, as well as attracting and retaining top talent, they will also be well served by effective laws preventing unfair competition. As United States Trade Representative Susan Schwab stated, 'the Chinese are beginning to understand that we expect China to conduct itself as a mature trading partner that benefits greatly from the rules-based trading system and should, therefore, reinforce that system by abiding by it' (Schwab, 2006).

CONCLUSION

Economic espionage, including the theft of trade secrets, is, indeed, a kind of warfare. Because offensive action and active deterrence are much more desirable compared to litigation once trade secrets have been infringed upon, the thrust of this article is to encourage employers to take action early. Important steps are to ensure that contractual provisions for employees in China are consistent with the law, and that effective prevention measures are in place. If so, Chinese courts are more likely to protect what a company claims are its trade secrets. All the recommendations in this chapter are designed to help firms develop best practices to protect themselves from unfair competition in China by former employees with the potential to disclose trade secrets and other proprietary information.

NOTES

1. Associate Professor of Legal Studies, Terry College of Business, University of Georgia, Athens, GA. The author gratefully acknowledges funding for this project from a Terry-Sanford research grant and a Coca Cola Center for International Business Programs award from the University of Georgia. The author is indebted to Grace Fei for her research assistance and case translations, as well the following individuals for their assistance: Yuming Bao, Taide Law Firm, Beijing; Jiang Lu, Tsinghua University, Beijing; Tao Peihua, Fudan University, Shanghai; Peter Thorpe and Mile Zhao, Allen & Overy LLP, Beijing; and Andreas W. Lauffs, Baker & McKenzie, Hong Kong.
2. It is interesting to note, however, that GM has been criticized for seeking patent protection in China for the Spark car, and instead relied on loss of trade secrets as a remedy (*Managing Intellectual Property*, 2004, p. 40).
3. China adopted the new Labor Contract Law on 29 June 2007 (Xinhua News Agency, 2007). The official translation of the Labor Contract Law was not available at the time of writing this chapter, but an unofficial translation is on file with the author.
4. A number of authors discuss problems associated with the protection of intellectual property in China (Mertha, 2005; Yu, 2000, 2006; Liu, 2004; Yong-Shun, 1998). Other authors discuss alternative ways to protect trade secrets. Hermann et al. (2005) discusses patenting as a strategy opposed to trade secret strategy for protecting nanotechnology in China, and Anton and Yao (2004) analyze the relationship between imitation, disclosures necessary to obtain a patent, and protection of the innovation as a trade secret.
5. For an interesting perspective about the Chinese legal system and the role of the rule of law, see Upham (2005), reviewing *Song fa xiaxiang: Zhongguo jiceng sifazhidu yanjiu* or *Sending Law to the Countryside: Research on China's Basic-Level Judicial System* by Zhu Suli, which was published in China in 2000.
6. 'China's Legislature Adopts' (2007). The official translation of the Labor Contract Law (hereinafter Labor Contract Law) was not yet available at the time of writing this chapter, but an unofficial translation is on file with the author.
7. For a provocative discussion about whether a company should seek patent protection or trade secret protection in China, see Bejesky (2004). This is an important issue in the context of business methods, because at this time the patentable status of business methods is in question in China.
8. This definition is also in the rules promulgated in accordance with the Unfair Competition Law (Jager, 2005).
9. 'Reverse engineering' refers to relevant technical information on any product acquired by dismantling, surveying, mapping and analyzing products obtained through open channels.
10. Only the People's Court has the power to award compensation; the AIC has the power to investigate acts of unfair competition and impose penalties.
11. Under the Criminal Law, 'obligee' as mentioned in this Article refers to owners of business secrets and their agents.
12. Translations of the cases discussed in this section are on file with the author.

REFERENCES

Agreement on Trade-Related Aspects of Intellectual Property Rights (1994), http://www.wto.org/english/tratop_e/trips_e/t_agm0_e.html.

Agreement on Trade Relations Between the United States of America and The People's Republic of China (1979), Art. 8 (October 23).
Alford, William P. (1995), *To Steal a Book is an Elegant Offense: Intellectual Property Law in Chinese Civilization*, Stanford, CA: Stanford University Press.
Anton, James J. and Dennis A. Yao (2004), 'Little patents and big secrets: Managing intellectual property', *Rand Journal of Economics*, **35**(1), 1–22.
Beijing Shiweige-Tide Electronic Engineering Co. v. Beijing Yin Lan Tech. Co. (1997), Beijing Han Dian People's Court.
Bejesky, Robert (2004), 'Investing in the dragon: Managing the patent versus trade secret protection decision for the multinational corporation in China', *Tulsa Journal of Comparative & International Law*, **11**, 437–89.
Bird, Robert C. (2006), 'Defending intellectual property rights in BRIC economies', *American Business Law Journal*, **43**, 317–63.
Buckley, Chris (2005), 'Pushed on patents, China shoves back', *International Herald Tribune*, http://www.iht.com/articles/2005/01/13/business/yuan.php.
Business Intell. Svcs., Inc. v. Hudson (1984), 580 F. Supp. 1068, 1073 (SDNY).
Cheng, Yuan (1996), 'Legal protection of trade secrets in the People's Republic of China', *Pacific Rim Law & Policy Journal*, **5**, 261–297.
Chow, Daniel C.K. (2002), *Primer on Foreign Investment Enterprises and Protection of Intellectual Property in China*, The Hague: Kluwer Law International.
Chow, Daniel C.K. (2006), 'Why China does not take commercial piracy seriously', *Ohio Northern University Law Review*, **32**, 203–25.
CIETAC (2005), *Arbitration Rules*, http://www.cietac.org.cn/english/rules/rules.html.
Clarke, Donald C. (2003), 'Economic development and the rights hypothesis: The China problem', *American Journal of Comparative Law*, **51**, 89–111.
Congressional-Executive Commission on China (2006), *Annual Report 2006*, http://www.cecc.gov/pages/annualRpt/annualRpt06/CECCannRpt2006.pdf.
Constitution of the People's Republic of China (1999), http://www.novexcn.com/prc_constitution_1999.html.
Continental Group, Inc. v. Kinsley (1976), 422 F. Supp. 838 (D. Conn.), 'Criminal Law of the People's Republic of China', (1979) (revised on 15 March 1997, effective 1 January 1998), http://www.cecc.gov/pages/newLaws/criminalLawENG.php.
'Detailed rules and regulations for the implementation of the Regulations on the Administration of Technology Import Contracts of the People's Republic of China' (1987), http://www.novexcn.com/admin_tech_export_k.html.
Economist, The (2003), 'Imitating property is theft', 15 May, http://www.economist.com/displaystory.cfm?story_id=1780818.
Evans, Donald L. (2005), US Commerce Secretary, 'Remarks forum on international property rights protection', http://usinfo.state.gov/ei/Archive/2005/Jan/14-57930.html.
Feng, Peter (2003), *Intellectual Property in China* (2nd edn), London: Sweet & Maxwell.
Fisk, Catherine L. (2001), 'Working knowledge: Trade secrets, restrictive covenants in employment, and the rise of corporate intellectual property, 1800–1920', *Hastings Law Journal*, **52**, 441–535.
Forney, Matthew (2005), 'Here come the really cheap cars', *Time*, http://www.time.com/time/magazine/article/0,9171,1015925,00.html.
Fuo Tao Group Ltd. Pottery Research Institute v. Jin Chang Pottery Factory (1995), Intermediate People's Court of Guangdong Province.
General Principles of the Civil Law of the People's Republic of China (1987), http://www.lawbridge.net/english/LAW/20065/1322572053247.shtml.
Greene, Nathan (2004), 'Enforceability of the People's Republic of China's Trade Secret Law: Impact on technology transfer in the PRC and preparing for successful licensing', *Idea*, **44**, 437.
Halverson, Karen (2004), 'China's WTO accession: Economic, legal, and political implications', *Boston College International & Comparative Law Review*, **27**, 319–70.
Hermann, Kirk et al. (2005), 'Protecting nanotechnology intellectual property in China', *Nanotechnology Law & Business*, **2**, 96–109.
International Herald Tribune (2007), 'Chrysler, China's Chery sign deal to export Chinese cars to

United States', *International Herald Tribune*, http://www.iht.com/articles/ap/2007/07/04/business/AS-FIN-China-Chrysler-Chery.php.
Jager, Melvin F. (ed.) (2005),'Several regulations concerning prohibition of acts of infringement of business secrets', art. 2 (effective November 23), in Melvin F. Jager (ed.), *Trade Secrets Throughout the World*, vol. 1, Appendix 8B, Thomson West.
Jones, William C. (2003), 'Trying to understand the current chinese legal system', in C. Stephen Hsu (ed.), *Understanding China's Legal System*, New York: New York University Press.
Liu, Chenglin (2004), 'Chinese law on trade, investment and intellectual property rights: A bibliography of selected English-language materials', *International Journal of Legal Information*, **32**, 1–33.
Managing Intellectual Property (2004), 'Secrets of Success in China', *Managing Intellectual Property*, October.
Maskus, Keith E. (2002), *Intellectual Property Rights in the WTO Accession Package: Assessing China's Reforms*, 16 December, http://siteresources.worldbank.org/INTRANETTRADE/Resources/maskus_tips.pdf#search.
Mertha, Andrew (2005), *The Politics of Piracy: Intellectual Property in Contemporary China*, Ithaca, NY: Cornell University Press.
Ministry of Commerce of the People's Republic of China (2007a), 'Chery to raise annual output to 1 mil vehicles by 2010', http://english.mofcom.gov.cn/aarticle/newsrelease/commonnews/200707/20070704866226.html.
Ministry of Commerce of the People's Republic of China (2007b), 'China's action plan on IPR protection 2007', http://www.china.org.cn/english/China/207534.html.
Office of the National Counterintelligence Executive (2006), 'Annual report to Congress on foreign economic collected and industrial espionage', 2005, http://www.ncix.gov/publications/reports/fecie_all/FECIE_2005.pdf.
Orts, Eric W. (2001), 'The rule of law in China', *Vanderbilt Journal of Transnational Law*, **34**, 43–115.
Porter, II, William G. and Michael C. Griffaton (2002), 'Using non-compete agreements to protect legitimate business interests', *Defense Counsel Journal*, **69**, p. 194.
PRC (1985), 'Regulations of the People's Republic of China on the Administration of Technology Acquisition Contracts', http://www.novexcn.com/tech_acquisit_contract.html.
PRC (1993), 'Law Against Unfair Competition of the People's Republic of China', http://www.sipo.gov.cn/sipo_English/flfg/xgflfg/t20020420_34756.html.
PRC (1994), 'Labor Law of the People's Republic of China', 8th Sess. of the Standing Comm. of the 8th NPC, http://www.jus.uio.no/lm/china.labor.law.1994/doc.html.
PRC (1995), 'Regulations of the Shanghai Municipality Against Unfair Competition'.
PRC (2002), 'Labour Contract Regulations of Shanghai Municipality', http://www.12333.gov.cn/english/rules/rule/t20041028_4648.html.
PRC (2006), 'Key Points of the 11th Five-Year Guidelines', http://www.china.org.cn/english/2006lh/160403.html.
PRC (2007), Labor Contract Law of the People's Republic of China.
PRC (n.d.), 'Labour Contract Measures', *Shanghai Municipality FAQS on Labour Contracts*, http://www.shanghai.gov.cn/shanghai/node8059/FAQ/node8462/node8464/index.html.
Prod. Action Int'l, Inc. v. Mero (2003), 277 F. Supp. 2d 919, 929 (SD Ind.), 'Provisional regulations of the state council on technology transfer' (promulgated 10 January, 1985), http://novexcn.com/technology_transfer.html.
Ribao, Fazhi (1995), 'Trade secrets lawsuit: A record of unfair competition tried by the Beijing municipality Haidian District Court', *Legal Daily*.
Riley, Molly (2002), 'China: Employment Contracts-Confidentiality-Non-Competition Agreements', ICCLR, **13**(10), N. 103–4.
Roberts, Dexter (2005), 'Did Spark spark a copycat?', *Business Week*, http://www.businessweek.com/magazine/content/05_06/b3919010_mz001.html.
Schwab, Susan C. (2006), 'To consider the nomination of Susan C. Schwab to be the United States Trade Representative: Hearing before the US Finance Comm.' 109th Cong. 13–14, 16 May (statement of Susan C. Schwab, US Trade Representative – Designate), http://www.ustr.gov/assets/Document_Library/USTR_Testimony/2006/asset_upload_file533_9447.htm.

Supreme People's Court's Interpretation of Several Issues Relating to Trial of Civil Cases of Unfair Competition (2006), *China Pat. & Trademarks*, Dec. 30, at 94, http://www.cpahkltd.com/Archives/elaw1.pdf.

Sun-Tzu (2002), *The Art of War* (trans. John Minford), New York, USA; Viking.

Tianjin Nutrexpa Food Co., Ltd. v. Li Shaochang (1994), (Tianjin Hexi People's Court), SCPC [1995:2] pp. 134–8.

United States Trade Representative (2006a), '2006 Report to Congress on China's WTO compliance', http://www.ustr.gov/assets/Document_Library/Reports_Publications/2006/asset_upload_file688_10223.pdf

United States Trade Representative (2006b), '2006 Special 301 Report (Executive Summary)', http://www.ustr.gov/assets/Document_Library/Reports_Publications/2006/2006_Special_301_Review/asset_upload_file473_9336.pdf.

United States Trade Representative (2006c), 'US–China trade relations: Entering a new phase of greater accountability and enforcement', *Top-to Bottom Review*, http://www.ustr.gov/assets/Document_Library/Reports_Publications/2006/asset_upload_file921_8938.pdf#search.

Upham, Frank K. (2005), 'Who will find the defendant if he stays with his sheep? Justice in rural China', *Yale Law Journal*, **114**, 1675–718 (reviewing *Song fa xiaxiang: Zhongguo jiceng sifazhidu yanjiu* or *Sending Law to the Countryside: Research on China's Basic-Level Judicial System* by Zhu Suli, published in China in 2000).

US–China Business Council (2006), '2006 USCBC Member Priorities Survey: US Companies Gain in China, Still Face Hurdles', http://www.uschina.org/public/documents/2006/08/member-priorities-survey.pdf.

Weinstein, Veronica and Dennis Fernandez (2004), 'Recent developments in China's intellectual property laws', *Chinese Journal International Law*, **3**, 227–37.

WTO Press Release (2006) 'Trade Policy Review: China', http://www.wto.org/english//tratop_e/tpr_e/tp262_e.html.

Xiamen Metal Powder Melting Factory v. Xiamen Hen Zhu Metal Manuf. Factory (1994), (Superior People's Court, Fujan Province).

Xinhua News Agency (2007), 'China's legislature adopts labor contract law' (29 June), http://news.xinhuanet.com/english/2007-06/29/content_6308557.html.

Xuji Electronic, Co. Ltd. v. Zheng Xueshen and Aite Electronic Equip. Co. (1998), (Intermediate People's Court of Hebei Province).

Yang, Deli (2003), *Intellectual Property and Doing Business in China*, Boston, USA: Pergamon Press.

Yong-Shun, Justice Cheng (1998), 'Juridical protection of intellectual property in China', *Duke Journal of Comparative & International Law*, **9**, 267–73.

Yongtu, Long (2000), H.E. Vice Minister, Head of the Chinese Delegation, 'Fourteenth Session of the Working Party on China', *WTO News*, 8 December, http://www.wto.org/english/news_e/news00_e/wpchina_longstatement_e.html.

Yu, Peter K. (2000), 'From pirates to partners: Protecting intellectual property in China in the twenty-first century', *American University Law Review*, **50**, 131–243.

Yu, Peter K. (2006), 'From pirates to partners (Episode II): Protecting intellectual property in China in the twenty-first century', *American University Law Review*, **55**, 901–1000.

Yu, Peter K. (2007), 'Intellectual property, economic development, and the China puzzle', *SSRN Legal Studies Research Paper Series*, No. 04-23.

Zhang, J. (1987), *A Survey of Legal History* (Fa Shi Jian Lue), Beijing, China: Mass House Publishing.

Zimmerman, James M. (2005), *China Law Deskbook: A Legal Guide for Foreign-Invested Enterprise* (2nd edn), Chicago, IL: American Bar Association.

8. The Indian patent matrix: issues in patent amendment 2005

V.C. Vivekanandan

INTRODUCTION

The emergence of the World Trade Organization from the erstwhile GATT (General Agreement on Tariffs and Trade) marks a new watershed in international law and its impact on international trade and business. With 150 nations[1] signing as members of the WTO, the organization and its agreements have set off unprecedented changes not just in the domain of international trade laws, but also in the domain of the national laws of the member states. The WTO has set differential deadlines and continuous deliberations to be compliant with the agreements for the member states. The agreements and rules of the WTO are officially negotiated by the representatives of the governments of the member countries. The table of contents of 'The results of the Uruguay Round of multilateral trade negotiations: The legal texts' is a daunting list of about 60 agreements, annexes, decisions and understandings. In fact, the agreements fall into a simple structure with six main parts: an umbrella agreement (the Agreement Establishing the WTO); agreements for each of the three broad areas of trade that the WTO covers (goods, services and intellectual property); dispute settlement; and reviews of governments' trade policies.[2]

Yet the content and its impact on the public of the member states have brought several non-governmental organizations, public interest groups, academic experts and policy watchers to oppose these agreements in various degrees. The official negotiating rounds at various venues around the world also serve as a venue for protestors of various interest groups. The WTO and its constituent agreements are signed by member countries voluntarily and to meet the contractual obligations of the agreements of which some are agreed upon and some still negotiated. Though it is considered as a sovereign decision, the dissemination of its contents, its implications on the society, economy and trade of a country, the legal analysis of its impact on the respective constitution of the member state, and the process of public policy making have triggered serious debates by various interest groups representing stakeholders. This debate and protests have also made governments reconsider and shift stances on the ongoing negotiation processes.

THE BASICS OF THE WTO

The WTO is charged with setting the legal ground rules for international trade. Its objectives are to promote: (1) non-discrimination; (2) progressive liberalization of barriers to trade; (3) predictable policies and transparency; (4) competition; and (5) special provisions for developing countries.

In joining the WTO, members adhere to 18 specific agreements annexed to the Agreement establishing the WTO. They cannot choose to be party to some agreements but not others (with the exception of a few 'plurilateral' agreements that are not obligatory). Of greatest relevance to the health sector are: the Agreement on Trade-Related Aspects of Intellectual Property Rights (TRIPS); the Agreement on the Application of Sanitary and Phytosanitary Measures (SPS); the Agreement on Technical Barriers to Trade (TBT); the General Agreement on Tariffs and Trade (GATT); and the General Agreement on Trade in Services (GATS). Of these agreements, TRIPS is expected to have the greatest impact on the pharmaceutical sector and thereby on the health sector. The TBT Agreement also should be of particular concern to producing countries, since its implementation may affect export markets.

The WTO Agreement is a treaty that creates international obligations among its members. These obligations include refraining from taking actions that are inconsistent with the agreement and implementing certain provisions via national legislation. The various parts of the WTO Agreement, including the TRIPS Agreement, require that such national legislation embody certain specific standards. However, in many areas, the WTO Agreement claims to afford considerable discretion in how its obligations are implemented. This discretion, combined with the potential impact of national legislation on health, makes it imperative that health officials work closely with other parts of government, such as the trade department, and use top-level legal, trade and pharmaceutical expertise when legislation is being drafted.

Disputes can arise when countries differ in their interpretation of the WTO Agreement. The WTO provides a dispute settlement process that may progress from a consultation phase, to the establishment of and decision by a dispute settlement panel, and finally to an appeal to the Appellate Body. Trade sanctions may only be implemented if the dispute settlement process has run its course and the losing country has failed to comply with the decision made. Thus, WTO members may not unilaterally impose trade sanctions based on alleged failures to comply with TRIPS.

KEY REQUIREMENTS OF TRIPS

Agreement

The TRIPS Agreement introduced global minimum standards for protecting and enforcing nearly all forms of intellectual property rights, including those for pharmaceuticals. The Agreement's 73 Articles cover basic principles, standards and use of patents, enforcement, dispute settlement and a range of other subjects.

Patent Protection

Members must provide patent protection for a minimum of 20 years from the filing date of a patent application for any invention, including that of a pharmaceutical product or process. The invention must fulfill the criteria of novelty, inventive step and utility.

Rights Conferred

TRIPS specifies the rights conferred on a patent owner, but allows for limited exceptions and compulsory licensing, subject to specified conditions. The Agreement also contains provisions on: protection of undisclosed information (including test data); actions to address anti-competitive practices; protection of trademarks (relevant to generic substitution and combating counterfeit drugs); and enforcement.

Transitional Arrangements

TRIPS provides transitional periods during which countries are required to bring their national legislation and practices into conformity with its provisions. The compliance dates specified for WTO members are: 1996 for developed countries; 2000 for developing countries (as a general rule); 2005 for developing countries who had not introduced patents before joining the WTO; and 2006 for least-developed countries. TRIPS specifically recognizes the economic, financial, administrative and technological constraints of the least-developed countries. It therefore provides the possibility for further extension of the transitional period.

IMPLEMENTATION OF TRIPS

Before TRIPS, international conventions did not specify minimum standards for patents. Over 40 countries provided no patent protection for pharmaceuticals; many provided only process and not product patents; and the duration of patents was much less than 20 years in many countries.

From the health sector's perspective, intellectual property standards, including those specified in TRIPS, should take protection of public health into account. However, current standards – historically derived from those of developed countries – are not necessarily appropriate for countries struggling to meet health and development needs. Developing countries can therefore use the flexibility of TRIPS provisions and its safeguards to protect public health.

In respect to patent law, the TRIPS Agreement provides a three-stage time frame for developing countries to comply with its obligations. These include:

i. Introduction of a facility ('mail box') from 1 January 1995 to receive and hold product patent applications in the fields of pharmaceuticals and agricultural chemicals until 1 January 2005. Further, on fulfillment of certain conditions, the granting of exclusive marketing rights (EMRs) for a period of five years or until the product patent is granted or patent application is rejected, whichever is earlier;
ii. Compliance, from 1 January 2000, with other obligations of the TRIPS Agreement, namely those related to rights of the patentee, term of patent protection, compulsory licensing, reversal of burden of proof, and so on; and
iii. Introduction of product patent protection in all fields of technology from 1 January 2005. (In India's case this means extension of product patent protection to food, drugs, pharmaceuticals and chemicals.) At this stage, the applications for product

patents filed and held in the 'mail box' from 1 January 1995 are also to be taken up for examination.

India has complied with the obligations in respect of (i) and (ii) in the following manner:-

a. In respect to obligations effective from 1 January 1995, India has amended the Patents Act, 1970 through the Patents (Amendment) Act, 1999 effective retroactively from 1 January 1995. This Act provides for a 'mail box' to receive and hold product patent applications in the fields of pharmaceuticals and agricultural chemicals and also, on fulfillment of certain conditions specified in the law, for granting of exclusive marketing rights (EMRs). It has also been provided in the law that product patent applications received shall not be referred for examination until 31 December 2004.
b. In respect to obligations from 1 January 2000, India has further amended the Patents Act through the Patents (Amendment) Act, 2002 passed by Parliament in May 2002 and notified in June 2002. The Act has been made effective from 20 May 2003.
c. The third amendment to the Patents Act was promulgated as an ordinance in December 2004 and later tabled in both Houses and passed as Patents (Amendment) Act 2005 in March 2005.

IMPACT OF TRIPS ON NATIONAL LEGISLATION

After signing of the WTO agreement in 1995, India amended the Patents Law in 1999, 2002 and finally in 2005.[3] The New Trade Marks act was enacted in 1999.[4] The Geographical Indications of Goods (registration and protection) Act was enacted in 1999.[5] The Protection of Plant Varieties and Farmers' Rights Act was enacted in 2001.[6] The official position of the Indian Government is that it is in full compliance with its international obligations under the TRIPS Agreement.

The amendment to the Patents Act, 1970 required from 1 January 2005 a substantive adjustment from the view point of the pharmaceutical and chemical industries, as it introduced a regime of product patent protection in addition to the existing process patent protection for food, pharmaceutical and chemical inventions. The approximately 5000 'mail box' applications have been taken up for examination from 1 January 2005. Apart from the implications for the chemical and pharmaceutical industries, this amendment also has other implications on the pricing and availability of drugs/medicines, on public health issues, and on the Indian industry that has hitherto basically operated (and flourished) through reverse engineering of drugs and pharmaceuticals emerging from R&D efforts of mostly MNCs.

In view of the high business and commercial stakes involved in any change in India's patent regime, the pharmaceutical sector has been sharply divided in its views, which range from maintenance of the status quo, to renegotiation of the TRIPS Agreement, to stronger provisions for protecting domestic industry, to introduction of product patent protection at the earliest opportunity, and so on. Besides these industry groups, several non-governmental organizations are also active in the field of WTO/TRIPS matters and these are generally apprehensive of the WTO and also the TRIPS Agreement.[7]

PERSPECTIVE OF THE GOVERNMENT OF INDIA

The Patent Act of 1970 was amended twice during 1999 and 2002 before the final amendment of 2005. The Third Amendment 2005 was viewed as the final one to comply with TRIPS provisions. The Indian Patents Act always provided for process patents in all fields, and product patents in all fields except drugs, food and chemicals. The law relating to patents is contained in the Patents Act, 1970 (39 of 1970) which came into force on 20 April 1972. This Act was amended in March 1999 and June 2002 to meet India's obligations under the Agreement on Trade Related Aspects of Intellectual Property Rights (TRIPS), which forms part of the agreement establishing the World Trade Organization (WTO).

The amendments primarily focused on the obligations which came into force from 1 January 1995 (in respect of amendments made in March 1999) and obligations which came into force from 1 January 2000 (in respect of amendments notified in June 2002). The first amendment to the Patents Act introduced a transitional facility ('mail box') from 1 January 1995 to receive and hold product patent applications in the fields of pharmaceutical and agricultural chemicals until 1 January 2005 and also for granting of exclusive marketing rights (EMRs) for a period of five years or until the product patent is granted or patent application is rejected, whichever is earlier.

Before making the latter amendment, a Joint Committee of both Houses of Parliament examined all aspects and recommended various provisions in order to provide necessary and adequate safeguards for protection of public, interest, national security, biodiversity and traditional knowledge, including effective flexibilities to enable appropriate and timely response to national and public interest concerns, especially those relating to public health and nutrition. These were included in the second amendment.

The earlier amendments had provided, *inter alia*, for the modalities for a ten-year transition facility (which India had negotiated at the time of its accession to the WTO), commencing from 1 January 1995. As a consequence, the law was required to be amended further in respect of India's obligations under the TRIPs Agreement, due by 1 January 2005.

According to the Government, the Act ensured that the reasonable requirements of the public with respect to availability and affordability of drugs are addressed. Public interest, particularly public health and nutrition, is protected. The law effectively balances and calibrates intellectual property protection with public health concerns and national security. By participating in the international system of intellectual property protection, India unlocks for herself vast opportunities both in exports and in her potential to become a global hub in the area of R&D-based clinical research outsourcing, particularly in the area of bio-technology.[8]

PERSPECTIVE OF APEX INDUSTRY ASSOCIATIONS

The apex industry associations like CII[9] and FICCI[10] took up positions for the compliance with the TRIPS provisions prior to the final amendment of the Patent Act. This was also reflected by major pharmaceutical firms[11] who were generic players in the absence of the Product Patent regime. The associations, through their position paper to the Government, reflected the views of the major pharmaceutical players, as follows:[12]

i. The TRIPS agreement is a legal fact and its obligations are equally binding on all signatories, including India.
ii. Only a consensus among all WTO members can lead to any change in the TRIPS Agreement. There are no indications at this stage that the obligations of developing countries in respect of product patent regime are being diluted/revised.
iii. Almost all drugs on the essential list of WHO and India are outside patent protection. Further, for essential drugs under patent protection, if any, alternatives are available in most cases.
iv. The existing patent law in the country, which provides for a strong and comprehensive set of safeguards, is fully equipped to deal with issues relating to non-availability of drugs and/or exploitative pricing. These provisions were recently revised and elaborate safeguards have been incorporated in the Indian patent law for compulsory licensing, government use, parallel imports and assumption/revocation of patent rights in cases of health-related national/public urgency.
v. After recent cases of public health crisis, especially those related to AIDS in Africa, the Anthrax scare in the USA, and also the Doha Declaration on TRIPS and Public Health, the protective provisions of the Indian Patent law (as also those of other developing countries) have acquired greater acceptability.
vi. India also has a strong drug price control mechanism to ensure availability of drugs at reasonable prices.
vii. The development of new drugs and pharmaceuticals to meet emerging challenges involves substantive R&D initiatives and huge investments. The near total reliance of the Indian pharmaceutical sector on reverse engineering adversely impacts substantial foreign investment in the pharmaceutical sector as well as India's emergence as a technology and R&D driven economy.
viii. It is also inappropriate to link the state of public health in India almost totally to the presence or absence of a product patent regime. The cost of medicine in treatment constitutes only a small fraction of the overall cost. Effective health care primarily depends on investments in infrastructure and development of efficient health delivery systems. In India, the expenditure on the health care system is reportedly around 2 per cent of GDP, which is quite low compared to 8 to 10 per cent recommended by the WHO. Health concerns are, therefore, to be primarily addressed through a more comprehensive set of initiatives involving investments, infrastructure development, HRD and so on.
ix It is also significant that the apprehensions raised prior to both sets of amendments made earlier in the patent law have proven to be unfounded and the drug availability/pricing scenario has not radically changed to the detriment of the Indian consumer.
x. India is developing a modern patent administration to cope with new challenges.

PERSPECTIVE OF NON-GOVERNMENTAL ORGANIZATIONS

Many non-governmental organizations working on public health opposed the mandated changes when the final bill was introduced in 2004. The standpoint of these organizations can be summarized as follows:[13]

- First, the Bill proposes to extend the scope of patentability beyond the TRIPS requirements by amending Section 3 (d) to allow patent protection for new use of known drugs. Patent for new use would help pharmaceutical companies to extend the monopoly of the drug even after the expiry of the original patent. There is no obligation under TRIPS to provide patent protection to new use of known drugs. Earlier, the Mashelkar Committee recommended limiting patent protection only to new chemical molecules.
- Second, the Bill proposes to eliminate the pre-grant opposition procedure. Currently, there are approximately 6000 applications pending in the mailbox. In the absence of pre-grant opposition, these 6000 applications would escape much-needed public scrutiny. Public scrutiny is crucial in light of the fact that fewer than 500 drugs have been granted marketing approvals in India between 1995–2004.
- Third, the Bill has not properly incorporated the 'August 30th Decision', which permits the granting of compulsory licenses for export purposes. The Bill proposes to permit compulsory licensing for export purposes if there is a compulsory license in the importing country having no or insufficient manufacturing capacity in the pharmaceutical sector. This ignores the fact that Least Developing Countries (LDCs) need not provide product patents until 2016. In the absence of patent protection, issuance of a compulsory license is impossible. In that event, the Indian drug companies would not be able to export to LDCs.
- Finally, the Bill fails to revamp the compulsory licensing mechanism. Even though the chapter on compulsory licenses in the Patents Act 1970 states the need for protecting the public interest, the same spirit is not reflected in the substantial provisions. Cumbersome procedures without any timeline for the final disposal of application makes the compulsory license mechanism an impractical option to curb abuse of patent monopoly.

The Civil Society Groups[14] advocated the following:

- Simplify and streamline India's compulsory licensing procedure. Routine issuance of compulsory licenses after 1 January 2005 in India is critical if the rapid entry of generic versions of important pharmaceuticals is to continue. However, compulsory licensing in India is considered cumbersome. The process must be changed to facilitate routine and expedited compulsory licensing of important medicines. A strictly enforced deadline of one to three months should be established for the granting of a compulsory license, and rights of appeal should not include permission for injunctive relief that would impede the use of the license.
- Retain India's pre-grant opposition procedure. India's pre-grant opposition procedure permits opposition to potentially frivolous patent applications, protecting consumers against high prices on non-innovative pharmaceutical products under consideration for patent protection.
- Remove draft provisions for new-use or second-use patents, currently described in Section 3(d) of the Patents Act. TRIPS does not require the granting of additional patents for new uses or new dosage forms for known medicines. New use or second use patents do not reward or encourage true innovation; they will however

increase the cost of important medicines, compromise patient access, and extend monopolies over a longer period of time.

- Fully implement the decision of the WTO General Council on the implementation of paragraph 6 of the Doha Declaration for countries that lack sufficient domestic pharmaceutical manufacturing capacity (the 'August 30th Decision'). The draft amendment to the Patents Act would not permit export of compulsorily licensed medicines from India without a compulsory license granted in the importing country. If the importing country does not have a patent for the compulsorily licensed medicine in force, it will not be allowed to import compulsorily licensed medicines exported by India, even though the August 30th Decision clearly permits this. Despite its flaws, the August 30th Decision should be implemented in as complete a manner as possible.

PROVISIONS OF THE 2005 AMENDMENT OF THE PATENT ACT

The Draft Bill of the Patents Act 2004 met stiff opposition from civil society groups and most notably from the left front political parties supporting the government. These parties, along with a substantial number of Members of Parliament, influenced the government, which finally resulted in the ordinance of the Patent Amendment of 2004, later becoming an Act in 2004. The final amendment had the following important changes which were a result of sustained pressure from various advocacy groups and also by the left parties which were supporting the Government from outside and whose vote was crucial for the passage of the legislation.

The major Amendments are:

1. In the definition of what are not inventions, the amendment now says '*Mere* new use for a known substance' is not an invention. In other words, if the applicant can substantiate that it is new use for a known substance with some technical input, such new use can be patented.[15]
2. A computer program per se is not patentable but its 'technical application to industry or a combination with hardware' is patentable. The scope of patentability of a computer program has now been widened and is more or less in line with the US Patent grant.[16]
3. A mathematical method or business method or algorithms are not patentable.
4. The provision prohibiting product patents for food, medicine, drug and chemical processes has been removed. In India with effect from *1 January 2005* product patents are available for medicine, drug, chemical processes and food. This is the most important amendment introduced by the new Ordinance. A product patent regime in respect of drug, medicine, food and chemical processes is implemented in India.[17]
5. If a patent application is accompanied by a provisional specification, the complete specification should be filed within 12 months of filing of the application. Otherwise the application shall be deemed abandoned.[18]
6. A patent application shall be examined only on request in a prescribed manner. Without a request the patent applications will not be examined as a matter of routine, as it was prior to the year 2003.[19]

7. Provisions relating to Exclusive Marketing Rights (EMR) have been removed. The EMR provision was introduced in India in the year 1999 in compliance with TRIPS as product patents for drug and medicine were not available in the Indian Act. As product patents can now be granted for drugs, medicines, food and chemical processes, the EMR provision has become redundant and has been repealed.
8. When a patent has been published but has not been granted, any person can make a representation to the Controller of Patents requesting him to refuse the application on the grounds of lack of novelty, inventive steps, or industrial applicability. The Controller shall consider such representation and disposition it. The person making the representation is not a party to the proceeding. After the granting of a patent but before the expiry of the period of one year from the date of publication of granting of a patent, any person interested may give notice of opposition to the Controller.[20]
9. Only after granting of the patent are the application, specification and documents related thereto opened for public inspection.
10. The Act now provides for a compulsory license for manufacture and export of patented pharmaceutical products to any country having insufficient or no manufacturing capacity in the pharmaceutical sector for the concerned product to address public health problems provided compulsory license has been granted by such country. To avail of this provision, the applicant should satisfy two conditions:
    (a) The country to which export has to be made has insufficient or no facility to manufacture.
    (b) The recipient country should grant compulsory license for import and sale of the drug.[21]
11. The ordinance also provides for appeal from the order of decision of the Controller to the Intellectual Property Appellate Board (IPAB). The power of revocation is also conferred with the IPAB.[22]

THE LEGAL CHALLENGE TO THE PATENTS AMENDMENT ACT

The first ever challenge to the Patent Amendment Act was mounted by Novartis[23] when its patent application No.1602/MI\S/1998 for the beta crystalline form of imatinib mesylate sold under the brandname Gleevec/Glivec used for treating blood cancer (leukemia) and Gastro-Intestinal Stromal Tumours (GIST) was rejected. This product earlier received an EMR Exclusive Marketing Right in November 2003. The patent application was rejected by the Assistant Controller of Patents of Chennai Patent Office, in pre-grant opposition proceedings filed by Respondents[24] for the beta crystalline form of imatinib mesylate sold under the brand name Gleevec/Glivec used for treating blood cancer (leukemia) and Gastro-Intestinal Stromal Tumours (GIST). The company, by way of writ petition, challenged the constitutional validity of section 3(d) as added to the Patents Act, 1970 by the Patents Amendment Act (15 of 2005).

A. The petitioners submitted that Section 3(d) is not in conformity with the provision of the TRIPS Agreement. As mentioned above, Article 27 thereof provides for uniform conditions of patentability.[25] The petitioners contended that the enacted section is narrower than the TRIPS provision which mandates that a product has to be new, inventive and industrially applicable for a patent.

B. Section 3(d) is also contrary to the provisions of Article 1(1) of the TRIPS Agreement.[26]
C. The amendment of Section 3(d) has ignored the obligation of the Parliament or the Court to mould municipal law in harmony with the International treaties. In a catena of Judgments, there has been recognition of the presumption that Parliament does not assert or assume jurisdiction which goes beyond the limits established by the common consent of nations, and statutes are to be interpreted provided that their language permits, so as not to be inconsistent with the comity of nations or with established principles of international law.
D. The use of the term 'derivative' in the explanation to Section 3(d) implies human intervention and an inventive step and not a discovery. The law seems thoroughly to recognize the supremacy of an invention to discovery but proposes to give the latter the status of an invention if it passes the test of efficacy.
E. The term 'efficacy' has not been defined in the Act, which makes the provision vague and arbitrary. Moreover, the requirement of 'efficacy' is unique to India; it is not to be found in any other Patent statute in the world.
F. The petitioner also contended that the amended act brought in Section 3 (d) to deny their patent, as the Minister of Commerce of Government of India formed an Expert Committee to look into the issue of criteria of patentability of new forms of known substances as well as the issue[27] of patentability of micro-organisms. Before the Expert Committee rendered its opinion, the provision was hurriedly introduced specifically to deny the patent claim of the petitioner.

A CRITICAL ANALYSIS OF THE CASE

The response of the defendants submitted to the Court on this petition can be summarized as follows:

1. Non-compliance with an international obligation does not afford a basis for challenging a domestic statute to a private party in a municipal court unless the international instrument itself specifically confers such a ground. The TRIPS Agreement does not confer rights on private parties nor does it confer jurisdiction on municipal courts to adjudicate disputes relating to actions or omissions of member states that possibly are not in conformity with the TRIPS Agreement.[28]
2. The Dispute Settlement Board of TRIPS is the sole and exclusive forum for any disputes on incompatibility with TRIPS provisions.[29]
3. They also contended that the TRIPS provisions allow flexibility to develop national legislation to protect Public Health.[30]
4. It was also contended that TRIPS only sets broad criteria of patentability by way of novelty, inventive step and industrial utility. The exact definition of the criteria is left to the member country through its legislation, including what is not patentable.[31]

5. This flexibility to define the criteria is also reinforced in TRIPS by incorporating the provisions of the Paris convention through Article 2 of TRIPS. The Paris Convention recognizes the freedom of the member countries to interpret the criteria of patentability.[32]
6. The Doha Declaration on Public Health has put the focus on the issue of public health and has clearly defined the interpretation of TRIPS within the ambit of public health. The provisions of the declaration are binding on the members.[33]
7. TRIPS insists on non-discrimination in fields of technologies, whereas the section 3(d) only interprets criteria of patentability which is for all fields of technology. This was also upheld in the WTO decision of 'Canada – Patent Protection of Pharmaceuticals Products' aimed at increasing competition for greater access to medicine.[34]
8. The provision also aims to contain 'evergreening' of patents which delays entry of generic products into the market. It was contended that patenting of salts and polymorphs is a method by which pharmaceutical companies, including the Petitioners, delay the entry of generic competitors into the market.
9. The TRIPS agreement again has no exhaustive list of exclusions and only in 27.2 and 27.3 are there specific exclusions from patentability of those inventions: (i) necessary to protect *ordre public* or morality; (ii) diagnostic, therapeutic and surgical methods for the treatment of humans or animals; and (iii) plant and animals other than micro-organisms. However, many countries exclude business method patents and data presentation methods which may not be based on 27.2 and 27.3 but nevertheless are based on the flexibility, and not on strict interpretation of article 27.[35]
10. It was also contended that India's constitutional obligations not only override international obligations, but are also in accordance with other international obligations on the issues of Public Health. Article 21 of the Indian Constitution has defined the fundamental right of public health, which has been affirmed by various court decisions.[36]

THE DECISION OF THE COURT

The Bench, comprised of the Hon. Mr Justice R. Balasubramanian and the Hon. Mrs Justice Prabha Sridevan, delivered their judgment on the case on 8 August 2007. The Judgment touched upon the content of the two writ petitions, namely:

a. the Constitutional validity of section 3(d) alone is in challenge;
b. on ground that it violates not only Article 14 of the Constitution of India but also on the ground that it is not in compliance with 'TRIPS'.

The Hon. Judges observed that India is a welfare country and its first obligation under the constitution is to provide good healthcare to its citizens. Every member country is given enough latitude in discharging their TRIPS obligations to introduce local laws that consider the various needs of their citizens.

The court framed the following issues for consideration in disposal of the writ petitions:

a. Assuming Section 3(d) of the Patents Act is in clear breach of Article 27 of TRIPS and thereby suffers the vice of irrationality and arbitrariness violating Article 14 of

Constitution of India, could the courts in India have jurisdiction to test the validity of amended section in the backdrop of such alleged violation of TRIPS.

Even if the amended section cannot be struck down by this court for the reasons stated above, cannot this court grant a declaratory relief that the amended section is not in compliance of Article 27 of 'TRIPS'?

b. If it is held that courts in India have jurisdiction to go into the above referred to issue, then, is the amended section compatible or non-compatible to Article 27 of 'TRIPS'?
c. Dehors issues (a) and (b) referred to above, could the amended section be held to be violative of Article 14 of the Constitution of India on the ground of vagueness, arbitrariness and conferring un-canalized powers on the Statutory Authority?

Counsels Mr Soli Sorabji and Mr Shanthi Bhushan, appearing for Novartis AG and Novartis India Ltd, argued that there is no legal bar for the Hon. Madras High Court to give a simplicitor declaratory relief that the amended section is incompatible with Article 27 of 'TRIPS'.

The Learned Judges observed that when a domestic law is challenged on the ground of it being in violation of an International Treaty, domestic courts would have no jurisdiction. When a comprehensive dispute settlement mechanism is provided under the WTO, it cannot be disputed that it is binding on the member states. The Learned Judges observed,

> we see no reason at all as to why the petitioner (Novartis), which itself is a part of that member State (Switzerland), should not be directed to have the dispute resolved under the dispute settlement mechanism referred to above. Several nations in the world are parties to 'TRIPS' as well as the 'WTO' agreement.

The Learned Judges held that Madras High Court has no jurisdiction to decide the validity of the amended section, being in violation of Article 27 of 'TRIPS', and that they are not going to address the question of whether any individual is conferred with an enforceable right under 'TRIPS' or not.

The next issue considered was when an enactment infringes upon fundamental rights and a challenge is made to that enactment on the grounds that, following the guidelines laid down by the Supreme Court of India, the court should not hesitate to grant declaratory relief under Article 32 of the Constitution of India. The Learned Judges considered the contention of the respondents that the petitioner is entitled to a proprietary right over the patent only for a fixed tenure and, beyond that, it gets nothing else. The Judges agreed with this point. The Learned Judges observed that

> we also find that ends of justice, on the facts of this case, is not in favour of the petitioner, which would disable us from exercising our discretionary jurisdiction . . . Therefore, for the reasons stated above, we find that the petitioner in each writ petition is not entitled to even the declaratory relief.

The main grounds of attack on the validity of the amended section are that it is vague, arbitrary and confers uncanalized powers on the Statutory Authority. The counsel for Novartis argued that though the expression 'efficacy' has a definite meaning, no definite meaning could be attributed to the expression 'enhancements of the known efficacy' and 'differ significantly in properties with regard to efficacy'. These expressions are ambiguous. According to them, if this ambiguity is not cleared, then there is every chance for the Statutory Authority to exercise its power to its whims and fancies.

The counsel for respondents argued that if the discretionary power vested in the Statutory Authority is found to have been wrongly exercised or abused, then such an error can always be corrected by higher forums, which is provided for in the Act itself and thereafter, by the courts of law. The amended section is not confined only to drugs, as it deals with machines and apparatuses as well. The Learned Judges observed that 'we are clear in our mind that the portions of the amended section and the Explanation under attack is definitely referable only to the pharmacology field, namely, drugs'.

The Judges then considered the argument advanced before the court by learned Senior Counsels for Novartis on the validity of the amended section on the touchstone of Article 14 of the Constitution of India.

The counsel for respondents argued that any patent applicant must place on record what is the therapeutic effect/efficacy of a known substance and what is the enhancement in that known efficacy. The amended section not only covers the field of pharmacology but also the other fields. Therefore, the amended section is a comprehensive provision covering all fields of technology, including the field of pharmacology. The explanation would operate only when discovery is made in the pharmacology field.

After considering the arguments by counsels the Learned Judge observed

> Therefore it is clear from the amended section and the Explanation that in the pharmacology field, if a discovery is made from a known substance, a duty is cast upon the patent applicant to show that the discovery had resulted in the enhancement of a known efficacy of that substance and in deciding whether to grant a Patent or not on such new discovery, the Explanation creates a deeming fiction that all derivatives of a known substance would be deemed to be the same substance unless it differ significantly in properties with regard to efficacy . . . . In our opinion, the amended section and Explanation give importance to efficacy . . . . Therefore in sum and substance what the amended section with the Explanation prescribes is the test to decide whether the discovery is an invention or not is that the Patent applicant should show the discovery has resulted in the enhancement of the known efficacy of that substance and if the discovery is nothing other than the derivative of a known substance, then, it must be shown that the properties in the derivatives differ significantly with regard to efficacy.

The Learned Judges observed that

> it is possible to show by giving necessary comparative details based on such science that the discovery of a new form of a known substance had resulted in the enhancement of the known efficacy of the original substance and the derivative so derived will not be the same substance, since the properties of the derivatives differ significantly with regard to efficacy.

The Learned Judges observed that

> Writ petitioner (Novartis) is not a novice to the pharmacology field but it, being pharmaceutical giant in the whole of the world, cannot plead that they do not know what is meant by enhancement of a known efficacy and they cannot show that the derivatives differ significantly in properties with regard to efficacy.

Extensive arguments were submitted by counsel that even if the Act is not complete, a Judge may not alter the material on which the Act is woven but he can and should iron out the creases. The Parliamentarians expressed the general object and purpose of the legislation when enacting the statutes, but did not foresee minute details that are likely to arise in future, nor did they intend to provide a solution for these details when the Act was enacted. The Court would interpret the statute to advance the object for which the Act was passed.

The Learned Judges held that Article 14 of the Constitution of India can be invoked only when it is shown that, in the exercise of discretionary power, there is a possibility of real and substantial discrimination and such exercise interferes with the fundamental rights guaranteed by the constitution. The Learned Judges observed that the amended section 3(d) does not discriminate and does not prohibit trade being carried on. The Learned Judges held that there is no ambiguity or vagueness in the expressions found in Section 3(d) of the Patents Act and the explanation attached to it. The Learned Judges held that 'Therefore there cannot be any doubt at all that the Patents Act as it stood then and as it stands today, is designed to safeguard the economic interests of this country and if that is so, the amended section must be viewed with greater latitude'. The court held that the amended section 3(d) has built-in measures to guide the Patent Controller in exercising his power under the Act. Amended Section 3(d) does not suffer from vagueness, ambiguity and arbitrariness. Amended Section 3(d) cannot be invalidated solely on the grounds that there is a possibility of misusing the power by the Controller of Patents.

In the concluding portion the Learned Judges observed 'we have borne in mind the object which the amending Act wanted to achieve viz. to prevent evergreening; to provide easy access to the citizens of this country to life saving drugs and to discharge their constitutional obligation of providing good healthcare to its citizens'.

The above judgment is a landmark in patent law in India after the product patent protection provided to medicines and foods by the Amendment Act of 2005. The Act has provided provisions to prevent evergreening of patents; a basic tenet of patent law all over the world. The judgment has analyzed the various provisions and case laws involved in detail and has upheld the validity of Section 3(d) of the Patents Act.

CONCLUSION

The current case is the first and most significant challenge on the Patent Amendment Act of India. It is significant for the following reasons:

1. The interpretation of National Legislation within the framework of TRIPS sets a precedent in other national legislations relating to intellectual property rights.
2. The outcome of the decision impacts on the balance of Innovators vs. Generics players.
3. The interpretation of the appropriate balance between IP monopoly rights and consumer and societal interests.

On the technical issue of the patent rejection, the court referred to the Intellectual Property Appellate Board which had been activated during the proceedings of the case. However, the major objection to the IPAB's hearing pertained to continuance in office of the Board's Technical Member (Patent), Mr S. Chandrasekharan, who was allegedly responsible for rejection of its patent application. It contended that the technical member was the former Patent Controller General and he was alleged to be behind the decision to reject the application for the patent. The plea, however, was rejected by the IPAB. Novartis filed a writ petition in the Madras High Court on this issue. The First Bench of the Madras High Court, consisting of Mr Chief Justice, A.P. Shah, and Mr Justice P. Jothimani, which heard the writ petition of Novartis, held that until further orders, the proceedings before the IPAB were stayed.

NOTES

1. http://www.wto.org/english/thewto_e/whatis_e/tif_e/org 6_e.htm.
2. http://www.wto.org/english/thewto_e/whatis_e/tif_e/agrm1_e.htm.
3. See http://ipindia.nic.in/ipr/patent/patents.htm.
4. See http://ipindia.nic.in/tmr_new/default.htm.
5. See http://ipindia.nic.in/ipr/gi/gi_act.PDF.
6. See http://www.plantauthority.in/download.htm.
7. See http://www.altlawforum.org/PUBLICATIONS/A%20critical%20view%20of%20the%20new%20Indian %20Patent%20Act.doc/ www.combatlaw.org/information.php?article_id=581&issue_id=23 - 46k/; www. patentmatics.org/pub2005.htm/www.cpim.org/marxist/200601_eco%20polciies%20of%20upa.doc.
8. http://pib.nic.in/release/release.asp?relid=6074-statement made by Shri Kamal Nath, Union Minister of Commerce & Industry, on the Ordinance relating to Patents (Third) Amendment.
9. The Confederation of Indian Industry (CII) is a non-government, not-for-profit, industry-led and industry-managed organization, playing a proactive role in India's development process. The organization works to create and sustain an environment conducive to the growth of industry in India, partnering industry and government alike through advisory and consultative processes. The confederation is headquartered in New Delhi. See http://en.wikipedia.org/wiki/Confederation_of_Indian_Industry.
10. Federation of Indian Chambers of Commerce and Industry (FICCI) is an association of business organizations in India. FICCI is one of the main organizations to fund and support many governmental and non-governmental educational institutes. http://en.wikipedia.org/wiki/FICCI.
11. http://www.ranbaxy.com/newsroom/rworld2007/ranbaxy_world-march2007.pdf.
12. http://www.ficci.com/media-room/ficci-in-news/march/march.htm.
13. http://hrw.org/english/docs/2004/10/22/india9556.htm.
14. http://www.healthgap.org/press_releases/04/121404_HGAP_FS_INDIA_patent.pdf.
15. 3. Amendment of section 3. In section 3 of the principal Act, for clause (*d*), the following shall be substituted, namely:

    (*d*) the mere discovery of a new form of a known substance which does not result in the enhancement of the known efficacy of that substance or the mere discovery of any new property or new use for a known substance or of the mere use of a known process, machine or apparatus unless such known process results in a new product or employs at least one new reactant.

    Explanation. For the purposes of this clause, salts, esters, ethers, polymorphs, metabolites, pure form, particle size, isomers, mixtures of isomers, complexes, combinations and other derivatives of known substance shall be considered to be the same substance, unless they differ significantly in properties with regard to efficacy.

16. 3(K) a mathematical or business method or a computer program per se or algorithms. A computer program product is claimed as 'A computer program product in computer readable medium', 'A computer-readable storage medium having a program recorded thereon', and so on. In such cases the claims are treated as relating to software per se, irrespective of the medium of its storage, and are not held patentable. Examples in respect of other categories of subject matter are Scheme or method of bookkeeping; business method in the field of accounting; method of tax collection.
17. Omission of Section 5. Section 5 of the principal Act shall be omitted: original act read as Chapter II- 5. Inventions where only methods or processes of manufacture patentable (1) In the case of inventions:

    a. claiming substances intended for use, or capable of being used, as food or as medicine or drug, or
    b. relating to substances prepared or produced by chemical processes (including alloys, optical glass, semi-conductors and inter-metallic compounds),

no patent shall be granted in respect of claims for the substances themselves, but claims for the methods or processes of manufacture shall be patentable. [(2) Notwithstanding anything contained in sub-section (1), a claim for patent of an invention for a substance itself intended for use, or capable of being used, as medicine or drug, except the medicine or drug specified under sub-clause (v) of clause (1) of sub-section (1) of section 2, may be made and shall be dealt, without prejudice to the other provisions of this Act, in the manner provided in Chapter IVA.]

18. Amendment of Section 9. In Section 9 of the principal Act: '(1) Where an application for a patent (not being a convention application or an application filed under the Patent Cooperation Treaty designating India) is accompanied by a provisional specification, a complete specification shall be filed within twelve months from the date of filing of the application, and if the complete specification is not so filed, the application shall be deemed to be abandoned.'
19. Amendment of Section 11A. In Section 11A of the principal Act: sub-section (2) The applicant may, in the prescribed manner, request the Controller to publish his application at any time before the expiry of the period prescribed under sub-section (1) and subject to the provisions of sub-section (3), the Controller shall publish such application as soon as possible.
20. Substitution of new sections for Sections 25 and 26. For Sections 25 and 26 of the principal Act, the following sections shall be substituted, namely:

> 25. Opposition to the patent. (1) Where an application for a patent has been published but a patent has not been granted, any person may, in writing, represent by way of opposition to the Controller against the grant of patent . . .
> (2) At any time after the grant of patent but before the expiry of a period of one year from the date of publication of grant of a patent, any person interested may give notice of opposition to the Controller in the prescribed manner . . .
> (3) (a) Where any such notice of opposition is duly given under sub-section (2), the Controller shall notify the patentee.
> (b) On receipt of such notice of opposition, the Controller shall, by order in writing, constitute a Board to be known as the Opposition Board consisting of such officers as he may determine and refer such notice of opposition along with the documents to that Board for examination and submission of its recommendations to the Controller.
> (c) Every Opposition Board constituted under clause (b) shall conduct the examination in accordance with such procedure as may be prescribed.
> (4) On receipt of the recommendation of the Opposition Board and after giving the patentee and the opponent an opportunity of being heard, the Controller shall order either to maintain or to amend or to revoke the patent.
> (5) While passing an order under sub-section (4) in respect of the ground mentioned in clause (d) or clause (e) of sub-section (2), the Controller shall not take into account any personal document or secret trial or secret use.

21. Insertion of new Section 92A. After Section 92 of the principal Act, the following section shall be inserted, namely:

> 92A. Compulsory licence for export of patented pharmaceutical products in certain exceptional circumstances.–(1) Compulsory licence shall be available for manufacture and export of patented pharmaceutical products to any country having insufficient or no manufacturing capacity in the pharmaceutical sector for the concerned product to address public health problems, provided compulsory licence has been granted by such country or such country has, by notification or otherwise, allowed importation of the patented pharmaceutical products from India.
> (2) The Controller shall, on receipt of an application in the prescribed manner, grant a compulsory licence solely for manufacture and export of the concerned pharmaceutical product to such country under such terms and conditions as may be specified and published by him.
> (3) The provisions of sub-sections (1) and (2) shall be without prejudice to the extent to which pharmaceutical products produced under a compulsory licence can be exported under any other provision of this Act.
> *Explanation.* For the purposes of this section, 'pharmaceutical products' means any patented product, or product manufactured through a patented process, of the pharmaceutical sector needed to address public health problems and shall be inclusive of ingredients necessary for their manufacture and diagnostic kits required for their use.

22. Substitution of new section for Section 117G. For Section 117G of the principal Act [as inserted by the Patents (Amendment) Act, 2002 (38 of 2002)], the following section shall be substituted, namely:

117G. Transfer of pending proceedings to Appellate Board. All cases of appeals against any order or decision of the Controller and all cases pertaining to revocation of patent other than on a counter-claim in a suit for infringement and rectification of register pending before any High Court, shall be transferred to the Appellate Board from such date as may be notified by the Central Government in the Official Gazette and the Appellate Board may proceed with the matter either *de novo* or from the stage it was so transferred.

23. In the High Court of Judicature at Madras (special original jurisdiction) w.p.no.24759 of 2006 – Novartis Ag VS Union of India and others.
24. M/s Natco Pharma, Cipla Ltd, Hetero Drugs Ltd, Cancer Patient Aid Association of India, Ranbaxy Ltd.
25. 'Subject to the provision of paragraph 2 and 3, patents shall be available for any inventions, whether products or processes, in all fields of technology, provided that they are new, involve an inventive step and are capable of industrial application. Subject to paragraph 4 of Article 65, paragraph 8 of Article 70 and paragraph 3 of this Article, patents shall be available and patent rights enjoyable without discrimination as to the place of invention, field of technology and whether products are imported or locally produced.'
26. 'Members shall give effect to the provisions of this Agreement. Members may, but shall not be obliged to, implement in their law more extensive protection than is required by this agreement, provided that such protection does not contravene the provisions of this Agreement . . .' (emphasis added).
27. Reply of Kamalnath on the Patentability issue on 22 March in Indian Parliament: 'When you recognise that India is capable of this leadership, then only and with your support can India effectively play that role. So having recognised that, I greatly appreciate your support on the two points which you have made and the two points on which I differ with you. I differ with you but I will refer it to an expert group to see whether there is enough elasticity and also whether it is in the interest of Indian pharmaceutical companies. I will be happy to bring an amendment when the House is reconvened. The two issues are related to the new chemical entity and the question of micro-organisms. That was the question which was raised, I will be happy to refer it to the expert group which will also be constituted in consultation with you because, as I said, our intentions are common.
28. See *M/s VO Tractoroexport v. M/S Tarapore*, 1963 (3) SCC 562, page 571, at para 16, in *Compilation of Judgments, volume 1, page 10*; *Gramaphone Company of India Ltd. v. Birendra Bahadur Pandey*, (1984) 2 SCC 534, page 540, at paras 5 and 6, in *Compilation of Judgments, volume 1, page 129*.
29. TRIPS, Article 64, in *Compilation of Documents, volume 3 (extracts), page 81* and World Trade Organization, *Understanding on Rules and Procedures Governing the Settlement of Disputes*, http://www.wto.org/english/docs_e/legal_e/index_u_e.htm.
30. Article 1.1 of the TRIPS Agreement states that '[m]embers shall be free to determine the appropriate method of implementing the provisions of this Agreement within their own legal system and practice.'

    Article 7 of the TRIPS Agreement states that 'the protection and enforcement of intellectual property rights should contribute to the promotion of technological innovation and to the transfer and dissemination of technology, to the mutual advantage of producers and users of technological knowledge *and in a manner conducive to social and economic welfare*, and to a balance of rights and obligations'. Article 8.1 of the TRIPS Agreement states that '*Members may in formulating or amending their laws and regulations, adopt measures necessary to protect public health* and nutrition, and to promote the public interest in sectors of vital importance to their socio-economic and technological development, provided that such measures are consistent with the provisions of this agreement'.
31. Article 27.1 of the TRIPS agreement states: 'Subject to the provisions of paragraphs 2 and 3, patents shall be available for any inventions, *whether products or processes*, in all fields of technology, provided that they are *new, involve an inventive step and are capable of industrial application*.'
32. Paris Convention, Article 4*bis*, declares that 'patents applied for in the various countries of the Union by nationals of countries of the Union shall be independent of patents obtained for the same invention in other countries, whether members of the Union or not.'
33. Paragraph 4 of the Doha Declaration provides, 'We agree the TRIPS Agreement does not and should not prevent Member from taking measure to protect public health. Accordingly, while reiterating our commitment to the TRIPS Agreement, *we affirm that the Agreement can and should be interpreted and implemented in a manner supportive of WTO Members' right to protect public health and, in particular, to promote access to medicines for all*'.
34. 'Canada – Patent Protection of Pharmaceutical Products', WT/DS114/R, the WTO Dispute panel examined whether a Canadian legal provision designed to promote competition in the pharmaceutical sector and thus increase the public's access to affordable medicines was valid under Article 27 of the TRIPS Agreement. In so doing, the Panel explained that Article 27 of TRIPS '*does not prohibit bona fide exceptions to deal with problems that may exist only in certain product areas*'.
35. See Brazil, Industrial Property Law, Article 10; Chile, Industrial Property Law, Section 37; Malaysia, Patents Act, Section 13; Philippines, Intellectual Property Code, Section 22; Sri Lanka, Code of

Intellectual Property Act, Section 59.3. See Argentina, Patent Law, Article 6; Austria, Patent Law, Section 2; Brazil, Industrial Property Law, Article 10; Russia, Patent Law, Article 4(2); South Africa, Patents Act, Section 25(2)], 'computer programs' [see Argentina, Patent Law, Article 6; Austria, Patent Law, Section 2; Brazil, Industrial Property Law, Article 10; Philippines, Intellectual Property Code, Section 22; Russia, Patent Law, Article 4(2); South Africa, Patents Act, Section 25(2); Thailand, Patent Act, Section 9], and 'aesthetic creations'. [See Argentina, Patent Law, Article 6; Austria, Patent Law, Section 2; Brazil, Industrial Property Law, Article 10; Philippines, Intellectual Property Code, Section 22; Russia, Patent Law, Article 4(2); South Africa, Patents Act, Section 25(2).]

36. *Vincent Panikurlangara v. Union of India*, (1987) 2 SCC 165.

9. Intellectual property, foreign direct investment and the China exception

Peter K. Yu*

INTRODUCTION

Since the 1980s, policy makers in the less developed world have undertaken considerable intellectual property law reforms to attract foreign direct investment (FDI) (Yu, 2007, pp. 892–901). Economists have defined FDI as 'the act of establishing or acquiring a foreign subsidiary over which the investing firm has substantial management control' (Maskus, 1998, p. 119). Stronger intellectual property protection, however, is not always needed for attracting such investment. In the case of China, foreign investors are usually not attracted by the strength of the country's intellectual property protection. Rather, they entered the Chinese market because of the drastically lower production costs, the country's enormous market, its inefficient economic system and the preferential treatment of foreign investors. Thus, some commentators have considered China a paradigmatic case for showing how rapid economic development can take place despite limited intellectual property protection (Abbott, 2005, p. 81; Chow, 2007, p. 199).

Although the piracy and counterfeiting problems in China have been widely reported by the media in the past decade, the protection of intellectual property rights was a rather recent development in the country. Modern copyright, patent and trademark laws were not introduced until after China reopened its market to foreign trade in the late 1970s (Yu, 2000, pp. 136–41). Since then, the country revamped its intellectual property system in response to US pressure in the late 1980s and early 1990s and did so again in preparation for its accession to the World Trade Organization (WTO) (Yu, 2000, pp. 141–51; 2006a, pp. 906–23). At present, China is a proud member of many multilateral intellectual property agreements, including the Berne Convention, the Geneva Convention, the Paris Convention, the Patent Cooperation Treaty and UPOV (International Union for the Protection of New Varieties of Plants).

Notwithstanding these developments, the enforcement of intellectual property rights in China remains inadequate. Every year, US industries are estimated to have lost billions of dollars due to piracy and counterfeiting in the country. As the International Intellectual Property Alliance stated in its recent Special 301 Report, copyright piracy in China resulted in $2.2 billion of US trade losses in 2006 alone (International Intellectual

* Copyright © 2008 Peter K. Yu. This chapter was abridged and adapted from Peter K. Yu (2007), 'Intellectual property, economic development, and the China puzzle', in Daniel J. Gervais (ed.), *Intellectual Property, Trade and Development: Strategies to Optimize Economic Development in a TRIPS Plus Era*, Oxford: Oxford University Press, pp. 173–220.

Property Alliance, 2007, p. 96). Of particular concern is the considerable quantity of the infringing products that have been exported to other foreign markets. To protect its industries, the United States has recently requested consultations with China over its failure to comply with the Agreement on Trade-Related Aspects of Intellectual Property Rights (TRIPS Agreement) concerning protection and enforcement of intellectual property rights.[1]

This chapter examines, with a focus on China, the causal relationship between the strength of intellectual property protection and the amount of FDI attracted to a country. It begins with a theoretical discussion of the conventional linkage between these two variables and challenges the claim that China is the proverbial exception to this causal relationship. Instead, the chapter argues that the country illustrates rather well the relationship's theoretical and empirical ambiguities and the complex interplay of the different location advantages that affect private investment decisions. The chapter then examines why China expanded its intellectual property protection even though such expansion was unnecessary for attracting FDI. Tracing the growing protection to both external pressure and internal push, the chapter contends that intellectual property reforms were introduced in China because they promoted economic development in certain parts of the country and resulted in the creation of local stakeholders who benefited from and lobbied for stronger protection.

INTELLECTUAL PROPERTY AND FOREIGN DIRECT INVESTMENT

Conventional wisdom holds that strong intellectual property protection is needed to attract foreign investment in less developed countries, because firms are reluctant to invest in a foreign country unless they are assured of protection of their intellectual assets and financial investment. However, recent empirical research questions this conventional wisdom. As Carsten Fink, Keith Maskus, Carlos Primo Braga and other economists have shown, intellectual property protection is more likely to attract FDI if two additional conditions are met (Maskus, 1998, pp. 130–31; 2000; Primo Braga and Fink, 1998, p. 164). First, the country needs to have a strong capacity to imitate foreign products and technologies. If local competitors are unable to copy these products and technologies, the business interests of foreign firms are unlikely to be threatened, and intellectual property protection will be unnecessary. Second, the country needs to have a sufficiently large market to enable foreign firms to capture economies of scale or scope (Heald, 2003, p. 266). In a country that lacks such a market, foreign firms are unlikely to find it advantageous to move their productions abroad.

Even if these two conditions are met, policy makers still have to question what form of protection needs to be strengthened in order to promote economic development. Paul Heald and Keith Maskus each suggested that firms that seek to establish manufacturing or research-and-development plants are unlikely to require more protection than what is needed to ensure the non-disclosure of technologies brought in by foreign firms (Heald, 2003, pp. 258–60; Maskus, 1998, pp. 119–28). While these firms need trade secrets and contractual protection, firms seeking to establish markets for finished products need copyright, patent and trademark protection instead. Thus, it is important to separate investment decisions that seek to relocate manufacturing or research-and-development facilities from those that seek to market finished products.

While strong intellectual property protection is a main concern for marketing decisions, a decision to relocate manufacturing facilities is likely to be determined by such 'location advantages' as 'market size and growth, local demand patterns, transport costs and distance from markets, low wage costs in relation to labor productivity, abundant natural resources, and trade protection that could encourage "tariff-jumping" investments' (Maskus, 1998, p. 123). Likewise, a decision to relocate research-and-development facilities is likely to be affected by 'the level of education and training of the local workforce, the condition of its financial sector, the health of its legal system, and the transparency of governmental procedures' (Heald, 2003, p. 259).

To make things more complicated, firms can resort to many different investment strategies, and FDI is only one of them. Using John Dunning's ownership–location–internalization framework (Dunning, 1981, pp. 110–12), economists have shown that, even in the presence of favorable location advantages, firms still need to decide whether they want to serve foreign markets through FDI, export finished products to the less developed market, conduct arm's-length technology licensing, set up joint ventures with local manufacturers or distributors or ignore the foreign market entirely (Maskus, 1998, p. 130). As Carlos Primo Braga and Carsten Fink explained:

> In order for firms to invest abroad, two further conditions must be met. First, the foreign country must offer location advantages that make it more profitable to locate business abroad. Location advantages are usually associated with factors such as high transportation costs and tariffs, low input prices, access to distribution networks, and local regulatory environments. Second, it must be more profitable for firms to internalize production rather than to sell or license their intellectual assets to independent local firms in the foreign country. Internalization advantages take the form of avoiding transaction costs with potential licensees, controlling inputs, and protecting quality. (Primo Braga and Fink, 1998, p. 170)

While the strength or weakness of intellectual property protection will 'influence a firm's decision to internalize or externalize its intellectual assets', it is only one of the many location advantages that influence such a decision (ibid., p. 171). As Keith Maskus put it in the FDI context, 'IPRs are an important component of the general regulatory system, including taxation, investment regulations, production incentives, trade policies, and competition rules. The joint implementation of an overall pro-competitive business environment matters most for FDI' (Maskus, 1998, p. 129).

Paradoxically, the strengthening of intellectual property protection may encourage firms to conduct more arm's-length technology licensing, which in turn will result in a reduction of FDI. As Primo Braga and Fink explained, intellectual property protection can affect foreign investment in two negative ways: 'First, stronger IPR protection provides title holders with increased market power and could, at least theoretically, cause firms to actually divest and reduce their service to foreign countries. Second, higher levels of protection may cause [transnational corporations] to switch their preferred mode of delivery from foreign production to licensing' (Primo Braga and Fink, 1998, p. 172). Whether a firm will choose to license will depend on transaction costs – in particular, the robustness of the local regulatory regimes, the existence of a contracting culture and experience and the availability of information needed to evaluate the transactions. In places where there is limited intellectual property protection, the firm's need to internalize foreign production to maintain direct control over their proprietary assets may also affect licensing decisions (ibid.). If the firm chooses to externalize its production through, say, licensing, stronger intellectual property protection arguably would have the 'cancel out' effect of reducing FDI.

Finally, most firms do not need to make the difficult decision between relocating their entire facilities and not relocating at all. They can simply decide which type of operations they want to relocate abroad and whether they want to combine FDI with other investment strategies, such as export, licensing or establishment of joint ventures. Even if they choose to relocate abroad, they can still decide 'where to invest and in what kind of facilities, whether to purchase existing operations or construct new plants (so-called "greenfield investments"), which production techniques to pursue, and how large an equity position to take with potential local partners' (Maskus, 1998, p. 113).

Economists generally distinguish between 'horizontal FDI' and 'vertical FDI'.[2] While the former refers to the investment made when 'firms establish plants abroad to produce the same or similar goods for local or regional markets', the latter 'occurs if plants in different countries produce outputs that serve as inputs in other plants' (Primo Braga and Fink, 1998, pp. 172–3). Although intellectual property protection affects both horizontal and vertical FDI, the amount and composition of FDI vary according to the impact of such protection on the particular production process.

For example, Edwin Mansfield observed in his influential study for the World Bank that,

> [w]hile US firms may be quite willing to invest considerable amounts in sales and distribution outlets and in rudimentary production and assembly facilities in countries with weak protection, their investments in R and D facilities or in facilities to manufacture components or complete products may be more likely to go to countries with stronger protection systems. (Mansfield, 1994, p. 17)

Because '[v]ertical FDI is more prevalent among [multinational enterprises] that invest in developing (low-wage) economies, while horizontal FDI tends to characterize the investment decisions of MNEs operating across borders within the industrialized, developed nations', the amount and proportion of each type of investment may fluctuate with the country's economic development (Maskus, 1998, p. 120). As the country becomes more developed economically, the amount of horizontal FDI may increase, while that of vertical FDI may decrease.

In sum, countries that lack a strong imitative capacity and a sufficiently large market are unlikely to benefit from stronger intellectual property protection. However, even if countries meet these two prerequisites, stronger intellectual property protection may be unnecessary for attracting FDI. It depends on the complex interactions between the different location advantages, especially when some of these advantages are significant enough to compensate for the lack or ineffectiveness of strong intellectual property protection. Thus, the relationship between the strength of intellectual property protection and FDI remains theoretically ambiguous.

THE CHINA EXCEPTION

Commentators often consider China as an exception to the causal relationship between the strength of intellectual property protection and the amount of FDI attracted to the country. However, China is not the exception they suggested. Rather, it illustrates well the ambiguity of this relationship and the complex interplay of the different location advantages that can affect private investment decisions.

To begin with, China has met the two prerequisites needed for a country to benefit from stronger intellectual property protection. Since the reopening of its market to foreign trade in the late 1970s, China has developed a strong imitative capacity. In fact, such capacity explains China's ability to produce a large amount of pirated and counterfeit products. Moreover, China has seen tremendous economic growth in the past two decades (Bergsten et al., 2006, p. 18; Yu et al., 2003, p. 3). Today, China boasts a healthy market of hundreds of millions of customers, even though it has yet to offer one billion customers as some would hope. It also has become one of the world's largest surplus countries, possessing one of the most sizeable foreign exchange reserves in the world (Bergsten et al., 2006, p. 4).

Nevertheless, intellectual property protection in the country remains inadequate and ineffective, and it is unlikely that foreign firms were attracted to China because of its intellectual property system. Instead, firms often relocate to China to take advantage of the lower production costs and the emerging market. To many of these firms, the lower costs and the promise of an enormous market would easily make up for the losses incurred by ineffective intellectual property protection (Tackaberry, 1998, p. 26). While these firms certainly welcome greater intellectual property reforms, they do not find stronger protection a prerequisite for obtaining profits in the first place. In fact, many major Western firms – such as Coca-Cola, Kodak, Motorola, Procter & Gamble and Siemens – have already been enjoying substantial profits for years despite serious piracy and counterfeiting problems (Sun, 2004, pp. 4–5). Thus, instead of seeing strong intellectual property protection as the necessary precursor to profitability, they see it more as a means to 'increas[e their] already acceptable profit ratios' (ibid., p. 5).

Other firms, especially those that are new to China or that are unfamiliar with the local conditions, have been less successful. Nevertheless, they consider the emerging Chinese market too large to ignore. While some consider the losses unavoidable as they build up their market share and improve their position in this emerging market, others write off their piracy-related losses as promotional expenses. The latter approach easily reminds one of the remark Microsoft's founder Bill Gates made a few years ago. When questioned about the widespread piracy of Microsoft software in China, Gates observed:

> Although about three million computers get sold every year in China, people don't pay for the software. Someday they will, though. And as long as they're going to steal it, we want them to steal ours. They'll get sort of addicted, and then we'll somehow figure out how to collect sometime in the next decade. (Schlender et al., 1998)

Recent research, however, has revealed a more complicated picture concerning FDI in China. The amount of FDI in a country does not depend only on 'pull' factors, but also on 'push' factors, such as those that have made the country unappealing for local production. As Huang Yasheng pointed out in his provocative book, *Selling China*, the inefficiencies of the Chinese economic system and the country's preferential treatment of foreign investors have led to a large amount of FDI in the country (Huang, 2005). Because commentators tend to focus on the attractions of the Chinese market, they often ignore how '[t]he poor profitability of the state sector, the credit constraints on the part of Chinese private firms, the insecurity of private property rights, and the weaknesses of domestic firms have all driven up China's demand for FDI' (ibid., p. 81).

To Professor Huang, the considerable amount of FDI in China may reflect the weakness, rather than the strength, of the Chinese market. As he explained:

> China's low labor – and land – costs do not automatically motivate a Hong Kong firm to *invest* in China; instead, they motivate a Hong Kong firm (or any other firm) *to do more business* with China, as opposed to doing more business with, say, Mexico. China's low labor costs tell us something about the location of a labor-intensive production facility, but not about who owns it. (Ibid, p. 57)

Professor Huang therefore credited the superior regulatory and legal treatments of foreign-invested enterprises as an important motivation for private entrepreneurs in China to seek out FDI from its neighbors (ibid., p. 90). His thesis also illuminates why a substantial amount of investment was derived from businesses in Hong Kong and Taiwan as well as those owned by the Chinese diaspora. After all, if local firms have to reach out for FDI, they are more likely to turn to firms in the so-called Greater China.

In sum, the drastically lower production costs, the country's enormous market, its inefficient economic system and the preferential treatment of foreign investors have all helped to attract FDI in China. Because these factors more than compensate for the country's weak intellectual property protection, FDI in China increased substantially despite limited intellectual property protection in the country. China therefore is not an exception to the causal relationship between intellectual property protection and FDI, but an ideal case study to illustrate the ambiguity of this relationship and the complex interactions between the many location advantages that affect private investment decisions. After all, as Keith Maskus pointed out, if stronger intellectual property protection always led to more FDI, 'recent FDI flows to developing economies would have gone largely to sub-Saharan Africa and Eastern Europe . . . [rather than] China, Brazil, and other high-growth, large-market developing economies with weak IPRs' (Maskus, 1998, p. 129).

INTELLECTUAL PROPERTY REFORMS IN CHINA

'Since 1983, FDI [in China] has grown from less than $1 billion a year to more than $60 billion, and it is projected to soon reach $100 billion annually' (Navarro, 2007, p. 13). Today, China is one of the world's largest recipients of FDI, with capital inflows of about $50 billion, behind the United States and the United Kingdom (Chow, 2007, p. 198). Such an influx of FDI not only provides China with the foreign capital needed for economic modernization, but also results in technology transfer, job creation, development of human capital and generation of tax revenues (Sherwood, 1990, pp. 191–9). Although economists have pleaded for caution in considering the benefits of FDI to recipient countries (Maskus, 1998, p. 146), there is no denial that the influx of foreign capital has contributed to China's recent rise to its status as an emerging economic superpower.

As pointed out earlier, strong intellectual property protection is not always needed for attracting FDI. In fact, stronger protection may reduce investment by encouraging investors to conduct arm's-length transactions by licensing their products. Such protection would also reduce the net gains in economic welfare from increased FDI by incurring significant costs, such as administrative and enforcement costs, adjustment costs due to labor displacement, social costs associated with monopoly pricing, higher imitation and innovation costs and potential costs resulting from the abuse of intellectual property rights (Maskus et al., 2005, pp. 302–6). Stronger intellectual property protection therefore would drain the country's scarce governmental resources, render cutting-edge foreign technologies inaccessible and stifle the development of local industries (Giunta and Shang, 1993, p. 331; Yu, 2000, pp. 189–90). Given the significant costs of strengthening intellectual property protection, Chinese policy makers and commentators understandably were worried that stronger protection would slow down the country's economic progress and therefore would make it difficult for the country to catch up with its Western developed neighbors.

Indeed, as Rod Falvey, Neil Foster and David Greenaway have shown recently, although intellectual property protection promotes innovation in high-income countries and technology flows in low-income ones, middle-income countries may suffer from offsetting losses due to the reduced scope of imitation (Falvey et al., 2006). Likewise, as the UK-based Commission on Intellectual Property Rights cautioned, 'rapid [economic] growth is more often associated with weaker IP protection. In technologically advanced developing countries, there is some evidence that IP protection becomes important at a stage of development, but that stage is not until a country is well into the category of upper middle income developing countries' (Commission on Intellectual Property Rights, 2002, p. 22).

If the costs of strong intellectual property protection are not enough, the costs of introducing an inappropriate intellectual property system can be quite high for less developed countries. Although overprotection of intellectual property rights harms both developed and less developed countries, it usually harms less developed countries more than it would harm their developed counterparts. Many less developed countries lack the economic strengths and established correction mechanisms to overcome problems created by an unbalanced system (Yu, 2006a, pp. 382–3; 2007, p. 890). As the Commission noted, 'if anything, the costs of getting the IP system "wrong" in a developing country are likely to be far higher than in developed countries. Most developed countries have sophisticated systems of competition regulation to ensure that abuses of any monopoly rights cannot unduly affect the public interest' (Commission on Intellectual Property Rights, 2002, p. 4). Even if stronger intellectual property protection is beneficial to less developed countries in the long run, they may lack the needed wealth, infrastructure and technological base to take advantage of the opportunities created by the system in the short run.

In sum, all of these potential negative impacts of stronger intellectual property protection lead one to wonder why China introduced reforms to offer stronger intellectual property protection at all. After all, both theories and actual practice have suggested that China would have limited net economic benefits from stronger intellectual property protection during the first decade of the reopening of the Chinese market to foreign trade. Acknowledging the Chinese leaders' lack of focus on these net benefits in the early development of the modern Chinese intellectual property system, this chapter traces the intellectual property reforms to both external pressure and internal push.

External Pressure

Shortly after China reopened its market to foreign trade in the late 1970s, China and the United States signed the Agreement on Trade Relations Between the United States of

America and the People's Republic of China, which, among other things, called for reciprocal protection of copyrights, patents and trademarks owned by the nationals of the other party. Pursuant to this agreement, China became a member of the World Intellectual Property Organization (WIPO). It also promulgated a new trademark law in 1982 and a new patent law in 1984 and joined the Paris Convention in 1985. Notwithstanding these new developments, China afforded authors and inventors very limited protection, due to the leaders' concern about establishing new private property interests in a socialist economic system, their belief that strong intellectual property protection is inappropriate for a less developed country like China, and their inexperience with Western forms of intellectual property protection (Alford, 1995, pp. 66, 70; Mertha, 2005, pp. 84–6). While the new laws granted individuals rights in their marks and inventions, these statutes included many limits that rendered the original grants largely insignificant.

Concerned about the lack of intellectual property protection in China, copyright in particular, US businesses lobbied their government heavily for stronger pressure on China. In the late 1980s and early 1990s, the US government repeatedly threatened China with a series of economic sanctions, trade wars, non-renewal of most-favored-nation status and opposition to China's entry into the WTO (Yu, 2000, pp. 140–51). Such threats eventually led to the issuance or signing of two memoranda of understanding in 1989 and 1992, an 'agreement' regarding intellectual property rights in 1995 (which appeared in the form of an 'exchange of letters' with an attached action plan) and an 'accord' reiterating China's commitment to strengthening intellectual property protection in 1996.

Although the seldom-mentioned 1989 memorandum of understanding reassured the United States that China would strengthen its protection for computer software, the 1992 memorandum was the 'first full bilateral IPR agreement' between China and the United States (Massey, 2006, p. 235). In retrospect, the 1992 memorandum was effective in revamping China's intellectual property system. Pursuant to that document, China acceded to the Berne Convention and ratified the Geneva Convention. China also amended its 1990 Copyright Law, issued new implementing regulations and adopted a new unfair competition law that provided trade secret protection.

Likewise, the 1995 Agreement was effective in helping China create an institutional infrastructure conducive to protecting and enforcing rights created under this new intellectual property regime. The Agreement formally introduced the State Council Working Conference on Intellectual Property Rights, which was later replaced by the State Intellectual Property Office, as well as the Enforcement Task Forces (Yu, 2000, p. 152). To protect CDs, laser discs and CD-ROMs, the agreement established a unique copyright verification system, proposing to punish by administrative and judicial means any manufacturer of audiovisual products who failed to comply with the identifier requirement. The agreement also called for title registration with the National Copyright Administration and local copyright authorities of foreign audiovisual products and computer software in CD-ROM format. In addition, the agreement required customs offices to intensify border protection for all imports and exports of CDs, laser discs, CD-ROMS and trademarked goods. The agreement further stipulated that relevant authorities would conduct training and education on intellectual property protection throughout China. Finally, the agreement provided that the Working Conference would develop a transparent legal system while compiling and publishing guidelines regarding application and protection in various areas of intellectual property law.

Notwithstanding these two agreements, piracy remained rampant in China in the mid-1990s, and the United States was estimated to have lost $2 billion of revenues annually due to copyright piracy (Faison, 1998). To make things worse, the ineffectiveness of the coercive tactics used by the United States Trade Representative (USTR) has become apparent to not just Chinese negotiators and seasoned commentators, but also to the US industries and the American public. Although the two countries reached another 'accord' in 1996, that document clearly revealed the limitation of the coercive approach. The document included neither significant new terms nor terms that improved market access of American products; instead, it merely reaffirmed China's commitment to protect intellectual property rights made under the intellectual property agreement signed the year before (Yu, 2001, p. 14).

As industry support decreased, the Clinton administration abandoned its strong-arm tactics shortly after the 1996 negotiations (Yu, 2003, p. 365). Although the United States continued to exert pressure on China during the negotiation of China's accession to the WTO and undertook frequent consultations with Chinese officials, the United States has yet to revive its coercive approach – partly because of the approach's limitations and partly because of its impracticality after China's WTO membership. Under the WTO, countries are prohibited from taking retaliatory measures before they have exhausted all of the actions permissible under the rules (World Trade Organization, 1999). Except in areas that are outside the scope of the TRIPS Agreement, China's WTO membership has greatly constrained the United States' ability to exert external pressure on China in the intellectual property area. To make up for the lack of external pressure, US businesses now exert pressure from within the country – through persuasion, business pressure and alliances with local stakeholders and authorities.

In February 2005, US policy makers and trade groups again urged the administration to file a formal complaint against China with the WTO Dispute Settlement Body concerning inadequate intellectual property protection (Yu, 2006a, p. 923). A few months later, the United States, in conjunction with Japan and Switzerland, invoked article 63(3) of the TRIPS Agreement to formally request 'clarifications regarding specific cases of IPR enforcement that China has identified for the years 2001 through 2004, and other relevant cases' (Allgeier, 2005). In April 2007, the United States finally requested consultations with China concerning its failure to protect and enforce intellectual property rights in pursuance to the TRIPS Agreement. Five months later, a WTO dispute settlement panel was established to resolve the dispute. If the United States did so, and if China were found to have violated the TRIPS Agreement, external pressure again might play an important role in unleashing and accelerating intellectual property reforms in China.

Internal Push

Alignment with the national modernization goals

While researchers have explored extensively the relationship between intellectual property protection and economic development, they rarely examine the rhetorical effects of the claim that stronger intellectual property protection will promote economic development. The lack of such an examination is understandable considering the difficulty in quantifying and assessing rhetorical effects. Nevertheless, rhetoric is needed to persuade the populace to accept a new government policy. It may also provide the direction and psychological incentives needed for promoting economic development.

To some extent, the rhetorical significance of the claim that stronger intellectual property protection will promote economic development is similar to the significance of the claim that intellectual property is property. Despite the uneasy analogy of intellectual property to real property, intellectual property rights holders have widely used the rhetoric of private property to push for stronger protection.[3] Meanwhile, foreign rights holders and governments have also used the economic development rationale to entice foreign leaders and policy makers to ratchet up intellectual property protection and, more specifically, to establish the TRIPS Agreement within the WTO. As Daniel Gervais recounted, developed countries and the lobbies that pushed for stronger intellectual property protection believed that 'TRIPS was a difficult but essential measure to jumpstart global economic development', while less developed countries 'were told to overlook the distasteful aspects of introducing or increasing intellectual property protection and enforcement in exchange for longer-term economic health' (Gervais, 2007, p. 43). Similarly, Edmund Kitch argued that less developed countries agreed to stronger intellectual property protection during the TRIPS negotiations because they found such protection in their own interests, although the negotiation records and the reactions of less developed countries offered very limited support for Professor Kitch's account (Kitch, 1994, p. 138; Maskus, 1998).[4]

While the rhetorical linkage of intellectual property to economic development is important to induce less developed countries to offer stronger protection, it is particularly important to a country like China, which has placed heavy emphasis on symbols and political movements and was emerging from autarky and diplomatic isolation. Since the reopening of the Chinese market to foreign trade in the late 1970s, Deng Xiaoping and other reformist leaders advocated a pragmatic 'economics in command' approach to replace Mao Zedong's 'politics in command' approach. Seeing economic wealth as the foundation of China's power, the reformist leadership believed 'whether China could have a rightful place in the world of nations depended on China's domestic economic development' (Zheng, 1999, p. 17). These leaders therefore vigorously pushed for the Four Modernizations to develop China's world-class strengths in agriculture, industry, science and technology and national defense. They also established Special Economic Zones to transform socio-economic conditions in coastal areas and renewed diplomatic and commercial ties with the United States, Japan and other Western developed countries. The 1979 US–China trade agreement was a product of this urgent push for greater internationalization.

While economic development was easily justified by the severe need for reforms following the Cultural Revolution, the death of Mao Zedong and the subsequent arrest of the infamous Gang of Four, the justification for intellectual property reforms remained elusive. Indeed, when China reopened its market to foreign trade in the late 1970s, both the Chinese leaders and the populace considered intellectual property an alien concept transplanted from Western soil. As William Alford pointed out in his seminal work, *To Steal a Book is an Elegant Offense*, the notion of intellectual property protection did not take root in China despite earlier attempts to transplant the concept onto the country through bilateral commercial treaties at the turn of the twentieth century and intellectual property reforms during the Republican era (Alford, 1995, pp. 36–55). Even if those reforms introduced the concept to the Chinese populace, the numerous class struggles, mass movements and the Cultural Revolution that rejected ownership of private property virtually eliminated from public consciousness the concept of intellectual property (Yu, 2001, pp. 21–2).

Thus, when this concept was *re*introduced in the 1980s, the justification for such a concept was badly needed. In his well-cited chapter concerning justifications for intellectual property protection, William Fisher identified four possible justifications – utility, labor, personality and social planning (Fisher, 2001, pp. 169–73). For a society that was making a transition from a command economy, rather than today's socialist market economy, the first and second justifications were easily deemed unsuitable. Indeed, early Chinese intellectual property laws were filled with compromises that resulted in what commentators called 'socialist legality with Chinese characteristics' (Alford, 1995, p. 70). While the Chinese leadership was anxious to create a stimulus for inventions and to rehabilitate scientists, inventors and academics to make up for the time lost to the Cultural Revolution (ibid., p. 65), the leaders remained gravely concerned about the impact of new intellectual property rights on the country's socialist economic system.

The third justification, which was based on personality theories, was attractive to the Chinese, because it sat well with Communist ideology and the Soviet notion of non-property-based protection of authorship. Recent research by Mira Sundara Rajan, for example, has shown that the Russian Copyright Act of 1928 granted limited recognition to the authors' property interests by 'plac[ing] them within the broader context of a non-property theory of authorship' (Sundara Rajan, 2005, p. 333). As a 1938 commentary on the Russian law noted, the Soviet author's right 'has the objective of protecting to the maximum the personal *and property* interests of the author, coupled with the assurance of the widest distribution of the product of literature, science and the arts among the broad masses of the toilers' (ibid., p. 334). Nevertheless, the personality justification – in particular, its emphasis on moral rights – was inconsistent with foreign demands for stronger intellectual property protection, which reflected the interests of and the more utilitarian approach embraced by Western rights holders.

The most suitable justification was therefore what Professor Fisher described as 'social planning', which ranges from the development of the economy to the nurturing of an attractive intellectual culture (Fisher, 2001, pp. 192–3; Netanel, 1996, p. 288). As he explained, '[t]his approach is similar to utilitarianism in its teleological orientation, but dissimilar in its willingness to deploy visions of a desirable society richer than the conceptions of "social welfare" deployed by utilitarians' (Fisher, 2001, p. 172). This justification therefore fitted well with China in the early 1980s, and economic modernization provided the needed 'social planning' justification for a new intellectual property system. Since then, intellectual property reforms have been linked to the country's rapid economic development and have benefited from the push for continuous economic reforms.

Politically, backing the newly-established intellectual property system with rhetoric that was consistent with the national modernization goals was very important. As David Zweig suggested, directions from the leadership and rhetoric that conveys these directions are critical to a country that is undergoing 'a fundamental change in [its] international orientation' (Zweig, 2002, p. 27). Because the Chinese leaders were inexperienced with intellectual property protection and had to constantly struggle with unfamiliar concepts and models introduced during the transitional period, the alignment of intellectual property reforms with the national modernization goals also allowed leaders to defend intellectual property reforms on more familiar terms.

In addition, because reformist leaders were constantly challenged by their more conservative counterparts, who were uncomfortable with the country's rapid socio-economic changes and the social ills brought about by these changes, the rhetoric allowed the reformist leaders to deflate criticisms of their kowtowing to foreign interests, especially in times of considerable external pressure from the United States. Instead, the leaders could highlight the economic benefits of stronger intellectual property protection and justify intellectual property reforms as an important leapfrogging tool to enable China to catch up with its more advanced trading partners. The reformist leadership could also tie the reforms to the growing nationalist sentiments that longed for China to regain its rightful place following centuries of humiliation and semi-colonial rule (Hsü, 2000, pp. 660–61).

Moreover, the fact that stronger intellectual property protection is unnecessary for attracting FDI does not mean that an increase in protection would not result in more economic development. In fact, it would, at least in certain parts of the country or in selected industrial sectors. The more profits a firm can obtain, the more likely it is to expand its business, and the greater is its investment in or trade with the country. This is particularly true with respect to a country that has a strong imitative capacity and an enormous growing market. Indeed, stronger intellectual property protection may also provide to foreign investors important signals of a favorable investment climate (Alford, 1995, p. 68; Maskus, 1998, pp. 137–8). As Claudio Frischtak noted, a country's overall investment climate is often more influential on FDI decisions than the strength of the intellectual property protection it offers (Frischtak, 1993, pp. 99–100). Likewise, Carsten Fink and Keith Maskus stated that '[a] poor country hoping to attract inward FDI would be better advised to improve its overall investment climate and business infrastructure than to strengthen its patent regime sharply, an action that would have little effect on its own' (Fink and Maskus, 2005, p. 7). Thus, stronger intellectual property protection might result in more foreign investment from existing investors as well as those who otherwise would not invest in the country. While serious questions remain concerning whether stronger protection would result in net gains in economic welfare within the country, and whether such protection, on balance, would benefit the country, those questions do not negate the fact that stronger intellectual property protection would induce *some* economic development in the country.

In sum, even though stronger intellectual property protection is unnecessary for promoting economic development, the claim that stronger intellectual property protection would promote economic development provided the needed internal push for intellectual property reforms in the first decade and a half following the reopening of the Chinese market to foreign trade. In retrospect, that claim, to some extent, was similar to what psychologists have termed a 'self-fulfilling prophecy'. Although people might not be able to prove conclusively whether stronger intellectual property protection would lead to greater economic development, they would accept a higher level of protection if they believed such a link existed. This higher level of protection, in turn, would result in greater economic development in certain parts of the country and in selected industrial sectors. As more local stakeholders stood to benefit from stronger protection, they would lobby for even stronger protection. Eventually, the belief in the benefits of stronger intellectual property protection would result in more economic development, regardless of whether the link existed in the first place. And the cycle would repeat itself.

Development of local stakeholders

China experienced major economic setbacks after Tiananmen in 1989 and the subsequent turbulent bilateral relationship with the United States and other Western countries. Fortunately, its economy quickly recovered following Deng Xiaoping's famous 'tour' of southern China in 1992. In March 1993, the National People's Congress incorporated into the Chinese Constitution the concept of the socialist market economy, which contrasted powerfully with a command or centrally-planned economy.[5] Four years later, the private sector was designated an important component of the changing economy, and 'red capitalists' were invited to join the Chinese Communist Party at the Sixteenth Party Congress in 2001 (Prestowitz, 2005, p. 27). Today, article 13 of the Constitution stipulates explicitly that '[c]itizens' lawful private property is inviolable', and booming real estate markets appear in many major Chinese cities. Most recently, the National People's Congress enacted a much-anticipated, yet controversial law to offer explicit protection to private property (Kahn, 2007).

Accompanying this rapid economic development and growth was the emergence of local stakeholders who stood to benefit from stronger intellectual property protection. Consider, for example, the software industry, which has experienced tremendous growth since the mid-1990s. By 1997, the value of the software market had doubled from RMB 6.8 billion in 1995 to RMB 12.6 billion (Xue and Zheng, 1999, p. 8). The Chinese government also has been active in developing the local software industry, establishing bases in Liaoning, Hunan, Shandong and Sichuan Provinces and in Beijing, Shanghai and Zhuhai districts (ibid., p. 9).

Today, the number of private software companies has greatly increased. Although state-owned enterprises once dominated the Chinese economy, a large number of employees of these enterprises are now entering the private sector – or, in the Chinese parlance, 'plunging into the sea' (*xiàhǎi*). As the late Zheng Chengsi and Xue Hong, two leading commentators on Chinese intellectual property law, observed:

> In recent years . . . many software engineers resigned from state enterprises or research institutes, taking software products (finished or unfinished) created during the course of employment with them, and joined private software companies or established their own companies. These private companies immediately produced and marketed the software products, and became competitors of state software enterprises. (Xue and Zheng, 2002, pp. 104–5)

In the late 1990s, intellectual property reforms were given a further push by the emerging consciousness of the need to develop a knowledge-based economy. As Lester Thurow noted,

> [k]nowledge is the new basis for wealth. . . . In the past, when capitalists talked about their wealth, they were talking about their ownership of plant and equipment or natural resources. In the future when capitalists talk about their wealth, they will be talking about their control of knowledge. (Thurow, 1999, p. xiii)

Perhaps under the influence of the Internet boom in other parts of the world, the phrase 'knowledge economy' suddenly began to appear in major Chinese newspapers, such as *The People's Daily* and *Guangming Daily*. Government officials used the phrase frequently in their presentations (Xue and Zheng, 1999, p. 7), while Chinese businesses quickly adopted words like 'e-commerce' and 'e-business' to enhance public image and stock market value (Xue and Zheng, 2002, p. xl).

Although the Internet bust a few years later slowed online developments throughout the world, the drive for the development of a knowledge-based economy in China continued, and the Chinese Internet population grew exponentially. In October 1997, there were only 299 000 computers connected to the Internet and 620 000 Internet users (Yu, 2003, p. 371). Based on the July 2007 survey by the China Internet Network Information Center (CNNIC), there are now 58.4 million computers connected to the Internet and 137 million Internet users, second only to the United States (China Internet Network Information Center, 2007, p. 5).

As the use of the Internet and new communications technologies continues to increase, Chinese policy makers have paid greater attention to issues concerning intellectual property rights in the digital environment. For example, the 2001 copyright law amendments addressed for the first time online copyright issues. In May 2006, the State Council promulgated the Regulations on the Protection of the Right of Communication Through Information Network. Most recently, China acceded to the WIPO Copyright Treaty and the WIPO Performances and Phonograms Treaty. These developments make a lot of sense. Greater certainty over the scope of rights protected on the Internet is important both to local and foreign content providers and will greatly facilitate electronic commerce and broadband deployment.

The biggest push for intellectual property reforms in the 1990s was China's accession to the WTO. As China prepared to join the international trading body, it undertook a complete overhaul of its intellectual property system, amending its copyright, patent and trademark laws. In addition, it introduced a large number of implementing regulations and administrative measures, such as those concerning the registration of computer software and those on the protection of topographies of integrated circuits. To help courts interpret these new laws and regulations, the Supreme People's Court also issued a number of judicial interpretations (Sun, 2004, pp. 66–7).

In November 2001, the WTO members finally approved the proposal to admit China to the international trading body during the Fourth Ministerial Conference in Doha, Qatar. After 15 years of exhaustive negotiations, China formally became the 143rd member of the WTO on 11 December 2001. Although the accession process was complicated and involved many inextricable factors, it would not be far-fetched to argue that China might still remain outside the WTO had it not strengthened its protection of intellectual property rights (Yu, 2003, p. 372). Indeed, some commentators considered the WTO membership a major impetus for China's recent improvements in intellectual property protection. As Professors Zheng and Xue explained:

> In general, China's entry to the WTO significantly influenced the speed and scope of the development of the Chinese IP law system. It is interesting to note that IP rights reforms kept pace with Chinese WTO negotiations. When the negotiations encountered obstacles, the IP rights reform slowed down; when the negotiations reached agreements to promote the accession process, the IP rights reform accelerated noticeably. Since China has become a member of the WTO, Chinese IP law reform has also peaked. (Xue and Zheng, 2002, p. xxxix)

To some extent, the economic benefits and reputational gains that were associated with China's accession to the WTO far exceeded the socio-economic costs incurred by increased intellectual property protection. By linking the two issues together, the Chinese began to understand that the stakes for the lack of intellectual property protection extended beyond the intellectual property arena, covering almost every other area that implicates international trade, including agriculture, banking, electronics, insurance, professional services, securities, telecommunications and textiles (Yu, 2003, p. 371). While they might not be excited about introducing stronger intellectual property protection, they certainly were reluctant to give up WTO-related trade benefits that were linked to such protection.

Moreover, the moderate costs of stronger protection required by the TRIPS Agreement were incomparable to the high costs of other reforms required by the WTO accession. If the leaders and the Chinese public were willing to accept the costs of these other reforms, it was natural for them to accept the costs of TRIPS-related reforms. In fact, one could make a strong claim that China could easily recoup its losses in the intellectual property area by obtaining gains in other trade areas, such as agriculture or textiles. Even critics of the overall economic benefits of China's accession had a tough time responding to the strong nationalistic sentiments that considered the WTO accession an important means for China to regain its past glory, not to mention the general excitement, rejuvenation and other psychological benefits brought about by the accession.

Nevertheless, one needs to be cautious about how much one attributes the recent intellectual property reforms to China's WTO accession. Although commentators and policy makers have widely credited the WTO accession for the recent changes in the Chinese intellectual property system, it is important not to overlook the many internal developments within the country, including the Chinese leaders' changing attitude toward the rule of law, the emergence of private property rights and local stakeholders, the increasing concerns about ambiguities over relationships in state-owned enterprises and the government leaders' active push for modernization (Yu, 2006a, p. 908). While the WTO accession may be important, China's *guóqíng*, or national conditions, continues to play a very important role in shaping intellectual property reforms in China.

Increasing shift toward an export-driven economy

Today, China is 'the world's fourth largest economy and the third largest trading nation' (Bergsten et al., 2006, p. 3). Its imports 'tripled from $225 billion in 2000 to $600 billion in 2005', and the country 'accounted for about 12 percent of the growth of global trade', an impressive jump from only 4 per cent in 2000 (ibid., p. 73). Its factories 'make 70 percent of the world's toys, 60 percent of its bicycles, half its shoes, and one-third of its luggage' (Shenkar, 2005, p. 2). China also 'builds half of the world's microwave ovens, one-third of its television sets and air conditioners, a quarter of its washers, and one-fifth of its refrigerators' (ibid., p. 3). As the Chinese economy becomes increasingly driven by exports to other countries, intellectual property protection will become even more important than it was a decade ago. As Daniel Chow explained:

> [g]lobal competitiveness in the modern age is directly linked to the level of technology in goods and services. Studies indicate that the higher the level of technology involved in goods and services, the higher the growth rate of exports. . . . In the 1990s, China began to build a trade surplus with many nations based upon its low manufacturing costs. While China has been able to dominate in low-technology/labor-intensive industries, China realizes that to continue its growth in exports, it must move up the ladder into more technology-intensive goods and services. To do so, China must acquire access to advanced technology. (Chow, 2006, p. 206)

Indeed, 'China, like most nations, encourages exports because export sales contribute to a favorable trade balance and can earn United States dollars or other forms of hard currency' (ibid., p. 214). While Chinese companies were content to serve as original equipment manufacturers (OEM) for foreign firms a decade ago, they have now moved into high-end technology markets, such as those for cars and regional jets, while seeking to maintain their competitive edge over low-cost products (ibid., pp. 207–8; Shenkar, 2005, pp. 161–2). Thus, some commentators and pundits suggested that China's export-driven economic growth is likely to lead to greater future confrontations with the United States. As Peter Navarro observed, '[a]ny complete understanding of the Coming China Wars must begin with this observation: China's hyper-rate of economic growth is export driven; and the ability of the Chinese to conquer one export market after another, often in blitzkrieg fashion, derives from their ability to set the so-called China Price' (Navarro, 2007, p. 2).

Consider, for example, trademark protection, which is particularly important to an export-driven economy. The usual criticism of strong trademark protection in an emerging economy is that such protection would force local consumers to pay a premium for well-known foreign brands in exchange for no or very limited benefits. This is particularly true when local consumers are brand-conscious or when their purchase decisions are distorted by their obsession with social status, which they seek to gain by buying or owning more expensive foreign products. Because most of the branded products are made in China, local consumers are often asked to pay a higher price even though the quality of the products is no different from that of products made by local brand owners.

Moreover, by intentionally not offering trademark protection, countries may be able to take a free ride on the investment of foreign trademark holders, by earning profits as if they were selling genuine goods that bear the infringing marks. As foreign brand owners continue to advertise and promote their products, the local copycats would also benefit from the goodwill of the original products without incurring any advertising expenses. Such a competitive strategy, however, is ill-advised, especially for a country that has now become one of the world's largest exporters. As Professor Kitch explained, that strategy 'will result in a parasitical business that will always be dependent on the willingness of the targeted countries to tolerate the infringing imports . . . [and that] will never have an established market position that can lay a foundation for the development of an internationally competitive business' (Kitch, 1994, p. 168).

To be certain, local firms can ensure the marketability of their products in foreign countries by using non-infringing trademarks in foreign markets. Indeed, global firms have used that strategy to avoid infringement in selected markets. Nevertheless, such a strategy is costly, because it will not allow for the economies of scale commonly found in global production. That strategy also makes it difficult for local firms to learn how to establish market position by experimenting in the local market with brand development and trademark portfolio management. To some extent, one can see the local market as a 'playground' for Chinese export businesses to acquire the needed skills to set up internationally competitive businesses.

A case in point is the leading Chinese personal computer manufacturer, Lenovo (*Liánxiǎng*). When the company sought to expand business overseas a few years ago, it found out that its English name 'Legend' had already been registered and used as a trademark or trade name in many foreign countries. To avoid potential infringement and to ensure that it could become an official sponsor of the 2008 Beijing Olympics, it had no choice but to develop the new 'Lenovo' mark, which combined the first two letters of the 'Legend' mark with the word 'novo' (Ling, 2006, pp. 334–5). Interestingly, the 'Lenovo' mark has now become famous as a result of the worldwide media coverage of its purchase of IBM's personal computers division.

Lenovo, however, is not the only one. Compared to a decade ago, a number of Chinese companies have now achieved prominence in the international market, with their trademarks being recognized as well-known outside China (Sull with Wang, 2005). Examples of these famous local brands include Galanz (for microwave ovens), Haier (for household appliances), Huawei Technologies (for telecommunications equipment), Konka (for televisions) and TCL (for televisions). As China increases its exports of goods branded with globally recognized local trademarks, the importance of intellectual property protection to the country's future economic development cannot be ignored.

From the standpoint of internal economic development in China, trademark protection is even more beneficial than the protection afforded by other forms of intellectual property. The development of globally recognized trademarks requires neither considerable technological expertise nor initial heavy capital investment. Although the global market has been dominated by brands developed by major corporations in developed countries, less developed countries and smaller enterprises have their fair share of famous trademarks that are recognized throughout the world, especially in the fields of beer and liquor production – Bacardi (for Bermuda rum), Corona (for Mexican beer) and Tsingtao (for Chinese beer) easily come to mind (MacLaughlin et al., 1988, p. 104).[6] In fact, according to Interbrand, 'Bacardi is the world's 75th most valuable global brand, and with a valuation in excess of $3 billion, is worth comfortably more than the GDP of the country which produces it' (Anholt, 2005, p. 60).

From the standpoint of consumer welfare and economic self-sufficiency, it is also helpful to encourage local companies to catch up and compete with famous Western brands by developing more attractive products and better brand positioning (Yu, 2006a, p. 996). Instead, this brand building strategy 'fits [well] with the government's strategy of consolidating strategic industries . . . to create national champions that can hold their own in global markets and . . . to restore its imperial glory' (Shenkar, 2005, p. 158). Compared to foreign firms, local firms thus far have been very successful in the Chinese market. In this dynamic, yet immature market, 'consumers are still experimenting, and brands come and go with great speed' (Chee with West, 2004, p. 30; Yan, 2004, p. 95). As a result, local firms have the opportunity to attain market position and develop the next promising brands.

The ability of local firms to improve consumer loyalty and establish market position has been further enhanced by the failure of foreign firms to understand or adjust to the local market conditions. Studies, for example, have 'estimated that less than 10 percent of Chinese consumers have the level of disposable income that can afford to buy Western products' (Chee with West, 2004, p. 31). Yet many foreign businesses ignore this financial reality and insist on focusing on the high-end market, perhaps due to benefits from economies of scope and scale in global production, or to the firms' reluctance to lower the quality, and often the international reputation, of their products.

A case in point is the microwave market, which Galanz has overtaken recently. '[I]n 1993 only 1 per cent of Chinese consumers had microwaves. Consumption grew – but not in the pattern expected. By early 2000, nearly 90 per cent of the market was in cheaper models, with the Chinese company Galanz dominating' (ibid.). Similarly, although Whirlpool and Kelon were competitors for the manufacture of washing machines, the local manufacturer quickly won the race (Huang, 2005, pp. 193–4). Today, '[a]fter losing more than $100 million and shutting down most of its factories, Whirlpool . . . manufactures washing-machines for Guangdong Kelon' – a scenario that Whirlpool certainly did not foresee when it began its investment in China (Anholt, 2005, p. 64).

As China continues to increase exports and develop products under globally recognized trademarks, especially after the much-anticipated push around the 2008 Beijing Olympics (and again during the 2010 World Expo in Shanghai), the existence of effective intellectual property protection is likely to be of paramount importance. Significant improvement in trademark protection is therefore likely to be more important to China than similar improvement in the protection of other forms of intellectual property. In fact, the improved ability of Chinese businesses to develop globally famous brands may ultimately hold the key to converting those Chinese who are skeptical of intellectual property protection to global missionaries for greater intellectual property reforms.

CONCLUSION

Commentators have considered China the proverbial exception to the causal relationship between the strength of intellectual property protection and the amount of FDI attracted to a country. However, this chapter has shown that this causal relationship is more ambiguous than experts have claimed and China illustrates rather well the ambiguity of this relationship. While stronger intellectual property protection may be unnecessary for attracting FDI, this chapter has documented an undeniably intertwined relationship between intellectual property protection and economic development in China. Intellectual property protection can therefore be seen broadly as an integral and essential part of a complex innovation system that serves as a catalyst for economic development. If a country is to be further developed economically, the implementation of an effective and robust intellectual property system that is tailored to local needs and conditions is likely to be significant.

Today, piracy and counterfeiting problems remain widespread in China, and rights holders continue to be frustrated by the lack of enforcement of intellectual property rights in the country. However, at some point in the near future, China may reach a crossover point at which it will find it in its own interest to offer stronger intellectual property protection. Indeed, similar transformations occurred in Japan in the 1970s, in Hong Kong, Singapore, South Korea and Taiwan in the 1980s, and even in Germany and the United States many decades ago (Assafa, 1996, p. 120; Kingston, 2005, p. 658). It is only a matter of time before China joins its more developed neighbors in championing the cause for stronger intellectual property protection.

NOTES

1. For discussions of the United States's potential WTO complaint against China before the WTO Dispute Settlement Body concerning a lack of general enforcement of intellectual property rights, see Yu (2005, 2006a, pp. 923–46).

2. Some commentators have added a third type of FDI, distribution FDI, referring to 'investment in local sales offices, distribution networks, and services facilities' (Kennedy, 2003, p. 79 n.5).
3. For discussions or critiques of the use of the private property rhetoric to expand intellectual property protection, see Bell (2003, pp. 273–7); Netanel (2003, p. 22); Stallman (2005); Sterk (2005, p. 420).
4. For my earlier discussion of this self-interest narrative, see Yu, 2006b, pp. 376–9.
5. The amended Article 15 of the 1982 Chinese Constitution now reads: 'The State has put into practice a socialist market economy. The State strengthens formulating economic laws, improves macro adjustment and control and forbids according to law any units or individuals from interfering with the social economic order.'
6. For a detailed discussion of emerging brands in less developed countries, see Anholt (2005, pp. 43–77).

REFERENCES

Abbott, Frederick M. (2005), 'Toward a new era of objective assessment in the field of TRIPS and variable geometry for the preservation of multilateralism', *Journal of International Economic Law*, **8**(1), 77–100.

Alford, William P. (1995), *To Steal a Book is an Elegant Offense: Intellectual Property Law in Chinese Civilization*, Stanford, CA: Stanford University Press.

Allgeier, Peter F. (2005), 'Letter to HE Mr Sun Zhenyu, Ambassador, Permanent Mission of the People's Republic of China to the World Trade Organization', http://www.ustr.gov/assets/Document_Library/Reports_Publications/2005/asset_upload_file115_8232.pdf.

Anholt, Simon (2005), *Brand New Justice: How Branding Places and Products Can Help the Developing World*, 2nd edn, Oxford: Butterworth–Heinemann.

Assafa, Endeshaw (1996), *Intellectual Property Policy for Non-industrial Countries*, Brookfield, Mass.: Dartmouth.

Bell, Tom W. (2003), 'Authors' welfare: Copyright as a statutory mechanism for redistributing rights', *Brooklyn Law Review*, **69**(1), 229–80.

Bergsten, C. Fred, Bates Gill, Nicholas R. Lardy and Derek Mitchell (eds) (2006), *China: The Balance Sheet: What the World Needs to Know Now about the Emerging Superpower*, New York: Public Affairs.

Chee, Harold with Chris West (2004), *Myths about Doing Business in China*, New York: Palgrave Macmillan.

China Internet Network Information Center (2007), *19th Statistical Survey Report on the Internet Development in China*, Beijing: China Internet Network Information Center.

Chow, Daniel C.K. (2006), 'Why China does not take commercial piracy seriously', *Ohio Northern University Law Review*, **32**(2), 203–25.

Chow, Daniel C.K. (2007), 'The role of intellectual property in promoting international trade and foreign direct investment', in Peter K. Yu (ed.), *Intellectual Property and Information Wealth: Issues and Practices in the Digital Age*, Westport, CT: Praeger Publishers, **4**, pp. 187–200.

Commission on Intellectual Property Rights (2002), 'Integrating Intellectual Property Rights and Development Policy: Report of the Commission on Intellectual Property Rights', London: Commission on Intellectual Property Rights, http://www.iprcommission.org/papers/pdfs/final_report/CIPRfullfinal.pdf.

Dunning, John H. (1981), *International Production and the Multinational Enterprise*, London: George Allen & Unwin.

Faison, Seth (1998), 'China turns blind eye to pirated disks', *New York Times*, 28 March, p. D1.

Falvey, Rod, Neil Foster and David Greenaway (2006), 'Intellectual property rights and economic growth', *Review of Development Economics*, **10**(4), 700–719.

Fink, Carsten and Keith E. Maskus (2005), 'Why we study intellectual property rights and what we have learned', in Carsten Fink and Keith E. Maskus (eds), *Intellectual Property and Development: Lessons from Recent Economic Research*, Oxford: Oxford University Press, pp. 1–15.

Fisher, William (2001), 'Theories of intellectual property', in Stephen R. Munzer (ed.), *New Essays in the Legal and Political Theory of Property*, Cambridge: Cambridge University Press, pp. 168–99.

Frischtak, Claudio R. (1993), 'Harmonization versus differentiation in intellectual property rights regime', in Mitchel B. Wallerstein, Mary Ellen Mogee and Roberta A. Schoen (eds), *Global Dimensions of Intellectual Property Rights in Science and Technology*, Washington, DC: National Academy Press, pp. 89–106.

Gervais, Daniel J. (2007), 'The TRIPS Agreement and the Doha Round: History and impact on economic development', in Peter K. Yu (ed.), *Intellectual Property and Information Wealth: Issues and Practices in the Digital Age*, Westport, CT: Praeger Publishers, **4**, pp. 23–72.

Giunta, Tara Kalagher and Lily H. Shang (1993), 'Ownership of information in a global economy', *George Washington Journal of International Law and Economics*, **27**(2–3), 327–58.

Heald, Paul J. (2003), 'Mowing the playing field: Addressing information distortion and asymmetry in the TRIPS game', *Minnesota Law Review*, **88**(2), 249–314.

Hsü, Immanuel C.Y. (2000), *The Rise of Modern China*, 6th edn, Oxford: Oxford University Press.

Huang, Yasheng (2005), *Selling China: Foreign Direct Investment During the Reform Era*, Cambridge: Cambridge University Press.

International Intellectual Property Alliance (2007), *2007 Special 301: People's Republic of China – Amended*, Washington, DC: International Intellectual Property Alliance.

Kahn, Joseph (2007), 'China approves property law, strengthening its middle class', *New York Times*, 16 March, p. A1.

Kennedy, Kevin C. (2003), 'A WTO agreement on investment: A solution in search of a problem?', *University of Pennsylvania Journal of International Economic Law*, **24**(1), 77–188.

Kingston, William (2005), 'An agenda for radical intellectual property reform', in Keith E. Maskus and Jerome H. Reichman (eds), *International Public Goods and Transfer of Technology Under a Globalized Intellectual Property Regime*, Cambridge: Cambridge University Press, pp. 653–61.

Kitch, Edmund W. (1994), 'The patent policy of developing countries', *UCLA Pacific Basin Law Journal*, **13**(1), 166–78.

Ling, Zhijun (translated by Martha Avery) (2006), *The Lenovo Affair: The Growth of China's Computer Giant and Its Takeover of IBM–PC*, Singapore: John Wiley & Sons.

MacLaughlin, Janet H., Timothy J. Richards and Leigh A. Kenny (1988), 'The economic significance of piracy', in R. Michael Gadbaw and Timothy J. Richards (eds), *Intellectual Property Rights: Global Consensus, Global Conflict?*, Boulder, CO: Westview Press, pp. 89–108.

Mansfield, Edwin (1994), *Intellectual Property Protection, Foreign Direct Investment and Technology Transfer*, Washington, DC: World Bank.

Maskus, Keith E. (1998), 'The role of intellectual property rights in encouraging foreign direct investment and technology transfer', *Duke Journal of Comparative and International Law*, **9**(1), 109–61.

Maskus, Keith E. (2000), *Intellectual Property Rights in the Global Economy*, Washington, DC: Institute for International Economics.

Maskus, Keith E., Sean M. Dougherty and Andrew Mertha (2005), 'Intellectual property rights and economic development in China', in Carsten Fink and Keith E. Maskus (eds), *Intellectual Property and Development: Lessons from Recent Economic Research*, Oxford: Oxford University Press, pp. 295–331.

Massey, Joseph A. (2006), 'The emperor is far away: China's enforcement of intellectual property rights protection, 1986–2006', *Chicago Journal of International Law*, **7**(1), 231–7.

Mertha, Andrew C. (2005), *The Politics of Piracy: Intellectual Property in Contemporary China*, Ithaca, NY: Cornell University Press.

Navarro, Peter (2007), *The Coming China Wars: Where they will be Fought and how they can be Won*, Upper Saddle River, NJ: Financial Times Press.

Netanel, Neil Weinstock (1996), 'Copyright and a democratic civil society', *Yale Law Journal*, **106**(2), 283–387.

Netanel, Neil Weinstock (2003), 'Impose a noncommercial use levy to allow free peer-to-peer file sharing', *Harvard Journal of Law and Technology*, **17**(1), 1–84.

Prestowitz, Clyde (2005), *Three Billion New Capitalists: The Great Shift of Wealth and Power to the East*, New York: Basic Books.

Primo Braga, Carlos Alberto and Carsten Fink (1998), 'The relationship between intellectual property rights and foreign direct investment', *Duke Journal of Comparative and International Law*, **9**(1), 163–87.

Schlender, Brent, Warren Buffett and Bill Gates (1998), 'The Bill & Warren show', *Fortune*, 20 July, pp. 48–52.

Shenkar, Oded (2005), *The Chinese Century: The Rising Chinese Economy and its Impact on the Global Economy, the Balance of Power, and Your Job*, Upper Saddle River, NJ: Wharton School Publishing.

Sherwood, Robert M. (1990), *Intellectual Property and Economic Development*, Boulder, CO: Westview Press.

Stallman, Richard M. (2005), 'Did you say "intellectual property"? It's a seductive mirage', http://www.fsf.org/licensing/essays/not-ipr.xhtml.

Sterk, Stewart E. (2005), 'Intellectualizing property: The tenuous connections between land and copyright', *Washington University Law Quarterly*, **83**(2), 417–70.

Sull, Donald N. with Yong Wang (2005), *Made in China: What Western Managers can Learn from Trailblazing Chinese Entrepreneurs*, Boston, MA: Harvard Business School Press.

Sun, Catherine (2004), *China Intellectual Property for Foreign Business*, Hong Kong: LexisNexis.

Sundara Rajan, Mira T. (2005), 'Copyright and free speech in transition: The Russian experience', in Jonathan Griffiths and Uma Suthersanen (eds), *Copyright and Free Speech: Comparative and International Analyses*, Oxford: Oxford University Press, pp. 315–55.

Tackaberry, Paul (1998), 'Intellectual property risks in China: Their effect on foreign investment and technology transfer', *Journal of Asian Business*, **14**(4), 1–38.

Thurow, Lester C. (1999), *Building Wealth: The New Rules for the Individuals, Companies, and Nations in a Knowledge-Based Economy*, New York: HarperBusiness.

World Trade Organization (1999), 'Panel Report: United States – Sections 301–310 of the Trade Act of 1974', WT/DS152/R.

Xue, Hong and Zheng Chengsi (1999), *Software Protection in China: A Complete Guide*, Hong Kong: Sweet & Maxwell Asia.

Xue, Hong and Zheng Chengsi (2002), *Chinese Intellectual Property Law in the 21st Century*, Hong Kong: Sweet & Maxwell Asia.

Yan, Rick (2004), 'Short-term results: The litmus test for success in China', in *Harvard Business Review: Doing Business in China*, Boston, MA: Harvard Business School Press, pp. 79–140.

Yu, Peter K. (2000), 'From pirates to partners: Protecting intellectual property in China in the twenty-first century', *American University Law Review*, **50**(1), 131–243.

Yu, Peter K. (2001), 'Piracy, prejudice, and perspectives: An attempt to use Shakespeare to reconfigure the US–China intellectual property debate', *Boston University International Law Journal*, **19**(1), 1–87.

Yu, Peter K. (2003), 'The copyright divide', *Cardozo Law Review*, **25**(1), 331–445.

Yu, Peter K. (2005), 'Still dissatisfied after all these years: Intellectual property, post-WTO China, and the avoidable cycle of futility', *Georgia Journal of International and Comparative Law*, **34**(1), 143–58.

Yu, Peter K. (2006a), 'From pirates to partners (Episode II): Protecting intellectual property in post-WTO China', *American University Law Review*, **55**(4), 901–1000.

Yu, Peter K. (2006b), 'TRIPS and its discontents', *Marquette Intellectual Property Law Review*, **10**(2), 369–410.

Yu, Peter K. (2007), 'The international enclosure movement', *Indiana Law Journal*, **82**(4), 827–907.

Yu, Peter K., Gordon G. Chang, Jerome A. Cohen, Elizabeth C. Economy, Sharon K. Hom and Adam Qi Li (2003), 'Symposium, China and the WTO: Progress, perils, and prospects', *Columbia Journal of Asian Law*, **17**(1), 1–29.

Zheng, Yongnian (1999), *Discovering Chinese Nationalism in China: Modernization, Identity, and International Relations*, Cambridge: Cambridge University Press.

Zweig, David (2002), *Internationalizing China: Domestic Interests and Global Linkages*, Ithaca, NY: Cornell University Press.

PART IV

Value capture and retention strategies

10. Protecting unconventional trademarks in the European Union and the United States

Willajeanne F. McLean*

INTRODUCTION

Businesses are always looking for ways to make their products and services memorable. Therefore, it should not be surprising that they have turned to the use of colors, sounds, slogans, scents and tastes and, in some instances, textures to distinguish their product(s) or service(s) from others in the market place. Nor should it be surprising that savvy businesses seek to protect these marketing tools from use by their competitors, and attempt to use intellectual property rights (more than likely, trademark law) to do so.

Although, in theory, trademark registration is possible for unconventional trademarks, both in the United States and in the European Union, such registrations are far from commonplace (Frost, 2004). The first part of the chapter will briefly discuss the statutory underpinnings for the protection of trademarks, both within the United States and the European Union.[1] The second part will examine individual decisions taken within the United States and the European Union in each of the abovementioned categories of unconventional marks. The third part of the chapter will address some of the questions that are implicated when protection is sought for unconventional marks.

TRADEMARK PROTECTION WITHIN THE UNITED STATES AND THE EUROPEAN UNION

In the United States, a trademark serves several purposes: it operates as a merchandising short cut, in that it lowers search costs for buyers (Landes and Posner, 1988), and it also signals the source of the good, even though that source is unknown (*Bayer Co., Inc., v. United Drug Co.*, 1921).

The legal basis for protection of marks within the United States comes from both the common law, and the statutory provisions of the Lanham Act, which permit the owner of a mark to attain federal registration. Some of the benefits of a federal registration of a mark are that registration acts as evidence of ownership of the mark; there is constructive notice nationwide of the owner's claim to the mark; registration within the United States may serve as a basis for foreign registration; and it provides access to federal courts.

The Lanham Act was enacted in 1946 to modernize trademark law. It was designed 'to dispense with mere technical prohibitions and arbitrary provisions'. Under the Lanham Act, Congress granted the right of registration to

> any word, name, symbol, or device, or any combination thereof (1) used by a person, or (2) which a person has a bona fide intention to use in commerce . . . to identify and distinguish his or her goods, including a unique product, from those manufactured or sold by others and to indicate the source of the goods, even if that source is unknown. (15 USC § 1052)

A broad reading of this language suggests that almost anything is capable of serving as a trademark, unless it fell within any of the specified restrictions (15 USC § 1052 (a–f)) and as long as consumers recognize that the 'thing' serves a signaling function.

Within the European Union,[2] it would be fair to say that there was a hostile attitude towards trademark law exhibited by the governing institutions. Trademarks were viewed as 'nothing more than a prop for advertising', and were thought to be inimical to the goals of free movement of goods and open competition (Wilkinson, 1990).

Over time, the climate changed and trademarks were recognized as enabling the consumer to distinguish one product from those which have another origin. The legislative organs of the European Community, such as the Council (Treaty of the European Union Art. 202),[3] determined that it was necessary to harmonize the national laws on trademark. The result was the First Directive 89/104/EEC of the Council, of 21 December 1988, to Approximate the Laws of the Member States Relating to Trade Marks (OJ L 40/ 1).[4] One of the stated purposes of the Trademarks Directive (Art. 249 EC)[5] was to approximate the laws of the member states to remove disparities which may impede the free movement of goods and freedom to provide services and may distort competition within the common market (Wurtenberger, 1996). The Trademarks Directive sets forth what constitutes a mark (Trademarks Directive. Article 2),[6] provides guidelines for the grounds for refusal or invalidity of a mark (Trademark Directive, Article 3)[7] and defines the scope of the rights conferred by the mark.

However, since the goal of the Trademarks Directive was to *harmonize* the national laws in order to promote the goals of free movement of goods and unfettered competition, problems of territoriality still remained (Annand, 2003). In 1994, the Community Trade Mark Regulation came into force (Meyer, 2006). The goals of the Regulation were to remove barriers to free movement of goods and services, ensure that competition is not distorted, and create legal conditions, such as trademarks, which allow businesses to distinguish their products and services, regardless of frontiers (Regulation 40/94, 1993).

The Regulation provides that the Community trademark has a 'unitary character'. This means that a single trademark registration will have equal effect throughout the Community (Meyer, 2006), but it does not replace domestic registrations (Regulation 40/94, 1993). Furthermore, it should be noted that substantive provisions of the Regulation, such as the definition of trademark subject matter, mirror the language employed in the Trademarks Directive (Blakely, 2000).

As with the Trademarks Directive, the scope of what might constitute a trademark is relatively broad (Roth, 2005). The Regulation states that: '[a] Community trade mark may consist of any signs capable of being represented graphically, particularly words, including personal names, designs, letters, numerals, the shape of goods or of their packaging, provided that such signs are capable of distinguishing the goods or services of one undertaking from those of other undertakings' (Regulation 40/94, 1993).

The European Court of Justice, along with the Office for Harmonization in the Internal Market, which was created to register both Community Trademarks and Designs, (Council Regulation 40/94; McCarthy, 2005), has been responsible for delineating the boundaries of what can properly be registered as a trademark. Similarly, the courts of the United States federal court system, and the administrative organs of the United States Patents and Trademark Office have also considered what protections can be granted to unconventional marks. The next section will discuss some of the cases which have been reviewed by the relevant authorities.

PROTECTION OF COLOR MARKS IN THE UNITED STATES AND THE EUROPEAN UNION

Prior to the passage of the 1946 Lanham Act, color alone could not be registered as a trademark (*A. Leschen & Sons Rope Co. v. Broderick & Bascom Rope Co.*, 1906). An often used argument against protection of color alone was that of color depletion, based upon the idea that the palette of colors is limited, and therefore an appropriation of a single color would deplete the colors remaining (*Campbell Soup Co. v. Armour & Co.*, 1949). After the entry into force of the Lanham Act, federal circuit courts differed as to whether or not use of color alone could qualify as a trademark (*NutraSweet Co. v. Stadt Corp.*, 1990; *First Brands Corp. v. Fred Meyer, Inc.*, 1987; *In re Owens-Corning Fiberglas Corp.*, 1985; *Master Distributors, Inc. v. Pako Corp.*, 1993).

The United States Supreme Court clarified the issue of use of a single color as a trademark in its decision *Qualitex Co. v. Jacobson Products, Co.* (1995). In the case, Qualitex, a manufacturer of dry cleaning press pads, sued a competitor, Jacobson, on grounds of unfair competition and trademark infringement, for its appropriation of the same green-gold color used, and registered, by Qualitex.[8] Qualitex won the lawsuit in the District Court (*Qualitex Co. v. Jacobson Prods. Co.*, 1991); however, the Court of Appeals for the Ninth Circuit set aside the trademark infringement judgment because the Lanham Act did not permit the registration of 'color alone' as a trademark (*Qualitex Co. v. Jacobson Prods. Co.*, 1994). Due to the split in the circuit courts of appeals regarding the ability of color per se to be protectable as a trademark, the Supreme Court granted certiorari, and held that there 'is no rule absolutely barring the use of color alone' (*Qualitex Co. v. Jacobson Prods. Co.*, 1995, p. 162).

The Court based its holding on several premises. First the Court noted that color alone meets the basic legal requirements for a trademark under the Lanham Act. Since the Act defines the term 'trademark' to 'include any word, name, symbol, or device, or any combination thereof' (15 USC § 1127), a color should therefore be able to act as a symbol, and thus, function as a mark.

The Court went on to say that color, more than likely, would not be inherently distinctive or capable of signaling source to a customer (*Qualitex Co. v. Jacobson Prods. Co.*, 1995, pp. 162–3). However, upon achieving consumer recognition, also known as secondary meaning (*Inwood Laboratories, Inc. v. Ives Laboratories, Inc.*, 1982), similar to a color, a word, should be able to serve as a mark (*Qualitex Co. v. Jacobson Prods. Co.*, 1995, p. 163). Nor did the Court find that the doctrine of functionality, which prevents a producer from controlling a useful product feature, and thereby inhibiting legitimate competition, by allowing a producer to control a useful product feature, created a bar to the use of color as a trademark (*Inwood Laboratories, Inc. v. Ives Laboratories, Inc.*, 1982).

As for the arguments that color depletion and shade confusion should preclude a finding that a single color could function as a trademark, the Court found them unpersuasive. With respect to shade confusion, the Court did not think that it would be any more difficult to determine the similarities or differences between shades of color than it was for words (*Qualitex Co. v. Jacobson Prods. Co.*,1995, pp. 167–8). Nor was the Court swayed by the argument of color depletion. It dismissed the argument as a 'blanket prohibition' which relied on an 'occasional problem' (*Qualitex Co. v. Jacobson Prods. Co.*, 1995, p. 168). The Court believed that should the situation of color scarcity arise, any anti-competitive effects would be prevented by the doctrine of functionality (*Qualitex Co. v. Jacobson Prods. Co.*, 1995, p. 169).

The Court also dismissed the precedential value of cases which prohibited the protection of a single color. Here the Court noted that those cases had been decided prior to the passage of the Lanham Act, which 'significantly changed and liberalized the common law' (*Qualitex Co. v. Jacobson Prods. Co.*, 1995, p. 171). The Court instead read the Lanham Act, and its subsequent amendment, as permitting the use of color alone as a trademark under appropriate circumstances (*Qualitex Co. v. Jacobson Prods. Co.*, 1995, p. 173).

In the European Union, the European Court of Justice clarified the requirements for the registration of a single color. In *Libertel Groep BV v. Benelux-Merkenbureau* (2003), the applicant, Libertel, wanted to register the color orange as a trademark for telecommunications goods and services. The Benelux-Merkenbureau (Benelux Trade Mark Office) provisionally refused registration of the mark unless Libertel could show that the mark had acquired distinctiveness (*Libertel Groep BV v. Benelux-Merkenbureau*, 2003, para. 16). Libertel appealed that decision, and the issue eventually was referred to the Court of Justice for a preliminary ruling (*Libertel Groep BV v. Benelux-Merkenbureau*, 2003, paras 16–19).[9]

The question referred, broadly speaking, was whether color alone possessed the requisite distinctiveness to serve as a trademark. The Court found that color must constitute a sign, capable of distinguishing the goods or services of one establishment from that of another (*Libertel Groep BV v. Benelux-Merkenbureau*, 2003, para. 23). However, whether a color constitutes a sign depends on a determination of the context of the use of the color; that is, whether it is recognized as functioning as a trademark.

Furthermore, the color (sign) must be capable of graphic representation (*Libertel Groep BV v. Benelux-Merkenbureau*, 2003, para. 23). Graphic representation, as set forth by the Court, means that the specimen submitted must be clear, precise, self-contained, easily accessible, intelligible, durable and objective. For registration of a color, this means that a sample of the color will not meet the requirement of durability. However, a written description may, under the right circumstances, suffice (*Libertel Groep BV v. Benelux-Merkenbureau*, 2003, paras 34–5).[10] The Court did approve the use of an internationally recognized identification code to constitute a graphic representation because these codes are deemed to be precise and stable (*Libertel Groep BV v. Benelux-Merkenbureau*, 2003, para. 37).

The Court acknowledged that a color per se does not inherently possess distinctiveness because of the widespread use of colors to advertise and market goods, without communicating specific information. Nevertheless, the Court found that the possibility that a color per se may serve as an indication of origin of goods or services could not be summarily rejected (*Libertel Groep BV v. Benelux-Merkenbureau*, 2003, para. 41).

The Court also addressed other concerns raised by the national court, such as the issue of color scarcity and depletion (*Libertel Groep BV v. Benelux-Merkenbureau*, 2003, paras 47–54). The Court acknowledged that in Community trademark law, there is a public interest in preventing undue restriction of colors available to other businesses *Libertel Groep BV v. Benelux-Merkenbureau*, 2003, paras 47–54),[11] and cautioned that the competent authority for registering trade marks must carry out an examination by reference to the actual situation, taking account of all the circumstances of the case and in particular any use which has been made of the mark (*Libertel Groep BV v. Benelux-Merkenbureau*, 2003, para. 77).

Recently, another case regarding the registration of color per se came before the European Court of Justice. In *Heidelberger Bauchemie GmbH* (2004), the company Heidelberger sought registration by the German Patent Office of the colors of blue and yellow, in every conceivable form, as a trademark for certain products used in the building trade (*Heidelberger Bauchemie GmbH*, 2004, para. 10). Although the Patent Office accepted that colors are in principle able to constitute a trademark, it rejected the application on the ground that the proposed mark lacked distinctiveness (*Heidelberger Bauchemie GmbH*, 2004, para. 12). Heidelberger appealed to the Bundespatentgericht (German Federal Patent Court), which referred two questions to the European Court of Justice.[12] The Court determined that the issue could be summed up thus: 'whether . . . colours or combinations of colours designated in the abstract and without contours are capable of constituting a trade mark for the purposes . . . of the [Trademark] Directive' (*Heidelberger Bauchemie GmbH*, 2004, para. 15).

In arriving at its judgment, the Court reiterated the criteria for a trademark as described in the Trademark Directive: that it must be a sign, sufficiently distinctive to be capable of indicating origin, and capable of being represented graphically (*Heidelberger Bauchemie GmbH*, 2004, para. 22).

The Court explained that a color or combinations of colors, under the proper circumstances (*Heidelberger Bauchemie GmbH*, 2004, para. 42), could function as a sign (*Heidelberger Bauchemie GmbH*, 2004, para. 23). The Court also noted that it was important that the protection of the color(s) did not provide an unfair competitive advantage to the proprietor of the mark (*Heidelberger Bauchemie GmbH*, 2004, para. 24).

In determining whether or not colors or a combination of colors could be sufficiently distinctive to indicate origin, the Court observed that colors 'possess little inherent capacity for communicating specific information' (*Heidelberger Bauchemie GmbH*, 2004, paras 38–9), and therefore colors per se were not distinctive. However, the Court did acknowledge that it was possible for colors to acquire distinctiveness (*Heidelberger Bauchemie GmbH*, 2004, para. 39), and thereby serve to distinguish the goods or services of one undertaking from those of another (*Heidelberger Bauchemie GmbH*, 2004, para. 40).

As for the criterion that a sign must be capable of being graphically represented, the Court held that such a graphic representation which consists of two or more colors, in the abstract and without contours, must be systematically arranged by associating the colors concerned in a predetermined and uniform way.[13] Without a systematic arrangement, the Court reasoned, a consumer would have difficulties in recalling a particular color combination, which would preclude the certainty of a repeat purchase.[14] Lack of uniformity in the color combination(s) also would prevent competitors (and competent authorities) from knowing the scope of protection afforded to the mark.[15]

PROTECTION OF SOUND MARKS IN THE UNITED STATES AND THE EUROPEAN UNION

In 1978, General Electric Broadcasting Company wanted a federal service mark[16] registration for the sound made by a ship's bell clock for radio broadcasting services (*In re General Electric Broadcasting Company, Inc.*, 1978). General Electric described the mark as 'a series of bells tolled during four, hour sequences, beginning with one ring at approximately a first half hour and increasing in number by one ring at approximately each half hour thereafter' (*In re General Electric Broadcasting Company, Inc.*, 1978, p. 561).' According to the Trademarks Examiner, registration of the service mark would be improper because the listeners would not associate the bells with the source of the service, the radio station, but with the time of day (*In re General Electric Broadcasting Company, Inc.*, 1978, p. 562).

The Trademark Trial and Appeals Board affirmed, in part, the decision of the Examiner (*In re General Electric Broadcasting Company, Inc.*, 1978, p. 563).[17] The Board reasoned that sounds, under certain conditions, may function as indicators of source.[18] In fact, there were several sound marks that had been successfully registered. However, sounds would be indicators of source where the hearer made an association between the sound and the service being offered.[19] The Board also made a distinction between sounds which are 'unique, different or distinctive', and those which are commonplace or are imitative of commonplace sounds. The former, according to the Board, would be registrable without necessitating a showing of secondary meaning. The latter, however, would only be registrable if 'supported by evidence to show that purchasers, prospective purchasers and listeners do recognize and associate the sound with services offered and/or rendered exclusively with a single, albeit anonymous, source' (*In re General Electric Broadcasting Company, Inc.*, 1978, p. 563).

In *Shield Mark BV v. Joost Kist* (2003)[20] two questions were before the European Court of Justice. The first question was whether Article 2 of the Trademarks Directive must be interpreted as precluding sound signs from being regarded as trademarks,[21] and whether that article implies that sound signs must be capable of being regarded as trademarks.[22] The second question concerned the conditions under which a sound could be represented graphically, as required by Article 2 (*Shield Mark BV v. Joost Kist*, 2003, para. 42).

According to the Court, the examples given in the Trademarks Directive such as personal names, designs, letters or numerals were not exhaustive (*Shield Mark BV v. Joost Kist*, 2003, paras 31–2). Therefore, the Court reasoned, sound is not excluded. The Court believed that 'sound signs are not by nature incapable of distinguishing the goods or services of one undertaking from those of other undertakings' (*Shield Mark BV v. Joost Kist*, 2003, para. 36).

Article 2 of the Trademarks Directive, however, requires that a sign be represented graphically. The Netherlands court, in its second question, asked whether 'musical notes, a written description in the form of an onomatopoeia, a written description in some other form, a graphical representation such as a sonogram, a sound recording annexed to the registration form, a digital recording accessible via the internet, a combination of those methods, or any other form' (*Shield Mark BV v. Joost Kist*, 2003, para. 42) would meet the requirements of graphical representation.

With respect to some of the methods of graphic representation proposed by the national court, the European Court of Justice declined to consider whether they would suffice (*Shield Mark BV v. Joost Kist*, 2003, paras 51–3).[23] The Court noted that it was for the national court to determine whether a sign was capable of being registered.[24] Nevertheless, it did offer some guidance as to what would constitute graphic representation of a sign which is incapable of being perceived visually: its graphic representation 'must be clear, precise, self-contained, easily accessible, intelligible, durable and objective' (*Shield Mark BV v. Joost Kist*, 2003, para. 62). In the case of music, the Court held that musical notes, without more, did not satisfy the requirements (*Shield Mark BV v. Joost Kist*, 2003, para. 64). However, those requirements are satisfied where the sign is represented by a stave divided into measures and shows, in particular, a clef, musical notes and rests whose form indicates the relative value and, where necessary, accidentals (*Shield Mark BV v. Joost Kist*, 2003, para. 64).

PROTECTION OF SLOGANS IN THE UNITED STATES AND THE EROPEAN UNION

Prior to the passage of the Lanham Act, slogans were neither recognized nor protectable as trademarks (Beran, 1967; Lunney, 1999). Any protection offered to a slogan came in the form of unfair competition (Beran, 1967; Lunney, 1999). The limitations of protection stemmed from the sentiment that consumers did not recognize the slogan as an indicator of source, but experienced the slogan as descriptive of the product or services. Furthermore slogans did not meet the requirement that a trademark must be affixed to the product (Beran, 1967; Lunney, 1999).

The first case that resolved the question of whether or not a slogan could be federally registered as a trademark was *American Enka Corp. v. Marzall* (*Am. Enka Corp. v. Marzall, 1952,* 92 U.S.P.Q.111 (D.D.C.)'. The plaintiff was a manufacturer of rayon yarn, and used the slogan 'THE FATE OF A FABRIC HANGS BY A THREAD' for its yarns. After having its trademark application rejected by the Patent and Trademarks Office, it appealed the decision. In a tersely written opinion, the District Court for the District of Columbia concluded that 'certain combinations of words, *albeit that they are also slogans*, may properly function as trade marks' (*Am. Enka Corp. v. Marzall*, 1952, p. 112) (emphasis added).

Although the United States case put to rest the question of whether or not a slogan could properly function as a trademark, there were requirements that the owner of the mark show that the slogan had acquired consumer recognition (Beran, 1967). It was not until the 1970s that the United States Patent and Trademark Office (USPTO) began to register slogans in their own right (Ramsey, 2006).

More recently in Europe, the European Court of Justice had an opportunity to determine whether a slogan met the requirements of the Trademark Directive (*Société des produits Nestlé SA v. Mars UK Ltd*, 2005). Nestlé is the owner of two marks registered in the

United Kingdom: one is a slogan, 'HAVE A BREAK . . . HAVE A KIT KAT'; the other is a conventional word mark, 'KIT KAT'. Nestlé wanted to register part of its slogan 'HAVE A BREAK'. The application was rejected on the grounds that the expression was devoid of distinctive character (*Société des produits Nestlé SA v. Mars UK Ltd*, 2005, para. 12). Nestlé appealed the decision to the High Court of Justice of England and Wales, Chancery Division, and then to the Court of Appeals (England and Wales) (Civil Division). The Court of Appeals made a preliminary reference to the European Court of Justice, asking, in essence, whether part of a mark may acquire such distinctiveness by its use in the whole mark so that it might function as a trademark (*Société des produits Nestlé SA v. Mars UK Ltd*, 2005, para. 19).

The Court answered that a determination of distinctiveness necessarily took into consideration the relationship of the mark to the goods or services with which it is used, and the presumed expectations of an average consumer of the category of goods or services in question, who is reasonably well-informed and reasonably observant and circumspect (*Société des produits Nestlé SA v. Mars UK Ltd*, 2005, para. 25). In addition, acquisition of distinctiveness is achieved when the relevant class of persons identify the mark as originating from a particular source (*Société des produits Nestlé SA v. Mars UK Ltd*, 2005, para. 29). The Court concluded that distinctiveness 'may be as a result both of the use, as part of a registered trade mark, of a component thereof and of the use of a separate mark in conjunction with a registered trade mark' (*Société des produits Nestlé SA v. Mars UK Ltd*, 2005, para. 30). The Court underlined that what is necessary is that the relevant class of persons actually perceive the product or service as emanating from a given undertaking, and that an assessment of that perception may be undertaken by taking into consideration the market share held by the mark; how intensive, geographically widespread and long-standing use of the mark has been; the amount invested by the undertaking in promoting the mark; the proportion of the relevant class of persons who, because of the mark, identify goods as originating from a particular undertaking; and statements from chambers of commerce and industry or other trade and professional associations (*Société des produits Nestlé SA v. Mars UK Ltd*, 2005, para. 31).

OLFACTORY TRADEMARKS IN THE UNITED STATES AND THE EUROPEAN UNION

In the case *In re Clarke* (1990), the Trademark Trial and Appeal Board reviewed an appeal from a decision refusing to grant registration for scented yarn. The applicant described her mark as 'a high impact, fresh, floral fragrance reminiscent of Plumeria blossoms' (*In re Clarke*, 1990, p. 1238). The Examiner refused to pass the mark to registration on the grounds that the mark was not capable of distinguishing the applicant's product from those of others, and therefore could not function as a trademark. The Examiner also contended that prospective purchasers would not recognize that the scent was indicative of origin, but would just assume that it was a 'pleasant feature' of the goods (*In re Clarke*, 1990 p. 1239).

The Trademark Trial and Appeal Board found the arguments against registration unavailing. It found that the applicant had demonstrated that the fragrance which impregnated the yarn could serve as a trademark.[25] The Board determined that the applicant presented a prima facie case of distinctiveness, and reversed the refusal of registration. However, it should be noted that the Trademark Trial and Appeal Board limited the application of its decision, stating that

> [i]t should be noted that we are not here talking about the registrability of scents or fragrances of products which are noted for those features, such as perfumes, colognes or scented household products. Nor is this a case involving the question of descriptiveness of a term which identifies a particular fragrance of a product. (*In re Clarke*, 1990, p. 1239 fn 4)

In these types of cases, the Board continued, the term would be unregistrable.

Since the registration of Clarke's fragrance for scented yarn, there have been very few registrations for olfactory marks (Hammersley, 1998). This may be because 'the amount of evidence required to establish that a scent or fragrance functions as a mark is substantial' (Trademark Manual of Examining Procedure, 2005, § 1202.13).

In a case with an issue deemed both 'stimulating and significant' (*Ralf Sieckmann v. Deutsches Patent- und Markenamt*, 2002), the European Court of Justice confronted the question whether an odor could be registered as a trademark, and if so, under what conditions.

Ralf Sieckmann applied in Germany to register a scent which he described as 'balsamically fruity with a slight hint of cinnamon'. In support of his application he submitted a container of the scent, and a written description of the mark, methyl cinnamate (= cinnamic acid methyl ester), and its chemical formula, C6H5-CH = CHCOOCH3 (*Ralf Sieckmann v. Deutsches Patent- und Markenamt*, 2002, para. 11). The Deutsches Patent- und Markenamt (German Patent and Trade Mark Office) refused to register the scent on the grounds that it was not capable of constituting a trademark or be represented graphically, and that it was not inherently distinctive (*Ralf Sieckmann v. Deutsches Patent- und Markenamt*, 2002, para. 12).

Sieckmann appealed to the Bundespatentgericht (Federal Patents Court). That court held that, in theory, odors may be capable of distinguishing the goods of one undertaking from those of another (*Ralf Sieckmann v. Deutsches Patent- und Markenamt*, 2002, para. 15), but it had doubts as to whether an olfactory mark can satisfy the condition of graphic representation as required by Article 2 of the Trademarks Directive (*Ralf Sieckmann v. Deutsches Patent- und Markenamt*, 2002, para. 17). The Federal Patents Court referred the question of whether a trademark may consist of a sign which cannot, in itself, be represented visually to the Court of Justice (*Ralf Sieckmann v. Deutsches Patent- und Markenamt*, 2002, para. 25). The Federal Patents Court also wanted to know whether 'the requirements of graphic representability [*sic*] are satisfied by a chemical formula, by a description in written words, by the deposit of an odour sample or by a combination of those elements' (*Ralf Sieckmann v. Deutsches Patent- und Markenamt*, 2002, para. 56).

The Court of Justice held that a trademark could consist of a sign which is not capable of being represented visually (*Ralf Sieckmann v. Deutsches Patent- und Markenamt*, 2002, para. 45). It made its determination by deconstruction of Article 2 of the Directive, whose purpose, according to the Court, is to define the types of signs of which a trademark may consist. Although the Directive does not mention odors in its list (*Ralf Sieckmann v. Deutsches Patent- und Markenamt*, 2002, para. 44), the Court decided that the list was not exhaustive, and therefore did not expressly exclude signs, such as odors, which are incapable of being represented graphically (*Ralf Sieckmann v. Deutsches Patent- und Markenamt*, 2002, para. 45).

The requirements are that the sign be able to function as a trademark; that is, guarantee the identity of the origin of the marked product or service to the consumer or end-user by enabling him/her, without any possibility of confusion, to distinguish that product or service from others which have another origin (*Ralf Sieckmann v. Deutsches Patent- und Markenamt*, 2002, para. 35). Furthermore, the trademark must offer a guarantee that all the goods or services bearing it have been manufactured or supplied under the control of a single undertaking which is responsible for their quality.[26] With respect to a mark such as an odor, the Court further found it necessary that the mark be capable of graphic representation (*Ralf Sieckmann v. Deutsches Patent- und Markenamt*, 2002, para. 45).[27] This was to ensure that the precise scope of the protection would be known to the owner of the mark (*Ralf Sieckmann v. Deutsches Patent- und Markenamt*, 2002, para. 48), and any competitors (*Ralf Sieckmann v. Deutsches Patent- und Markenamt*, 2002, para. 51), as well as national authorities (*Ralf Sieckmann v. Deutsches Patent- und Markenamt*, 2002, para. 50).

The Court next discussed the specimens that were submitted as part of the application. It found that the chemical formula would not fulfill the requirements of a graphic representation because few people would recognize the formula as representative of the scent. Furthermore, the Court found that a chemical formula is neither sufficiently clear and precise nor representative of the odor, but rather stands for the substance itself (*Ralf Sieckmann v. Deutsches Patent- und Markenamt*, 2002, para. 69).

As for the sample of the scent, the Court found that the 'deposit of an odour sample, does not constitute a graphic representation' (*Ralf Sieckmann v. Deutsches Patent- und Markenamt*, 2002, para. 71) and, moreover, is not sufficiently stable or durable.[28]

More recently, the European Court of First Instance[29] had an opportunity to review a decision made by the Office for Harmonisation in the Internal Market,[30] which rejected an application for the smell of ripe strawberries (*Eden SARL v. Office for Harmonisation in the Internal Market* (Trade Marks and Designs) (OHIM), 2005).[31]

The applicant, Eden SARL, wanted to use the smell for soaps, face cream, stationery, leather goods and clothing (*Eden SARL v. OHIM* (Trade Marks and Designs), 2005, para. 3) It appealed the decision of the OHIM to the Court of First Instance, arguing that the *Sieckmann* case allowed for registration of scent marks if they were capable of being represented graphically (*Eden SARL v. OHIM* (Trade Marks and Designs), 2005, para. 13). Eden claimed that its representation of the mark – a description of the mark, and the photo of a strawberry – should satisfy the requirements set forth in *Sieckmann*.

Eden also claimed that the description, 'the smell of ripe strawberries' was sufficient, in that it is 'unequivocal, precise and objective'. The Court disagreed, and based its finding on a study that showed that 'it was possible to differentiate the varieties [of strawberries] by their smell in five of the nine crops' (*Eden SARL v. OHIM* (Trade Marks and Designs), 2005, paras 31–2). The Court held that since the description 'smell of ripe strawberries' could refer to several varieties and therefore to several distinct smells, the description was 'neither unequivocal nor precise', and did not meet the criteria as set forth in *Sieckmann*. In addition, the Court noted that 'there is no generally accepted international classification of smells which would make it possible, as with international colour codes or musical notation, to identify an olfactory sign objectively and precisely through the attribution of a name or a precise code specific to each smell' (*Eden SARL v. OHIM* (Trade Marks and Designs), 2005, para. 34).

PROTECTION OF FLAVORS IN THE UNITED STATES AND THE EUROPEAN UNION

In 2002, N.V. Organon, a Netherlands corporation, filed an application before the United States Patent and Trademark Office to register an 'orange flavor' as a trademark for 'pharmaceuticals for human use, namely anti-depressants in quick-dissolving tablets and pills' (*In re N.V. Organon*, 2006, p. 1639). According to the rules of the Trademark Office, only a detailed description of the mark, if it consists of a sound, scent, or other completely non-visual matter, is required.[32] The Examining Attorney rejected the application on two grounds: that it neither identified nor distinguished the goods of applicant from those of others and, thus, did not act as a source identifier; and that the mark was functional.

Organon appealed the rejection of its application to the Trademark Trial and Appeal Board (TTAB). In its appeal, Organon conceded that flavor as a trademark was unconventional, but argued that flavor was entitled to be protected as a trademark, just as scent and sound were entitled to that protection, as long as it functioned as a trademark (*In re N.V. Organon*, 2006, Appeal Brief, p. 1). In addition, Organon argued that the addition of the flavor was not functional, in that it did not add to the efficacy of the anti-depressant trademark (*In re N.V. Organon*, 2006, Appeal Brief, p. 6).

It was a case of first impression for the Trademark Trial and Appeals Board (*In re N.V. Organon*, 2006, p. 1643). The Board acknowledged that the Lanham Act gives a broad definition of the term 'trademark', which essentially includes unconventional trademarks because it does not exclude them. Nevertheless, the Trademark Trial and Appeal Board did not agree with the assertions made by Organon that the orange flavor was not, in fact, functional. Rather, the Board found: '[a]pplicant's orange flavor makes its antidepressant tablets and pills more palatable for patients, resulting in increased patient compliance, and thereby supplying applicant with a competitive advantage. Registration by applicant would hinder competition by placing competitors at a substantial competitive disadvantage' (*In re N.V. Organon*, 2006, p. 1649).

As for the assertion that flavor was capable of functioning as a trademark, the Board noted that 'consumers would not view the orange flavor of an antidepressant tablet or pill as a trademark; rather, they would consider it only as just another feature of the medication, making it palatable' (*In re N.V. Organon*, 2006, p. 1649). Furthermore, the Board observed that the applicant had not shown that the flavor of its anti-depressant had acquired distinctiveness (*In re N.V. Organon*, 2006, p. 1650).

The Board concluded that the applicant's flavor failed to function as a trademark for several reasons. First, flavor is generally seen as a characteristic of the goods and, therefore, is not inherently distinctive (*In re N.V. Organon*, 2006, p. 1649). Also, there is the more practical problem of acquiring secondary meaning, particularly when 'there generally is no way for consumers routinely to distinguish products by sampling them before they decide which one to purchase' (*In re N.V. Organon*, 2006, p. 1650). The Board noted it would not be expected that prescribed antidepressants would be tasted prior to purchase so that a consumer, in conjunction with a physician, could distinguish one antidepressant from another on the basis of taste.[33] Lastly, the Board could not conceive of an acceptable specimen of use- a placebo might not have the same taste as the actual medicine (*In re N.V. Organon*, 2006, p. 1650, fn 11) and taste buds vary (*In re N.V. Organon*, 2006, p. 1650, fn 10–11). Based on all those reasons, the Board affirmed the decision of the Examining Attorney.

Earlier, in 2000, Eli Lilly and Company submitted an application for a Community Trademark for the taste of artificial strawberry flavor for pharmaceutical preparations (*Eli Lilly and Company v. OHIM*, 2003). The Examiner rejected the application on the grounds that the mark was not capable of being represented graphically (*Eli Lilly and Company v. OHIM*, 2003, para. 12),[34] and that the mark lacked distinctive character (*Eli Lilly and Company v. OHIM*, 2003, para. 2).

Eli Lilly appealed the decision to the Board. It contended that the taste of artificial strawberry flavor in a pharmaceutical substance is uncommon, and unnecessary to the product (*Eli Lilly and Company v. OHIM*, 2003, para. 8). Further, Lilly argued that it was irrelevant that the taste would only be ascertained after purchase, but that the prescribing physician would favor this product because it would be more palatable to the patient.

The OHIM Board upheld the findings of the Examiner that the mark lacked distinctive character. In its holding, the Board found that to give Lilly an exclusive right to use the flavor of artificial strawberries would interfere with the freedom of other pharmaceutical companies to add the same flavor to disguise any unpleasantness of the medication (*Eli Lilly and Company v. OHIM*, 2003, paras 14–15). In reaching its decision, the Board noted that the European Court of Justice, in the *Libertel* case, held that there is a public interest in not unduly restricting the availability of colors for other traders who offer for sale goods or services of the same type as those in respect of which registration is sought. The Board thought that the same reasoning would apply to tastes (*Eli Lilly and Company v. OHIM*, 2003, para. 14). In addition, the Board found that taste could not function as a trademark in that it could not distinguish one pharmaceutical product from another. It would be unlikely that a consumer would perceive it as a trademark, but would instead believe that it was an additive to mask the unpleasant taste of the product (*Eli Lilly and Company v. OHIM*, 2003, para. 16).

BUSINESS IMPLICATIONS FOR THE PROTECTION OF UNCONVENTIONAL TRADEMARKS

With respect to the protection of color per se, both the United States and European Union recognize that most colors will not be inherently distinctive, and therefore require a showing of secondary meaning. However, the requirements for registration are different. In the United States, a drawing of a color mark is required (Trademark Manual of Examining Procedure, 2005, § 807.07(a)). In addition, the drawing must be accompanied by a claim of color.[35] Furthermore, the claim is properly worded if it reads as follows: '[t]he color(s) <*name the color(s)*> are claimed as a feature of the mark.'[36]

In the European Union, while a written description of the mark, under certain circumstances, might satisfy the requirement that a graphic representation be clear, precise and self-contained, it is entirely likely that supplemental information, such as an international color code, would be necessary. Furthermore, it is unclear, when dealing with a combination of colors, what would constitute a systematic arrangement of colors in a 'predetermined and uniform way' (Heidelberger Bauchemie GmbH, 2004, para. 33).

As for sound marks, the United States does not require a drawing of the mark, but the applicant must submit a detailed description of the mark (37 C.F.R. § 2.52(e).[37] Specimens submitted for sound marks include audio cassettes, compact discs or musical scores (Trademark Manual of Examining Procedure, 2005, § 1202.15). If the applicant is filing online, a musical score is submitted in .wav format.[38] In contrast, the European Union requires that the sound mark be graphically represented. However, the use of a score, in the case of music composition, only allows those who are trained to read music to understand the scope of the claimed mark. It is an open question as to what types of graphic representation may be used for the registration of a non-musical sound mark.

Both the United States and the European Union require that protectable slogans must not be descriptive, but that they be distinctive (Trademark Manual of Examining Procedure, § 1213.06; *Société des produits Nestlé SA v. Mars UK Ltd*, 2005). In the United States, the acceptance of slogans as trademarks is now rather commonplace – the only stricture placed on the slogan according to the Trademark Manual of Examining Procedure is that if a mark consists entirely of a slogan which is merely descriptive or which is not being used as a mark, then registration should be refused.[39] However, in Europe acceptance of the judgement in the Nestlé case has been mixed (European Perspectives, 2005; Melnitzer, 2005). One commentator finds that the preliminary ruling allows businesses more protection in their marketing investments, without sacrificing the principle of distinctiveness (European Perspectives, 2005), while another noted that some thought the Nestlé decision, if followed by the UK courts, would obviate the purpose of a trademark as a badge of origin (Melnitzer, 2005).[40]

As for the protection of scents, the requirement in the European Union that the scent be able to be graphically represented leads one to believe that registrations of olfactory marks will be forestalled, if not prohibited altogether (Hidaka et al., 2004; Vaver, 2005; Roth, 2005). On the other hand, the position in the United States on the registration of olfactory marks is much less onerous (Hammersley, 1998; Roth, 2005).

By all indications, marks proposed for the 'flavor of something' will have a difficult time meeting the registrability requirements of both the United States and European Union. A major impediment would be overcoming the arguments of functionality – that the flavor is needed to mask the bad taste of medicine (Cooper, 1980; Gilson and LaLonde, 2005). Another problem would be providing the evidence needed to show that consumers associated the flavor with the source of the product (Gilson and LaLonde, 2005). Practically speaking, it is unclear how one might clear these hurdles. Furthermore, assuming, arguendo, that a flavor mark might be deemed registrable, the question of how one might enforce the registration looms large (Clarke, 1993).

CONCLUSIONS

Both the United States and the European Union protect, in some fashion, unconventional trademarks. In the United States courts and the United States Patents and Trademark Office, protection of unconventional marks has been extended due to the broad language of the Lanham Act itself which seemingly encompasses such marks by not excluding them

(15 USC § 1127). In order to protect unconventional marks, the general requirement is that the proposed mark be able to function as a mark – identify the good or service – and be recognized as such by the consumer (Gilson and LaLonde, 2005; Roth, 2005). It should be noted that there are those who favor imposing more strict controls on the registration of unconventional marks, given that such marks are not readily perceived by consumers as functioning as trademarks (Roth, 2005; Pisarsky, 2008).

The situation regarding unconventional marks in the European Union is a bit different. It cannot be said that these newer forms have been welcomed with open arms. Yet, similarly, the language in both the Trademark Directive and the Regulation also suggests (and has been interpreted to mean) that unconventional marks are registrable because they have not been expressly excluded from the ambit of a 'sign'. However, the criterion of graphic representation, for example, imposed by the European Court of Justice, sets up hurdles which may prove, under certain circumstances, to be insurmountable.

In addition, there is the requirement within the European Union that there is an assessment of secondary meaning. The criteria for making a showing of secondary meaning include: consideration of the market share held by the mark; how intensive, geographically widespread and long-standing use of the mark has been; the amount invested by the undertaking in promoting the mark; the proportion of the relevant class of persons who, because of the mark, identify goods as originating from a particular undertaking; and statements from chambers of commerce and industry or other trade and professional associations. These conditions seem to ensure that unconventional trademarks will rarely be granted protection (Llewellyn, 2005).

Nevertheless, businesses seeking to use, and protect, unconventional marks should not lose hope; given that the preliminary reference procedure only allows the European Court to give preliminary rulings on specific questions posed by the national courts. It is still necessary for the competent national authority to ascertain whether the proposed marks fulfill the requirements of registrability. Inevitably, there will be national divergences on these matters. Furthermore, it is important to note that an inability to receive registration does not preclude use; it only limits the amount of protection one can receive.

As one commentator has put it, 'the history of the law of trademarks – indeed, the history of all of intellectual property law – has been one of expanding subject matter and scope of protection: both what is protected and how deep protection should run, and also where and against whom it should run . . .' (Vaver, 2005). The use of nonconventional trademarks, and the attempts to protect such use, is just another chapter in the history of the law of trademarks.

NOTES

* Professor of Law, University of Connecticut School of Law. The author acknowledges, with gratitude, the helpful suggestions of her colleagues, and those of the CIBER participants.

1. It is beyond the scope of this chapter to discuss in any detail individual trademark protection or registration practices of individual European member states.
2. The European Union is comprised of 27 countries: Austria, Belgium, Bulgaria, Cyprus, Czech Republic, Denmark, Estonia, Finland, France, Germany, Greece, Hungary, Ireland, Italy, Latvia, Lithuania, Luxembourg, Malta, the Netherlands, Poland, Portugal, Romania, Slovakia, Slovenia, Spain, Sweden and the United Kingdom.

3. The Council is the principal legislative body of the EU, a power which it frequently shares with the Parliament. It acts on proposals referred to it by the Commission, which is charged with 'the proper functioning and development of the Common Market'.
4. First Directive 89/104/EEC of the Council, of 21 December 1988, to Approximate the Laws of the Member States Relating to Trade Marks, OJL 40/1 (hereinafter 'Trademarks Directive').
5. A directive is a legislative act. According to the Treaty, 'a directive shall be binding, as to the result to be achieved, upon each Member State to which it is addressed, but shall leave to the national authorities the choice of form and methods.' See Art. 249 EC (ex 189).
6. See Article 2 of the Trademarks Directive. This states: 'A trade mark may consist of any sign capable of being represented graphically, particularly words, including personal names, designs, letters, numerals, the shape of goods or of their packaging, provided that such signs are capable of distinguishing the goods or services of one undertaking from those of other undertakings' (Council Directive 89/104/EEC, 1988, OJ L 40/1 at Art. 2).
7. Article 3 of the Directive provides, in pertinent part: 'The following shall not be registered or if registered shall be liable to be declared invalid:

   (a) signs which cannot constitute a trade mark
   (b) trade marks which are devoid of any distinctive character . . .' (Council Directive 89/104/EEC, 1988, OJ L 40/1 at Art. 3).

8. The green-gold color for use on press pads was registered as a trademark in the United States Patent and Trademark office on 5 February 1991 as Registration No. 1,633,711.
9. Libertel appealed the case to the Gerechtshof te 's-Gravenhage (Regional Court of Appeal, The Hague) (Netherlands), and upon its dismissal, appealed to the Hoge Raad der Nederlanden. The Hoge Raad then referred the case to the European Court of Justice. The preliminary ruling procedure is intended to ensure the uniform interpretation and application of Community Law in the Member States (Article 234 EC). Note that under Art. 234 EC, a distinction is made between discretionary references (lower courts or tribunals) and mandatory references (courts of last resort).
10. The Court notes that the sufficiency of a written description would need to be evaluated on a case by case basis.
11. The emphasis on Community trademark law reflects the tension between the monopolistic effects of protecting intellectual property with the Community goals of free movement and unfettered competition.
12. Under the EC Treaty, a member state court may refer questions to the ECJ concerning the interpretation of EC law unless it is a court or tribunal of last resort, in which case it 'shall' refer such questions to the ECJ. See EC Treaty Article 234.
13. Heidelberger (2004, para. 33).
14. Heidelberger (2004, para. 35).
15. Heidelberger (2004, para. 35).
16. A service mark serves to indicate and distinguish the source of a service. See 15 USC, § 1127.
17. The Board concluded that the record was insufficient to allow it to decide whether the proposed sound functioned as a service mark.
18. The Board noted that there was already a history of registering sound marks.
19. *In re General Electric Broadcasting Company, Inc.*, 1978, p. 563.
20. Case C-283/01, *Shield Mark BV v. Joost Kist*.
21. *Shield*, paragraph 26.
22. *Shield*, paragraph 26.
23. The Court has a long history of refusing to answer hypothetical questions.
24. *Shield*, paragraph 57.
25. The applicant's case was helped, somewhat, by the fact that it was the only yarn with a scent. *In re Clarke*, 1990, p. 1239.
26. *In re Clarke*, 1990, p. 1239.
27. According to the Court, that graphic representation must enable the sign to be represented visually, particularly by means of images, lines or characters, so that it can be precisely identified. *Ralf Siechmann v. Deutsches Patent- und Marhenamt*, 2002, paragraph 46.
28. Siechmann, paragraph 71.
29. The Court of First Instance is an independent court, attached to the European Court of Justice. Created in 1989, it has jurisdiction to hear actions relating to Community Trademarks. Appeals of its decisions may be made to the European Court of Justice but are limited to questions of law.
30. Office for Harmonisation in the Internal Market (hereinafter OHIM) is the agency responsible for the registration of trademarks for the European Union, and is the equivalent of the USPTO. See McCarthy, (2007), § 29:35 (4th edn).

31. The examiner rejected the application on the grounds that the mark was neither distinctive nor capable of being represented graphically. The Board of Appeals upheld the decision.
32. The description was simply '[t]his trademark application is for an orange flavor'. *In re NV Organon*, 2006, p. 1639.
33. *In re NV Organon*, 2006, p. 1639.
34. The Examiner later waived the objection that the flavor could not be represented graphically. The waiver came before the ECJ gave its judgment in *Sieckmann* (where the Court held that in respect of an olfactory sign the requirement of graphic representability [*sic*] is not satisfied by a description in written words).
35. Trademark Manual of Examining Procedure, § 807.07 (a). A statement describing where the color(s) appear on the mark is also required.
36. Trademark Manual of Examining Procedure, § 807.07 (a).
37. The applicant is not required to submit a drawing if the applicant's mark consists *solely* of a sound, a scent, or other completely non-visual matter. For these types of marks, the applicant must submit a detailed written description of the mark that clearly explains the sound or scent. 37 CFR, § 2.52 (e) (2008).
38. Trademark Manual of Examining Procedure, § 1202.15.
39. Trademark Manual of Examining Procedure, § 1213.06.
40. Melnitzer also noted that there was sentiment that the European Court's ruling was moving European trademark law too close to the United States' model. Melnitzer, 2005.

REFERENCES

A. Leschen & Sons Rope Co. v. Broderick & Bascom Rope Co. (1906), 201 US 166 (S.Ct.).

Am. Enka Corp. v. Marzall (1952), 92 USPQ 111 (DDC).

Annand, R. (2003), 'The International Trademark Association and the community trade mark', *Trademark Reporter*, **93**, 113–21.

Bayer Co., Inc., v. United Drug Co. (1921), 272 F. 505 (SDNY).

Beran, M.J. (1967), 'Protection of slogans in the Patent Office and the courts', *Trademark Reporter*, **57**, 219–54.

Blakely, T.W. (2000), 'Beyond the international harmonization of trademark law: The community trade mark as a model of unitary transnational trademark protection', *University of Pennsylvania Law Review*, **149**, 309–54.

Campbell Soup Co. v. Armour & Co. (1949), 175 F.2d 795 (3rd Cir.), cert. denied., 338 US 847.

Clarke, N.L. (1993), 'Issues in the federal registration of flavors as trademarks for pharmaceutical products', *University of Illinois Law Review*, pp. 105–32.

Cooper, I.P. (1980), 'Trademark aspects of pharmaceutical product design', *Trademark Reporter*, **70**, 1–46.

Council Regulation (EC) 40/94 (1993), as amended by Council Regulation (EC) No. 422/2004 (2004).

Eden SARL v. OHIM, 2005 ECR II-04705.

Eli Lilly and Company v. OHIM (2003), from http://oami.europa.eu/legaldocs/boa/2001/EN/R0120_2001-2.pdf.

Europa (2007), 'European Union at a glance', http://www.europa.eu/abc/european_countries/index_en.htm.

European Perspectives (2005), 'Giving Nestlé a break', http://www.jenkins-ip.com/mym/autumn_2005/t_news 02.htm.

First Brands Corp. v. Fred Meyer, Inc., 809 F.2d 1378, 1382 (9th Cir. 1987).

First Directive 89/104/EEC of the Council, of 21 December 1988, to Approximate the Laws of the Member States Relating to Trade Marks (1988), OJ L 40/ 1.

Frost, R. (2004), 'Trademarking: Senses and sensibility', 26 April, Brandchannel.com

Gilson, J. and A.G. LaLonde (2005), 'Cinnamon buns, marching ducks and cherry-scented racecar exhaust: Protecting nontraditional trademarks', *Trademark Reporter*, **95**, 773–824.

Hammersley, F.M. (1998), 'The smell of success: Trade dress protection for scent marks', *Marquette Intellectual Property Law Review*, **2**, 105–56.

Heidelberger Bauchemie GmbH (2004), Case C-49/02, ECR I-6129.

Hidaka, S., N. Tatchell, M. Daniels, B. Trimmer and A. Cooke (2004), 'Sign of the times? A review

of key trade mark decisions of the European Court of Justice and their impact upon national trade mark jurisprudence in the EU', *Trademark Reporter*, **94**, 1105–14.
In re Clarke (1990), 17 USPQ 2D 1238 (TTAB).
In re General Electric Broadcasting Company, Inc. (1978), 199 USPQ 560 (TTAB).
In re N.V. Organon (2006), 79 USPQ 2D 1639 (TTAB).
In re N.V. Organon Appeal Brief, http://ttabvue.uspto.gov/ttabvue/v?pno=76467774&pty=EXA&eno=4
In re Owens-Corning Fiberglas Corp., 774 F.2d 1116, 1128 (CAFC, 1985).
Inwood Laboratories, Inc. v. Ives Laboratories, Inc., 456 US 844, 850, n. 10 (1982).
Lanham Act (1946), S. Rep. No. 1333, 79th Cong., 2d Sess. 3.
Landes, W.M. and R.A. Posner (1988), 'The economics of trademark law', *Trademark Reporter*, **78**, 267–306.
Libertel Groep BV v. Benelux-Merkenbureau (2003), Case C-104/01, ECR I-3793.
Llewelyn, D. (2005), 'Struggling for coherence: A review of recent developments in European Trade Mark Law', pp. 1–41, http://www.ipria.com/events/Llewelyn.pdf.
Lunney, G.S., Jr. (1999), 'Trademark monopolies', *Emory Law Journal*, **48**, 367–487.
Master Distributors, Inc. v. Pako Corp., 986 F.2d 219, 224 (8th Cir. 1993).
McCarthy, J. Thomas (2007), Trademarks and Unfair Competition § 29:35 (4th edn).
Melnitzer, J. (2005), 'Nestlé catches a break with Kit Kat trademark', *Corporate Legal Times*, http://www.insidecounsel.com/issues/insidecounsel/15_167/global_views/41-1.html.
Meyer, L. (2006), 'Much ado about nothing? Characteristics, benefits, and practical implications of the European Community trademark', *Chicago-Kent Journal of Intellectual Property*, **5**, 158–76.
NutraSweet Co. v. Stadt Corp., 917 F.2d 1024, 1028 (7th Cir. 1990).
Pisarsky, N. (2008), 'Po TAYto–Po TAHto – let's call the whole thing off: trademark protection of product sounds', *Conn. L. Rev.*, **40**, 797–842.
Qualitex Co. v. Jacobson Prods. Co. (1991), 21 USPQ 2d 1457 (C.D. Cal.).
Qualitex Co. v. Jacobson Prods. Co. (1994), 13 F.3d 1297, (9th Cir).
Qualitex Co. v. Jacobson Prods. Co. (1995), 514 US 159 (S. Ct.).
Ralf Sieckmann v. Deutsches Patent- und Markenamt (2002), Case C-273/00, ECR I-11737.
Ramsey, L.P. (2006), 'Intellectual property rights in advertising', *Michigan Telecommunications and Technology Law Review*, **12**, 189–263.
Roth, M. (2005), 'Something old, something new, something borrowed, something blue: A new tradition in nontraditional trademark registrations', *Cardozo Law Review*, **27**, 457–95.
Shield Mark BV v. Joost Kist (2003), Case C-283/01, ECR I-14313.
Société des produits Nestlé SA v. Mars UK Ltd (2005), Case C-353/03, ECR I-06135.
Trademark Manual of Examining Procedure (2005), http://tess2.uspto.gov/tmdb/tmep.
Vaver, D. (2005), 'Recent trends in European Trademark Law: Of shape, senses and sensation', *Trademark Reporter*, **95**, 895–913.
Wilkinson, D.C. (1990), 'The community trade mark regulation and its role in European economic integration', *Trademark Reporter*, **80**, 107–39.
Wurtenberger, G. (1996), 'References to the European Court of Justice for preliminary ruling in trademark matters', *Trademark Reporter*, **86**, 203–15.

11. National IPR policies and multinational R&D strategies: an interactive perspective

Minyuan Zhao and Bernard Yeung

INTRODUCTION

TRIPs, the Agreement on Trade-Related Aspects of Intellectual Property Rights administered by WTO, has prompted extensive discussions on the optimal international IPR arrangement and its enforcement. For developing countries eager to speed up their technological progress, how strictly should they enforce the protection of IPR?

Developing countries often argue that they need the time and freedom to learn from the advanced countries and nurture their indigenous industries. The experiences of the United States in the nineteenth century and Japan in the twentieth century are cited as examples of the imitate-first-innovate-later policy. The Commission on Intellectual Property Rights (2002),[1] for example, observed that 'there has generally been an association with "weak" rather than "strong" forms of IP protection in the formative period of economic development'.

Meanwhile, endogenous growth models in economics suggest that a strong IPR regime is crucial to R&D investment and economic growth (Romer, 1990). This view is echoed by Ambassador Susan Schwab, the US Trade Representative, in a recent news conference: 'Any country that aspires to be a knowledge-based economy, to promote its entrepreneurial and artistic classes sees the value of protecting intellectual property.' In particular, weak IPR protection may keep away valuable foreign direct investments (Lai, 1998; Smith, 2001), especially in technology-intensive sectors that rely heavily on intellectual properties (Smarzynska Javorcik, 2004).

A missing piece in the whole debate is the fact that firms are heterogeneous. Large conglomerates may be able to use their internal organizations to substitute for inadequate social and legal institutions in the economy (Khanna and Palepu, 2000). Multinational enterprises (MNEs), meanwhile, have the advantage of allocating complementary R&D projects across national borders. By protecting the key components in the home country, MNEs with the right organizational and technological capabilities can minimize the imitation risk in countries with weak IPR protection (Zhao, 2006).

In fact, China, the country frequently cited for its inadequate IPR enforcement, has become 'a global magnet of R&D' in recent years (*Wall Street Journal*, 13 March, 2006). According to the World Investment Report by UNCTAD, over 750 foreign-funded R&D centers had been set up in China by 2005, and 61 per cent of the surveyed enter-

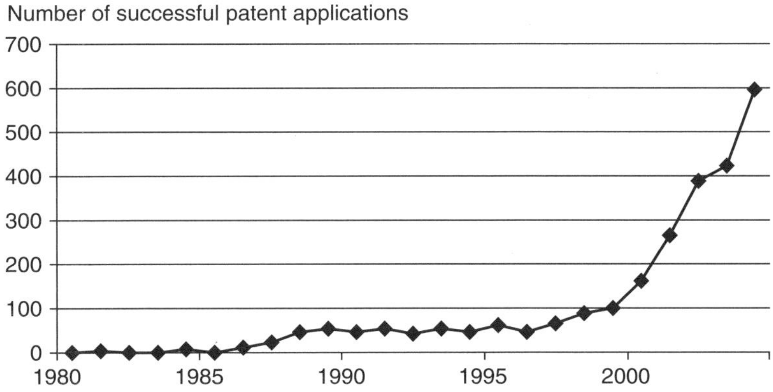

Figure 11.1 US patents invented in China

prises named China as the most active country for new R&D facilities. As shown in Figure 11.1, the number of patents developed in China and filed with the US Patent and Trademark Office (USPTO) is growing rapidly in recent years. More than 75 per cent of them are owned by multinational companies such as General Electric, Microsoft, IBM and Intel.

The purpose of this study is to include the strategic R&D organization of firms into policy considerations, and analyze how national IPR policies may change in the presence of multinational R&D activities. To address this question, I construct a simple framework in which IPR protection affects human capital investment, innovation and imitation. The government chooses a protection level given the distribution of heterogeneous firms. When the country opens up, MNEs are allowed to utilize local talents and create knowledge for global applications. Thanks to their cross-border organizations, MNEs are less reliant on the local institutions for knowledge protection. Thus, the competing demand from MNEs prompts the government to adjust the IPR policy accordingly. The policy response to MNE entries, however, differs widely across countries, depending on the initial industry structures. For example, multinational R&D may have little impact on an economy dominated by entrenched power or special interest groups. In contrast, if the domestic players are mainly small homogeneous firms, a sound legal system is critical to their competition with MNEs.

This chapter is not intended to challenge the large literature on IPR policies. Instead, it is to build on the current literature and shed light on a new channel of interaction between firms and institutions: the flow of resources across heterogeneous firms. The rest of the chapter is organized as follows. The second section describes firm R&D strategies in detail, particularly MNEs that expand their R&D networks across multiple institutional environments. The third section incorporates strategic R&D organization into a simple model to highlight the impact of firm heterogeneity on the market equilibrium. Various factors, such as initial industry structure and rent-seeking incentives by the government, are also discussed in this section. The fourth section concludes.

ENDOGENOUS R&D ORGANIZATION

Firm Heterogeneity in the Domestic Economy

Instead of relying solely on the legal institutions, firms can partially protect the value of their innovation using alternative mechanisms, including complicated hierarchies, strategic innovation structures, social ties as well as government relationships. Heterogeneity in firm organization has been addressed in various fields. Khanna (2000) shows substantial evidence that large business groups in emerging economies substitute for missing outside institutions with internal capital and labor markets. Firms affiliated with such business groups perform significantly better than their unaffiliated counterparts. Consequently, poor legal environments are associated with the prevalence of family-controlled businesses (La Porta et al., 1998), whereby the entrenched families are given preferential access to capital and lobbying power (Morck et al., 2000).

Similar arguments apply to the protection and appropriation of IPR. First, imitation is costly (Mansfield et al., 1981) and often challenging (Rivkin, 2000), so it will happen only when imitators can profit from the technologies. Teece (1986) suggests that specialized and co-specialized complementary assets are critically important to the successful commercialization of an innovation. Connection to related products or services (Anand and Galetovic, 2004) can all be important factors in the appropriation of value from innovation. Thus, innovating firms can discourage imitation by developing technologies that require complementary resources unavailable to potential imitators. Market leaders not only rely on innovation, which may be susceptible to imitation, but also the ability to put innovation into immediate, large-scale manufacturing and move down the cost curve quickly. Competitors are thus discouraged from investing in costly imitation once they see the limited market potential for their own products.

Imitation is also restricted by absorptive capacity – the ability to identify, assimilate and implement new technologies. The internal development of knowledge often involves intensive interaction among various components and with the firm's existing expertise. The more firm-specific the technologies are, the longer it takes for other firms to decipher the information. Thus, innovating firms can take advantage of the constraint on absorptive capacity and win out on lead time. Obviously, large established firms are more likely to benefit from such knowledge transfer barriers.

Note that such firm heterogeneity is endogenous. In an environment with weak legal institutions, firms are more wiling to invest in alternative mechanisms of value appropriation, and those who successfully obtained the alternative mechanisms tend to dominate the market, driving out their pure-play competitors. Casual observations are also consistent with this argument. Under weak IPR regimes, R&D activities tend to concentrate in large conglomerates, often with strong government connections, whereas technology start-ups are more likely to prosper in environments with an efficient financial market, well-developed market institutions and sound legal systems. The reverse is also true: once the dominating firms develop alternative mechanisms of value appropriation, there is less pressure for the government to make improvements. We will elaborate this point later in the next section.

R&D across National Borders

Strategies to overcome local institutional constraints are best illustrated in the geographically dispersed R&D of MNEs. In a 2004 survey by the Economists Intelligence Unit (EIU), 84 per cent of executives cited inadequate IPR protection in emerging economies as a challenge for R&D globalization. Yet R&D spending by US firms is growing rapidly in a wide range of emerging economies. From 1995 to 2004, the number of US patents obtained by US firms based on technologies developed in non-OECD countries more than doubled.

This may seem a paradox at first sight. However, there is a simple arbitrage explanation once we take factor prices into consideration. Due to the poor IPR protection, local talents cannot realize the full value from their innovative activities. Human capital is underutilized as a result. Such low-cost human capital is attractive to R&D-intensive MNEs that possess alternative mechanisms to appropriate value from their intellectual properties.

The unique advantage of MNEs is that their R&D networks span multiple institutional environments. In Figure 11.2, we plot (1) the average number of distinct R&D locations and (2) the Herfindahl Index of geographic concentration in terms of patent inventors for each of the top 100 innovating firms in the medical and drug industry. Clearly, large firms are increasingly spreading out their R&D activities in the past two decades, facilitated by the rapid development of information technologies. Further examination reveals the crucial role played by firms' internal organizational structures. A typical research lab in China or India is separated from the firm's local operations, but maintains extensive communications and collaborations with the technology department at headquarters. The locally developed technologies are quickly integrated into the firms' global R&D projects,

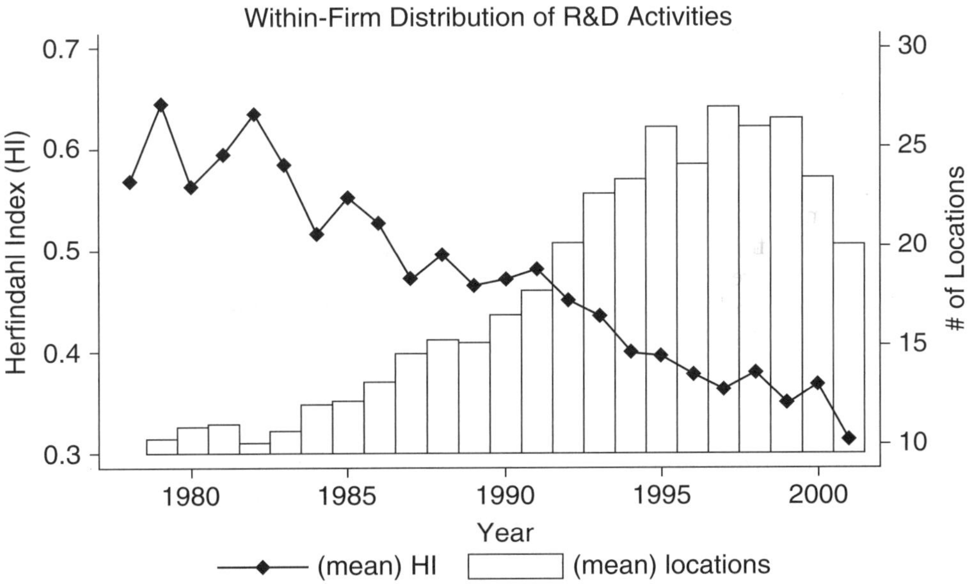

Figure 11.2 Geographically dispersed R&D in the medical and drug industry

and the final products are marketed worldwide, especially in regions with strong IPR protection.

By leveraging their home institutions and protecting the complementary technologies at headquarters, MNEs are less vulnerable to the imitation risk in the host countries. A major success of Microsoft Research Asia in Beijing was 'AutoMovie', a technology that can intelligently generate edited movies from home videos. It was later integrated into 'Microsoft Movie Maker', which was further integrated into the new Windows operating system. Similar examples are the 'Mobile HTML Optimizer' used in Microsoft FrontPage, the 'Ink Parsing' technology used in Tablet PC, and the 'error-resilient video transmission' technology used in the MPEG4 Standard. These are all considered important contributions by the Beijing lab, but they themselves do not bring direct commercial value to potential imitators. The closely-knit internal structure, therefore, serves as an immune system against the adverse external environments.

Large MNEs usually have a wide spectrum of R&D activities under management, ranging from basic research to product development to manufacturing. Some technologies are inherently more tacit and less likely to diffuse across firms (Kogut and Zander, 1993). Thus, they can tailor the tasks accordingly to capitalize on the strengths of particular locations and at the same time minimize costs and risks. Looking across firms and industries, we identify two typical strategies of internalization used by MNEs.

The first one is secrecy of architectural knowledge, with the help of geographic distance across subsidiary labs. Take the famous KFC sauce for example. The sauce is composed of eleven different herbs and spices, none of which is protected by IPR. However, the ingredients are mixed at two different locations and then combined at a third location. Because knowledge tends to be locally bounded, KFC maintains the secrecy of the recipe without the secrecy of any individual ingredients. In fact, many firms are doing what KFC does. Pharmaceutical companies, for instance, are hiring scientists around the world to screen chemical compounds and conduct lab tests, but only few managers at the top of the hierarchical ladder know exactly how these test results fit into the drugs being developed. Without seeing the whole picture, the local scientists find it very difficult to transfer the knowledge to or even communicate with researchers from other firms.

The secrecy strategy works for some industries but has serious drawbacks for others. For R&D projects that cannot be easily specified or new technologies that require significant initiatives from local scientists and engineers, keeping the big picture from local R&D units hurts morale and productivity. It may even create distrust across global subsidiaries, increasing coordination costs. In such circumstances, MNEs often rely on what they do best: global networks that create and integrate knowledge efficiently (Bartlett and Ghoshal, 1990). For example, GE Healthcare integrates technologies from its labs in China, Israel, Hungary, France and India into everything from new X-ray devices to million-dollar CT scanners (*BusinessWeek*, 3 February, 2003). Information leakage may happen at any of these places – a Chinese engineer may reveal an important piece of technology without effective legal restriction and an Israeli scientist may decide to change jobs every six months – but nobody is able to integrate the array of technologies better and faster than GE. By the time competitors catch up, GE has already rolled out the second or third generation products. By developing an efficient and closely-interlinked organization, innovating firms are able to maintain their technological lead without secrecy. For imitators, circumventing a patent is much easier than imitating a dynamically evolving organization.

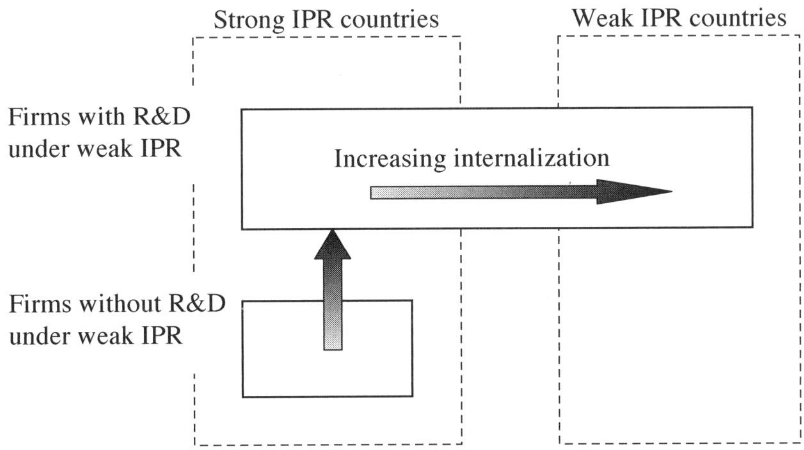

Figure 11.3 Within- and cross-firm variations with internalization strategies

Empirical evidence is supportive of this argument. Examining a sample of 1567 innovating firms headquartered in the US, Zhao (2006) finds that within the same firm, technologies developed in weak IPR countries are used more internally than those developed in other foreign countries. In addition, across all firms, those doing R&D in weak IPR countries feature significantly stronger internal linkages than those staying out. Because extensive internal linkages may compromise efficiency and incur excessively high coordination costs, only a small group of firms with strong organizational capabilities will find it worthwhile to enter weak IPR countries. The relationships are illustrated in Figure 11.3.

The above discussions on endogenous R&D organization are the building blocks for our analysis of policy implications. In the face of strategic responses by heterogeneous firms, policy makers may have to reevaluate the implications of IPR enforcement. In the next section, we model an economy comprised of heterogeneous firms. We first show that the government's policy choice is highly dependent on the initial composition of firms in the economy. The results are then compared with the policy dynamics after the country's opening-up to foreign competition, assuming the same initial profile of firms.[2]

POLICY DYNAMICS

Model Set-up

To keep the model simple, we assume an economy with fixed population L. Individuals are each endowed with one unit of labor, with which they can earn the same basic wage in production. They can also spend time on education and obtain one unit of human capital, so the education cost can be considered the opportunity cost of time that can otherwise be spent on production. Because of the idiosyncratic learning capabilities across individuals, those with high capabilities will invest in education first. Therefore, the aggregate human capital investment in the economy is featured by increasing marginal cost: $C'(H) = aH > 0$, where H is the aggregate amount of human capital in the economy. In market equilibrium, the last agent who enters the human capital market will find the marginal cost equal to marginal return: $C'(H) = aH = r$, where r is the price of human capital that is endogenously determined by the market.

Firms hire human capital and profit from their innovative activities. Assume that with human capital h, a firm experiences innovations with a Poisson arrival rate $\dot{n} = b \cdot h$. The reason for such a linear function is that, at this stage, we do not want the scale effect to complicate the analysis. An innovation will generate expected value v (the net present value of future cash flows), which will be held exclusively by the innovator until imitation occurs. This is where the protection of IPR plays a role. The risk of imitation is associated with the effectiveness of IPR protection enforced by the government. With IPR enforcement λ $(0 < \lambda < 1)$ and in the absence of alternative mechanisms by firms, the expected value that an innovating firm can appropriate from an innovation is λv. So the inventor appropriates the whole value v if IPR protection is perfect, and gets zero if there is no protection at all.

In a competitive market, demand for human capital is determined by the condition $r \cdot h = \dot{n}\, \lambda\, v$. That is, the cost of hiring human capital h should be equal to the return that the firm expects from the resulting innovations. Hence, $r = b \cdot \lambda v$. Because $aH = r$, $H = r/a = (b/a) \cdot \lambda v$. Obviously, the lower the IPR protection λ, the lower is the equilibrium value for human capital (r), and the lower is the investment in education (H). Human capital investment is also positively related to the productivity in innovation (b), and negatively related to the cost of education (a).

As discussed in the previous section, firms are not relying exclusively on legal enforcement for their IPR protection. Rather, they take advantage of the internal complementarities among technologies and strategic organization of R&D to appropriate value from innovation. We use the parameter z $(0 < z < 1)$ to measure the degree to which a firm can internalize its value of innovation; only $(1 - z)$ part of the value is exposed to potential imitation. So the value appropriated is $zv + (1 - z)\lambda$. We assume that all firms, including the extant firms and potential entrants, are continuously distributed along z following the distribution density function $f(z)$.[3] Those with high z's are the privileged firms that are relatively independent of the external institutions.

Thus, for each unit of h, firm profit $\pi(z, \lambda) = b \cdot [zv + (1 - z)\lambda \cdot v] - r$. To the extreme, $\pi(z, \lambda) \rightarrow b \cdot \lambda v$ when $z \rightarrow 0$ (fully exposed) and $\pi(z, \lambda) \rightarrow b \cdot v$ when $z \rightarrow 1$ (fully internalized). It immediately follows that, for all firms, the appropriable value from R&D is increasing in the strength of IPR protection. However, the sensitivity to λ varies in z: $\partial\pi/\partial\lambda = b(1-z)v$. Those with high z's are less sensitive to the environmental variable λ. As will be clear soon, for the most privileged firms, the adverse external environment may even induce higher profits, thanks to the lower equilibrium price of human capital.

Market Equilibrium in a Domestic Economy

The supply of human capital is determined by $r = aH$, the upward-sloping curve along which people's investment in human capital increases in the expected return r. In a closed economy, the aggregate demand is determined by firms who can appropriate higher returns from human capital than the cost r. The marginal firm with internalization level z_0 will have zero profit: $\pi(z_0 \lambda) = 0$. Thus, the demand function is $H = \int_{z_0}^{1} f(z)dz$.

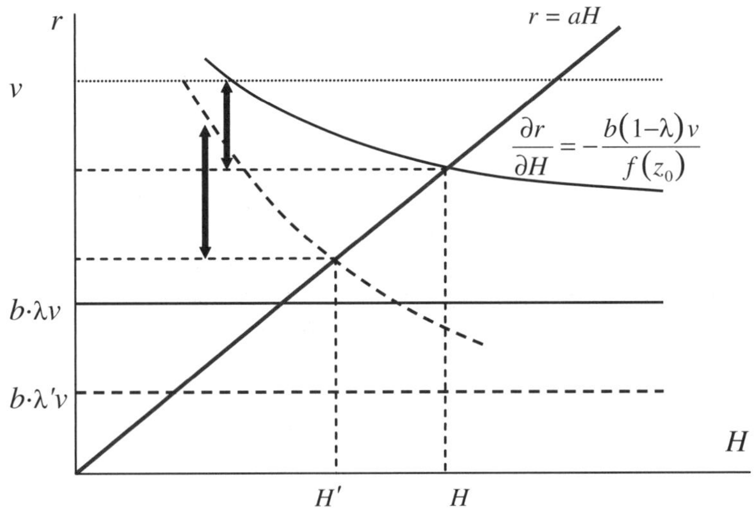

Figure 11.4 Market equilibrium under different levels of IPR protection

The downward sloping curves track the appropriable returns of the marginal firm, as the R&D sector expands and less privileged firms enter.

The slope of the demand curve at the market equilibrium point z_0 is $(\partial r/\partial H) = (\partial r/\partial_{z_0})/(\partial r/\partial_{z_0}) = -b(1-\lambda)v/f(z_0)$, which is affected by two key factors. The curve will be steeper if (1) the economy is composed of more heterogeneous firms dispersed from the marginal point (low $f(z_0)$), and (2) the IPR protection is weak (that is, λ is closer to 0). With a steep demand curve, even a significant drop in cost can only introduce limited entries of new firms (the expansion of the equilibrium H to the right).

More importantly, the slope of the demand curve affects the distribution of returns in the economy. Although profits are always higher for more privileged firms: $\partial\pi/\partial z = b(1-\lambda)\cdot v > 0$, a strong IPR regime attenuates the difference: $\partial^2\pi/\partial z\ \partial\lambda = -bv < 0$. Intuitively, it is crucial for firms under a weak legal environment to possess alternative means of value appropriation, while strong IPR protection provides a level playground for all types of firms. For policy makers, it is important to realize that IPR policies affect not only the *level* of R&D activities, but also the *distribution* of resources across heterogeneous firms. The implication of IPR policies to profit distribution is obvious with the two double-arrows in Figure 11.4, which represent the profit margins that high-z firms can expect under two different IPR regimes. Weak IPR protection suppresses the demand for human capital, and, by keeping the price of human capital low, allows higher profits for the most privileged firms in the economy.

The Policy Rules

Strong IPR protection (large λ) increases the return to human capital and encourages human capital investment. At the same time, the costs of strong IPR enforcement can be prohibitively high when λ gets closer to 1. The costs include the establishment and

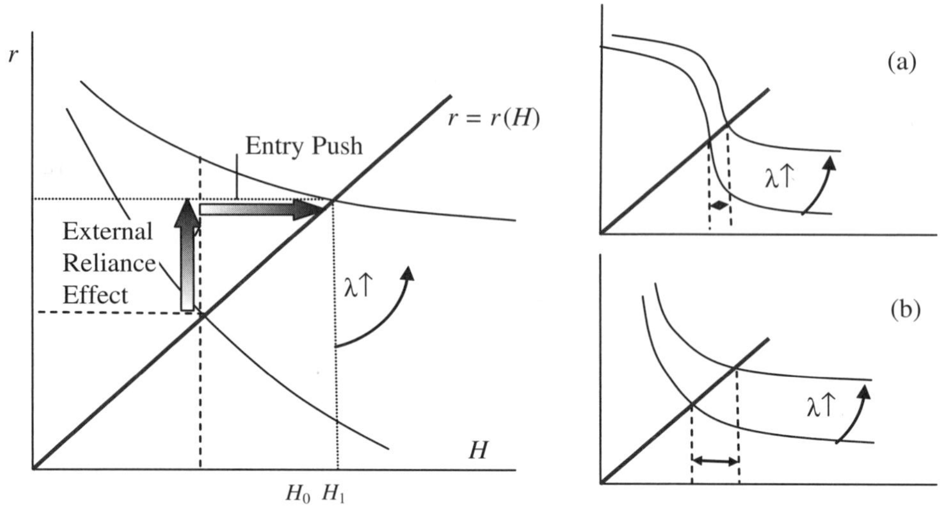

Figure 11.5 Effect of IPR reform and distribution of firm types

maintenance of an effective legal infrastructure by the government and the litigation costs borne by firms. Over-strong IPR also slows down the spread of new technologies to the competitive sector, incurring the deadweight loss of monopolistic pricing. The government's objective is to encourage innovation while keeping the enforcement costs in check.

Institutions are path-dependent and change slowly, so it is reasonable to assume that a country cannot jump to an optimal level of protection overnight. The government improves institutions only if the near-term expected benefit outweighs the near-term expected cost, which again depends on the composition of firms in the economy, that is, $f(z)$. The impact of institutional development will be larger in countries where existing firms have invested less in institution substitution mechanisms such as complicated business group structures and preferential ties with the government, and in countries with a longer queue of potential entrants who are ready to enter the market upon incremental institutional improvements.

We call the first mechanism of institutional improvement the *external reliance effect*, which is illustrated by the upward vertical arrow in Figure 11.5. An increase in institutional environment makes everyone better off, but the marginal benefit is much larger for firms with little alternative in knowledge protection. Secondly, because of the increased return to R&D, more firms with low institution-substitution capabilities are able to enter the market. We call it the *entry push effect*. In an economy whose initial institutions are weak, the entry barrier is high and the population of entrepreneurs prepared for entry is likely to be small (Fogel et al., 2006). In other words, marginal improvement in IPR protection will not induce significantly more R&D investment in the economy. The government will be likely to see a large impact of its policies if there is a 'ready' population of entrepreneurs previously constrained by the weak IPR regimes. Otherwise, with low external reliance effect and low entry push effect, even a benevolent government will have little incentive to engage in costly institutional reforms.

Figure 11.5 illustrates the marginal benefits of an IPR improvement, decomposed into the external reliance effect and the entry push effect. Panels (a) and (b) depict two economies with different initial distributions of firms. Panel (a) features a polarized structure, with a group of elite firms and the rest of the economy that will not engage in R&D without significant policy support. The marginal impact of an IPR reform, therefore, is much smaller than in the economy in panel (b), where there exists a concentration of marginal firms.

This comparison highlights the path dependence of IPR environment changes over time. The weaker the environment, the more likely that the surviving firms have developed alternative means of value appropriation independent of the legal system, hence the lower incentives that the government has to initiate changes. In addition, because the distribution of firm types is usually the endogenous result of overall institutional environments, including the development of the financial market and judiciary systems, any discussions of IPR policies should not be isolated from the general context of institution development in the country.

The Impact of Multinational R&D

The path-dependency of institutional changes may result in economically undesirable, but stable, political economy equilibriums. Globalization, particularly the entry of MNEs, may disrupt such equilibriums, and facilitate institutional reforms by reducing the incumbents' abilities and incentives to preserve the status quo.

What is special about the MNEs is that they can strategically organize R&D activities across multiple institutional environments, and therefore make their value less vulnerable to particular national IPR regimes. Of course, MNEs usually have more resources (for example, the existing knowledge base of the firm, deeper pockets, and so on) to work with human capital, thus making human capital more productive. They are also able to utilize the resulting technologies in a larger scale and broader scope, thus deriving more value from R&D (Cohen and Klepper, 1996). Nevertheless, in this study we want to focus on the influence of institutional environment and exclude other factors at the moment. The objective is to show how the host country's IPR policy affects the relative competitiveness of MNEs versus domestic firms, and what this means for policy choices.

Due to the features of multinational R&D discussed above, MNEs only expose a small proportion of the value (z_f) to the local environment. Then, the return of human capital to MNEs is: $r_f = b[z_f v + (1 - z_f)\lambda \cdot v] - c$, where c is the additional coordination cost incurred by the cross-border arrangements. Until recent years, the cost of communication and collaboration across national borders was prohibitively high. Moreover, in most traditional industries, decomposing projects for offshore R&D is costly and inefficient. If r_f is lower than the pre-entry market price for human capital (r) in the host country, there will not be any multinational R&D. Hence, R&D is historically concentrated at the firm headquarters.

The development in information technologies, however, has dramatically reduced the coordination costs across geographic distance. The adoption of task-oriented R&D organization and standardized interfaces has also facilitated R&D internationalization. With $r_f > r$, it is profitable for MNEs to take advantage of the inexpensive human capital in the host country.

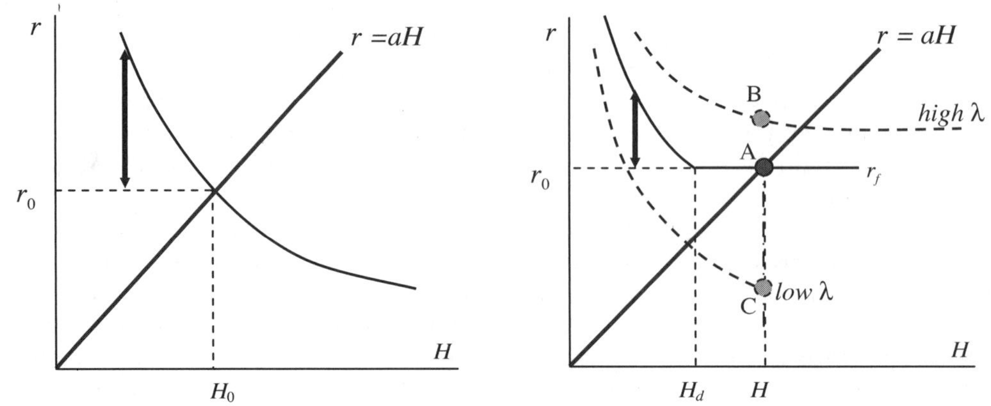

Figure 11.6 Market equilibrium before and after MNE entries

Assume that the demand for human capital by MNEs is fully elastic at the price r_f. This is a simplistic but not unrealistic assumption given the number and scale of MNEs involved in R&D internationalization. Relaxing the assumption from full elasticity to high elasticity does not affect our analysis. As a result, multinational entries – as well as potential entries – change the marginal conditions of the local human capital market. The market price of human capital, instead of being constrained by the human capital supply, is now bounded from below at r_f.

The profit of a domestic firm becomes: $\pi(z) = [zv + (1-z)\lambda \cdot v] - r_f$. Apparently, the marginal domestic firm needs to have a $z = z_d$, larger than the pre-globalization z_0. Figure 11.6 illustrates the change in market equilibrium upon the presence of fully elastic demand from MNEs. Compared with the domestic economy, now the value of human capital is not only higher, but also more homogeneous across firms, thus leaving narrower profit margin to the privileged domestic firms. Corresponding to the higher r, the total amount of human capital H increases from the domestic equilibrium H_0 to H, but human capital employed by the domestic firms decreases to H_d.

The entry of multinational R&D brings a one-time shock to domestic economy, inducing the government to re-evaluate the costs and benefits of IPR reforms. As shown in Figure 11.6, with the competing demand from the MNEs, the amount of human capital available to the domestic sector is now more sensitive to the IPR policies. If the IPR protection is extremely bad, the expected returns from R&D will not be enough to cover the fixed coordination cost c. In that case, MNE entries will not happen even if the country opens up. Once entries occur, the sensitivity of human capital in the domestic sector to IPR protection will significantly increase if (1) the density of domestic firms around the new critical point is high (large $f(z_d)$), and (2) MNEs are insensitive to the local policies (high z_f). Under these conditions, a weak IPR regime corresponds to a sharp decline of H_d due to the brain drain to MNEs.

Using this framework, we can discuss how firm heterogeneity and the internalization strategies of MNEs affect the catching-up argument proposed by many developing countries. The strong presence of MNEs and their hiring of local talents per se should not be the reason for concern. Because of locally bounded knowledge spillover (Jaffe et al., 1993), the presence of multinational R&D in developing countries should also provide great learning opportunities for the host country. Following the conventional wisdom, a lax IPR environment should facilitate the spillover of foreign technologies to local competitors. But is it true? Let us examine two aspects of the knowledge spillover process: (1) the types of technologies being transferred, and (2) the recipients of the technologies.

First, because of the endogenous strategies that MNEs employ, the weaker the external IPR protection, the more the MNEs are willing to incur higher organizational costs for the purpose of internalization. Hence, technologies developed in weak IPR countries tend to be more internalized, even within the same firm (Zhao, 2006). Without the complementary resources residing in the MNEs, local competitors cannot easily understand or build on the highly firm-specific technologies. In contrast, when local IPR protection strengthens, MNEs are more willing to transfer technologies applicable to local needs (Branstetter et al., 2006), which are potentially more valuable for the development of indigenous R&D.

Secondly, labor mobility has been identified as the most effective means of knowledge transfer (Agrawal et al., 2006; Almeida and Kogut, 1999; Song et al., 2003). Researchers in an MNE may have incentive to leave the company and start their own businesses or to join a local competitor, if they are able to appropriate higher value from their intellectual capital (that is, point B in Figure 11.6). The weaker the external institutions, the more reluctant they will be in leaving the highly internalized MNE (that is, from point A to point C in Figure 11.6). As a result, while lax IPR policies may help the locals to copy a product design or circumvent a patent of a tangible technology in the short run, they discourage entrepreneurship and the mobility of talents – and the intangible, tacit knowledge that is carried with them – from MNEs to the domestic sector. All this may hurt the technological catch-up in the long run.

Combining the above two factors, we believe that any argument for a lax IPR environment should take firms' strategic R&D organization into consideration. When the IPR protection is weak, the source of knowledge spillover does not remain fixed. Rather, MNEs would adjust their R&D strategies according to the imitation risks that they foresee in the host countries. More internalized innovation structures in weak IPR countries not only make the information less comprehensible by local competitors, but also reduce the possibility of employees leaving the multinational sector. Both factors may reverse the effort to learn advanced technologies from foreign countries.

The competing demand for, and keeping of, human capital by MNEs gives additional reasons for the government to engage in costly IPR reforms. However, just as in the closed economy, the degree to which foreign entries affect policy decisions depends on the initial economic structure of the country. IPR reforms are most likely to happen if, at the new equilibrium price r_f, there exist strong external reliance effect and entry push effect. That is, firms would benefit from or respond to the external policy changes. In an economy controlled by elite business groups, the entry of MNEs simply expands the horizon to areas that have never been reached by local entrepreneurs, but does not impose much threat to the interest of the incumbents. In such circumstances, policy re-evaluation will not generate significant changes in IPR enforcement.

The two panels in Figure 11.7 feature exactly the same initial price (r_0) and the same level of human capital investment (H_0) prior to the entry of MNEs. However, in the left panel there are two distinct groups of firms: one privileged class with high z, and one

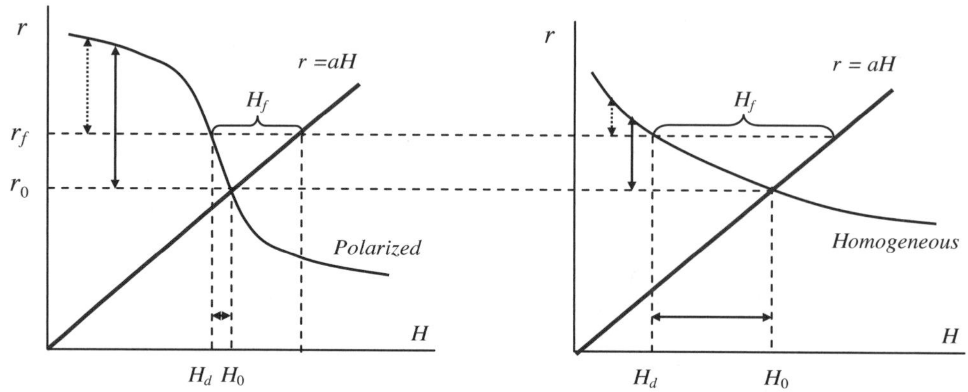

Figure 11.7 Impact of multinational entries depending on initial structure of the economy

entrepreneurial class vulnerable to external environments. In contrast, firms in the right panel are relatively homogeneous in their ability to appropriate value.

As discussed earlier, even in a purely domestic economy, the government of the left panel is more likely to settle with a weak IPR regime. Higher imitation risk makes the return curve steeper, which keeps the factor prices low and the profits high for the privileged firms. When MNEs enter with r_f, the two economies experience the same increase in factor prices. While the economy with a cluster of privileged firms does not lose much ground, the economy with relatively homogeneous firms sees a large wave of brain drain to MNEs (see the double arrows between H_0 and H_d). To shore up domestic R&D, a shift towards stronger IPR protection is expected in the right panel – which was in a better condition to begin with – but not in the left one. In that sense, globalization may simply magnify, rather than change, the institutional differences already there across countries.

Rent-seeking and Policy Implications

The above discussions are based on the assumption that there is a benevolent government aiming for technological progress. In most parts of the world, however, side payments from firms are an important part of the governments' considerations, only to various degrees. Since IPR policies affect not only the level but also the distribution of resources across heterogeneous firms, firms will show different willingness as well as ability to make side payments. Knowing this, a rent-seeking government is likely to approach the policy decisions differently. In this subsection, we incorporate the possibility of rent-seeking into our model and see how it may change the policy outcomes.

It is reasonable to assume that the firm-specific parameter z is associated with their side payments to the government, that is, privileged firms are privileged partly because they are paying higher contributions. Therefore, the total amount of side payments expected by the government is determined by two factors: (1) the payment propensity of all incumbent firms, and (2) the overall size of the contributing base.

First, under strong external protection, firms are more reluctant to build a costly relationship with the government: alternative mechanisms of value appropriation become less important when legal protection is readily available to everyone. Moreover, the higher market price of human capital – as a result of the strong protection – cuts into the profit enjoyed by the highly privileged firms, who are usually the largest contributors. Namely, there is less monopoly profit left in a more competitive environment. These two effects lower the firms' willingness as well as their ability to make side payments. When $\lambda = 1$, there is no room for rent-seeking. In contrast, a poor institutional environment transfers profits to institution-independent firms, who can return the favor to government officials in the form of higher side payments.

Second, the distribution of firms also affects the concern for the overall contribution base. Weak IPR protection reduces the contributing base by driving the marginal firms out of business. However, the negative impact will be very limited if there are limited entrepreneurship activities. Hence, with the presence of rent-seeking incentives, a polarized economic structure – as is often the case in developing countries – pushes the policy maker further away from institutional improvements.

The presence of multinational R&D generally discourages rent-seeking for two reasons. First, given r_f, the government can no longer induce higher rents by keeping the costs low. Although r_f may still be decreasing in the imitation risk λ, it is not as sensitive as r in the closed economy. Second, facing the competition from MNEs (instead of the upward-sloping supply curve in a closed economy), the domestic sector of an economy without adequate IPR protection is likely to shrink rapidly. This reduces the pool of firms potentially making side payments to the government. Consequently, globalization mitigates the effect of rent-seeking on a government's decision on IPR enforcement.

This mitigation effect, however, still varies with the prior distribution of firm types. Although foreign competitors might be less sensitive to the local institutions than some domestic firms, they may be no match for those with extensive investments in substitutive mechanisms. Thus, in a polarized economy with weak IPR protection, the most privileged firms may lobby for even weaker protection to deter foreign competition from entry and to safeguard their profits. Therefore, with side payments predominantly coming from the privileged firms, we may actually see deterioration of IPR enforcement with the prospect of globalization. More generally, this also explains why externally forced open-door policies, without taking the composition of domestic players into consideration, do not work in most cases. It is not unusual to see anti-competition behaviors from the government right upon opening up – just to protect the existing interest (for example, Siegel, 2004). Such policy responses are more likely to occur when the rent-seeking incentive is high.

In summary, rent-seeking reduces the government's incentive to improve IPR protection because weak institutions channel profits to privileged firms who convert them as side payments to the government. Moreover, when potential entries are limited, weak institutions do not erode much of the government's base for rent revenues. Hence, rent-seeking aggravates the impact of the external reliance and entry push effects discussed earlier. Globalization tends to mitigate this effect as open competition constrains the government's ability to channel profits. Yet the impact is limited if the rents are predominately from a group of highly privileged firms, who may even persuade the government to utilize adverse institutions to preserve the domestic interests from foreign competition.

CONCLUSION

There has been a large amount of literature analyzing globalization and IPR protection. Most studies take the framework of an innovating 'North' and an imitating 'South', with a representative firm in each country. However, this framework is not adequate in two aspects. First, different firms react differently to public policies and thus have important implications for policy effectiveness. Second, with MNEs strategically allocating their R&D activities across different IPR regimes, national policies affect not only the domestic economy, but also the international allocation of resources. The purpose of this chapter is to bring firm strategies explicitly into the analysis of policy outcomes.

Emphasizing firm heterogeneity allows us to reach a richer understanding of the impact of MNE entries on institutional changes in the host countries. Depending on the initial distribution of domestic firms, there has been a large cross-country variation in the impact of MNE entries. In a country dominated by strong entrenched power or large business groups, a poor institutional environment serves as a de facto entry barrier against competition. After opening up, MNEs take advantage of the human capital that would otherwise have been kept out of the market, but they do not impose an immediate threat to the entrenched powers. Thus, the government will not have a strong incentive to improve IPR protection. In contrast, if the domestic players are mainly small homogeneous firms, a sound legal system is critical to their competition with MNEs. The implication of the analysis goes beyond human capital and intellectual properties and applies to more general settings.

NOTES

1. http://www.iprcommission.org/.
2. For a complete description of the model and its mathematical solutions, see Zhao (2004).
3. We treat f as exogenous at any given point in time, fully acknowledging that it could well be the equilibrium outcome of a firm's decisions to invest in substitutes for weak institutions. Thus, the worse the institutional environment, the more likely that firms form large business groups or establish political relationships with the government, which shifts the distribution to the right.

REFERENCES

Agrawal, A., I. Cockburn and J. McHale (2006), 'Gone but not forgotten: Knowledge flows, labor mobility, and enduring social relationships', *Journal of Economic Geography*, **6**(5), 571–91.

Almeida, P. and B. Kogut (1999), 'Localization of knowledge and the mobility of engineers in regional networks', *Management Science*, **45**, 905–17.

Anand, B.N. and A. Galetovic (2004), 'How market smarts can protect property rights', *Harvard Business Review*, **82**(12), 72–9.

Bartlett, C.A. and S. Ghoshal (1990), 'The multinational corporation as an interorganizational network', *Academy of Management Review*, **15**(4), 603–25.

Branstetter, L., R. Fisman and C.F. Foley (2006), 'Do stronger intellectual property rights increase international technology transfer? Empirical evidence from US firm-level panel data', *Quarterly Journal of Economics*, **121**(1), 321–49.

Business Week (2003), 'The new global job shift', February 3.

Cohen, W.M. and S. Klepper (1996), 'A reprise of size and R&D', *Economic Journal*, **106**(437), 925–51.

Fogel, K., A. Hawk, R. Morck and B. Yeung (2006), 'Supply of entrepreneurs and institutional obstacles to advancement', in Mark Casson, Bernard Yeung, Anuradha Basu and Nigel Wadeson (eds), *Oxford Handbook of Entrepreneurship*, Oxford, UK and New York, USA: Oxford University Press.

Jaffe, A.B., M. Trajtenberg and R. Henderson (1993), 'Geographic localization of knowledge spillovers as evidenced by patent citations', *Quarterly Journal of Economics*, **108**(3), 577–98.

Khanna, T. (2000), 'Business groups and social welfare in emerging markets: Existing evidence and unanswered questions', *European Economic Review*, **44**(4–6): 748–61.

Khanna, T. and K. Palepu (2000), 'Emerging market business groups, foreign intermediaries, and corporate governance', in Randall Morck (ed.), *Concentrated Corporate Ownership*, Chicago, USA: The University of Chicago Press.

Kogut, B. and U. Zander (1993), 'Knowledge of the firm and the evolutionary theory of the multinational corporation', *Journal of International Business Studies*, **24**(4), 625–45.

La Porta, R., F. Lopez-de-Salinas, A. Shleifer and R. Vishny (1998), 'Law and finance', *Journal of Political Economy*, **106**(6), 1113–57.

Lai, Edwin (1998), 'International intellectual property rights protection and the rate of product innovation', *Journal of Development Economics*, **55**(1), 133–53.

Mansfield, E., M. Schwartz and S. Wagner (1981), 'Imitation costs and patents: An empirical study', *Economic Journal*, **91**(364), 907–18.

Morck, R., D. Stangeland and B. Yeung (2000), 'Inherited wealth, corporate control, and economic growth', in Randall Morck (ed.), *Concentrated Corporate Ownership*, Chicago, USA: The University of Chicago Press.

Rivkin, J.W. (2000), 'Imitation of complex strategies', *Management Science*, **46**(6), 824–44.

Romer, Paul M. (1990), 'Endogenous technological change', *Journal of Political Economy*, **98**(5), 71–102.

Siegel, J.I. (2004), 'Is political connectedness a paramount investment after liberalization? The successful leveraging of contingent social capital and the formation of cross-border strategic alliances involving Korean firms and their global partners (1987–2000)', *Harvard NOM Working Paper* No. 03–45.

Smarzynska Javorcik, B. (2004), 'The composition of foreign direct investment and protection of intellectual property rights: Evidence from transition economies', *European Economic Review*, **48**(1), 39–62.

Smith, P. (2001), 'How do foreign patent rights affect US exports, affiliate sales, and licenses?', *Journal of International Economics*, **55**, 411–39.

Song, J., P. Almeida and G. Wu (2003), 'Learning-by-hiring: When is mobility more likely to facilitate inter-firm knowledge transfer?', *Management Science*, **49**(4), 351–65.

Teece, D.J. (1986), 'Profiting from technological innovation: Implications for integration, collaboration, licensing and public policy', *Research Policy*, **15**(6), 285–305.

Zhao, M. (2004), 'Essays on multinational R&D, intellectual property rights, and knowledge spillover', Doctoral dissertation, Stern School of Business, New York University.

Zhao, M. (2006), 'Conducting R&D in countries with weak intellectual property rights protection', *Management Science*, **52**(8), 1185–99.

PART V

Perspectives of emerging nations

12. The vulnerability of middle developed countries to changes in foreign direct investment arising from intellectual property appropriation

Robert C. Bird* and Daniel R. Cahoy**

INTRODUCTION

Intellectual property has become an increasingly important facet of global commerce. It is hard to imagine a negotiation concerning trade between nations that does not address the protection or use of these key property rights. Whether the issue is piracy, investment or development, both the developed and developing worlds now recognize a significant interest in designing functional intellectual property systems.

Significantly, beliefs regarding the appropriate degree of intellectual property rights are not universally shared among nations. Industrialized nations – generally in control of the most valuable IP assets – view strong, dependable protection as a cornerstone to an efficient global business environment. Developing nations may share these ideals to a great degree, but many see the additional need for significant limitations in order to promote local interests, such as health care. This difference of opinion can lead to significant conflict.

The most studied aspect of developed–developing nation conflict in intellectual property rights protection has been in its effect on innovation. However, a secondary effect involving foreign direct investment may be more important for its ability to influence the debate. In particular, a firm's reduction in foreign direct investment in response to a relaxation of intellectual property rights is a function that can have dramatic effects in some countries, but not others. The most important determinate of impact may be the economic structure of the countries involved; evidence suggests that, as a class, middle-developed countries are most open to influence. Understanding these relationships is of great importance to the international trade framework as well as general international relations. This chapter discusses the intellectual property–foreign direct investment relationship and endeavors to provide insight on the most important motivating factors.

* Assistant Professor of Business Law, University of Connecticut. A related version of this chapter was published in volume 45 of the *American Business Law Journal*. Our thanks for comments and support go to the participants of the CIBER conference, 'The global challenge of intellectual property rights', hosted by the University of Connecticut School of Business in May 2007, at which an earlier draft of this chapter was presented.

** Associate Professor of Business Law, Smeal College of Business, the Pennsylvania State University.

INVESTMENT IMPACTS OF INTELLECTUAL PROPERTY APPROPRIATION

Intellectual property rights are at their core investment-inducing mechanisms. The idea is to trade limited market exclusivity for the increased production and disclosure of useful goods, research or services (Scotchmer, 2004). By providing a limited right to exclude competitors, intellectual property rights permit their owners the ability to extract monopoly rents, thus providing the primary investment incentive. In exchange, society obtains access to goods or services that may not have been created but for the incentive, or at least not widely disseminated. While some view the possibility of monopoly rents as a reward, most consider it better articulated as the product of an *ex ante* gamble: make an intelligent investment and, depending on the market, you may win a great return (Kitch, 1977; Lemley, 2004). In that regard, it is similar to any business investment seeking the greatest return for the least investment. This paradigm could theoretically be applied to all types of intellectual property, but it fits best with copyrights and patents, which therefore form the basis of the following discussion.

To be sure, other models of innovation development and dissemination have been proposed. For example, in the context of useful inventions, patent buyouts and patent prizes occasionally surface as alternative mechanisms (Kremer, 1998). However, it is not at all clear that such models can replace a meaningful amount of private research. They are subject to several important weaknesses, including the difficulty in setting the correct incentives and administrative costs (Abramowicz, 2003). At best, they may provide an important complement to traditional incentives for innovation and creativity. To encourage the private funding of high-cost, high-risk endeavors such as public health invention, it is generally accepted that intellectual property rights are necessary.

Not surprisingly, strict innovation investment may be accompanied by substantial parallel investment in business facilities and personnel, amplifying the effect of the rights on economic development (Hall, 1996). In developing countries, a significant amount of such investment may come from outside the country, stimulating the growth of local industry beyond that which would be possible through endogenous investment alone (Chon, 2006). It is this broad impact on a country's economic wealth that purportedly justifies the global establishment of strong intellectual property regimes. Strong rights should lead to greater investment, all things being equal.

The primary downside to intellectual property rights is, of course, that the lack of competition will usually result in higher prices than would otherwise exist (Kitch, 2000). This is particularly problematic when the good or service covered by the right constitutes a socially-important good, such as a pharmaceutical used to treat a life-threatening disease. For example, significant advancements in medicine are often accompanied by a cost premium (DiMasi, 2000). This tradeoff is the classic conundrum in the use of intellectual property rights in the context of socially-important goods. A nation with sufficient wealth may be able to shoulder the burden of high costs if the information provides important advantages, but for impoverished nations, even moderate costs may mean that some individuals will go without (Kapczynski et al., 2005). A second obstacle is the potential for conflicting rights to preclude optimal treatment. Again, this is common with patents. A combination of several inventions may be required when, for example, an integrated delivery mechanism would be preferable and available, if not for the intellectual property rights

(Hamilton, 2006). Therefore, many believe that, in a strong intellectual property rights regime, developing countries may suffer disproportionately.

It is possible to adjust the balance between intellectual property rights and access by contracting or expanding the boundaries of intellectual property rights. Effective revision can be achieved through the manipulation of various aspects of the rights (Cahoy, 2006). For example, if a country wished to limit the temporal power of patent rights, the term could be shortened to a few years. Alternatively, a country could declare patent infringement remedied only through the award of monetary damages as opposed to injunctions. By attenuating intellectual property 'levers', a country could reduce the capture of information from the public domain.

The consequences of intellectual property rights limitations are important. Primarily, economic theory strongly suggests that investment incentives will be negatively affected, reducing innovation and development. The notion that economic progress and strong intellectual property rights are so highly connected has been a key component of the continued push for Western-style intellectual property protections in developing nations. While this relationship may be valid, empirical evidence supporting this proposition is a bit muddied due to the complex interaction of a number of factors (Maskus, 2001). The lingering ambiguity has probably contributed to some resistance on the part of developing countries to adopt strong rights as soon as possible (Yu, 2006; Bird, 2006). Nevertheless, it is widely accepted by developed countries.

In practice, a country's re-balancing options are somewhat limited. Recent international accords, particularly the Trade-Related Aspects of Intellectual Property ('TRIPS') agreement, have gone a long way toward harmonizing the basic attributes of intellectual property (TRIPS, 1994). Arbitrarily reducing rights could lead to trade sanctions if the move violates the basic protections agreed to by treaty members. On the other hand, expanding rights is generally not in conflict with international agreement unless it reduces another's existing property protections.

If harmonization has been so predominant and successful, one might be surprised at the continued debate over the allocation of rights in various countries. It occurs because there are in fact flexibilities in a few important areas, leaving open the possibility of significant differences in intellectual property rights between countries (Cahoy, 2006; WIPO, 2007). Under certain circumstances, common intellectual property rights can be relaxed or even eliminated. The most prominent mechanisms include (1) *ex post* elimination of existing property rights through compulsory licensing or a similar government-imposed mechanism and (2) *ex ante* limitations on the ownership of intellectual property in certain technologies. Many of these flexibilities are reserved to developing and least-developed countries, as they are viewed as essential breathing room for broader economic development.

Ex Post Elimination of Established Property Rights

Because the rationale for enshrining information with the legal protection of property is the dependability and predictability of investment return, eliminating that protection after the investment occurs is generally prohibited. If such a move could occur without obligation, one presumes a government would be inclined to do so whenever a property right covers information that turns out to have great value. The private investor assumes all of the risk, and government simply allows the market to identify the best cherries to pick. Of course, this would only have to occur a few times before potential innovators and creators decide that high risk investments in public goods are not worthwhile, reducing the utility of the system. On the other hand, a system designed to provide unwavering protection to intellectual property owners is not without significant downsides. Times may arise in which immediate public need should not be held hostage to the arbitrary whims of a single property owner. Attempting to achieve a difficult balance in these competing priorities is the legal mechanism known as the compulsory license.

Compulsory licenses provide a means for addressing the effects of property hold-ups without entirely eliminating the right. Essentially, they are a mandatory license to the government in exchange for some measure of compensation or remuneration to the property owner. By intruding on the right to exclude, a government (or entity specifically authorized by the government) can more flexibly make use of the information. Essentially, the patent holder is forced to give up a bit of her/his property right to benefit the public. The benefit to the public can be direct, as in the case of a license to provide availability for a previously withheld good, or indirect, as in the case of a license to improve marketplace conditions (Correa, 1999). The loss is usually restricted in time or by the continued occurrence of a triggering event. As a general matter, the patent holder retains the right to exclude others not licensed by the government, and to compete against the licensee. The aforementioned TRIPS agreement actually requires that compulsory licenses be non-exclusive (TRIPS, 1994).

Simple in concept, the term 'compulsory license' can actually apply to a rather bewildering array of government incursions that have distinctly different impacts on investment incentives. In perhaps the most important (and contentious) context, it is used to describe an unexpected, *ex post* deprivation of property rights in response to some emergent need. In these cases, negotiation may not be practical and the license acts as a simple mechanism for providing the necessary access. Additionally, it may increase access when barriers preclude optimal use of the property. High prices due to monopoly control would certainly be one example (Reichman and Hasenzhal, 2004). It has also been suggested that patent compulsory licenses can also address concerns regarding a patent's ability to convey paternalistic control or exploitation on the part of industrialized countries over developing nations (May and Sell, 2006; Yu, 2007). Under this view, compulsory licensing could be a mechanism for reasserting indigenous power and promoting the development of home industries.

Such unanticipated compulsory licenses are decidedly retrospective in nature. The measures are generally imposed only after considering property that already exists, determining that it is valuable, and then reallocating ownership rights through a form of nationalization. As a general matter, intellectual property owners are likely to consider it an appropriation of private ownership that suggests danger in investment, unless full compensation is available (Cahoy, 2007). Although the incentive to invent or create with respect to the licensed invention cannot be changed (since invention has already taken place), innovation policy advocates argue that the incentive to create future information is decidedly reduced (Chien, 2003). In other words, it is posited that some ideas or expressions that would have been created in view of the full power of the intellectual property rights, will never come to be in the face of compulsory licensing. This may be an acceptable tradeoff; a compulsory license is predicated on the assumption that the beneficial effects from the limitation will be significant, outweighing the loss of any innovation investment. Whether that is true is open to debate, and may depend on the particular circumstances surrounding the license.

On the other side of the spectrum is the use of compulsory licenses as a remedial measure. This may occur in the context of antitrust litigation concerning a property owner's abuse of a dominant market position (Scherer and Watal, 2002). Similar issues arise from litigation in which a court refuses to grant permanent injunctive relief in favor of continued royalty payments in a given case (as opposed to making injunctions more difficult in all cases). In these instances, the reason for the license is tied to the property owner's behavior instead of the country's desire to attenuate intellectual property strength. Thus, a broader investment disincentive is not likely, and the licenses falling within this group are not as relevant for policy analysis (Cahoy, 2007).

The imposition of a compulsory license for patent rights is explicitly endorsed in international law. One of the earliest expressions of this right was contained in the nineteenth-century Paris Convention for the Protection of Industrial Property (Paris Convention, 1883). More recently, the TRIPS agreement, which came into effect in 1995 as part of the Uruguay Round of trade discussions, provides for the 'use without the authorization of the right holder'. Article 31 permits member states to issue licenses under certain circumstances, including: (1) after efforts to obtain a license from the patent holder on 'reasonable commercial terms and conditions' have failed, (2) in the case of national emergency or other circumstances of extreme urgency and (3) for public non-commercial use (TRIPS, 1994). The latter two circumstances are significant in that they do not require prior negotiation with the patent holder (which should theoretically make a compulsory license easier to obtain). As a result of the flexibilities in international law, at least one hundred countries make patent compulsory licenses available in one form or another (Correa, 1999; Dratler, 2001).

The most prominent context for considering the ability of *ex post* compulsory licenses to balance innovation and access is the invention and delivery of essential medicines. Factors such as the amount of investment at stake, dependence on intellectual property rights, great likelihood of rights reduction, and social importance combine to create great contention. To be sure, compulsory licensing is not a comprehensive answer to global health; it is only one tool in a much larger toolbox (Attaran and Gillespie-White, 2001). In fact, it is probable that other methods for improving public health may actually be more important in the long term. Many problems in the developing world are remedied by ensuring a sufficient supply of clean water, nutritional food and even education on the dangers of certain social behaviors (WHO, 2006). However, the option of compulsory licensing of pharmaceuticals is gaining an ever more prominent place in world health policy, and it appears to be a permanent fixture of international trade.

An important limitation to TRIPS article 31 as originally drafted was a provision requiring that licensed rights be practiced domestically, for the benefit of the home market. Under this restriction, third-party countries with the ability to produce licensed products could not effectively export the products to a needy nation without a pharmaceutical manufacturing base. It has been suggested that it might be possible for a country such as India or Brazil to impose a compulsory license 'predominantly for the supply of the domestic market', and export additional production to non-manufacturing developing countries under a separate license (Abbott and Van Puymbroeck, 2005). However, that non-predominant quantity may be insufficient to satisfy the needs of a country facing a growing public health crisis. Recently, WTO members agreed to relax the domestic production rule in the context of essential medicines by permitting the manufacture and export of products from a non-licensing country to a licensing country (Doha Para. 6 Implementation, 2003). In response, several governments amended or proposed to amend their patent laws to permit the manufacture and sale of pharmaceuticals under such circumstances, though only one country has taken advantage of the more flexible rules to date (WTO, 2007a; Cahoy, 2007). Outside of public health, the original domestic manufacturing requirement still applies.

Ex Ante Limitations on IPR Ownership

Another significant means by which a government can capture the value of intellectual property rights is by failing to extend protection over categories of inventions supplied by foreign firms. Although technically not 'appropriation' since the rights never existed in the first place, it can have the same effect. Because intellectual property rights have no extraterritorial application (beyond agreements to grant regional rights), a county may reap the benefits of foreign inventive or creative efforts by refusing to grant intellectual property rights on a par with those that exist in the product's primary markets. Thus, IPR-granting countries shoulder the burden of providing the return on investment, while the non-IPR granting country can benefit from the lower costs of a fully competitive environment.

A primary context for this form of appropriation is again in the pharmaceutical arena. For years, several countries refused to extend patent protection to pharmaceutical compounds (Abbott, 1989). Drugs protected by these patents might be introduced into countries by foreign firms only to find that generic competitors could arise and legally undercut profits. In some cases, sufficient public knowledge could exist to permit domestic generic producers to copy the pharmaceutical without introduction of the branded compound, effectively eliminating much of the profit on the invention in that country. The non-IPR granting country benefits from the research investment incentives in other countries without the costs of high pharmaceutical prices.

At least in the case of India, the lack of pharmaceutical protection appears to be a direct case of appropriating foreign R&D for the benefit of home industries. Prior to 1970, India provided patent protection to pharmaceutical compounds. However, in a bid to encourage the development of the generic drug industry, India eliminated that protection from its laws. Not surprisingly, an extraordinarily robust generic industry developed to produce compounds created in other nations (primarily the US and Europe). Interestingly, that industry was no 'open source' model of free collaboration. Indian generic pharmaceutical companies competed on the basis of efficient manufacturing processes, and such processes were often proprietary and patentable (Gupta, 2003). In other words, it can be argued that India was never against patent rights related to pharmaceuticals, but rather it was against patent rights that would enable foreign firms to outcompete local ones. In any case, now that India has instituted patent protection over pharmaceutical compounds, investment in drug development may well increase.

To be sure, one should not conclude that all *ex ante* limitations on IPRs serve a naked economic purpose. In fact, some of the most prominent are fairly the result of social policy. A very broad such exclusion exists in the law of the European Patent Convention

(EPC), the signatories of which encompass the European Union along with Switzerland, Liechtenstein, Turkey, Monaco and Iceland. According to Article 52 of the Convention concerning patentable inventions, among the information not recognized as an invention subject to protection are '[m]ethods for treatment of the human or animal body by surgery or therapy and diagnostic methods practiced on the human or animal body' (EPC, 1973). Clearly, this eliminates some of the incentive to invest in uncovering, *inter alia*, new methods of administering pharmaceutical or biotechnology compounds. To compensate somewhat for the reduction in patent incentives, the EPC permits recapturing patent protection over a substance's 'first medical use', even if the compound or substance is in the prior art. This is obviously an imperfect solution, particularly if a new method of treatment is possible but some other medical use of the involved pharmaceutical already exists.

As with *ex post* appropriations, the TRIPS agreement has curbed some historic activity in this area by placing some rather strong restrictions on a country's ability to arbitrarily eliminate intellectual property protection for whole categories of information. According to the Berne Convention, as confirmed by the TRIPS agreement, copyright protection must be accorded to broad categories of works (Berne Convention, 1971). Very little 'expression' is available for outright exclusion save for unfixed works. On the other hand, more openings exist in the context of patents. Article 27 of the TRIPS agreement permits the exclusion of inventions necessary to 'protect *ordre public* or morality', as well as those related to diagnostic, therapeutic or surgical treatments and higher-level animals and plants (TRIPS, 1994). Additionally, Article 30 allows members to create exceptions to patent rights if such exceptions do not 'unreasonably conflict with a normal exploitation of the patent' or 'unreasonably prejudice the legitimate interests of the patent owner'. However, this provision has generally been viewed as relatively narrow in application and limited to circumstances like experimental use (UNCTAD-ICTSD, 2005). Finally, because some widely held limitations, such as those on pharmaceutical patents, have been grandfathered in for developing and least-developed nations, flexibilities continue to exist for a very limited time. By working within an exception that is protected in one or more revenue-producing countries, a government may appropriate value.

In addition to the outright exclusion of rights, it is possible to appropriate more narrowly through the elimination of enforcement powers against particular entities. One of the most interesting examples actually occurred recently in the United States. In 1996, legislation entitled 'Limitations on Patent Infringements Relating to a Medical Practitioner's Performance of a Medical Activity' was enacted that prohibited the enforcement of patent rights on medical procedures against physicians. The law was a clear response to the repugnant notion that a lifesaving medical procedure might be withheld by (or permitted subject to a payment to) the property owner (Mossinghoff, 1996). However, patents on lifesaving medical procedures could still be obtained and in some cases enforced through third-party liability. Similarly, one could view the debate on patent exhaustion as a form of enforcement limitation. In some countries, the sale of a patented good anywhere in the world exhausts a patent owner's control over that particular item (Cahoy, 2005). However, other countries deem rights exhausted only when they occur in the *situs* of enforcement. In the latter case, revising national rules to provide universal exhaustion of patent rights upon the first sale would be a reduction in property rights (opening the country to parallel importation). Public availability is maximized at the expense of the patent owner.

A related *ex ante* appropriation option is to restrict enforcement through the automatic imposition of a compulsory license for certain uses. In other words, a country could preclude injunctive relief and set a royalty scheme as the exclusive compensation for another's unauthorized use of the intellectual property. This is different from an *ex post* compulsory license because its imposition does not depend on the nature or value of the intellectual property being licensed; rather, the license option is known to the prospective property owner before any investment is made. Perhaps the most prominent example of this exists in US copyright law. One may make use of music on copyrighted 'phonorecords' upon the payment of a royalty to the copyright owner, and no injunction can be issued to stop the use (Merges, 1996). Other compulsory licenses exist for various uses of copyrighted material such as satellite rebroadcast of television programs. Established compulsory licenses can also exist for patents.

One important fact about *ex ante* limitations is that they are only appropriations under specific contexts. If a category of possible intellectual property protection is unrecognized across the world, the consequence (if any) would simply be a lack of investment in that area. That may be an undesirable outcome, but it can be addressed by the international community as an innovation policy question. Arguably, this is the current state of the law concerning patents on business methods, which are prominently recognized only in a few countries (Thomas, 2002). A true appropriation – which may subject a country to some measure of punishment – occurs only when significant investment does take place with the expectation of monopoly rents, and those expectations are dashed in particular countries or regions.

One should also keep in mind that 'appropriation' is not necessarily a normative label, though it is easy to assume a negative connotation. In fact, it is perfectly reasonable and common to hold the belief that some appropriation is necessary under the current international intellectual property scheme (Sell, 2002; Lanjouw, 2003). The short-term goal of immediate access in particular countries may outweigh whatever additional strain is imposed, at least from a global perspective. That said, one should not be surprised if firms that end up providing the majority of investment support believe that both *ex post* and *ex ante* appropriations should be discouraged. Such firms may be inclined to use financial disincentives to counter the economically-motivated desire to appropriate. The prospect of withholding private investment funding may be the most powerful and effective, depending on the country.

RETRIBUTION THROUGH FOREIGN DIRECT INVESTMENT DISINCENTIVES

Stated simply, foreign direct investment (FDI) is the flow of people, capital and technology from a source country to a destination country. FDI frequently takes the form of the acquisition or production of subsidiaries in the host country by a multinational enterprise ('MNE'). FDI usually grants control through management or outright ownership of the enterprise in the host country to the MNE. Passive investment or non-equity investment through instruments such as bonds, debt securities and notes does not generally constitute FDI activities (Hunter et al., 2003; Maskus, 1998).

MNEs may pursue three types of FDI – vertical, horizontal and distributional. Distributional FDI, the least discussed and least invasive of the three, involves establishing sales offices, distribution networks and services facilities in the target nation. Vertical FDI ('VFDI') refers to investment of a component of a larger product in different countries. The location of each stage of product production is chosen to minimize production costs. Firms locate facilities to mine mineral resources near the mineral itself. High labor processes exist where labor costs are lowest. Horizontal FDI comprises the manufacture of the entire good in one place. This may include manufacturing, research and development, and distribution of the product. As firms mature, they generally move from vertical to horizontal FDI activities (Kennedy, 2003).

The choice to pursue FDI by an MNE is principally a profit motive, but the factors that impact that decision are more complex. An MNE planning FDI must have some efficiency advantages that can be leveraged by placement of production assets within a foreign country. These efficiency advantages many manifest in three forms – ownership, localization and internalization – known collectively as the OLI theory (Maskus, 1998).

An ownership advantage usually involves the exportation of an intangible asset such as marketing power, technological expertise, and intellectual property ownership to a foreign country where those assets can be optimally utilized. MNEs export such knowledge-based assets to take advantage of a supportive information infrastructure. Through multi-plant production, MNEs receive economies of scope by producing technical knowledge in one location and applying it to plants across different nations. Less commonly, ownership advantages many manifest themselves in tangible forms, such as an exclusive claim to a valuable natural resource.

Location advantages provide geographic efficiency benefits to MNE production in target countries. Such advantages include distance to markets, low wage costs, natural resources and even trade protection from manufacturing 'inside' an external trade barrier. MNEs also seek supporting infrastructure, such as transportation in order to bring goods to market, marketing outlets in order to develop brand equity reliably, and a financial network from which to receive loans, grant credit, or pursue local investments.

Finally, internalization advantages occur when MNEs exploit advantages in multinational operations by acquiring established enterprises in the region. In essence, this involves buying a subsidiary with the local knowledge and expertise to produce the product for a given national or regional market (Maskus, 1998). An internalization advantage occurs when the profits gained from exploiting the firm's assets are greater when the assets are kept within the company as compared to licensing the use of those assets to a foreign firm (Kennedy, 2003).

One ameliorating factor to external impacts on the FDI profit motive is the vertical nature of certain industries. High barriers to entry and lower level of competition between countries can make it somewhat less likely that a compulsory license imposed on one product will impact FDI related to other companies or have horizontal effects across other industries (Levy, 1999). In other words, if an individual nation is willing to accept the possible loss of investment in this segregated industry segment, FDI in other areas may make it less significant.

Differential Impact of Foreign Direct Investment Threats

Intellectual property laws are widely believed to have a signaling effect for the nations that enact them. The passage of such laws indicates to investors that a nation recognizes the rights of foreign firms and a government is willing to let foreign investors make strategic business decisions without undue government interference. Stronger intellectual property rights also signal a nation's shift toward a more transparent legal system with unbiased application of commercial laws and reduced corruption in government activities. Although the evidence supporting the conclusion that these signals impact on MNE behavior is inconclusive, several poor nations, including those with limited technical capabilities, have unilaterally improved their intellectual property rights during the 1990s (Maskus, 1998).

There is also significant evidence that patents work as signaling devices for the firms that own them. Patents signal to financial markets and customers that a firm holds a strong market position and can potentially achieve dominant status. Patents also act as symbolic markers of progress in research and development and as product differentiators. Patents also signal strong firm productivity, innovation, and research and development activity. Patents signal to venture capitalists that a company is well managed and has defined a market niche for itself (Long, 2002; Lemley, 2000).

If patents can readily convey broad information beyond the mere possession of an intellectual property, it stands to reason that when a patent is placed in jeopardy in a particular market it may send a variety of negative signals about the firm. A pharmaceutical enterprise entering a market where its patents are readily vulnerable to a compulsory license may cause firm observers, such as those who recommend or sell the firm's stock, to question the firm's projected revenue streams from conducting FDI in that new market. Questions may arise as to whether the target nation's economy will be a breeding ground for sales-impeding parallel imports. Just as the sale of a product through a low-status selling channel of a product can signal a diminution in brand status to the consumer, exposure of a patent to an uncertain legal environment can signal that the firm may not consider the patent to be as valuable as others believe. Even the threat of an 'anti-patent' such as a compulsory license can impair firm equity, thereby reducing the attractiveness of a country as an investment partner. Any firm calculating its returns from FDI will have account for the possibility of these signaling-based losses.

While the relationship between compulsory licensees and foreign direct investment is straightforward in theory, the actual economic mechanism can vary dramatically in practice. Most pronounced is the difference between countries at different income and investment attraction levels. Depending on inflow of FDI relative to compulsory licensing savings, the association may or may not be strategically important. Some general observations are possible using the broad categories of 'least-developed countries' and 'middle-developed countries'.

The Susceptibility of Middle Developed Countries to FDI Losses

A least-developed country's ('LDC') – a category of voluntary inclusion defined by the WTO – issuance of a compulsory license might not impact future foreign direct investment decisions of an MNE. LDCs cannot significantly impact the ownership advantage of a large firm. LDC markets are generally too small and not lucrative enough to impact the decision to pursue the exportation of an intangible asset abroad. LDCs will also have little influence over the location advantage. LDCs usually lack the infrastructure to present a location advantage to an MNE and are usually located geographically distant from key markets. Given the lack of influence of ownership and location advantages that LDCs can offer, there is little influence that an LDC can offer in an internalization advantage. Instead of licensing the drug or building a plant, a pharmaceutical MNE might simply resort to exporting that drug from a foreign manufacturer, thus keeping investment in LDCs as limited as possible.

On the other hand, the ability of certain countries to impact on MNE foreign direct investment behavior was highlighted in a thoughtful study by Lee and Mansfield, who in 1996 reviewed the perceptions about intellectual property rights in various countries by 100 American firms. The authors sampled one hundred major US firms in the chemical (including pharmaceutical), machinery, food, metals, electrical equipment and transportation industries. Each firm was asked whether any of a selected group of countries had intellectual property protection that was too weak to transfer its newest technology to a wholly-owned subsidiary in that country. The authors concluded that, depending upon the magnitude of the improved perception, increased perception by firm representatives that a given nation has strong intellectual property rights can result in as much as hundreds of millions of dollars in FDI. The authors found that weak intellectual property rights more negatively impact on the production of research and development facilities and less negatively impact on firms with limited ownership of local affiliates (Lee and Mansfield, 1996).

While the survey establishes important evidence that US firms consider intellectual property rights in foreign direct investment decisions, the other countries surveyed are particularly instructive. The authors surveyed fourteen countries – Argentina, Brazil, Chile, Hong Kong, India, Indonesia, Mexico, Nigeria, Philippines, Singapore, South Korea, Taiwan, Thailand and Venezuela – most of which are considered Middle-developed countries ('MDCs') as opposed to LDCs. According to the Human Development Index (HDI), a measure used annually by the United Nations Development Programme to measure social welfare within and across nations according to a variety of variables, every nation on this list except Nigeria is listed as having medium or high levels of human development. More focused tables measuring technology diffusion and creation and economic performance measure these nations similarly (Chon, 2006; UNDP, 2005). This implies the impact of intellectual property rights practices, and by extension granting compulsory licenses, might have a greater impact on middle developed countries than their least developed brethren.

Egypt's Declining FDI

Consider Egypt, a developing nation that ranks 119 out of 177 countries surveyed by the HDI, above South Africa and India but a few places below Guatemala and Indonesia on a human development scale. Egypt is similarly ranked on the HDI's technology diffusion and creation scale and the economic performance scale (UNDP, 2005).[1] Egypt is a quintessential middle-developed country (MDC) having the potential for significant economic growth but plagued with a variety of social ills such as high unemployment that hinder its advancement. Most interesting, although the Egyptian government has aggressively sought to attract foreign direct investment, FDI flows have continued to decline from $948 million in 1987 to $598 million in 1995 to $428.2 million in 2001–02 (Maskus, 2005).

In spite of this decline, Egypt receives more foreign direct investment than most other countries in Africa (A.T. Kearney, 2005). Egypt possesses an economic environment that can attract companies seeking to exploit their FDI ownership, internalization and localization advantages. Egypt is widely believed to possess a strong education system, a cheap labor force, and citizens who speak English on a widespread basis (Guerrera, 2001). Egypt has taken numerous steps in order to liberalize its investment laws, including the abolishing of export taxes, eliminating foreign exchange controls, and reducing bureaucratic procedures (Metwally, 2004). Egypt is also the largest consumer of medicines in Africa and the Middle East (Guerrera, 2001).

Egypt's position on intellectual property rights has shifted demonstrably over the past fifty years. Egypt's first modern patent law was enacted in 1949 and protected the manufacturing process of pharmaceutical production but excluded the product itself from protection. This law was most recently updated in 2002, when Law No. 82 of 2002 Promulgating Intellectual Property Law was passed after seven years of drafting and two years of formal debate. The 2002 law expanded protection for pharmaceutical products and other areas to comply with the TRIPS agreement which Egypt signed (Aziz, 2003; Al-Ali, 2003).

TRIPS does not explicitly establish detailed compulsory licensing rules. Article 31, however, permits the use of patents without authorization from the owner of the patent, effectively authorizing compulsory licenses (TRIPS, 1994). Of particular interest is Egypt's compulsory licensing statute. Egypt's compulsory licensing statute has many components that might concern foreign investors. Article 17 allows the head of Ministry of Health, the Ministry of Internal Affairs or other Ministers to oppose any patent application if that application 'relates' or is of 'significance' to those fields (Law on the Protection of Intellectual Property Rights, 2002). If any of these agencies oppose the patent filing, the patent process stops and no judicial review of the decision appears available (Al-Ali, 2003). The obvious connections between pharmaceuticals and health and the limitless discretion of Ministers to halt the patent process leave drug-producing MNEs vulnerable.

Articles 23 and 24 discuss procedures and requirements for compulsory licensing. Article 23(2) allows the Minister of Health to grant compulsory licenses when the quantity of medicine available fails to meet national needs due to the poor quality or prohibitive price, or where there are incurable or endemic diseases. This article also applies to inventions related to the associated manufacturing processes of raw materials necessary to develop the medicines. Article 23(3) allows the Egyptian government to grant licenses of patents when necessary to support 'national efforts in vital sectors for economic, social, and technological development, without unreasonable prejudice to the rights of the patent holder and taking into consideration the legitimate interests of third parties' (Law on the Protection of Intellectual Property Rights, 2002).

Egypt's 2002 law also addresses compensation. Article 31(h) of TRIPS requires that 'the right holder shall be paid adequate remuneration in the circumstances of each case, taking into account the economic value of the [compulsory license]' (TRIPS, 1994). Article 24(8) of Egypt's law by contrast states that the patent holder is entitled to 'fair compensation for the exploitation of his invention. The amount of the compensation shall be fixed on the basis of the economic value of the invention' (Law on the Protection of Intellectual Property Rights, 2002). Egypt's compensation provision uses the world 'fair' instead of 'adequate', which may give the Egyptian government greater flexibility in establishing the appropriate level of compensation. Whereas 'adequate' may imply a compensatory quasi-contractual requirement, a 'fair' determination might involve value judgments or justice considerations, a factor that MNEs would find troubling as issues of public need might weigh against them in the equation. This interpretation may be unnecessarily nuanced, and the subsequent compulsory language in the Egyptian statute fixing compensation on the basis of economic value might contain any discretion afforded by a 'fair' term. Yet, at the very least, a compensation provision under Egyptian law that varies from the TRIPS language places in question whether the two systems are the same and whether Egyptian law will provide adequate compensation for compulsory licenses.

Even more troublesome would be a differing translation of the statute described by Aziz, whose source translates the second sentence of article 24(8) as stating that '[t]he economic value of the invention must be considered while determining said compensation' (Aziz, 2003). This translation of article 24(8) would merely require economic factors to be considered rather than the sole measure, permitting more opportunity to political and social considerations to effect the appropriate compensation for a compulsory license.

Egypt's compulsory licensing statute is broad and ambiguous (IIPA, 2006). This may be a product of legislative compromise between differing factions over a controversial provision. The statute's vagueness, however, does give the Egyptian government some advantages. Under the current statute, Egypt can issue compulsory licenses for pharmaceutical drugs in a wide variety of circumstances – including whenever it determines that high prices fail to satisfy national demands. The possibility of high prices accompanying stronger patent protection is a significant one. For example, in Egypt the price of an anti-adhesive substance Intergel rose 70 per cent over a four-month period in 2002 (Al-Ali, 2003). In India prices of pharmaceutical drugs can increase as much as 50 per cent after the implementation of a stronger patent regime (Maskus, 2001; Watal, 2000). In China, stronger pharmaceutical patent laws are a possible reason why pharmaceutical prices have risen as much as fourfold in small Chinese pharmacies in Beijing and Shanghai (Maskus, 2001). The current statute allows Egypt to issue compulsory licenses if drug prices are outside the reach of most consumers or simply because they are too expensive to be ignored politically.

What cost, however, does Egypt's flexible compulsory license impose upon its economy? There is little doubt that reckless use of its compulsory licensing statute will provoke strong reactions from affected pharmaceutical MNEs. As the leader of a major pharmaceutical trade association is apparently attributed as stating, 'you can compel a private company once [with a compulsory license]. After that they probably leave your borders, and you lose the opportunity to get the access and the technology transfer in the future' (Mayer, 2002, p. 668).[2] In 2002, after four years of effort, Pfizer finally received regulatory approval to enter the Egyptian market with their popular drug Viagra. Local well-connected drug manufacturers responded by pressuring the Egyptian Ministry of Health, accusing the Ministry of helping MNEs to exploit Egypt's poor. Only two months after Pfizer's entry into the Egyptian market, the Ministry decided to grant similar authorization to produce Viagra to all Egyptian companies who applied to do so. The Ministry of Health cited the interests of the poor and the fact that the 2005 deadline for developing countries to comply with TRIPS had not yet expired. Pfizer was, naturally, 'furious' at the decision. The decision led Pfizer to halt construction on a state of the art production facility in Egypt (Castellano, 2006; Allam, 2002). The government's decision prompted a Pfizer Middle Eastern representative to remark that allowing generic Viagra to be sold will 'send a chill down foreign investors' spines' and that 'there are many other countries in the region who are competing for these new high-tech investments'(Castellano, 2006, p. 289).

Examining the dispute more closely reveals that the issuance of this compulsory license was far from the purpose for which such licenses were intended: to safeguard the health of poor nations in medical emergencies. A number of more dubious reasons were at work and 'the interests the poor people', as the President of Ministry of Health described the purpose of the license, were far from the primary reason for the license (Castellano, 2006). First, this compulsory license does not stand within the idealized class of licenses such as for example a least-developed country issuing a license for an anti-AIDS drug to save the lives of citizens afflicted with a debilitating disease. Viagra treats erectile dysfunction, a significant problem, but far from the life-threatening health crisis that compulsory licenses were envisioned to prevent. Second, the government process carried out to determine whether the license should be issued was far from an independent one. For example, the Chairman of a large generic drug manufacturer is also the Chairman of the Health Committee in Egypt's upper house of Parliament (Allam, 2002). Third, the decision to issue the license did not comply with TRIPS. Even though Egypt had until 2005 to comply with TRIPS, its refusal to attempt early compliance with the treaty when it had the opportunity to do so signals that its interest in compliance is at best lukewarm and that it might do only the minimum necessary to protect intellectual property rights under the agreement. Fourth, legal experts state that even without TRIPS in place, Viagra is protected by a Prime Ministerial Decree which prohibits any company from using an undisclosed trade secret that would injure the commercial success of the firm that developed that trade secret. If the Egyptian Ministry of Health is willing to flout current Egyptian law when it is to the disadvantage of local interests, then MNEs have reason to find any future claims of government adherence to intellectual property laws dubious at best. Fifth, the companies themselves seeking the compulsory license may have little interest in improving Viagra's access to Egypt's poor beyond their own self-interest. According to Dr Ahmed El Hakim, Pfizer's director of health policy and external relations for the Middle East, of the two loudest proponents of the compulsory license, one wants to license because it is hemorrhaging money and the other is trying to inflate his company's net worth before placing it on the auction block. This dilutes the accusations by local press supporting the license that Pfizer is attempting to monopolize the market and profit from the misfortunes of Egyptian men (*Business Today*, 2002).

Egypt badly needs foreign direct investment from companies like Pfizer to jumpstart a faltering economy. The Egyptian government has stated the importance of foreign direct investment and has made pledges in the past to raise the amount received (Guerrera, 2001). In addition, unlike LDCs that might have little to lose in issuing a compulsory license, Egypt and nations similarly positioned have much to lose when mishandling their intellectual property regime. In 2001, the year before Egypt enacted its sweeping intellectual property laws, the government suffered withering criticism for its lack of protections that impair receipt of foreign direct investment. The ambassador to Egypt from the United States in 2001 stated that, 'Egypt's ability to attract foreign investors in many fields will hinge on adequate protection of copyrights, patents and other intellectual property', and may be a precondition for any free trade agreement between Egypt and the United States (Guerrera,

2001, p. 8). A US official reported in 2001, '[a]t the moment Egypt is just not getting billions of foreign investment and this is the most damning evidence that the system is not working' (Guerrera, 2001, p. 8). The Pharmaceutical Research and Manufacturers Association of American (PhRMA) informed Egypt that its weak intellectual property laws deterred PhRMA from investing $300 million in Egypt's pharmaceutical sector (Aziz, 2003).

The statements above were made before the passage of Egypt's 2002 law. Yet Egypt's open-ended compulsory licensing scheme can undermine the strengthened patent protections Egypt worked so long and hard to legislate for. Even if the broad compulsory licensing statute is never used, its mere presence transmits negative signals to an interested MNE that pharmaceutical patents and FDI in Egypt are vulnerable.

If the mere presence of a broad compulsory license statute can impact on the perception of its investment climate, it remains to be seen whether Egypt (or any country in a similar position) should leave the statute in place at all. The best course for Egypt might not be to revoke the statute outright, but to bargain away the statute's discretion in exchange for investment guarantees. Egyptian representatives, in a future hypothetical negotiation with pharmaceutical interests, could find low 'cost' and high 'benefit' in curtailing compulsory license protection in selected industries where Egypt already has a competitive foothold. Egypt's pharmaceutical industry is one of the oldest strategic industries in Egypt and produces more medicines than any country in the North Africa and Middle East region. As Egyptian pharmaceutical companies mature from a distribution to a research focus, patent applications will inevitably increase (Aziz, 2003). Excluding or curtailing compulsory licensing powers away from these industries will provide needed security for foreign enterprises without the attendant increase in risk from higher prices, national undersupply, or emergency crises because a developing industry is already in place. This concession would be far from costless, but would be negotiated in an area where Egypt would have a modicum of competitive strength.

Brazil's Response to Foreign Pressure

Meanwhile, as Egypt struggles to attract foreign direct investment in spite of an unnecessarily broad compulsory licensing statute, Brazil has made significant steps toward solving public health problems while using its compulsory licensing statute as an asset. Brazil, like many countries, suffers from a spreading AIDS epidemic. However, the Brazilian government has responded by providing aggressive prevention services and free access to anti-retroviral drugs for over ten years. Hailed as an international model, Brazil avoided pessimistic projections by the World Bank that Brazil would have 1.2 million citizens suffering from the HIV virus by 2000. Instead, roughly 600 000, or 1 per cent of the adult population, are infected with the disease. This stands in stark contrast to South Africa, which in 2000 had an infection rate of 4.2 million people, or 20 per cent of its adult population. Brazil's efforts have been used as a model around the world (Marques et al., 2005; Russell, 2000).

Why has Brazil been so successful? The primary reason has been the government's early implementation of an aggressive anti-AIDS program. Launched in 1983 when the scientists in Brazil first isolated the HIV virus, Brazil's anti-AIDS program has provided extensive support services to infected people. This program includes prevention – advocating communication with controversial high-risk groups such as sex workers, drug users and homosexuals. These programs have included targeting intravenous drug users with information on methods of safe practice and an aggressive promotion of contraception devices such as condoms. This program has grown to provide 159 000 infected Brazilians with free anti-retroviral drugs and support services (Marques et al., 2005; National STD and AIDS Programme, 2005).

Anti-retroviral drugs, however, can potentially come only at a steep price. Brazil's skillful negotiation with pharmaceutical companies as well as its savvy use of its compulsory licensing statute has allowed the government to provide these drugs on a broad scale. Prior to TRIPS, Brazilian patent laws did not provide protection for pharmaceutical processes or products. The United States responded to lobbying efforts by the Pharmaceutical Manufacturers Association by imposing Special 301 sanctions against Brazil for failing to protect intellectual property rights. On 20 October 1988, President Reagan increased duties on various Brazilian products by 100 per cent. The Brazilian government announced one year later that it would seek improved patent legislation for pharmaceutical products and processes. During this period Brazil led a coalition of developing countries that resisted increases in global intellectual property protections through TRIPS (Bird, 2006; Bass, 2002). That resistance failed, and after the enactment of TRIPS Brazil enacted Intellectual Property Law number 9.279, which went into effect on 15 May 1997 (Brazilian Patent Law, 1997). This law recognized the relevant TRIPS provisions, including patent protection for pharmaceutical drugs and processes. Drugs manufactured in Brazil before 1995, however, were not eligible for patent protection (Marques et al., 2005).

Embedded in the 1997 law are Brazil's compulsory licensing statutes. These statutes, like their Egyptian counterpart, are similarly broad and are thus similarly controversial to MNE pharmaceutical providers and other patent holders. For example, Article 71 states that through an act of the Federal Executive Authorities a compulsory license may be granted in cases of 'national emergency or public interest' (Brazilian Patent Law, 1997). Then Brazilian President Fernando Henrique Cardoso reinforced this provision through an Executive Decree. While President Cardoso limited narrowed 'national emergency' to conditions of 'imminent public danger', he also declared that matters of public health were of public interest, by inference giving pharmaceutical drugs a particular focus of compulsory licensing statutes (Marques et al., 2005).

Brazil's most controversial provision has been the 'local working' requirement of Article 68. Article 68 requires that within three years of obtaining a patent, the patent holder must manufacture the subject matter of the patent in Brazil unless the patent holder can show that local production is not economically feasible or reasonable. If the patent holder fails to do so then Brazilian companies may apply to manufacture the patented product through compulsory licensing in Brazil (Marques et al., 2005; Valach, 2005).

The United States responded to this provision by bringing a complaint against this legislation with the World Trade Organization (WTO). The US argued that Article 68 was incompatible with the non-discrimination provision of Article 27(1) of TRIPS, which required that national patent protection cannot discriminate as to the place of its invention (Mathews, 2004).

The WTO complaint triggered global criticism because it would arguably impair Brazil's ability to distribute low cost anti-AIDS drugs to its citizens. At an NGO global meeting in Brazil, 250 delegates organized a march to the US consulate to protest the complaint. Similar demonstrations took place in other major Brazilian cities (Passarelli and

Terto, 2002). AIDS activists accused the US government of prioritizing MNE profits at the expense of Brazilians infected with the HIV virus (Bass, 2002). A widespread NGO signature campaign, which included organizations such as Oxfam and Doctors without Borders, brought further attention to the complaint. One article called the US complaint a public relations disaster (Raghavan, 2001).

Most interesting was Brazil's skillful response to the American threat to its intellectual property system. First, Brazil negated the moral high ground of the United States by immediately filing its own complaint challenging portions of the US patent code (Yerkey and Pruzin, 2001). The US code Brazil cited requires funding arrangements with non-profits and small business to state that products made with government funding must be manufactured in the United States. Brazil also cited statutory language requiring that licenses of federally-owned inventions be manufactured in the United States (Mota, 2005). India also wished to join Brazil in its request for consultations regarding US law, claiming that it was 'well known that India has a substantial trade as well as systemic interest in these consultations' (WTO, 2004). In the Brazilian government's own words, 'Brazil has requested consultations with the United States in order to examine these and other provisions of the US Patents Code, with a view to understand how the United States justifies the consistency of such requirements with its obligations under the TRIPs Agreement, specially Articles 27 and 28' (WTO, 2001).

Second, the Brazilian government also leveraged its role as a developing country leader to present a resolution to the United Nations Human Rights Commission. The resolution called for appropriate medicines to be made available at accessible prices and for access to AIDS treatment to be recognized as a human right. The motion received the support of all but one of the 52 countries present: the United States (Passarelli and Terto, 2002).

Third, Brazilian government officials issued a number of statements framing the dispute in its favor. Jose Serra, the Brazilian Minister of Health, reiterated that Brazil's patent law complies with WTO guidelines and stated that 'the simple fact we have been prepared to use [our compulsory license] has led to a number of foreign laboratories to lower their prices, as is the case of Merck-Sharp, which reduced the price of two AIDS drugs for Brazil by two and a half times' (Brennan, 2001, pp. 2–3). Serra also characterized the dispute as a clash between a rich, bullying America and the downtrodden, stating that, 'There is no way that the Brazilian Government will retreat on this issue. The United States is not at all accustomed to Latin American countries also defending their own interests' (Brennan, 2001, p. 3). Brazilian Ambassador Celso Amorim hinted at the fallout from the complaint that would follow, stating that the US's '[complaint] is not only legally unfounded, but it may prove politically disastrous' (Brennan, 2001, p. 3).

Brazil's counter-campaign combined with global public pressure forced the United States to withdraw its complaint from the WTO. Brazil responded with a promise to consult and negotiate with the United States and its pharmaceutical manufacturers before granting any future compulsory licenses. One wonders whether the US choice to file the complaint was a mistake from the start. According to one author, Brazil could have produced the same drugs under a 'public non-commercial use' exception authorized in article 31 of TRIPS because Brazil produced the medicine in state-owned labs and distributed it to the public for free (Wilson, 2005).

Brazil could defend the compulsory license because although Brazil is a developing country, it has the resources to develop the technology necessary to manufacture pharmaceuticals. Brazil can thus more readily implement a compulsory license than its poor neighbors, giving threats to compulsory licensing a greater sense of immediacy and importance. Also, Brazil has for years had the economic resources to passively resist American sanctions that could strong-arm a weaker nation into not issuing compulsory license. For example, in 1987 negotiations between Brazil and the United States failed to reach an agreement regarding pharmaceutical patent rights. The United States announced tariffs on a variety of products, including pharmaceuticals, paper products, chemicals, television cameras, microwave ovens, answering machines, jewelry and tape recorders. General Electric protested the tariffs against imported electrical breakers, Xerox opposed the inclusion of copy paper, Dow Chemical objected to the tariffs on carbon tetrachloride, Ford Motor called for the removal of amplifiers and windscreen wipers, and Carrier sought the removal of air conditioners from the tariffs target list. The firms claimed that the proposed sanctions harmed their interests because they relied on the importation of the targeted products to satisfy consumer needs. Brazil's interests were protected by the American firms who reaped economic benefits from trading with Brazil and did not want to suffer the losses the tariffs would impose (Bird, 2006; Getlan, 1995).

As characterized by Valach (2005), Brazil has used a three-pronged attack in order to protect its compulsory license. First, Brazil produces locally any HIV drugs that are not subject to patent protection in Brazil because they predate legal protection. Second, if the needed drugs are covered by Brazilian patents, then the Brazilian government attempts to negotiate a deal with the patent holder for a lower price that would allow the Brazilian government to provide the drugs to citizens for free (Valach, 2005). Over the past ten years Brazil has successfully negotiated deep discounts for different kinds of anti-retroviral and other drugs from a variety of pharmaceutical enterprises (Sell, 2004). Only when these negotiations fail does Brazil threaten to issue a compulsory license for the needed drugs. Brazil has successfully used this threat to secure an affordable price for anti-retroviral drugs (Mathews, 2004), and other countries have taken notice. A not-for-profit group is coaching groups in Ghana, Kenya, South Africa and Uganda how to mount legal bids for compulsory licenses from pharmaceutical companies (Caroll, 2003). Until recently, Brazil was the only country to use compulsory licenses for anti-retroviral drugs successfully. Other developing countries are now following Brazil's lead (Kapczynski et al., 2005).

Unlike Egypt, Brazil's compulsory license statute does not appear to come at a price of lost foreign direct investment. Brazil's compulsory license practices have done little to hamper their ability to attract foreign direct investment. According to a pharmaceutical industry executive, Brazil has received $2 billion of FDI in the pharmaceutical and chemical sectors since their modern patent law was adopted in 1996 (Mayer, 2002). Although Brazil may be a useful model, not every developing country has the political savvy, economic might and technological infrastructure to resist pressure from MNEs to avoid issuing compulsory rights.

CONCLUSION

Intellectual property rights play an increasingly important role in global commerce. Investment in innovating activities amplifies economic development for firms by giving them a competitive advantage that can not be easily replicated by competitors. Nations also use intellectual property rights to attract foreign direct investment, which can stimulate the growth of local industry, increase employment, and enhance research and development activities. Intellectual property rights, however, come at a price. That price is the lack of competition, which may result in higher prices for consumers.

This problem becomes particularly acute for products without adequate substitutes, such as lifesaving pharmaceutical drugs. High prices can deny poor consumers medicines that could improve their quality of life or simply keep a person alive. Developing countries have increasingly relied on compulsory licenses, or the threat of compulsory licenses, to force medicines to be sold at affordable prices for consumers.

Issuing compulsory licenses, however, may come at a cost in the form of reduced foreign direct investment. Conventional thinking may be that all nations would suffer proportionally equal foreign direct investment losses, but it is likely that middle-developed countries would suffer the most. Unlike least developed countries, who receive little investment anyway, middle developed countries such as Egypt, Brazil and others, have investment to lose.

Nations must employ different strategies for issuing compulsory licenses depending upon their placement on the economic continuum. As the Brazilian government has shown, a middle-developed nation can use the threat of a compulsory license combined with savvy public relations to good effect. The result is that each nation can leverage its unique position in the global economy to maximize the issuance of compulsory licenses to protect the lives of its citizens while minimizing the effect on foreign direct investment losses.

NOTES

1. The technology scale measures nations according to telephone, cellular and Internet use. It also measures patent granted, royalties received, and research and development commitments. The economic performance scale measures nations according to GDP and change in consumer prices.
2. This quote is attributed to a 'Harvey Bell of IPFMA' in the remarks of Susan Kling Finston, Assistant Vice President, Intellectual Property and Middle East/Africa/South Asian Affairs, PhRMA. Finston is probably referring to Harvey E. Bale, Director General of the International Federation of Pharmaceutical Manufacturers Associations (IFPMA), an organization that represents the research-based pharmaceutical industry and other manufacturers of prescription medicines through over 55 industry member associations worldwide. The misstatement of the name is probably a transcriber's error and not attributable to Ms Finston.

REFERENCES

Abbott, Frederick M. (1989), 'Protecting first world assets in the third world: Intellectual property negotiations in the GATT Multilateral Framework', *Vanderbilt Journal of Transnational Law*, **22**(4), 689–745.

Abbott, Frederick M. and Rudolf V. Van Puymbroeck (2005), 'Compulsory licensing for public health: A guide and model documents for implementation of the Doha Declaration paragraph 6 decision', World Bank Working Paper No. 61.

Abramowicz, Michael (2003), 'Patent prizes', *Vanderbilt Law Review*, **56**(1), 115–236.

Al-Ali, Nermien (2003), 'The Egyptian pharmaceutical industry after TRIPS – A practitioner's view', *Fordham International Law Journal*, **26**(2), 274–314.

Allam, Abeer (2002), 'Seeking investment, Egypt tries patent laws', *New York Times*, 4 October, W1.
A.T. Kearney (2005), '2005 Foreign Direct Investment Confidence Index: Regional findings', http://www.atkearney.com/main.taf?p=5,3,1,140,12.
Attaran, Amir and Lee Gillespie-White (2001), 'Do patents for antiretroviral drugs constrain access to AIDS treatment in Africa?', *Journal of the American Medical Association*, **286**, 1886–92.
Aziz, Sahar (2003), 'Linking intellectual property rights in developing countries with research and development, technology transfer, and foreign direct investment policy: A case study of Egypt's pharmaceutical industry', *ILSA Journal of International and Comparative Law*, **10**(Fall), 1–34.
Bass, Naomi A. (2002), 'Implications of the TRIPS Agreement for developing countries: Pharmaceutical patent laws in Brazil and South Africa in the 21st century', *George Washington International Law Review*, **34**(1), 191–222.
Bird, Robert C. (2006), 'Defending intellectual property rights in the BRIC economies', *American Business Law Journal*, **43**(2), 317–63.
Brazilian Patent Law (1997), Brazilian Patent Law 9.279 of 14 May 1996, Art. 68 (enacted 15 May 1997), http://www.ftaa-alca.org/intprop/natleg/Brazil/ENG/L9279eB.asp#lic.
Brennan, Terrence M. (2001), 'The United States and Brazil agree to disagree over Brazil's Patent Law', *Intellectual Property and Technology Law Journal*, **13**(9), 1–6.
Business Today (Egypt) (2002), 'A tough pill to swallow', *Business Today (Egypt)*, 1 August.
Cahoy, Daniel R. (2005), 'Patent fences and constitutional fence posts: Property barriers to pharmaceutical importation', *Fordham Intellectual Property, Media and Entertainment Law Journal*, **15**(3), 623–708.
Cahoy, Daniel R. (2006), 'An incrementalist approach to patent reform policy', *N.Y.U. Journal of Legislation and Public Policy*, **9**(2), 587–661.
Cahoy, Daniel R. (2007), 'Confronting myths and myopia on the road from Doha', *Georgia Law Review*, **42**(1), 131–92.
Caroll, Rory (2003), 'Africa's Aids drugs trapped in the laboratory', *The Guardian*, http://www.guardian.co.uk/aids/story/0,,960116,00.html. 21 May 2003.
Castellano, Richard A. (2006), 'Patent law for new medical uses of known compounds and Pfizer's Viagra patent', *IDEA*, **46**(2), 283–315.
Chien, Colleen (2003), 'Cheap drugs at what price to innovation: Does the compulsory licensing of pharmaceuticals hurt innovation?', *Berkeley Technology Law Journal*, **18**(1), 853–907.
Chon, Margaret (2006), 'Intellectual property and the development divide', *Cardozo Law Review*, **27**(6), 2821–912.
Convention on the Grant of European Patents (1973), 1065 UNTS 254.
Correa, Carlos M. (1999), 'Intellectual property rights and the use of compulsory licenses: Options for developing countries', South Centre, http://www.southcentre.org/publications/complicence/toc.htm.
DiMasi, Joseph A. (2000), 'Price trends for prescription pharmaceuticals: 1995–1999', http://aspe.hhs.gov/health/reports/Drug-papers/dimassi/dimasi-final.htm.
Dratler, Jay, Jr. (2001), *Licensing of Intellectual Property*, New York, NY: Law Journal Seminars Press.
Getlan, Myles (1995), 'TRIPS and the future of Section 301: A comparative study in trade resolution', *Columbia Journal of Transnational Law*, **34**(1), 173–218.
Guerrera, Francesco (2001), 'Investors rue weak patent protection: Much needed foreign investment is being held back because international rules on patents and brands are not enforced', *Financial Times*, 9 May, p. 8.
Gupta, Rishi (2003), 'TRIPS compliance: Dealing with the consequences of drug patents in India', *Houston Journal of International Law*, **26**(3), 599–648.
Hall, Bronwyn H.(1996), 'The private and social returns to research and development', in Bruce L.R. Smith and Claude E. Barfield (eds), *Technology, R&D, and the Economy*, Washington, DC: Brookings Institution Press.
Hamilton, David P. (2006), 'New AIDS pill simplifies treatment', *Wall Street Journal*, 10 July, B8.
Hunter, Richard J., Robert E. Shapiro and Leo V. Ryan (2003), 'Legal considerations in foreign direct investment', *Oklahoma City University Law Review*, **28**(Summer–Fall), 851–73.

IIPA (International Intellectual Property Alliance) (2006), 'International Intellectual Property Alliance, 2006 Special 301 Report (Egypt)', pp. 53–62, http://www.iipa.com/rbc/2006/2006SPEC301EGYPT.pdf.

Implementation of Paragraph 6 of the Doha Declaration on the TRIPS Agreement and Public Health (1 September 2003), Doc. WT/L/540, http://www.wto.org/English/tratop_e/trips_e/implem_para6_e.htm.

Kapczynski, Amy, Samantha Chaifetz, Zachary Katz and Yochai Benkler (2005), 'Addressing global health inequities: An open licensing approach for university innovations', *Berkeley Technology Law Journal*, **20**(2), 1031–114.

Kennedy, Kevin C. (2003), 'A WTO Agreement on investment: A solution in search of a problem?', *University of Pennsylvania Journal of International Economic Law*, **24**(1), 77–188.

Kitch, Edmund W. (1977), 'The nature and function of the patent system', *Journal of Law and Economics*, **20**(2), 265–90.

Kitch, Edmund W. (2000), 'Elementary and persistent errors in the economic analysis of intellectual property law', *Vanderbilt Law Review*, **53**(6), 1727–41.

Kremer, Michael (1998), 'Patent buyouts: A mechanism for encouraging innovation', *Quarterly Journal of Economics*, **113**(4), 1137–67.

Lanjouw, Jean O. (2003), 'Intellectual property and the availability of pharmaceuticals in poor countries', in Adam B. Jaffe et al. (eds), *Innovation Policy and the Economy*, Vol. 3, Cambridge, MA: MIT Press.

Law on the Protection of Intellectual Property Rights (2002), http://www.egypt.pibs.info/brl-egypt-ipr-law-2002.pdf.

Lee, Jeong-Yeon and Edwin Mansfield (1996), 'Intellectual property protection and US foreign direct investment', *Review of Economics and Statistics*, **78**(2), 181–6.

Lemley, Mark A. (2000), 'Reconceiving patents in the age of venture capital', *Journal of Small and Emerging Business Law*, **4**(1), 137–48.

Lemley, Mark A. (2004), 'Ex ante versus ex post justifications for intellectual property', *Chicago Law Review*, **71**(1), 129–49.

Levy, Roy (1999), 'The Pharmaceutical Industry: A Discussion of Competitive and Antitrust Issues in an Environment of Change', Bureau of Economics Staff Report: Federal Trade Commission, http://www.ftc.gov/reports/pharmaceutical/drugrep.pdf.

Long, Clarissa (2002), 'Patent signals', *University of Chicago Law Review*, **69**(2), 625–79.

Marques, Ubirajara Regis Quintanilha, Vateska Santos Guimarães and Caitlin Sternberg (2005), 'Brazil's AIDS controversy: Antiretroviral drugs, breaking patents, and compulsory licensing', *Food and Drug Law Journal*, **60**(3), 471–7.

Maskus, Keith E. (1998), 'The role of intellectual property rights in encouraging foreign direct investment and technology transfer', *Duke Journal of Comparative and International Law*, **9**(1), 109–161.

Maskus, Keith E. (2001), 'Intellectual property challenges for developing countries: An economic perspective', *University of Illinois Law Review*, no. (1), 457–73.

Maskus, Keith E. (2005), 'The role of intellectual property rights in encouraging foreign direct investment and technology transfer', in C. Fink and K. Maskus (eds), *Intellectual Property and Development: Lessons from Recent Economic Research*, New York, NY: World Bank and Oxford University Press, pp. 41–73.

Mathews, Duncan (2004), 'WTO Decision on implementation of Paragraph 6 of the Doha Declaration on the TRIPS Agreement and public health: A solution to the access to essential medicines problem?', *Journal of International Economic Law*, **7**(1), 73–107.

May, Christopher and Susan K. Sell (2006), *Intellectual Property Rights: A Critical History*, Boulder, CO: Lynne Rienner Publishers Inc.

Mayer, Haldane R. (2002), 'United States Court of Appeals for the Federal Circuit 20th Anniversary Judicial Conference: "A salute to the federal circuit" ', *Federal Rules Decisions*, **217**, 548–771.

Merges, Robert P. (1996), 'Contracting into liability rules: Intellectual property rights and collective rights organizations, *California Law Review*, **84**(5), 1293–393.

Metwally, M.M. (2004), 'Impact of EU FDI on economic growth in Middle Eastern countries', *European Business Review*, **16**(4), 381–9.

Mossinghoff, Gerald J. (1996), 'Remedies under patents on medical and surgical procedures', *Journal of the Patent and Trademark Office Society*, **78**(11), 789–801.
Mota, Sue Ann (2005), 'TRIPS: Ten years of disputes at the WTO', *Computer Law Review and Technology Journal*, **9**(Summer), 455–78.
National STD and AIDS Programme (2005), 'National programme history: 20 years of AIDS', http://www.aids.gov.br/data/Pages/LUMISBD1B398DITEMID0FE488C7CE8E4EB1A093265 28B487409ENIE.htm.
Paris Convention (14 July, 1967), 21 UST 1583, TIAS No. 6295, 828 UNTS 305.
Passarelli, Carlos and Veriano Terto, Jr (2002), 'Good medicine: Brazil's multifront war on AIDS', *NACLA Report on the Americas*, **35**(5), 35–52.
Raghavan, Chakravarthi (2001), 'US beats a (tactical) retreat over Brazil's patent law', *Third World Network*, http://www.twnside.org.sg/title/tactical.htm. 25 June 2001.
Reichman, Jerome H. and Catherine Hasenzahl (2004), 'Non-voluntary licensing of patented inventions', UNCTAD-ICTSD Issue Paper No. 5, http://www.ictsd.org/pubs/ictsd_series/iprs/CS_reichman_hasenzahl.pdf.
Russell, Sabin (2000), 'AIDS experts to meet in eye of epidemic / 20% of South Africa's adults are infected', *San Francisco Chronicle*, http://www.aegis.com/news/sc/2000/SC000701.html, 7 July.
Scherer, F.M. and Jayashree Watal (2002), 'Post-TRIPS options for access to patented medicines in developing countries', *Journal of International Economic Law*, **5**(4), 913–39.
Scotchmer, Suzanne (2004), *Innovation and Incentives*, Cambridge, MA: MIT Press.
Sell, Susan K. (2002), 'TRIPS and the access to medicines campaign', *Wisconsin International Law Journal*, **20**(3), 481–522.
Sell, Susan K. (2004), 'The quest for global governance in intellectual property and public health', *Temple Law Review*, **77**(2), 363–99.
Thomas, John R. (2002), 'The responsibility of the rulemaker: Comparative approaches to patent administration reform', *Berkeley Technology Law Journal*, **17**(2), 727–62.
Trade-Related Aspects of Intellectual Property Rights (TRIPS) (1994), Marrakesh Agreement Establishing the World Trade Organization, Annex 1C, Legal Instruments – Results of the Uruguay Round, 33 ILM 81.
United Nations Conference on Trade and Development & International Centre for Trade and Sustainable Development (2005), *Resource Book on TRIPS and Development*, New York, NY: Cambridge University Press.
United Nations Development Programme (UNDP) (2005), Human Development Report, http://hdr.undp.org/reports/global/2005/pdf/HDR05_HDI.pdf.
Valach, Anthony P., Jr. (2005), 'TRIPS: Protecting the rights of patent holders and addressing public health issues in developing countries', *Chicago-Kent Journal of Intellectual Property*, **4**(Spring), 156–85.
Watal, Jayashree (2000), 'Pharmaceutical patents, prices and welfare losses: Policy options for India under the WTO TRIPS Agreement', *The World Economy*, **23**(5), 733–52.
Wilson, Clark A.D. (2005), 'The TRIPS Agreement: Is it beneficial to the developing world, or simply a tool used to protect pharmaceutical profits for developed world manufacturers?', *Journal of Technology Law and Policy*, **10**(2), 243–64.
World Health Organization (2006), 'Burden of disease and cost-effectiveness estimates', http://www.who.int/water_sanitation_health/diseases/burden/en/.
World Intellectual Property Organization (WIPO) (2007), 'Advice on flexibilities under the TRIPS Agreement', http://www.wipo.int/ip-development/en/legislative_assistance/advice_trips.html.
World Trade Organization (WTO) (2001), 'Request for Consultations by Brazil', WT/DS224/1. 7 Feb 2001. http://www.worldtradelaw.net/cr/ds224-1(cr).pdf.
World Trade Organization (WTO) (2004), 'Request to Join Consultations, US–US Patents Code', WT/DS224/2. 19 Feb 2004.
World Trade Organization (WTO) (2007a), 'TRIPS and public health: Notifications by importing WTO Members', http://www.wto.org/English/tratop_e/trips_e/public_health_notif_import_e.htm.
World Trade Organization (WTO) (2007b), 'Least Developed Countries', http://www.wto.org/english/thewto_e/whatis_e/tif_e/org7_e.htm.

Yerkey, Gary G. and Daniel Pruzin (2001), 'United States drops WTO case against Brazil over HIV/AIDS patent law', *WTO Reporter*, http://www.cptech.org/ip/health/c/brazil/bna06262001.html.
Yu, Peter K. (2006), 'TRIPS and its discontents', *Marquette Intellectual Property Law Review*, **10**(2), 369–410.
Yu, Peter K. (2007), 'The international enclosure movement', *Indiana Law Journal*, **82**(4), 827–907.

13. Intellectual property reform in developing countries: trade and investment dimensions

Douglas Lippoldt[1]

INTRODUCTION

In recent decades, the global economy has become increasingly integrated as technological advances, trade and investment liberalization, reform in transition countries, institutional change and other factors have come together to break down barriers and increase international economic possibilities. The multilateral trading system has played a major role in promotion of economic integration, in part by influencing the evolution of institutions related to intellectual property rights (IPRs) in developing and transition countries. A key element in this regard is the World Trade Organization's (WTO) Agreement on Trade-Related Aspects of Intellectual Property Rights (TRIPS), which came into effect in 1995. The TRIPS Agreement established minimum IPR standards and a framework to review and enforce these standards. In parallel with the advent of TRIPS, the World Intellectual Property Organization (WIPO) witnessed a significant increase in adherence to the various international treaties that it administers. One result of these developments has been a strengthening of IPRs around the world, including in a number of developing countries where the initial protection of IPRs was weak at best.

Drawing in part on recent OECD studies, this chapter begins with an examination of the extent of institutional change with respect to IPRs in developing and transition countries. It then presents analysis employing statistical and regression techniques in order to assess developments in international trade and investment associated with IPR reform. The chapter highlights the tendency – with some notable variation by sector or level of development – for strengthened IPRs to be associated with increased inflows of foreign direct investment (FDI) and imports, flows which can represent an important channel of technology transfer into developing countries. It concludes that IPR reform can play a useful role as one element in national development strategies, particularly where there exist notable shortfalls in IPR protection and where appropriate complementary policies are included in the strategies.

THE IMPORTANCE OF INSTITUTIONS

During the 1990s, reform of institutions governing IPRs was given particular impetus through the conclusion of the Uruguay Round of multilateral trade negotiations and the economic transition in the formerly socialist countries. As is underscored in a large and growing swath of economic literature, institutional reform can influence the functioning of an economy in important ways. Douglass North, in the introduction to a 1997 paper examining problems of economic transition, provides a useful summary:

> Institutions and the way they evolve shape economic performance. Institutions affect economic performance by determining (together with the technology employed) the cost of transacting and producing. They are composed of formal rules, of informal constraints and of their enforcement characteristics; while formal rules can be changed overnight by the polity, informal constraints change very slowly. (North, 1997, p. 1)

Given that institutions are but one factor influencing the evolution of a given economy, it is useful to examine the relative importance of institutions in shaping growth. Rodrik, Subramanian and Trebbi (2002) conducted one such study, yielding a particularly striking comparison of the deep sources of economic growth. Striving to peer beyond the first-level determinants (capital accumulation – human and physical – and productivity change), they consider three 'strands of thought' from the literature on the underlying drivers of growth. These consider geography, international trade integration and institutional quality, respectively, as central factors accounting for differences in average income levels among nations. Using a series of regressions to relate incomes to indicators for geography, integration and institutions,[2] Rodrik et al. (2002) find that the quality of institutions is the key factor. The institutional indicator exhibits a relatively large, positive and statistically significant relationship to income. Once institutional quality is controlled for, 'integration has no direct effect on incomes, while geography has at best weak direct effects' (Rodrik et al., 2002, p. 4). Moreover, in further assessments of the relationships among these variables, institutional quality is found to have a positive and significant effect on international trade integration, while trade in turn can have a positive influence on institutional quality (suggesting an indirect influence on incomes). However, the authors do not offer policy prescriptions with respect to institutions, rather citing evidence that 'desirable institutional arrangements have a large element of context specificity, arising from differences in historical trajectories, geography, political economy or other initial conditions' (Rodrik et al., 2002, p. 22).

A recent article by Bénassy-Quéré, Coupet and Mayer (2007) underscores the importance of institutional conditions as a determinant of FDI. The authors consider the impact of the quality of institutions on FDI using: i) first, a standard gravity model; ii) then, cross-country regression estimations and an instrumental variable approach[3] drawing in part on the new and detailed Institutional Profiles database constructed by the French Ministry of Economy, Finance and Industry; and iii) finally, a panel data assessment drawing in part on the Fraser Institute time-series data set (which has less institutional detail, but better country coverage). The authors conclude that host-country institutions matter as determinants of FDI, independently of GDP per capita, with good institutions almost always associated with increased amounts of FDI received. Good institutions with respect to bureaucracy, corruption, information, banking sector and legal institutions are found to be especially important positive determinants of inward FDI.[4] Convergence in institutions between host country and source country was found to tend to help increase inflows of FDI. Summing up, the authors note, 'The orders of magnitude found in the paper are large' (Bénassy-Quéré et al., 2007, p. 781), meaning that moving from a low level to a high level of institutional quality could have a substantial impact on FDI. These findings are promising in the context of the present paper, in that the enhancement of IPRs – as an institutional change – would appear to be potentially relevant to FDI inflows.

In light of the central role that institutions appear to play in the functioning of economies, it may be expected that reform of IPR institutions would be associated with economic impacts. For example, it may be that change in IPR stringency will alter the incentives to innovate or to provide access to technology embodied in intellectual property. Technological progress plays a central role in boosting productivity (output per worker), which in turn is a first-level determinant of income levels and growth.[5] The issue of international access to intellectual property is critical to developing countries, especially in the earlier stages of development, because these countries may face particular limitations in domestic sources of innovation.[6] If inward trade, direct investment and licensing can be influenced by the strength of IPRs in an economy, then governments may be able to exploit IPR policy as one element in a broader policy framework aiming to enhance these flows. Inflows of goods, direct investment and licenses embody various types of intellectual property and represent a channel of technology transfer. Indeed, Article 7 of the TRIPS Agreement provides that 'the protection and enforcement of intellectual property rights should contribute to the transfer and dissemination of technology'.[7]

THE NATURE OF INTELLECTUAL PROPERTY

Intellectual property has particular characteristics that differentiate it from physical goods. Unlike a material resource, the same bit of intellectual property can be made available simultaneously and repeatedly on a non-exclusive basis to multiple users, generally at a low marginal cost. New ideas embodied in intellectual property, being non-rivalrous, can contribute to technical progress with 'disproportionate' impacts on economic growth due to the big potential returns to scale when one idea is applied many times (Jones, 2004; Warsh, 2006). Given this economic potential, policy makers may be particularly motivated to reform policies with a view to boosting development of new domestic intellectual property[8] and improving access to existing intellectual property from abroad.

IPRs help to ensure that innovators are able to capitalize on their innovations. This is because IPRs provide the owners of intellectual property with legal means to prevent abuse of their rights.[9] At the same time, under the various systems governing IPRs, the rights of the owner are balanced against certain obligations (for example the public disclosure of certain information related to patents), limits on the extent of protection (for example in terms of duration of patents or copyrights, granting of research exemptions, or public health waivers) and some other constraints (for example, with respect to anti-competitive practices in contractual licenses).[10] Seen from an economic perspective, the incentives for innovators need to provide for an appropriate degree of protection without conferring excessive market power.[11]

The absolute size of the stock of relevant and available intellectual property appears to be an important factor in relation to productivity. As Jones (2004, p. 13) notes, 'Because of the non-rivalrous nature of ideas, output per person depends on the total stock of ideas in the economy instead of the per capita stock of ideas.' Since intellectual property can cross borders easily, the scope of the available stock can be nearly global, subject to an appropriate international framework and the willingness of rights holders to facilitate access. Singapore and Hong Kong-China are examples of economies that have overcome scale limitations in their domestic stocks of intellectual property, in part, through their integration into the global economy; among other initiatives in this regard, they have undertaken commitments with respect to the international framework agreements governing intellectual property.

The importance of IPR protection to rights holders may vary depending on the ease with which the ideas can be imitated. An exporter of specialty steel with a unique manufacturing process may not be especially concerned about patents in a particular destination market if the exported good cannot be easily reverse engineered. On the other hand, a software producer whose code can be easily copied by anyone with a laptop computer may hesitate to sell into a market where technological literacy is high and piracy is commonplace. While a goods producer in a competitive and freewheeling market may get paid the full amount of his or her marginal product, in the absence of a mechanism to protect IPRs there is a risk of little or no return to the originators of ideas, and hence insufficient incentives to innovate.

Developing country perspectives vary on the importance of IPRs in their economic policy frameworks. Public debate on IPRs in these countries is sometimes caught up in emotive issues such as implications for public health and access to medicine[12] or the need to prioritize among many competing demands for limited government resources. Critics point to significant implementation costs that can be associated with IPR commitments undertaken in the various international agreements.[13] Correa (2005) and others have challenged the legal and economic implications of strengthening of IPR, alleging that the system of international IPR rules is imposing a burden on developing countries.[14] The accusation is that the emerging standards raise the cost of intellectual content in products sought by developing countries, while developing countries may not have the capacity to capitalise on their own potential in a similar manner. Moreover, Correa alleges that the implicit bargain underlying the strengthening of the international IPR regime has not been satisfied, namely, that promises of technology transfer (for example as contained in TRIPS, Article 66.2) and FDI do not appear to be yielding results in a manner to benefit developing countries, whereas the strengthened IPRs may raise costs for developing countries seeking to upgrade their technological capabilities.[15]

On the other hand, some developing countries have sought to exploit strengthened IPRs strategically as a development tool. For example, they may see IPR policy as a means to draw in investment and to encourage domestic innovation, with the potential to boost development on both the extensive dimension (overall size of the economy) as well as the intensive dimension (that is, the value-added per employee). Government officials from a range of economies have pointed to strengthened IPRs as a plank in their strategies to enhance FDI inflows (Box 13.1) and trade.[16] For example, experts in some poor developing countries have seen the institution of trademark protection as a vehicle for reassuring investors in manufacturing industries that they can combat knock-offs. For wealthier countries, enhancement of IPRs may be seen as a means to draw in high technology that can boost worker productivity and contribute to intensification of growth.

Strengthening of IPRs since 1990

The years since 1990 have been marked by a significant strengthening of IPRs in developing and transition countries (Park and Lippoldt, 2005). The starting point for many of these countries was a relatively weak national system of IPR protection sometimes based on poorly adapted systems dating from a former colonial era, or sometimes, in effect, non-existent systems. The strengthening of IPRs has come about, in part, as a result of an increase in the number of ratifications of instruments administered by WIPO and the establishment of minimum IPR standards for the members of the WTO applicable as a consequence of the TRIPS Agreement.

BOX 13.1 FOREIGN DIRECT INVESTMENT: DESTINATION OF INFLOWS

Foreign direct investment refers to cross-border investments made with the objective of establishing a lasting interest in an entity that is resident in a market other than the investor's home market.[17] The investment may consist of equity capital, reinvested earnings and other capital contributions. Flows of FDI have exhibited impressive growth in recent years, particularly since 1990 but with significant year-to-year variation. OECD countries attract the bulk of the inflows (see Figure 13.1), but China has grown in importance and has been a top destination in recent years (for example accounting for about 10 per cent of global net inflows in 2002). The large volumes of the flows and their potential relationship to technology transfer have drawn the attention of some policy makers in developing countries who aim to attract greater shares, in some cases partly through IPR and other institutional reforms (for example Singapore).

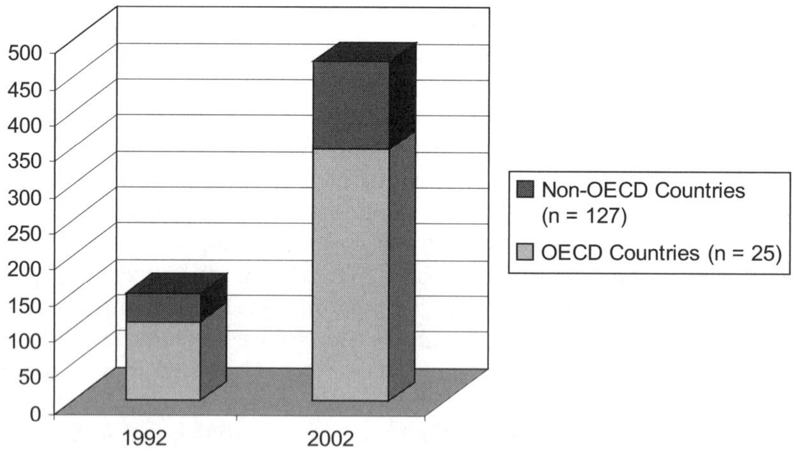

Notes: Figures for OECD do not include Belgium, Luxembourg, Korea, the Czech Republic or the Slovak Republic. 'BoP' indicates 'on a balance of payments basis'.

Source: World Bank, *World Development Indicators*, on-line edition.

Figure 13.1 Net inflows of FDI, USD millions (BoP)

Ratifications

WIPO administers a series of international IPR treaties developed over many years. Since 1990, the geographic coverage of these treaties was notably extended via increased numbers of ratifications (Figure 13.2). This occurred, in particular, in relation to the launching of economic reforms in the former socialist countries and in association with the coming into effect of the TRIPS Agreement. During the 1990s, for example:

a) The Berne Convention for the Protection of Literary and Artistic Works (ref. copyrights and neighboring rights) experienced 59 new ratifications (as of 5 May 2007, the total number was 163);
b) The Paris Convention for the Protection of Industrial Property (ref. patents, trademarks, industrial designs, utility models, geographical indications) experienced 60 new ratifications (as of 5 May 2007, the total number was 171);
c) The Rome Convention for the Protection of Performers, Producers of Phonograms and Broadcasting Organisations experienced 30 new ratifications (as of 5 May 2007, the total number was 86).

Particularly for the Berne and Paris Conventions, this was a considerable burst of activity in a relatively short period, given that both treaties date originally from the 1880s.

The effect of these ratifications was to extend specific protections for intellectual property as countries moved to comply with the various provisions. For example, the Paris and Berne Conventions include provisions on 'national treatment', meaning that within the terms specified in the conventions, the ratifying country must offer non-nationals the same protection as it grants to its own nationals.[18]

TRIPS and Regional or Bilateral Trade Agreements

Particular impetus to the strengthening of IPRs came from the advent of the TRIPS Agreement, which came into effect on 1 January 1995, covering the main types of intellectual property[19] and establishing more effective – and geographically inclusive – international minimum standards of protection for IPRs than had existed previously. The agreement specifies WTO member obligations to enforce IPRs; through the WTO's framework for trade policy review, dialog and dispute settlement it also provides pathways for redress among WTO members in cases of non-compliance by governments.

According to the TRIPS Agreement, WTO Members may implement in their law more extensive IPR protection than the minimum required under the agreement, provided that this does not contravene the agreement. In this spirit, regional and bilateral trade agreements involving OECD members and developing countries often include IPR references going beyond the TRIPS Agreement, as do some agreements among developing countries (for example Mercosur) (Lippoldt, 2003). In a review of 15 selected regional accords, Lippoldt found that most included one or more provisions going beyond the strict requirements of the TRIPS Agreement. Often these additional requirements concerned conformity with, or accession to, other relevant international agreements. For example, some agreements go beyond the TRIPS Agreement in requiring adherence to WIPO's

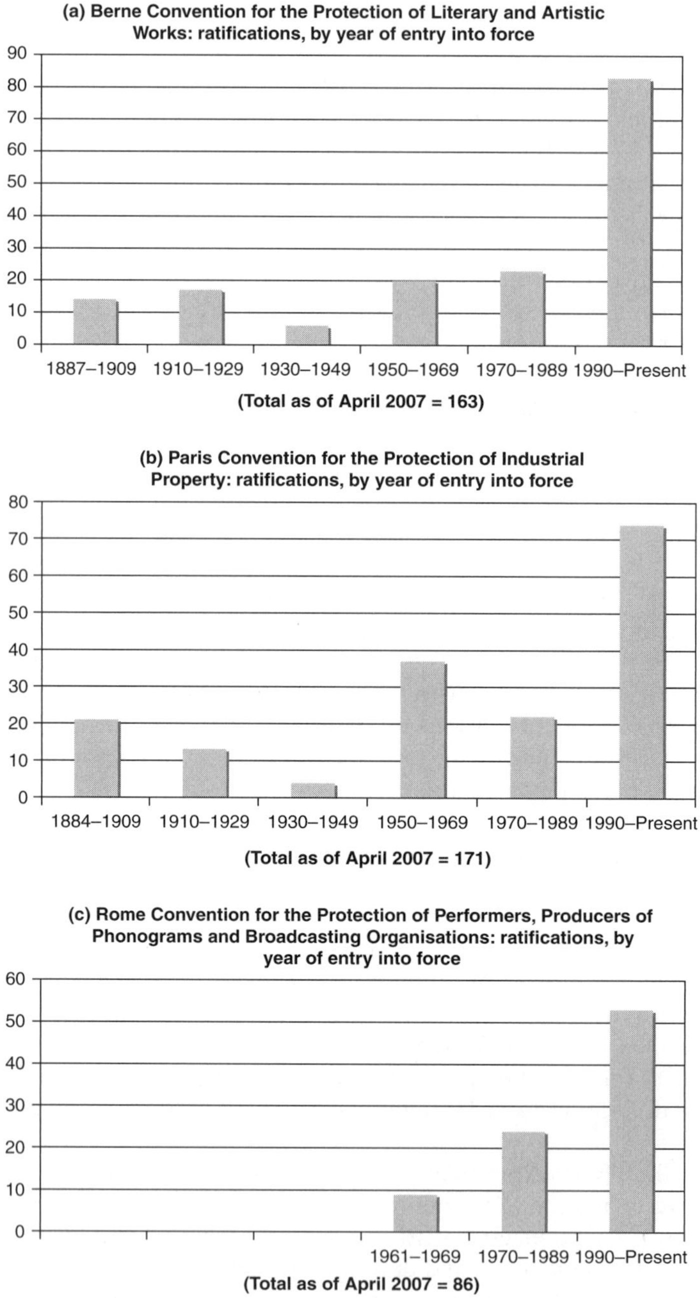

Note: The TRIPs Agreement also references the Treaty on Intellectual Property in Respect of Integrated Circuits adopted in Washington, 1989.

Source: WIPO, http://www.wipo.int/treaties/en/SearchForm.jsp?search_what=C .

Figure 13.2 Selected WIPO conventions referenced in the WTO TRIPS Agreement

Table 13.1 Evolution of average IPR index scores for developing countries, 1990–2000

Year	Patent Rights Index	Copyrights Index	Trademark Rights Index	Enforcement Effectiveness Index
1990	1.98	2.12	1.98	0.70
1995	2.36	2.53	2.24	0.87
2000	2.72	2.85	2.71	1.80
Total Observations	n=215	n=157	n=108	n=129

Notes: The maximum range of scores is 0–5 for the indices. The Copyright, Trademark and Enforcement indices were rebased from their original range of 0–1. See Appendix 13.A and Park and Lippoldt (2005) for an overview of the composition of these indices.

Source: Park and Lippoldt (2005).

Copyright Treaty and Performances and Phonograms Treaty (for example under the EU–Mexico or US–Jordan trade agreements). There are also examples of regional trade agreements that have special provisions concerning shortened transition periods, enforcement or cooperation, among other issues.

Indicators of IPR Strengthening

The impact of the expanded recognition of internationally established IPRs is evident in the evolution of various indices employed in this chapter to assess the strength of IPRs in developing countries. These include the four distinct indices of IPR strength (developed by Walter Park et al.[20]) covering patents, copyrights, trademarks and enforcement effectiveness. The patent, copyright and trademark indices are based on laws on the books, regardless of their application in practice. However, as noted by Douglass North (1997), there is sometimes a difference between formal and informal institutions, with the latter changing more gradually. And, a change in a formal institution may also be subject to implementation difficulties. Thus, the enforcement index was developed based on business perceptions (as reported to the Office of the US Trade Representative), in order to get a better sense of the application of the IPR laws in practice.

A second source was used in this section to extend the monitoring of IPR change into the current decade. This is an index for respect of intellectual property rights, which is drawn from the Institutional Profiles database at CEPII (Paris). The index scores are based on a survey of French government economic officials resident in countries around the world. As of the time of drafting, two waves have been conducted (2001 and 2006).

Table 13.1 presents, for a sample of developing and transition countries, the average score for each of the 'Park et al.' indices over the course of the 1990s. They each show a substantial increase in IPR strength over this period, particularly with respect to the indices for laws on the books. However, with respect to the wave of IPR reform of the first half of the 1990s, enforcement of the strengthened laws on the books seems to have lagged a bit. Then, during the second half of the decade, the Enforcement Effectiveness Index saw a substantial increase, with the average score more than doubling (probably at least partly related to the implementation of the TRIPS Agreement). While the score for the

Enforcement Effectiveness Index still remained well below the scores for the other indices, the importance of these changes should not be minimized. The strengthening of laws on the books and partially improved enforcement provide economic agents with a signal as to the future course of government policy – even if enforcement lags a bit behind in some areas.

Figure 13.3 provides an indication of business and government perceptions of the application of the IPRs in practice in a panel of 38 countries grouped by income level.[21] The top panel presents the evolution of the Enforcement Index during the 1990s. While the high-income OECD countries had a high and stable average score, the other country groups showed significant increases in their average score. However, perhaps not surprisingly given resource constraints and transition periods under TRIPS, the average score for the low-income countries did not increase as much as for the other groups. Drawing on the 'CEPII' index for respect of IPRs, the lower panel shows a relatively stable situation during the 2000s, although the low-income country group did catch up somewhat (in part as a consequence of the winding up of a key transition period for phase-in of IPR commitments by India).

Table 13.2 highlights the correlation between several indicators from the CEPII database and the Park et al. indices for Enforcement and Patent Rights. A strong relationship is found between the CEPII indicator of Respect for Intellectual Property and the Park indices. Given the different sources for the two data sets, this provides some independent confirmation of the variation captured in the Park et al. indices (which are used in the empirical assessments described below). Interestingly, the CEPII indicator for 'Security of Contracts Between Private Agents' is also fairly strongly correlated with the two part indices and very strongly correlated with the CEPII 'Respect' indicator. Thus, confidence in contractual relations is strongly associated with respect for intellectual property and fairly strongly associated with IPR laws on the books and perceptions of enforcement. Also, the Park et al. Enforcement Effectiveness Index is strongly correlated with the Patent Rights Index, indicating that countries with relatively strong laws on the books tend to have relatively strong enforcement.

Countries Acceding to the WTO

As the multilateral trading system evolves over time, continued participation through membership in GATT and, subsequently, the WTO drives change. Countries take on new commitments and obligations that now go beyond the 'traditional' trade-related border issues. This is particularly true for newly acceded countries. Evenett and Braga (2005) note the expanding demands that are being placed on countries acceding to the World Trade Organization since 1995, including in the service sector and with respect to rules that in some cases may not be obviously trade-related.

Figure 13.4 highlights change in the strength of IPRs (in terms of laws on the books) in six countries newly acceded to the WTO, according to type of property (that is patent, copyright or trademark) and compared to the average score for a broad group of developing countries. As the figure shows, each of the countries moved to strengthen its legal framework to a level roughly comparable to – or above – the average for the sample of developing and transition countries.

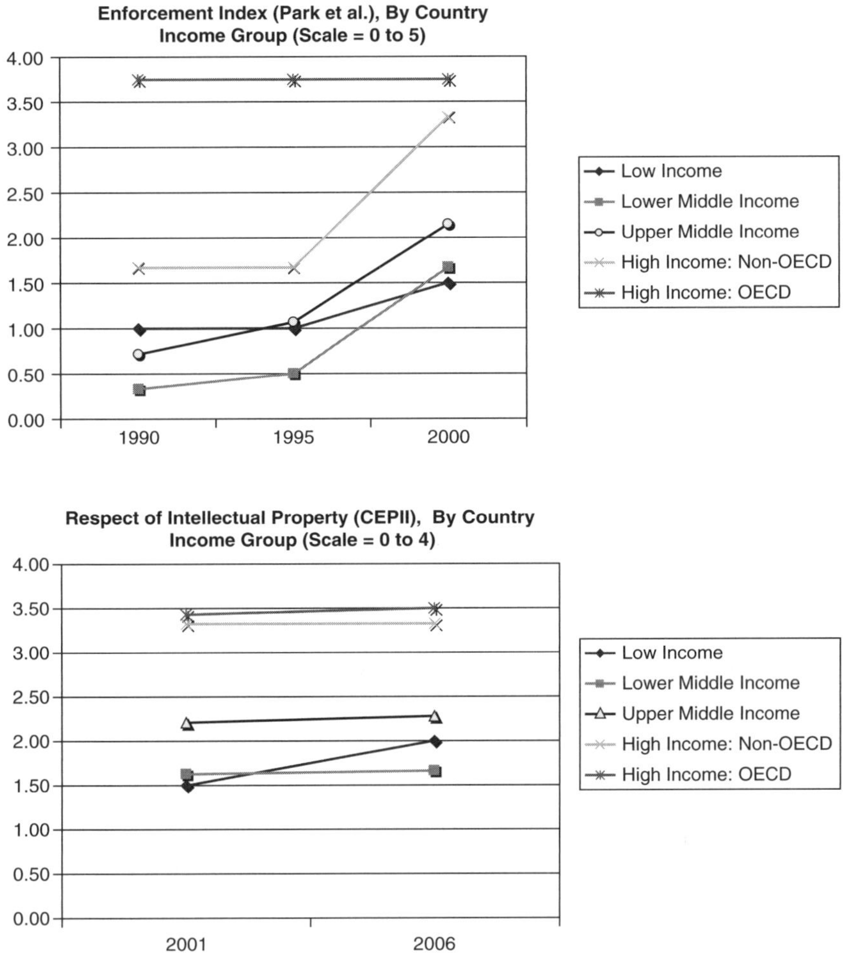

Notes:

1) The 38 countries covered in the two panels are the following: Low Income (Cameroon, Ghana, India, Pakistan, Zimbabwe), Lower Middle Income (Brazil, Bulgaria, China, Colombia, Egypt, Indonesia, Peru, Philippines, Romania, Russia, South Africa, Thailand, Tunisia, Turkey, Ukraine), Upper Middle Income (Argentina, Chile, Hungary, Malaysia, Mexico, Poland, Venezuela), High Income Non-OECD (Hong Kong, Israel, Singapore), High Income OECD (France, Germany, Greece, Ireland, Japan, Korea, Norway, Portugal).
2) The scores within each group were equally weighted. Both indicators are based on perceptions of observers.
3) The indicators in the top panel draw on reporting collected by the Office of the US Trade Representative and the bottom panel on a database built by the French Ministry of Economy, Finance and Industry (MINEFI) and the French Development Agency (AFD) based on a survey conducted by MINEFI and AFD agencies in 51 countries.

Sources: The top panel is based on data underlying Park and Lippoldt (2005); the lower panel is based on CEPII (2007).

Figure 13.3 Intellectual property rights in practice, 38 selected countries, by income group

Table 13.2 Correlation of selected institutional indicators: CEPII Institutional Profiles *database (2001) versus the* 'Park et al.' *Enforcement and Patent Indices (2000)*

	CEPII: Respect for Intellectual Property (e.g. counterfeiting)	CEPII: Arrangements for protection of IP (e.g. TRIPS or local systems)	CEPII: Security of contracts between private agents	Park: Enforcement Effectiveness Index
CEPII: Arrangements for protection of IP (e.g. TRIPS or local systems)	0.741442	1		
CEPII: Security of contracts between private agents	0.750967	0.669304	1	
Park: Enforcement Effectiveness Index	0.636504	0.470192	0.603324	1
Park: Patent Rights Index	0.713383	0.558154	0.604138	0.641282

Note: The CEPII data series referenced in the column titles above correspond, left to right, to the CEPII database indicators B603, B604 and A603.

Sources: CEPII (2007) and data underlying Park and Lippoldt (2005).

A SAMPLE OF EVIDENCE FROM THE LITERATURE

Business decisions to invest and trade are complex and based on a variety of considerations, with higher-level considerations sometimes trumping lower-level concerns.[22] While an effective IPR regime may not be sufficient in and of itself to attract FDI or trade, an inadequate IPR regime can be in some cases a deal-breaker for a firm looking to invest or trade. As IPR standards improve in countries around the world, the competitive advantage that provision of basic IPR protection affords to a given host country shrinks. Some firms have come to require a basic level of protection. On the other hand, depending on the technology concerned, it may be that a strategy of trade secrecy can adequately protect a firm's intellectual property in some cases, even in the face of some weakness in the local IPR system. In some cases, factors such as market scale (that is access to a large market) or strategic positioning prove to be dominant factors motivating investment or trade.[23] Such factors, for example, may help to account for the large number of pharmaceutical FDI projects in China (which has had a mixed performance on IPR enforcement since its entry into the WTO in 2001).[24]

Moreover, variation in IPR strength may influence not only the volume of FDI or trade but also the nature of the projects (for example for distribution, production or R&D). For example, an analysis of data from a 1995 EBRD enterprise survey in Eastern Europe and the republics of the former Soviet Union found that weak IPR regimes tended to discourage foreign investors in technology-intensive sectors that rely heavily on IPRs (Smarzynska, 2002). In all sectors, weak IPR regimes tended to deter investors from undertaking local production and rather focus on distribution of imported products. An earlier study of

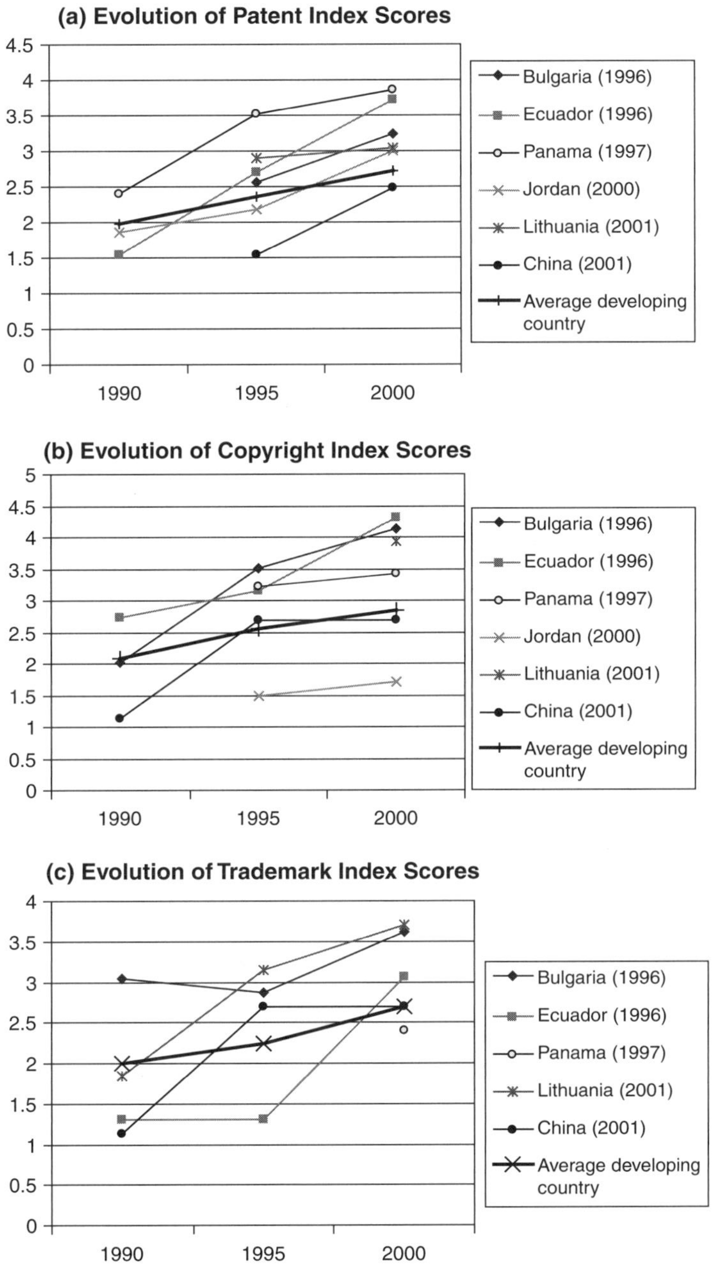

Note: Numbers in parentheses indicate the year of WTO accession. Developing country average index scores based on available country data as follows, e.g., for 1995: patents n =74, copyrights n = 53, trademarks n = 35. Trademark data were not available for Jordan.

Source: Based on data underlying Park and Lippoldt (2005).

Figure 13.4 WTO accession and IPR strengthening

intellectual property managers from 94 major US firms revealed that IPRs mattered less for protecting sales and distribution outlets, than for protecting production and R&D facilities (Mansfield, 1994; Lee and Mansfield, 1996). The proportion of FDI invested in production and R&D facilities was positively and significantly related to the perceived strength of IPRs. In addition, firms tended to regard strong IPRs as being more important for decisions concerning transfer of advanced technology than for FDI decisions as a whole.

In a further study on these issues, Nunnenkamp and Spatz (2003) also find that the importance of IPRs as a determinant of FDI flows varies according to the sector and host country, especially as those factors relate to the imitative capacity. They 'find that host countries can not only attract more FDI, but also derive more benefits from FDI by strengthening IPR protection. R&D expenditure by US affiliates as well as the value added and exports created by them tend to rise with stronger IPR protection' (p. 39). At the same time, they note that the extent of these positive effects tends to be limited and subject to the specific conditions more broadly in the sector and country concerned. Other factors, such as market scale, often play a determinant role and may attract investment despite shortcomings in the IPR environment. Also, as more countries raise their standards for IPR protection, the harder it becomes for a country to derive particular advantage from moves to strengthen the protection afforded to rights holders.

As for the technology transfer dimension of these flows, Branstetter et al. (2006) consider the response within US multilateral firms to IPR reform in 16 economies during the period from 1982 to 1999. Their analysis of firm-level data 'reveals that royalty payments for technology transferred to affiliates increase at the time of reforms, as do affiliate R&D expenditures and total levels of foreign patent applications' (p. ii). The findings point to prospects of increased technology transfer from US firms to affiliates in countries that engaged in IPR reform. Bascavusoglu and Zuniga (2002) find that French firms are also responsive to enhanced patent protection in foreign markets in line with their commercial potential, meaning the technological capacity and market scale in the destination market. However, for low-income markets they find the implications are not significant and in the case of low-technology sectors they find that strengthened patent protection may actually deter technology flows.

THE ASSOCIATION OF IPR CHANGE WITH CHANGE IN ECONOMIC INDICATORS

This section presents the results of two OECD studies that examine empirically the economic implications of strengthened IPRs in developing countries during the 1990s, with a principal focus on patents, copyrights and trademarks.[25] At the heart of both OECD studies is regression analysis whereby indicators for selected types of economic activity are related to indicators of the strength of particular IPRs (controlling for other factors that influence the corresponding economic activity).

IPRs, International Trade and FDI

The first OECD study presented here (Park and Lippoldt, 2003, as expanded in Park and Lippoldt, 2007, forthcoming) considered the relationship of patent rights to trade and

Table 13.3 The relationship between merchandise import flows and patent protection, 1990–2005

Sector	Destination	Coefficient estimate	N	Pseudo-R^{2} (%)
All industries	Developing countries	1.34*** *(0.16)*	164	36.5
	LDCs	0.54* *(0.31)*	31	74.0
High-tech sectors				
Pharmaceuticals	Developing countries and LDCs	1.18*** *(0.21)*	124	54.0
Office telecoms	Developing countries and LDCs	1.45*** *(0.21)*	172	54.6
Chemicals	Developing countries and LDCs	1.26*** *(0.15)*	162	47.2
Optics	Developing countries and LDCs	1.29*** *(0.17)*	162	53.6
Electronics	Developing countries and LDCs	1.54*** *(0.19)*	162	54.9
Aerospace	Developing countries and LDCs	2.03*** *(0.36)*	161	32.0

Notes: The dependent variable for this regression is import flows in real 2000 US dollars. All variables are in natural logarithmic units (except governance). The coefficient estimates represent the percentage change in the respective sector's imports per 1% change in the importing country's index of patent rights. N denotes number of observations and Pseudo-R^2 an estimate of the fraction of the variation in the data explained by the model. The estimates were obtained via a Feasible GLS regression which controlled for other determinants of trade including: real GDP per capita and indicators for freedom to trade internationally, Doing Business rank (business environment), perceptions of IPR enforcement, legal effectiveness, physical property rights and governance. ***, ** and * denote significance levels at the 1, 5 and 10% levels, respectively. To conserve space, coefficient estimates of the control variables are not reported.

Source: Park and Lippoldt (2007, forthcoming).

FDI in developing countries at both the macro and sectoral levels. Using regression analysis, the study estimated the relationship of change in the Patent Rights Index (referenced above) with change in indicators of trade and the stocks of FDI, while controlling for a variety of other factors (enumerated in the notes to Table 13.3). The analysis covered the period from 1990 to 2005, focusing on a sample of developing and OECD countries.[26]

With respect to trade, the strength of patent rights was found to be significantly associated with changes in total imports (Table 13.3). A 1 per cent increase in the strength of patent rights was found to be associated with a 1.3 per cent increase in merchandise imports in developing countries, controlling for other factors. A weaker, but still significant, relationship was found for Least Developed Countries (LDCs). A significant positive relationship between the strength of patent rights and imports was also found for imports in a range of high-technology sectors.

The study found that the patent rights as described by the Patent Rights Index generally were associated positively with the stock of inward FDI in developing countries and LDCs (Table 13.4). A 1 per cent increase in the Patent Rights Index was associated with

Table 13.4 Estimates of relationship between inward FDI stock and patent protection, 1990–2005

	Developing countries	LDCs
Change in stock of inward FDI associated with a 1% change in the Patent Rights Index	1.65*** *(0.19)*	1.66** *(0.76)*
Number of observations	163	31
Pseudo-R^2	35.1%	57.3%

Notes: The dependent variable is inward stock of FDI in real 2000 US dollars. Other notes are the same as for Table 13.3 above.

Source: Park and Lippoldt (2007, forthcoming).

Table 13.5 Estimates of relationship between outward US FDI stock in developing countries and patent protection, by industry, 1990–2005

Sector	Coefficient estimate	N	Pseudo-$R^{2\,(\%)}$
Chemicals	1.14*** *(0.37)*	81	25.8
Machinery	1.40*** *(0.49)*	59	22.1
Electronics	−0.43 *(0.51)*	55	21.2
Service	1.74*** *(0.32)*	76	30.8
Computers	0.96 *(1.49)*	41	32.3

Notes: The dependent variable is the amount of total assets of foreign affiliates of US multinational firms in real 2000 US dollars. Other notes are the same as for Table 13.3.

Source: Park and Lippoldt (2007, forthcoming).

a 1.7 per cent increase in the stock of FDI. Table 13.5 presents results of a similar analysis for developing countries using data for outward US FDI by sector. A statistically significant relationship exists in three of the five sectors considered. This variation may be in part related to variation in the ability of investors to appropriate the returns on the intellectual property embodied in the FDI. If firms operate using technologies where they are able to ensure returns even in environments with weak IPRs (for example which are difficult to reverse engineer), this weakness may be less dissuasive to investment than in other sectors where firms might be more vulnerable. Firms may also have other advantages that reduce the importance they place on IPR strength in making investment decisions. For example, they may have a strong lead-time advantage or an ability to protect their interest through trade secrecy. As Park and Lippoldt (2003, p. 5) note, 'In these cases, given the costs of acquiring intellectual property rights, firms may forgo seeking IPRs and rely on "natural" protections.' This may have contributed to the results in the analysis, whereby FDI in certain industries (that is electronics or computers) was found to be insignificantly associated with the index of patent rights in the host country. On the other hand, the strength of patent protection (as measured by the index) appears to matter more for FDI in services, chemicals and machinery; this may be due to the relative ease with which competitors can imitate the technology embodied in those sectors.

Licensing

The second OECD study referenced here (Park and Lippoldt, 2005) concerns the relationship between international licensing and the strengthening of IPRs. Licensing was singled out for special consideration, in particular, because of its potential role in technology transfer (Box 13.2). Licensing plays an important role in the large and increasing volumes of income earned globally each year from commercial transactions related to technology transfer (for OECD countries, these receipts amounted to more than USD 140.8 billion in 2001).[27]

As Park and Lippoldt note, theoretical reflections generally do not lend themselves a priori to absolute statements as to the relationship between stronger IPRs and licensing activity. Stronger IPRs may be expected to reduce the costs of reaching and enforcing contracts, thereby encouraging expanded licensing activity. However, depending on the initial level of protection, ever stronger IPRs could eventually reach a level where they confer

BOX 13.2 LICENSING AND TECHNOLOGY TRANSFER

Maskus (2004) points to five main channels for technology transfer through market-mediated mechanisms: trade in goods and services; foreign direct investment; joint ventures; cross-border movement of personnel; and licensing.[28] While flows via each channel embody technology, it is at present not possible to determine precisely the relative magnitudes of their technology content. However, Maskus points out that '[l]icenses typically involve the purchase of production or distribution rights (protected by some intellectual property right) and the technological information and know-how required to make effective the exercise of those rights' (p. 1). Citing balance of payments data, Maskus notes that in 2001 OECD member countries earned more than USD 70 billion in royalty revenue from licensing and other types of arm's length trade in technology (that is, excluding intra-firm flows).

Park and Lippoldt (2005) note that licensing transactions are an important means by which technology and expertise can be acquired by licensees, saving them the expense of independent research and development. At the same time, licensors not only derive fees and royalties, but may also be able to capitalize on the licensee's local reputation and knowledge. As a mode of market entry, licensing can offer firms strategic advantages under certain circumstances. Some companies (particularly small ones) may use licensing as a means to test a market before engaging in FDI or to overcome a lack of capacity to penetrate a market on their own. Also, as Park and Lippoldt note, licensing can involve relatively minimal commitment and make it easier for firms to enter and exit a market, whereas other means of entry may be less flexible (for example export sales may face tariff and non-tariff barriers and FDI may be costly or may face local restrictions). In addition, businesses may look to licensing as a means of earning an early return on their research and development efforts, rather than depending exclusively on internally-developed end products as the sole source of return on their investment in R&D.[29]

excess market power, thereby risk constraining licensing as rights holders boost license fees or refuse to license. Moreover, weak IPRs may prompt a defensive reaction whereby some rights holders are willing to license local producers in order to have a local interested party to safeguard against infringement.

The literature points to some evidence of a generally positive relationship between IPR strength and licensing, subject to certain conditions and with some variation by sector (for example Yang and Maskus, 2001). Park and Lippoldt (2005) build upon and extend this previous work by exploring in more detail the determinants of licensing flows, the variation in flows by level of economic development, and the relationship of licensing to FDI and exports.

The OECD licensing study uses two analytical approaches. In the first, the four quantitative 'Park et al.' IPR indexes (referenced above) are used to characterize the strength of intellectual property regimes with respect to patent rights, copyrights, trademark rights and enforcement effectiveness. Regression analysis is then employed to estimate the relationship during the 1990s between licensing fees received for use of intangible assets and indicators for the strength of IPRs, while controlling for other factors. The regression analysis is based on firm-level data for US parent firms and their licensing receipts from the rest of the world (a separate linked data set provides firm-level control variables).[30] While the regression analysis as specified here does not demonstrate causality, it can highlight statistically significant relationships between variables.

The second analytical approach used by Park and Lippoldt (2005) draws on the Securities Data Corporation database on Joint Ventures and Strategic Alliances to focus on counts of international licensing transactions between firms in a developed country and firms in a developing or emerging economy (for example Korea, Singapore, Brazil) during the period 1989 to 2002. Overall, for the purposes of the analysis, the database included transactions involving 28 developing or emerging market nations.[31, 32] A large number of these deals involved Asian economies.

Regression Analysis

Table 13.6 presents the distribution of the licensing fees received by these firms in 1999 for use of intangible assets. As can be seen, the bulk of these fees originate in high-income countries and from affiliated sources. Tables 13.7 and 13.8 then present the results from the regression analysis with respect to IPRs and licensing (the details of the basic equation are presented in the Appendix). They focus on licensing to unaffiliated sources, which may be more sensitive to variation in IPR strength than affiliated licensing because there is potentially less control of the intellectual property after it is transferred to the licensee.

Table 13.7, column 1, presents the results from estimating a broad formulation of the equation.[33] This reveals that patent rights are the most important form of intellectual property protection for unaffiliated licensing. A 1 per cent strengthening of patent rights is associated with a 0.6 per cent increase in the receipts of *unaffiliated* licensing fees. An increase in the level of protection either raises the ability of firms to appropriate the returns to technology or increases the incentive of firms to license. Both Sales and R&D Intensity also influence licensing positively. As Park and Lippoldt (2005) note, the statutory level of protection is an important explanatory factor even after controlling for a measure of enforcement effectiveness (which itself is a statistically significant determinant of licensing, albeit only moderately so). Thus, 'laws on the books' have an important effect

Table 13.6 Royalty and licensing fees for the use of intangible assets, received from abroad by US parent firms

	Annual value of fees for 1999 (billions, USD)	Percentage share from affiliated sources	Percentage share from unaffiliated sources
All countries	33.4	72.6	27.4
Nations with per capita GDP > USD 18 000	26.7	74.5	25.5
Nations with per capita GDP < USD 18 000	6.7	64.8	35.2

Source: Park and Lippoldt (2005).

independent of the actual implementation of the laws. The copyrights and trademark rights variables are not statistically significant in this specification.

Additional country-level control variables are included in the equation to control for country risk, corruption and trade restrictiveness (via the mean tariff rate). The tariff variable turns out not to be a significant factor, while country risk and corruption are significant at the 1 per cent level. The results indicate that corruption negatively contributes to licensing, and that lower country risk contributes positively to licensing.[34]

Columns 2 and 3 in Table 13.7 report the results of splitting the sample between countries whose GDP per capita is above and below USD 18 000, respectively. Column 2 shows that both patent rights and copyrights stimulate US parent firms' licensing in relatively rich countries. US firms are more sensitive to licensing copyrightable works in developed countries than in less developed countries, possibly since the imitative potential of foreign firms is higher in the developed markets. Copyrights have a negative effect on licensing in the relatively poorer countries. Park and Lippoldt hypothesize that stronger copyrights enable US parent firms to exercise stronger monopoly power in the developing markets, which would increase the return for each license while having a negative effect on overall licensing in those markets. For both developed and developing regions, trademark rights exert a negative influence on licensing. Stronger protection for trademarks seems to enable firms to enjoy greater market power in all markets. The authors suggest that one possible reason may be that, whereas stronger patent rights may lead to further innovation, stronger trademark rights tend to allow for a stronger exercising of existing rights. In less-developed markets, the index of enforcement effectiveness does not appear as an important influence on licensing. The main reason is that most countries in this sub-sample score low on enforcement effectiveness and thus the index does not have much variability.

In Table 13.8, Park and Lippoldt re-specify the model in order to consider whether change in IPR strength at the margin affects licensing relative to other channels of technology transfer, such as FDI and exports. The dependent variable is the log of the ratio of unaffiliated licensing to either FDI (Panel I) or exports (Panel II). For the purposes of this exercise, 'FDI' refers to investment in physical plant and equipment (net of accumulated depreciation) and 'exports' refers to US parent firm exports to unaffiliated parties.

The results in Panel I of Table 13.8 point to a bias in favor of licensing over FDI in association with a strengthening of patent rights in both developed and less developed

Table 13.7 Intellectual property rights: royalty and licensing fees from unaffiliated sources, firm level

	(1) All Countries	(2) GDP per capita > USD 18 000	(3) GDP per capita < USD 18 000
Constant	−8.739***	0.902	1.551***
	(1.516)	*(0.663)*	*(0.330)*
Log (Patent Rights)	0.647***	1.560***	0.359***
	(0.170)	*(0.349)*	*(0.095)*
Log (Copyrights)	0.162	0.948***	−0.450***
	(0.157)	*(0.232)*	*(0.126)*
Log (Trademark Rights)	−0.029	−0.360*	−0.197**
	(0.111)	*(0.190)*	*(0.091)*
Enforcement Effectiveness	0.250*	0.363**	0.177
	(0.137)	*(0.162)*	*(0.137)*
Log (Firm R&D Intensity)	0.026***	0.026***	0.013**
	(0.006)	*(0.008)*	*(0.007)*
Log (Firm Sales)	0.254***	0.235***	0.260***
	(0.016)	*(0.019)*	*(0.018)*
Log (Tariff Rate)	0.079		
	(0.058)		
Log (Country Risk Index)	2.66***		
	(0.363)		
Log (Corruption Index)	−0.545***		
	(0.108)		
Industry group fixed effects	Yes	Yes	Yes
Time fixed effects	Yes	Yes	Yes
Adjusted R-squared	0.13	0.10	0.16
Number of observations	5280	3773	3246

Notes: Dollar amounts here or in the underlying data are denominated in real 1995 US dollars. The dependent variable, Licensing, denotes the royalty and licensing fees received by US parent firms from unaffiliated sources. The unit of analysis is the US parent firm. Firm R&D Intensity is defined as the ratio of the parent firm's R&D expenditure to its sales. See the Appendix to this chapter for more information on key variables and sources. The model is estimated over three time periods: 1992, 1995 and 1999. Standard errors are in parentheses and italicized. ***, ** and * denote significance at the 1%, 5%, and 10% levels, respectively.

Source: Park and Lippoldt (2005), Table 2.

markets. Stronger copyrights favor licensing relative to FDI in richer markets and FDI relative to licensing in developing markets. Stronger trademark protection is found to favor FDI in developing markets. More effective enforcement favors licensing in richer markets but has a neutral effect in developing markets. A higher R&D intensity is found to favor FDI. When R&D intensity is high, FDI may be the preferred mode of technology transfer for internalization reasons – that is, the risk of imitation and copying may be higher when the firm licenses to unaffiliated third parties than when the firm does its own production abroad. An increase in market size (that is sales) also favors FDI relative to unaffiliated licensing.

Table 13.8 Intellectual property rights and US royalty and licensing fees relative to trade and foreign direct investment

	I. Dependent variable: Log (licensing/FDI)			II. Dependent variable: Log (licensing/Exports)		
	All countries	GDP per capita > USD 18 000	GDP per capita < USD 18 000	All countries	GDP per capita > USD 18 000	GDP per capita < USD 18 000
	(1)	(2)	(3)	(4)	(5)	(6)
Constant	5.58***	1.44***	5.24***	7.91***	5.93***	9.01***
	(0.31)	*(0.74)*	*(0.39)*	*(0.66)*	*(1.49)*	*(0.89)*
Log (Patent Rights)	0.42***	1.45***	0.40**	0.61**	1.21	0.57**
	(0.11)	*(0.39)*	*(0.11)*	*(0.23)*	*(0.79)*	*(0.26)*
Log (Copyrights)	0.16	0.89***	−0.31**	0.38	0.75	0.06
	(0.13)	*(0.26)*	*(0.15)*	*(0.28)*	*(0.52)*	*(0.34)*
Log (Trademark Rights)	−0.15	−0.31	−0.23**	−0.36*	−0.25	−0.54**
	(0.097)	*(0.21)*	*(0.11)*	*(0.20)*	*(0.42)*	*(0.24)*
Enforcement Effectiveness	0.41***	0.39**	0.13	0.32*	0.32	−0.003
	(0.091)	*(0.18)*	*(0.16)*	*(0.19)*	*(0.36)*	*(0.36)*
Log (Firm R&D Intensity)	−0.012**	−0.015*	−0.014*	−0.37***	−0.36***	−0.40***
	(0.006)	*(0.009)*	*(0.008)*	*(0.012)*	*(0.018)*	*(0.017)*
Log (Firm Sales)	−0.80***	−0.81***	−0.79***	−0.56***	−0.53***	−0.61***
	(0.016)	*(0.022)*	*(0.021)*	*(0.033)*	*(0.045)*	*(0.049)*
Industry Group Fixed Effects	Yes	Yes	Yes	Yes	Yes	Yes
Time Fixed Effects	Yes	Yes	Yes	Yes	Yes	Yes
Adjusted R-squared	0.34	0.33	0.36	0.41	0.38	0.45
Number of observations	7019	3773	3246	6801	3684	3117

Notes: FDI refers to expenditures on plant and equipment abroad and Exports to the export of goods and services to unaffiliated parties (both in real 1995 US dollars). Standard errors are in parentheses.. Also, see Table 13.7 notes.

Source: Park and Lippoldt (2005), Table 5.

Panel II of Table 13.8 examines the effect of IPRs on the ratio of licensing to exports. Here, an increase in patent strength is found to favor licensing in poorer markets, but it is not statistically significant in the regression focused on richer markets. An increase in trademark strength favors trade relative to licensing in developing markets. Given that trademark strength can augment the market power of firms, it may be that as these rights are strengthened, firms choose to exercise their market power via exports rather than licensing to competitors. Higher R&D intensity and sales of firms have a positive influence on exporting relative to licensing.

Summing up the findings from the regression analysis, IPR strength is found to be generally associated positively with international licensing receipts. The models yield statistically significant coefficients for many of the IPR variables, although they explain only a limited portion of the overall variation. Moreover, the extent of the influence of IPRs varies according to the type of intellectual property right and the effectiveness of IPR enforcement. In particular, in the case of patent rights and enforcement effectiveness, most specifications of the model found a significant positive relationship to licensing. Certain dimensions of IPR strength were found to influence the choice of channel for international technology transfer, albeit with some variation depending on the model specification.

Licensing Transactions

The next exercise drawn from Park and Lippoldt (2005) focuses on international licensing transactions between firms in a developed country (for example US, Japan or European Union countries) and firms in less developed or emerging economies (for example Korea, Singapore, Brazil).[35] Information on such transactions was drawn from the *Joint Ventures and Strategic Alliances* database, which contains information on over 100 000 transactions conducted since the mid-1980s and covering both private and public sector parties.[36] For the analysis, the authors selected only those licensing transactions where firms in a developed country licensed intellectual property to firms in a developing or emerging economy during the period from 1989 to 2002 (about 1000 transactions). Licenses granted by a developing country firm to a developed country firm or to another developing country firm were excluded.[37] This selection permits a focus on the impact of changes in patent regimes in developing or emerging economies on inward technology inflows via licensing agreements with developed countries.

Overall, there were 28 developing and emerging market economies in the sample that had firms which were licensees of firms in developed nations.[38] The transactions range in initial value from USD 300 000 to USD 200 million dollars. Unfortunately, less than 10 per cent of the transactions report the initial licensing fee. Thus, the focus in the following analysis is on 'counts' or numbers of licensing deals concerning intellectual property (rather than on the fees associated with the transactions).

Table 13.9 shows the change in licensing transactions between two periods: 1989–1994 versus 1997–2002. As can be seen, developing countries which least strengthened their patent regimes experienced a modest overall reduction in the count of licensing deals. In contrast, developing countries which most strengthened their patent regimes experienced an overall increase of 28 deals over the same time period. Countries with a medium degree of patent reform saw an increase of two more licensing deals. The table points to a positive correlation between changes in numbers of licensing deals and changes in patent

Table 13.9 The relationship between patent reform and high-tech licensing transactions in developing countries

Strengthening of patent regime	Number of licensing transactions		
	1989–1994	1997–2002	Change
Low	55	53	−2
Medium	24	26	2
High	33	61	28

Notes:
1) Each row in the table shows the levels and changes over time in the volume of licensing transactions between developing nation licensees and developed nation licensors, as experienced by the developing nations with the specified degree of patent reform. The change in the volume of transactions is for the developing nations in the reform group as a whole.
2) The strengthening of patent regime refers to the change in the index of patent rights of the recipient (licensee) nation. The strengthening of patent rights is considered low if the index grew by less than 7% over the period 1989–2002, and medium if the index grew by more than 7% but by less than 20% over the same period.
3) All deals are 'high-tech' licensing transactions (involving computer equipment and software, communications including telecommunications, biotechnology or electronics).

Source: Park and Lippoldt (2005).

regimes. This may provide an indication that increased IPR strength is contributing to an environment conductive to more technology transfer transactions and not simply increasing the flow of royalties to developing country licensors.

CONCLUSION

The 1990s witnessed an international wave of reform and institutional change with respect to IPRs, driven in part by international trade liberalization and economic transition (the latter in the former socialist countries). Many developing countries undertook new commitments in various international agreements administered by the WTO and WIPO. These commitments were subsequently reflected through changes in domestic law and practice that tended to strengthen IPRs – albeit in some cases with a significant lag and variation in application.

Are stronger IPRs associated positively with trade, foreign direct investment and licensing in developing countries? This review has found that the answer tends to be 'yes'. Patent rights and enforcement effectiveness, in particular, tend to be associated positively with these flows. In turn, these flows can represent important channels for technology transfer. The results do not imply that stronger protection for patents or other IPRs will always increase trade, FDI, licensing and the associated transfer of technology. IPR protection, accounting for only a portion of the variation in the flows, is not a 'silver bullet' development solution. Nevertheless, appropriate IPR standards do appear to contribute to an environment conducive to the growth of these flows.

A general policy implication of the analysis with respect to developing economies is that IPR reform should be assessed as one potential part of a broad strategy for promoting economic development. In view of the increasing globalization of markets and the establishment of international standards for IPR protection, competitive pressures are challenging growth-oriented developing countries to address any basic shortcomings in their national IPR regimes. Conformity with the minimum global IPR standards has become, in effect, a prerequisite for developing countries wishing to access and exploit the full range of global technologies and know-how.

NOTES

1. Douglas Lippoldt, OECD and Groupe d'Economie Mondiale, Sciences Po, Paris. The views expressed are those of the author and do not necessarily reflect those of the OECD, OECD member countries or GEM-Sciences Po. Correspondence concerning this chapter may be sent to: douglas.lippoldt@oecd.org.
   The author wishes to thank colleagues for their comments and suggestions on an earlier draft and, in particular, Robert C. Bird, Daniel Cahoy, Donald Richards, Jayashree Watal and other participants at the conference on the Global Challenges of Intellectual Property Rights held at the University of Connecticut, 10–12 May 2007. Special thanks go out to Kelly Aceto, Michelle Metcalf and Laura Munro for their assistance.
   Portions of this document, as noted in the text, draw on analysis undertaken in collaboration with Walter Park, American University, Washington, DC.
2. Due to problems of endogeneity and reverse causality, Rodrik et al. (2002) rely on instrumental variables drawn from the literature to proxy for international trade integration and institutional quality.
3. Bénassy-Quéré et al. (2007) use an instrumental variable approach to address problems of endogeneity and correlation between income and institutional indicators.
4. While significant in the gravity estimation, Bénassy-Quéré et al. (2007) found that property right protection was no longer significant once the correlation with GDP per capita was controlled for using the instrumental variable approach. However, from the database it appears that this protection variable refers primarily to real property, means of production and private property (for example protection from government expropriation), rather than intellectual property.
5. For example see WTO (2002) for a discussion and bibliographic references.
6. See UNCTAD (2003), p. 129.
7. A full text of the TRIPS agreement is available on the WTO website: http://www.wto.org. NB: the text of the TRIPS Agreement refers at various points to 'technology transfer', 'transfer of technology' and 'transfer and dissemination of technology', but does not define these terms.
8. Although, with respect to domestic innovation, as Branstetter et al. (2006) note, there are mixed findings in the literature on the impact of strengthened IPRs on domestic innovation in reforming countries. A footnote in their article provides a helpful list of key references on this issue.
9. The non-rivalrous, non-exclusive nature of intellectual property presents a challenge to the original innovator (or subsequent rights holder) wishing to appropriate an economic benefit from the intellectual property. Weak IPRs in a particular market may discourage the foreign rights holder from making the intellectual property available there because of a potential inability to enforce IPRs and appropriate the returns from the use of the intellectual property. This could be doubly damaging to the rights holder in the event that a competitor makes use of the intellectual property.
10. WTO (2006) provides a useful summary of some of these issues in relation to the TRIPS Agreement and pharmaceutical patents.
11. Overly-stringent protection could, in theory, risk conferring excess market power (for example from patents that are too broad), thereby diminishing competition and encouraging some rights holders to continue exploiting existing innovations while postponing new innovation efforts. For a discussion of this issue with respect to patents and an extensive reference list, see Encaoua et al. (2003).
12. At the Doha Ministerial Conference in 2001, WTO members issued the Declaration on The TRIPS Agreement and Public Health, to make clear their intention for the TRIPS Agreement to contribute positively to public health; this document is available at: http://www.wto.org/english/thewto_e/minist_e/min01_e/mindecl_trips_e.htm.
13. Finger and Schuler (2001) provide an assessment of costs related to the implementation of WTO Uruguay Round commitments with respect to IPR reform, among other issues.
14. The criticism is certainly not limited to developing country observers. Scholars such as L. Lessig and M. Boldrin and D.K. Levine have questioned the strengthening of IPRs more generally. For example, Lessig has challenged the privatization of the so-called 'intellectual commons' (Lessig, 2002) and the expanded range of patentable innovation in the US that now includes such areas as Internet business

methods (Lessig, 1999). Boldrin and Levine (2007) recognize the need for innovators to be rewarded and to have the right of sale with regard to their ideas. However, they challenge the right to regulate the use of innovations after their sale, proposing instead that innovators should make better efforts to capitalize on their first-mover advantages when they first sell their ideas.

15. Expressing similar concerns, Brazil and Argentina made a proposal in 2004 for WIPO to launch a new development agenda. The text of their proposal is available here: http://www.wipo.int/documents/en/document/govbody/wo_gb_ga/pdf/wo_ga_31_11.pdf .
16. For example, Cambodia, China and Singapore have integrated IPRs in their national economic strategies and affirmed the importance of IPRs on their national intellectual property office websites: http://www.moc.gov.kh/laws_regulation/development_of_cambodia's_ipr.htm; http://www.sipo.gov.cn/sipo_English/gysipo_e/fzgh/t20020430_33893.htm; http://www.ipos.gov.sg/main/aboutus/aboutipos/visionmission.html.
17. For statistical purposes, a 'lasting interest' is defined as investments to obtain a share of 10 per cent or more of the voting power in the foreign enterprise. For a more detailed definition of direct investment and related terms, see OECD (2006b, Box 1.1, p. 20).
18. Other examples: i) With respect to works covered under the Berne Convention, protection is 'automatic' in that it is not to be conditional upon compliance with any formality. ii) The Paris Convention provides for the 'right of priority' by which the filing of the first regular application for a patents, utility model, mark or industrial design entitles the applicant to apply subsequently in other contracting states with such applications regarded as if they had been filed on the same date as the first (for up to 12 months for patents and utility models, 6 months for industrial designs and marks).
19. These IPRs include: copyright and related rights, trademarks, geographical indications (of origin), industrial designs, patents, layout-designs (topographies) of integrated circuits, and protection of undisclosed information (trade secrets).
20. These indices were developed by Walter Park (American University, Washington, DC) et al. The relevant references are: Index of Patent Rights: Ginarte and Park (1997), Park and Wagh (2002); Index of Copyrights and Index of Trademark Rights: Reynolds (2003); Enforcement Effectiveness Index: Park and Lippoldt (2005). See the Appendix for an overview of the composition of the indices and further references.
21. The selection of the panel was based simply on the availability of data under both the Park et al. Enforcement Effectiveness Index and the CEPII Respect for Intellectual Property indicator; observations were available for all 38 countries for each of the time periods shown for each data set.
22. The choice of whether and where to invest depends on locational advantages of the home and foreign markets and the profitability of internalizing production or selling or licensing the technology to another firm that is active in the market (Braga and Fink, 1998). The extent of protection for intellectual property rights can constitute an important locational advantage.
23. In a survey on investment issues affecting the world's largest 1000 firms, business leaders characterized the most critical risks to their corporations as they invest abroad (A.T. Kearney, 2003). At the top of the list were government regulation, country financial risk, currency risk, and risk of political and social disturbances (each of which were cited by 60 per cent or more of respondents). Theft of intellectual property was cited by 17 per cent of the respondents and ranked 12th on the list of concerns.
24. Among the top 10 locations for pharmaceutical FDI projects during January 2002 to February 2005, China ranked second with 44 projects. The US ranked first with 52 FDI projects in the sector. Other countries ranked as follows: India (30 projects), Ireland (29), Spain (27), Canada (27), UK (23), Singapore (23), Brazil (22) and Germany (18). ('Pharma pulls in $15bn', 12 April 2005, accessed15 September 2006 at: www.fdimagazine.com).
25. Other areas covered in international accords include geographical indications (concerning the origins of goods), industrial designs, layout-designs of integrated circuits and undisclosed information (trade secrets). Discussions are underway in such forums as UNCTAD or the WTO concerning other dimensions such as the relationship of the TRIPS Agreement to protection of traditional knowledge and folklore.
26. Their sample included 25 developed countries (23 OECD countries, plus Israel and Malta), 78 developing and transition countries, and 27 Least Developed Countries (LDCs). The sample did not include developing countries that receive substantial amounts of FDI due to their status as tax havens or centres for 'offshore holding companies' rather than as the ultimate destination or host for investment funds (that is economies such as Bermuda, the Bahamas and Netherlands Antilles were excluded from the sample).
27. This amount (USD 140.8 billion) refers to data for 2001 from 17 OECD Member countries concerning receipts from the sale and use of patents, licenses, trademarks, designs, know-how and closely related technical services including technical assistance, and for industrial research and development carried out abroad, among other elements. For details, see OECD (2005a), pp. 53 and 71.
28. Maskus (2004) also identifies several non-market channels for international technology transfer including imitation, departure of employees, publicly-available test and patent application data, and temporary migration.

29. This point is sometimes made by representatives of multinational enterprises. For example, it was raised at the *High-Level Workshop on Intellectual Property Rights and Economic Development in China: Meeting Challenges and Opportunities Following WTO Entry*, Beijing, China, 20–21 April 2004, organized by the OECD in cooperation with the State Intellectual Property Office and the Development Research Centre of the State Council, China. The proceedings of this workshop and a related event are available on the OECD website: http://www.oecd.org/document/49/0,2340,en_2649_34269_31505201_1_1_1_1,00.html.
30. Park and Lippoldt (2005) thank C. Fritz Foley, Harvard Business School, for providing a concordance mapping between the two relevant BEA surveys used for the analysis.
31. Licenses granted by a developing country firm to a developed country firm or to another developing country firm were excluded as were transactions among developed nations (the latter transactions account for the vast majority of licensing deals).
32. Since less than 10 per cent of the transactions in the database report the initial licensing fee, the analysis instead focused on 'counts' or numbers of licensing deals.
33. The model captures 12 per cent of the variation in international licensing by US parent firms.
34. The sign for country risk is positive because a higher value of the index is associated with a lower country risk.
35. Note that the definitions of developed country and less developed country differ between this analysis and the regression analysis. In the regression analysis, the distinction was made based on an income threshold. Here, developed countries are categorized as those countries that were OECD Members as of 1989 (except Turkey) and the less developed and transition countries are those that were not OECD Members at that time.
36. The database contains various types of transactions (for example licensing, research, manufacturing or marketing).
37. The vast majority of international technology alliances are within or among developed nations.
38. The licensing fees refer to the initial flat fees or costs of the deal. The stream of future income or payments associated with royalties or profit-sharing arrangements is not included in this initial estimate.

REFERENCES

Bascavusoglu, Elif and M.P. Zuniga (2002), 'Foreign patent rights, technology and disembodied knowledge transfer cross borders: an empirical application', Université de Paris I Panthéon Sorbonne, TEAM, Théorie Macroéconomique et Microéconomique Appliquées, CNRS, available at: http://www.econ.kuleuven.ac.be/smye/abstracts/p 502.pdf .

Bénassy-Quéré, Agnès, Maylis Coupet and Thierry Mayer (2007), 'Institutional determinants of foreign direct investment', *The World Economy*, **30**(5).

Boldrin, Michele and David K. Levine (2007), 'Against Intellectual Monopoly', posted on UCLA Department of Economics website at: http://www.dklevine.com/general/intellectual/againstnew.htm.

Braga, Carlos A. Primo and C. Fink (1998), 'The relationship between intellectual property rights and foreign direct investment', *Duke Journal of Comparative and International Law*, **9**, pp. 163ff, http://www.law.duke.edu/journals/djcil/articles/djcil9p 163.htm.

Branstetter, Lee G., Raymond Fisman and Fritz Foley C. (2006), 'Do stronger intellectual property rights increase international technology transfer? Empirical evidence from US firm-level panel data', *Quarterly Journal of Economics*, **121**(1), February, available at: http://www.people.hbs.edu/ffoley/IPRReform.pdf.

CEPII (2007), 'Profils Institutionnels-database (Institutional Profiles database, 2001–2006)', Paris, available at: http://www.cepii.fr/ProfilsInstitutionnelsDatabase.htm.

Correa, Carlos Maria (2005), 'How intellectual property rights can obstruct progress', SciDev.Net, 4 April.

Encaoua, David, Dominique Guellec and Martínez Catalina (2003), 'The economics of patents: from natural rights to policy instruments', Cahiers de la maison des sciences économiques, CNRS, Série verte no. 2003.124, Paris, October.

Evenett, Simon J. and Carlos A. Primo Braga (2005), 'WTO accession: Lessons from experience', Trade Note No. 22, World Bank.

Finger, Michael J. and Philip Schuler (2001), 'Implementation of Uruguay Round commitments: the development challenge', World Bank Working Paper No. 2215, Washington, DC.

Ginarte, Juan and Walter G. Park (1997), 'Determinants of patent rights: A cross-national study', *Research Policy*, **26**, 283–301.
Gwartney, James and Robert Lawson (with Walter G. Park and Charles Skipton) (eds) (2001), *Economic Freedom of the World Annual Report*, Vancouver, BC: Fraser Institute.
Hoekman, B. and B. Smarzynska Javorik (eds) (2006), *Global Integration & Technology Transfer*, Washington, DC: World Bank Publications.
Jones, Charles I. (2004), 'Growth and ideas', Working Paper 10767, National Bureau of Economic Research, Cambridge, MA, USA, September.
Kearney, A.T. (2003), 'FDI confidence index', Global Business Policy Council, **6**, Alexandria, VA, USA, September.
Lee, J.-Y. and E. Mansfield (1996), 'Intellectual property protection and US foreign direct investment', *Review of Economics and Statistics*, **78**, 181–6.
Lessig, Lawrence (1999), 'The problem with patents', *The Industry Standard*, 23 April.
Lessig, Lawrence (2002), 'The architecture of innovation', *Duke Law Journal*, No. 51, 1783–801.
Lippoldt, Douglas (2003), 'Intellectual property rights', in *Regionalism and the Multilateral Trading System*, Paris: OECD, pp. 111–26.
Lippoldt, Douglas (2006), 'Can stronger intellectual property rights boost trade, foreign direct investment and licensing in developing countries?', in M. Pugatch (ed.), *The Intellectual Property Debate: Perspectives from Law, Economics and Political Economy*, Cheltenham, UK and Northampton, MA, USA: Edward Elgar Publishing.
Mansfield, Edwin (1994), 'Intellectual property protection, foreign direct investment, and technology transfer', Discussion Paper No. 19, International Finance Corporation.
Maskus, Keith (2004), 'Encouraging international technology transfer', Issue Paper No. 7, UNCTAD-ICTSD Project on IPRs and Sustainable Development, May.
North, Douglass C. (1997), 'The contribution of the New Institutional Economics to an understanding of the transition problem', WIDER Annual Lectures 1, United Nations University, World Institute for Development Economics Research (WIDER) Helsinki.
Numenkamp, Peter and Julius Spatz (2003), 'IPR and FDI: the role of industry and host-country characteristics', Working Paper No. 1167, Kiel Institute for World Economics, June.
OECD (2005a), *Main Science and Technology Indicators*, Vol. 1, Paris: OECD.
OECD (2005b), *Science, Technology and Industry Scoreboard: 2005*, Paris: OECD.
OECD (2006a), *Innovation in Pharmaceutical Biotechnology: Comparing National Innovation Systems at the Sectoral Level*, Paris: OECD.
OECD (2006b), *International Investment Perspectives: 2006*, Paris: OECD.
Park, W.G. and D. Lippoldt (2003), 'The impact of trade-related intellectual property rights on trade and foreign direct investment in developing countries', *OECD Papers*, **3**(11), paper 294; draft available at: http://www.oecd.org/dataoecd/59/46/2960051.pdf.
Park, W.G. and D. Lippoldt (2005), 'International licensing and the strengthening of intellectual property rights in developing countries during the 1990s', *OECD Economic Studies*, **40**, Paris.
Park, W.G. and D. Lippoldt (2007, forthcoming), 'Technology transfer and the economic implications of the strengthening of intellectual property rights in developing countries', Working Paper, Paris: OECD.
Park, W.G. and Smita Wagh (2002), 'Index of patent rights, 2000 update', Chapter 2, in James Gwartney and Robert Lawson (eds), *Economic Freedom of the World Annual Report 2002*, Vancouver, BC: Fraser Institute, pp. 33–42.
Reynolds, Taylor W. (2003), 'Quantifying the evolution of copyright and trademark law', American University, doctoral dissertation.
Rodrik, Dani, Arvind Subramanian and Francesco Trebbi (2002), 'Institutions rule: The primacy of institutions over geography and integration in economic development', CID Working Paper No. 97, Harvard University, October.
Smarzynska, B. (2002), 'Composition of foreign direct investment and protection of intellectual property rights: Evidence from transition economies', The World Bank, Working Paper Series No. 2786, http://econ.worldbank.org/files/12031_wps 2786.pdf, February.
Tufts (2003), 'Total cost to develop a new prescription drug, including cost of post-approval research, is $897 million', press release, Tufts Center for the Study of Drug Development, 13 May.

UNCTAD (2003), *World Investment Report. FDI Policies for Development: National and International Perspectives*, United Nations Conference on Trade and Development, New York: United Nations Publications.
UNCTAD (2005), *World Investment Report 2005: Transnational Corporations and the Internationalisation of R&D*, United Nations Conference on Trade and Development, New York and Geneva: United Nations Publications.
Warsh, David (2006), *Knowledge and the Wealth of Nations: A Story of Economic Discovery*, New York: W.W. Norton and Company.
WTO (2002), 'Trade and transfer of technology', WT/WGTTT/W/1, Geneva, 2 April.
WTO (2006), 'TRIPS and pharmaceutical patents', Fact Sheet, Geneva, September, as of 1 October, available at: http://www.wto.org/english/tratop_e/trips_e/factsheet_pharm00_e.htm.
Yang, Guifang and Keith E. Maskus (2001), 'Intellectual property rights and licensing: An econometric investigation', *Weltwirtschaftliches Archiv*, **137**, 58–79.

APPENDIX – DATA AND METHODS

Intellectual Property Rights Indices: Components

This section of the appendix summarizes the components of each IPR index employed in the present study. In calculating each index, the scores for the main elements are combined in an unweighted fashion. For measurement and scoring details see Park and Lippoldt (2005, Appendix).

Patent Rights Index: Ginarte and Park (1997), Park and Wagh (2002)

1. *Membership in international treaties* including: i) Paris Convention and Revisions; ii) Patent Cooperation Treaty; iii) Protection of New Varieties (UPOV).
2. *Product coverage*, in terms of patentability: i) pharmaceuticals; ii) chemicals; iii) food; iv) plant and animal varieties; v) surgical products; vi) micro-organisms; vii) utility models.
3. *Restrictions on patent rights* (positive, if these do not exist): i) 'working' requirements; ii) compulsory licensing; iii) revocation of patents
4. *Enforcement*: i) preliminary injunctions; ii) contributory infringement; iii) burden-of-proof reversal
5. *Duration of protection*: proportion of 'full duration' (i.e., 20 years from the date of application or 17 years from the date of grant for grant-based patent systems).

(NB, for Tables 13.3, 13.4 and 13.5, an expanded Patent Rights Index was used drawing on Park and Lippoldt (2007, forthcoming). The main differences include a longer time series (1990–2005), addition of the Budapest Treaty and TRIPS Agreement to the list of treaties covered by the Index and inclusion of software in the product coverage.)

Copyrights Index: Reynolds (2003)

1. *Coverage*: i) general (literary and artistic works); ii) performances; iii) sound recordings; iv) films; v) broadcasts; vi) *droit de suite* (shares in resale); vii) computer programs. Scoring: i)–v) based on availability measured as a proportion of 70-year duration; vi) share as percentage of max (top censored at 5%); vii) based on availability.
2. *Usage* – extent of private use: i) full use or no mention of private use; ii) private study or fair dealing; iii) use but with tax on devices or media; or iv) no private use allowed.
3. *Enforcement*, availability of: i) criminal sanctions; ii) preliminary injunctions; iii) seizure and destruction; iv) anti-circumvention provision.
4. *International treaties*, membership: i) Berne Convention 1886; ii) Universal Copyright Convention 1952; iii) Rome Convention 1961; iv) Geneva Convention 1971; v) Universal Copyright Convention 1971; vi) Brussels Convention 1974.

Trademark Rights Index: Reynolds (2003)

1. *Coverage*: i) service marks; ii) certification marks; iii) collective marks; iv) colors; v) shapes (3-dimensional, packaging, etc.); vi) well-known marks.

2. *Procedures*, availability: i) prohibition of marks in bona fide use; ii) licensing restrictions; iii) use or lose provisions in law; iv) international exhibition protection; v) criminal penalties; vi) local lawyer requirements; vii) marks can become generic; viii) transferability of mark without business; ix) priority goes to first to use a mark.
3. *International treaties*, membership: i) Paris Convention 1883; ii) Madrid Agreement 1891; iii) Nice Agreement 1957; iv) Lisbon Agreement 1958; v) Vienna Agreement 1973; vi) Trademark Law Treaty 1994.

Enforcement Effectiveness: Park and Lippoldt (2005) and derived from USTR National Trade Estimate: Report on Foreign Trade Barriers, various issues

This index is a qualitative measure of the effectiveness of IPR enforcement in practice. It is based on reports filed with the US Trade Representative documenting experience and perspectives in relation to enforcement in countries outside the US. The reports describe complaints (with all the limitations and biases such may contain), if any, about enforcement procedures and about the failure of the proper authorities to carry out the laws on the books. The failure to enforce may be due to some inability on the part of the authorities to carry out those laws or due to a conscious policy choice. The absence of substantive laws (other than enforcement provisions) is already incorporated in the previous indexes, and thus complaints about the lack of substantive laws are not incorporated here. The Enforcement effectiveness index is scored as follows: 0 if enforcement measures are not available or inadequate to deter abuse; ½ if enforcement measures are available but not effectively carried out (for example due to lag in policy implementation or resource barriers); 1 otherwise.

Respect for intellectual property rights – An alternative indicator

The alternative indicators for respect of IPR and adherence to appropriate IPR arrangements were drawn directly from the Institutional Profiles database, CEPII (2007), available at: http://www.cepii.fr/ProfilsInstitutionnelsDatabase.htm.

Data Sources

1. Import and FDI assessment (Tables 13.3, 13.4 and 13.5)

- Merchandise trade: WTO Statistics Database, Time-Series on Merchandise and Commercial Services Trade, http://www.wto.org/english/res_e/statis_e/statis_e.htm.
- Inward FDI stock: United Nations Conference on Trade and Development (UNCTAD), Foreign Direct Investment Database, http://stats.unctad.org/fdi.
- US Foreign Direct Investment Assets: US Department of Commerce, Bureau of Economic Analysis, Financial and Operating Data Interactive Tables, http://www.bea.gov/international/index.htm#omc.
- Control variables: IPR survey and Physical property rights, World Economic Forum, *Global Competitiveness Reports*; Legal effectiveness and Freedom to trade internationally, Economic Freedom Network, 2006 dataset; Real GDP per capita, World Bank, *World Development Indicators*, 2007; Doing Business and Governance, World Bank (on-line).

2. Licensing and related data

- Firm Level: Bureau of Economic Analysis, US Department of Commerce, International Investment Division, Cross Border Trade Database (BE-93 Survey), Annual Survey of Royalties, Licensing Fees, and Other Receipts and Payments for Intangible Rights between US and Unaffiliated Foreign Persons.
- Firm Level: Bureau of Economics Analysis, US Department of Commerce, International Investment Division, US Direct Investment Position and Related Balance of Payments Flows (BE-10 Survey).
- Licensing Transactions: Securities Data Corporation (SDC) Platinum Version 2.3: Joint Ventures and Strategic Alliances Database, Thomson Financial Inc. (by subscription).

3. Other variables in licensing analysis

- GDP per capita & GDP deflator (1995 = 100): World Bank Development Indicators 2001, CDROM.
- Tariff Rate: Gwartney and Lawson (2001).
- Corruption Perceptions Index: Transparency International (www.transparency.org).
- Country Risk: International Country Risk Guide (www.countrydata.com).

Discussion of the Regression Models

1) Park and Lippoldt (2007, forthcoming): Patent Rights, Imports and FDI (Tables 13.3, 13.4 and 13.5)
The regression analysis employed an equation of the following type, which was fitted to the data: $\ln y_{it} = \alpha + \beta \ln x_{it} + \gamma \ln z_{it} + u_i + \varepsilon_{it}$, where y is the variable to be explained (that is, imports or FDI), and x and z are the variables to explain y. In this case, x is an index of the strength of patent rights and z the control variables (for example Real GDP per capita, Physical property rights). Country-specific effects are represented by u. The error term is represented by ε. Subscripts i and t denote country and year. Additional technical explanations and a more detailed description of the data sources are provided in the Appendix of Park and Lippoldt (2007, forthcoming). The pooled regression was run using a Feasible generalized least squares method.

2) Park and Lippoldt (2005): Analysis of IPRs and Licensing at the Firm Level
The regression analysis employed by Park and Lippoldt (2005) employs a model, taking into account firm-specific and environmental factors:

$$\text{Log (Licensing}_{i,n,t}) = \alpha_0 + \alpha_1 \log (Z_{1i,t}) + \alpha_2 \log (Z_{2i,t}) + \alpha_3 \log (\text{IPR}_{n,t}) + \text{`Industry Dummies'} + \text{`Time Dummies'} + \text{Error}_{i,n,t}$$

where the subscript i denotes the firm, n denotes country, and t denotes time. IPR is the key variable of interest, representing the strength of intellectual property rights (characterized using indices for patent rights, copyrights, trademark rights and enforcement effectiveness). Z_1, Z_2 and the dummies are control variables. The selection of specific variables was based on insights from the literature, intuition and data availability. In operationalizing the various permutations of the model, the control variables Z were specified as firm-level covariates (market size and the R&D intensity) or key environmental factors (tariff levels, country risk and corruption). Dummy variables were included to control for industry group and macro effects (time period). The error term was included to pick up factors that have not been explicitly captured by the other variables.

By expressing the variables as logarithms, the regression yields coefficients indicating the 'elasticity' of response. For example, if the dependent variable is the log of 'licensing receipts' and the independent variable is the log of 'IPR', then the coefficients provide an estimate of the relationship such that a 1 per cent increase in 'IPR' is associated with a α_3 per cent increase in licensing fees, holding other factors constant.

14. A skeptic's view of intellectual property rights

Donald G. Richards*

INTRODUCTION

Over the past nearly decade and a half the question of intellectual property rights (IPRs) has risen to the forefront of academic and international economic policy debates. The issue was intimately connected to the negotiation in the early 1990s of the Uruguay Round of the General Agreement on Tariffs and Trade (GATT) that led to the establishment of this institution's successor organization, the World Trade Organization (WTO). IPRs were an acute bone of contention between the developed countries, led by the United States, and the less developed countries (LDCs) who were accused by the former of IP piracy. The LDCs themselves see cheap, or free, access to technology as a necessary means of catch-up with the industrialized, developed countries, and legal restraints on such appropriation as an obstacle to their economic growth and development aspirations.

The result of the bargaining process leading to the conclusion of the Uruguay Round of GATT/WTO negotiations was the inclusion in the accord of an ancillary agreement on Trade-Related Intellectual Property Rights (TRIPS). The TRIPS agreement represents a significant victory for the holders of patents, copyrights, trademarks and designs who mostly reside in the developed countries. It represents an equally serious setback for the producers and consumers of protected goods, services, and production processes, many of whom, of course, reside in poor countries that lack the technical and human capital capacity to develop suitable substitutes.

Naturally one can ask why the LDCs agreed to the inclusion of the TRIPS agreement in the design of the new multilateral institutional infrastructure. This is a complicated question, deserving more discussion than space allows in this chapter. But the short answer to the question is that the LDCs lacked the negotiating power to prevent the establishment of the TRIPs relative to the well-organized, developed country interests that insisted on the agreement. Had they not acceded to the agreement there was a strong possibility that the Uruguay Round would never have been completed.

Why was the Uruguay Round important to the poorer countries? It was important because it dangled in the faces of the poor countries the prospect of increased access to the rich countries' markets for their export goods, especially agricultural production and textiles. It also held out the more intractable threat of unilateral sanctions against countries that refused to comply with the IPR demands of the rich countries. The United States, for example, is well-armed with, and has shown a willingness to employ, domestic legislation designed to pressure trading partners who are not sufficiently respectful of the intellectual property rights claims of their influential domestic interests.

The cost to the LDCs of this Faustian bargain, however, has been increased pressure by the developed countries to get them to respect not only IPRs on such goods as entertainment products, such as music CDs and motion picture videos, but also life-saving drugs and therapies for diseases such as HIV/AIDS. While the LDCs have not passively accepted this outcome and work to interpret the TRIPS agreement in ways most conducive to meeting their needs for access to needed technologies and knowledge, so too have IPR holders in the developed countries pressed their lawyers and trade representatives to insist on an interpretation of the agreement in the interest of their profits. The actual developmental implications of the TRIPS for the poor countries will be determined in some measure by their relative ability to sway the global court of public opinion regarding the legitimacy of their claims for free, or reduced-cost, access to knowledge-based goods and services. Likewise, the case for strong enforcement of the provisions of the TRIPS will be conducted by IPR holders both in terms of 'natural rights' arguments as well as by the global welfare benefits associated with strong IPRs. Major testimony in this ideological struggle has been provided by, and will continue to be offered by, social scientists and, especially, economists. In what follows I provide my own objective, and not so objective, views of the debate.

A BASIC COMPLAINT WITH INTELLECTUAL PROPERTY RIGHTS

The central welfare-based claims to be made against intellectual property rights are that they are an inefficient method of providing incentive to innovation and they tend to reduce social welfare rather than expand it. How do they do this? First, by creating monopoly power over the innovations that they purport to create. This monopoly power enables the owners of knowledge and knowledge-based commodities to restrict outputs and raise prices to users. The result, familiar to most students of the economic effects of monopoly, is a loss of consumer surplus and a diminution of total social welfare. Normally considered, this impact of the exercise of monopoly power calls out for government intervention in the form of either antitrust legislation or regulatory control to rectify these adverse welfare outcomes. The irony of intellectual property rights in the form of patents and copyrights, however, is that they are precisely the *creation* of law, and thereby of the state.

A second source of social welfare loss associated with the creation of IPRs resides in the fact that by enclosing new knowledge and knowledge-based commodities behind the wall of legal protections, the holders of IPRs are able to restrict the spillover effects (externalities) associated with technological progress. This will have precisely the opposite effect to the one that motivates the creation of IPRs in the first place. The creation of new knowledge is more often than not an incremental and cumulative process. New discoveries build on the insights of past discoveries.[1] Patents and copyrights impede this cumulative process of discovery–learning–discovery and reduce the rate of technological progress generally. In the so-called Third World, where the lack of technological progress is often cited as a major constraint on the processes of economic development and growth, the harmonization of IPRs according to the standards of the First World seems especially irrational.

Another way to look at the problem is to say that knowledge has a public good aspect to it. Knowledge, in the language of economics, is non-rivalrous in use. The use of an idea by one person does not impede its use by another. It is also difficult, in some cases impossible, to guarantee exclusiveness of use where knowledge is concerned. Ideas are frequently very easy to transmit. It is this latter characteristic of knowledge that presumably requires IPRs to provide incentives for its production. If incentives take the form of monopoly protections, however, the non-rivalry characteristic of knowledge is rendered mute and its ability to drive economic growth and development is thereby diminished.

THE QUESTION OF INNOVATION AND INCENTIVE

We are driven then to ask the following question: don't innovators need profits to innovate? The impulse to create and to innovate is intrinsic to human beings. There can be no realistic presumption that the profit incentive is either necessary or sufficient for creation or innovation. There is too much evidence to the contrary to suggest that innovation would shrink to insignificance in the absence of monopoly profits. A great deal of innovation and discovery comes from scientists and other creative people who pursue new ideas for reasons having little or nothing at all to do with the prospect of large pecuniary payoffs.

Bill Gates is a useful example. Gates is universally recognized as the highly successful creator of Microsoft, the computer software that runs the operating systems of the bulk of the world's personal computers. At the same time he is widely considered the richest, or one of the richest individuals in the world with wealth in the $100 billion range. The relevant question is, did Gates's inventions depend on his anticipation of amassing such a large fortune, or would he have developed them in the absence of this wealth? I do not pretend to have any special insight into Gates's personality or personal history to provide a definitive answer to this question. It is well known, however, that the inventions that made Microsoft a household name were actually begun when he was a Harvard University undergraduate and preceded by many years Gates's rise to the top of the *Fortune 500*. It is also clear that it was his business acumen, as much as his creative genius as a software developer, that drove Microsoft to the top of the industry, but not before, it is alleged, he appropriated some ideas from others, including Steve Jobs at Apple Computer. One also suspects that Gates's standing as 'the richest man in the world' owes in part to his ability to ignore a substantial body of US antitrust law in his business dealings, as Microsoft has been the target of several antitrust prosecutions. None of this is to deny that Microsoft has taken full advantage of US patent law to protect its IP and advance its corporate mission. It is to suggest, however, that the billions earned by Microsoft and Gates's personal fortune are the coincidental manifestations of their success rather than their fundamental purpose.

Are there alternatives to monopoly profits that may serve as incentives to life-changing technological innovations? Certainly recognition has always been a powerful incentive. Even if we grant the argument that material incentives are an inducement to invention and new product development, it does not follow that long-term patents provide an optimal path to research and development (R&D). Firms may profit from 'first to market advantage' and quality reputation effects to provide an appropriate incentive. Boldrin and Levine (2006) present a theoretical model to show that first to market advantages are generally sufficient to provide socially optimal incentives for innovation. They argue on empirical grounds that there are few exceptions to their main finding and that social welfare would be best served by the elimination of patent-based monopolies.[2] Ultimately, from the prospective of capitalist production, the trick is to discover what the reservation price of R&D is, and to devise institutions that generate desired flows of discovery that maximize flows of welfare-improving knowledge and knowledge-based commodities. Patent rights may have a role to play in an efficient institutional set designed to promote technological advance and innovation. Shortening patent life to the amount of time required to provide innovators with a decided 'first to market' advantage would provide innovators with market incentive without granting them monopoly power from which to extract rents.

If the market itself is shown to be incapable of the task of developing social welfare-maximizing institutions, then we must recognize this as a case of market failure and look to public institutions and policies for answers. There are those who are agnostic about the ability of the state to deliver a steady stream of useful innovations, or at least an ability to perform this function as well as the free market. Pro-market proponents of private sector entrepreneurialism will point to the disproportionate flow of new commodities and production processes that emanate from the quintessential capitalist culture, the United States, as evidence in favor of this argument. It is easy to demonstrate, however, the important role the state has played and continues to play in fomenting both basic science and applied R&D in the US economy in the form of public and quasi-public institutions including the nation's universities. Offhand I can see no reason why the same scientists who work on behalf of the research departments of large corporations to turn out important innovations could not be as successful working in nationally supported public research labs. Moreover I suspect that this work would be far less costly without the need to employ armies of patent lawyers to complicate and slow down the innovative process. Significant cost savings would also be realized by the lack of any need to spend the billions of dollars in marketing campaigns.

THE BAYH–DOLE ACT

The recent trend towards the patenting of university research encouraged by the Bayh–Dole Act is, in my view, lamentable. While the law has been very successful in inspiring private sector 'spinoffs' of tax-supported research, it has also had the effect of changing the culture in American higher education, at least in those universities where the law has had significant application. The *Economist* magazine in 2005, for example, cites a report by the American Association for the Advancement of Science that 35 per cent of academic biotech researchers experienced difficulties getting hold of patented technologies that they needed to conduct their own research. Moreover, lawsuits between universities and between universities and their own researchers, over patents and royalties have proliferated. Even industry leaders themselves have complained about a 'gold-digger' mentality that has emerged among academic administrators seeking to strike it big with a patented finding or technology.

Industry, of course, would prefer a modified version of the Bayh–Dole legislation that somehow keeps university researchers in their labs producing new products and processes, in addition to their familiar function of basic research, and then transferring the marketable ideas to them for a 'reasonable' licensing fee. They object when these same researchers turn instead to their own or their universities' lawyers and act as capitalist enterprises themselves. They complain when universities attempt to 'game' the patent laws the same way they themselves do when they are in control of the patented technologies. These criticisms made by corporations of the distortions introduced into university behavior by the patent system are valid in my estimation. This is, however, a lot like the proverbial pot calling the kettle black.[3] A logical alternative to the corporate development model, or the university-as-corporation development model, is to establish a development function within non-profit institutions that can make use of research breakthroughs and which ensures that the corresponding risks and rewards are socialized.

An additional concern of the unintended outcomes of the Bayh–Dole Act involves its implications for the nature of university research in terms of the disinterested pursuit of the common good. Clearly to the extent that university research becomes increasingly proprietary, universities themselves will have an incentive to emphasize research that has demonstrable market value and to undervalue research, including basic research, that does not have such value. Inasmuch as it is often impossible to know *a priori* what might have market value in the future, this could well result in the loss of economically important knowledge. It also skews incentives away from knowledge that is of potential importance to groups lacking purchasing power and to knowledge that has a wholly or largely public aspect to it. One thinks about, for example, the development of a bird flu vaccine.

Finally, there seems to be a great danger to the character and content of knowledge production that occurs when the culture of patent prospecting becomes endemic to the university and to the culture, including the global culture, as a whole. Consider the recent reluctance on the part of the Indonesian government to allow the World Health Organization to have access to biological samples of recent bird flu victims in that country. These government officials were understandably concerned that providing free and unrestricted access to these samples would result in the development of a vaccine or other treatment for bird flu by a private pharma corporation which would then patent the treatment for sale at a price that victims of the disease in the poor countries would find prohibitive. The stand-off ended only after the World Health Organization (WHO) promised the Indonesian health minister not to send the specimens to the corporations without the permission of the Indonesian government (AsiaNews.it, 2007).

THE TRIPS AGREEMENT

The agreement on Trade Related Intellectual Property Rights (TRIPS) was negotiated in the 1990s as an ancillary and precursor agreement to the Uruguay Round of the GATT/WTO. As noted above, it was in fact negotiated as a condition for US participation in the Uruguay Round without which the broader trade agreement would never have been struck.

The essence of the TRIPS agreement was to establish a global, harmonized system of minimum IPRs to which all signatory nations would be bound modeled on the standards of the US system of IPR law. Among the specific provisions of the TRIPS are minimum periods of patent protection of 20 years and periods of copyright protection that extend to a minimum of 50 years. Copyright protection is extended to sound and video recordings as well as to computer software and compilations of data that represent a reasonable degree of intellectual creativity. Industrial design and trademarks are also given minimum levels of protection.

All signatory nations were expected to abide by bringing their national law into conformity with the provisions of the agreement and constructing the administrative infrastructure for their enforcement. Especially poor nations were given a grace period of five years' exemption to accomplish these tasks following the enactment of the agreement. International oversight, including adjudication and settlement of disputes, was made the responsibility of the Disputes Settlements Procedures of the WTO. Countries found in violation would be subject to the normal sanctions that apply to other trade-related disputes. An important point that applies to IPR disputes is that the burden of proof in disputes falls on the alleged violator rather than the claimant.

TRIPS and the Welfare of Poor Countries

Proponents of the TRIPS agreement typically argue that a stronger and more harmonious international IPR regime is likely to benefit LDCs via a number of avenues.

First they note the correlation between national IPR standards and the domestic production of R&D. The obvious argument is that stronger IPR protection provides greater incentive to R&D and greater domestic technological dynamism. Countries that aspire to the technological frontier must then start by providing a legal environment that is propitious to R&D, and this means strong IPRs. Second, it is argued that a strong IPR regime will help to promote international technology diffusion via international trade and direct foreign investment. The lack of IPRs, it is argued, inhibits trade in knowledge-based products and foreign direct investment (FDI) because exporters and investors cannot capture the benefits of their innovations in legal environments that do not provide protections against piracy.

What these rather standard arguments overlook, however, is that the true causal relationship between IPRs and such performance variables as R&D capacity, trade and investment may actually run in the reverse direction. One can reasonably argue from theory and history that countries become interested in strong IPR regimes only *after* they have established a strong indigenous R&D capacity. The prior establishment of this capacity occurs as a result of the more or less free ability to appropriate or imitate existing inventions and knowledge. Constraints on the ability of poorer nations to appropriate and imitate will have the effect of delaying the day when they are able to join the world's club of innovators. History demonstrates the truth of the sequence of imitation followed by innovation followed by the institutionalization of IPRs for virtually every currently industrialized nation in the world with the possible exception of Great Britain – the first industrialized power. To suggest that today's non-industrialized nations follow a different path speaks more of the opportunism of the currently developed nations than it does of the science of development.

What do economists have to say about the likely welfare consequences of stronger IPRs? The simple answer to this question is that technology-importing countries are likely to benefit from stronger IPR regimes only under some fairly strong assumptions and circumstances. One of these assumptions is that the dominate share of the market for new knowledge-intensive goods exists within the poor countries themselves (Deardorff, 1992). But consider how innovation and product diffusion actually work. Under present circumstances, new goods are typically developed in the richer countries in response to local profit opportunities. After they have demonstrated a local potential for profit they are then exported to the markets of other similarly development countries and then only subsequently to the markets of poorer countries. That is, the incentive for innovation and product development is well-established prior to a consideration of market opportunities in the poorer countries of the world. A strengthening and harmonization of global IPRs will perhaps improve the profits of the transnational corporations (TNCs) that are the important agents of international investment, but this is unlikely to improve the indigenous innovation capacity of the poor countries. In addition, given this historical pattern of innovation and diffusion it is unlikely that the *kinds of innovations* that should have the greatest impact on Third World welfare will be developed. (There are three or more multibillion dollar efforts to develop treatments for erectile dysfunction, but no effective treatments for malaria!)

Second, the TRIPS agreement strengthens restrictions on the ability of nations to compel either compulsory licensing, local working of patents, or local production of patent-related production. These provisions of the agreement will tend to decrease the potential for technology spillovers that could potentially be a source of welfare improvement for the poorer countries.[4]

Third, an economic study by Subramanian (1991) of the welfare implications of discriminatory IPRs that grant greater rights to local innovators over foreign innovators finds that such a regime is welfare-superior to a regime that harmonizes IPRs. The TRIPS agreement, however, provides most favored nation (MFN) treatment in the area of IP protection and hence denies this potential source of welfare improvement for the poorer nations. Also, as noted by another economic study (Helpman, 1993), the MFN provision of the TRIPS agreement will have the effect of improving the comparative advantage in knowledge-based production in the nations where it currently exists and weakening it in countries where it does not. That is, the TRIPS agreement fails to recognize the applicability of the infant industry argument as it might apply to knowledge-based production and industries.

Fourth, while Subramanian argues that a stronger IPR regime is more likely to improve welfare in poor countries if it inspires innovation rather than imitation, the TRIPs agreement has been motivated precisely in order to provide protection to industries whose outputs are easy to imitate. Intellectual property is often characterized as involving commodities with high fixed costs of production, but minimal marginal costs of production. It is precisely the ease of imitation that drove the push for a stronger global IPR regime. It is to be expected then that this strengthening will result in transforming the welfare gains associated with imitation into producer rents.

EMPIRICAL EVIDENCE

The challenge to doing meaningful empirical work on the effects of IPRs and economic performance that is relevant to the less developed countries is coming up with measures that accurately assess the strength of these rights in the poorer countries. Early studies of

IPRs typically noted the degree to which nations had endorsed the standard international conventions on IPRs without investigating the degree to which these had been made effective by the enactment of national legislation or the extent of its enforcement. There were attempts made in the 1990s to come up with more sophisticated measures. The first was made by Rapp and Rozek (RR) (1990) who developed an index based on national legislation with respect to IP law along with the exclusions allowed for by that law. A second attempt was made by Ginarte and Park (GP) in 1997 that sought to improve on the Rapp and Rozek measure by examining in greater detail the patent law of individual countries to consider the duration of protection, extent of coverage, provisions for loss of protection, memberships in international agreements, and existence of enforcement measures. It also made an attempt to assess the strength of IP protection law by considering such matters as the availability of preliminary injunctions, reversibility of burden of proof, and contributory infringement actions. In neither the RR nor the GP indexes is there an attempt to gauge the effectiveness of enforcement. There is a clear strong direct correlation between each of these indexes and the level of per capita income of a nation and one or the other of them has been used in a number of recent empirical studies of the impact of the strength of IPRs and economic performance.

IPRs and Trade

Maskus and Penubarti (1995) ask the question, do differential patent laws influence international trade flows? Before they investigate this particular question they note an important theoretical ambiguity which they describe as the 'market expansion' effect of strong IPRs versus the 'market power' effect of strong IPRs. The first of these occurs when stronger IPRs reduce the cost of exports of knowledge-intensive goods and services. The second occurs when stronger IPRs provide firms with greater monopoly power which they exercise to restrict supply and raise prices, thus discouraging exports to poorer countries.

Maskus and Penubarti specify an estimable version of the Helpman-Krugman (1985) trade model that expresses bilateral gross imports as a function of a variety of variables including size of market in the importing country, the importer's per capita income, production of the exporting country, and measures of trade resistance, for example tariff rates. The authors also include the RR index of patent strength. The country data includes a set of OECD exporters and a set of 77 developed and less developed country importers. The model is estimated for a pooled data set for 29 categories of manufactured goods as well as separately for the individual 29 industries. The data set is also disaggregated into patent-sensitive industries and patent-insensitive industries. For the largest, pooled data set, Markus and Penubarti's regression results show a positive relationship between patent strength and imports. When the data set is disaggregated by industry, however, no such significant relationship between these variables is found for patent-sensitive industries, although in a few cases involving patent-insensitive industries, statistical significance is indicated. These findings suggest then that for patent-sensitive industries, the market power effect dominates the market expansion effect and vice versa for patent-insensitive industries. One is tempted to conclude from these findings that if the goal of the TRIPS is to promote trade, then the agreement ought to be extended only to patent-insensitive industries. The paradox, of course, is that the TRIPS was promoted at the behest of patent-sensitive industries such as the pharma industry.

A more recent empirical study of the trade consequences of the TRIPS was conducted by Smith (1999) who asks 'Are weak patent rights a barrier to US exports?' In this model US state level data are employed in a gravity trade model of export performance. The independent, explanatory variables include per capita income of exporters (states) and importers (countries), the populations of the exporters and importers, the distance between them, and tariff rates. This framework is augmented by the inclusion of patent right/dummy variable interaction terms. Two dummy variables are used in alternative specifications of the basic model. The first relates to level of development while the second relates to the threat of imitation. Both the RR and GP indexes of IPRs are employed in the analysis though Smith only reports the results using RR.

Smith's results show that patent strength matters for US exports for only one of the four levels of development groups she identifies (the lower middle income group). This group covers about 30 per cent of the sample of 96 countries. The patent right/development group interaction terms turn out to be negative in all other cases where statistical significance is indicated. Thus, for most of these groups the market power effect seems to dominate the market expansion effect, or neither effect dominates the other.

When the 'level of development term' is replaced by 'threat of imitation' in the interaction term the sample of countries is divided into four groups according to their ability to imitate. The regression results show that the market power effect dominates the market expansion effect in the case of the weakest threat to imitate while the effects are reversed in the case of the strongest threat to imitate group. (Threat to imitate here is measured in terms of a nation's R&D capabilities and its educational attainment.) For the intermediate threat to imitate groups the results are ambiguous in sign and lack statistical significance.[5]

Smith also estimates the effect of stronger patent rights on the volume of US exports and finds that this volume is likely to increase in the case of countries with strong imitative abilities but currently weak rights, and to decrease in the case of countries with weak imitative abilities and weak rights. Again, none of this is surprising. What is rather remarkable is her estimate that the combined effects of market power and market expansion that result from raising IPR standards to the level envisioned by the TRIPS agreement is likely to reduce US exports by anywhere from 2.6 to 5.4 per cent in the most patent-sensitive industries over the next ten years.

Foreign Direct Investment

On the matter of IPRs and foreign direct investment (FDI) the theory and evidence also paints a very ambiguous picture of the likely impacts of the TRIPS agreement. The most frequently cited study was published by Lee and Mansfield in 1996. This empirical paper surveyed a random sample of 100 major US companies regarding their views on the quality of IPR protections provided in 14 less developed countries. The respondents were mostly top executives and corporate patent attorneys who were asked about their willingness to transfer their latest technologies to subsidiaries operating in these countries. These responses were then developed into an index of IP weakness. The index was then used to determine the willingness to invest in these countries. The authors found a direct relationship between IP weakness and FDI on the basis of their data.

My own research (Richards, 2004) tells a different story, however. Increasing the sample size but otherwise employing the same set of countries used in the Lee and Mansfield study, replacing the authors' subjective measure of IP weakness with a more objective measure of IPRs (Ginarte and Park, 1997), and re-specifying their model to include an explanatory variable that captures the quality of a nation's infrastructure (a variable found to be an important determinant of FDI by Wheeler and Mody, 1992), provides empirical evidence that US FDI is more likely in countries that have *weaker* IPR regimes. A possible theoretical explanation for this empirical finding is that foreign firms are more likely to invest in (as opposed to merely export to) nations with weaker IPR treatment precisely in order to maintain arm's-length control over their innovations.

There are to be sure other studies that paint a more optimistic picture of the potential for the TRIPS agreement to improve welfare in the global economy, including the poorer countries. My own reading of the weight of the evidence is that technological progress and development in the Third World are *not* aided, but I admit the evidence is ambiguous. Notwithstanding this ambiguity, the TRIPS agreement is now a part of the global international system and this fact requires some explanation. The correct explanation in my view involves the exercise of power politics that dominate notions of ethical conduct and fair play. This fact raises important questions about why we are concerned about ethical conduct for businesses but we are content to allow our national policy makers to pursue global policies as if equity and fair play are quaint irrelevancies.

IPRS AND FIRST WORLD HYPOCRISY

The insistence on a harmonized global system of intellectual property rights is fraught with hypocrisy. History is clear in showing that the currently developed countries were not shy about appropriating inventions and innovations from other parts of the world without respecting the patents and copyrights of foreign innovators. While the United States Constitution institutionalized protection for intellectual property for its citizens in the late eighteenth century, these protections were not extended to foreigners until much later. In the interim, US industrialists were free to appropriate foreign inventions as part of a process of technological transfer that enabled the nation to climb to the summit of global industrial power a little more than two centuries later. The ability to imitate as a necessary pre-condition to innovate is likewise easy to identify in the economic histories of the European countries, Japan, and the East Asian NICs as well.

Also, the fact of the existence of the TRIPS agreement does not debar countries from using other means to achieve its commercial ends via bilateral measures. The United States in particular has shown a willingness to use bilateral pressure in the form of 301 and Special 301 trade legislation to pressure countries into respecting IPRs in cases where the TRIPS agreement is not sufficiently favorable to US industry, or where it feels that less developed trading country partners have not been sufficiently forthcoming with national legislation to make TRIPS effective, or in the case where less developed countries have attempted to invoke the agreement's compulsory licenses and exceptions clauses.

The issue of exception clauses is particularly telling. Article 27 of the TRIPS agreement allows governments to exclude a pharmaceutical patent from protection in the circumstance where the interests of public health or the environment are at stake. Article 31 provides that countries can compel licensing of a protected technology under certain conditions such as a national health emergency. Each of these 'escape clauses' from the requirements of the TRIPS is qualified, however. Article 30 that permits countries an exception to the exclusive right to a patented technology or product also requires that the exception should not *unreasonably* conflict with a normal exploitation of the patent and not *unreasonably* prejudice the legitimate interests of the patent holder. Article 31 includes the condition that the patent holder receive appropriate compensation for the patent before a compulsory license is granted and that this compensation take into consideration the economic value of the license and be subject to judicial review. Moreover, a compulsory license may only be granted after an effort is made to negotiate an authorization agreement with the patent holder on *reasonable* commercial terms.

It is clear from this language that these conditions are subject to wide interpretation and that outcomes to disputes over their application will depend heavily on the amount and skill of countries' respective legal and negotiating abilities. These kinds of abilities are in short supply in poor countries who also, as already mentioned, face additional bilateral pressures to conform to the goals and expectations of developed country negotiators.

A well-known case where this negotiating conflict came into play, a conflict that I prefer to characterize as an exercise in a struggle for hegemonic control, concerned the rights to compel licensing, or allow parallel imports, of the anti-viral drug technology to combat HIV/AIDS. Brazil insisted on its rights to this technology in its relatively successful campaign against the disease. The drug manufacturers insisted that Brazil respect its IPRs in the treatments. An important breakthrough in the impasse occurred in late 2001 at a ministerial meeting of the WTO held in Doha, Qatar where an agreement was reached to permit LDCs to import generic versions of patented drugs to treat HIV/AIDS and other public health crises. The United States Trade Representative (USTR) and US pharmaceutical companies waged a campaign against the agreement citing the detrimental impact on the incentive to engage in R&D leading to the development of new treatments, but were unable to overcome an intense effort by a large number of governmental and non-governmental organizations to secure it.

A telling moment in the battle over the Doha Agreement came in the immediate aftermath of the attacks on the World Trade Center in September 2001 when there was an increased concern about the possibilities of bioterrorism involving anthrax. In reaction to this fear US Secretary of Health Tommy Thompson declared his readiness to appropriate the patent on Cipro, an antibiotic to fight anthrax owned by Bayer AG, unless the German-based company agreed to lower its price. This obviously undermined the ability of United States Trade Representative head Robert Zoellick's ability to resist similar arguments involving health security pressed by the nations afflicted with the AIDS crisis.

While the Doha Agreement was a significant victory for the LDCs seeking low-cost treatments for AIDS, it must be recognized as an incomplete victory inasmuch as it does not change the status of IPRs as embodied in the TRIPS agreement and many Big Pharma representatives regard it mostly as a political declaration rather than a legal challenge to the WTO rules. Industry analyst Hemant K. Shaw was quoted in the press as saying, 'It's a public relations black eye, but it has no consequences whatsoever to the bottom line.' Pfizer CEO Henry McKinnell echoed that sentiment saying that the agreement 'will have zero effect on company profits'. These comments undoubtedly contain more than a small grain of industry spin designed to soothe the nerves of investors, but they also contain an element of truth.

Maybe they reveal several truths. The first is that lost sales to Brazil and Africa and other poor countries where AIDS has reached the crisis stage are not going to imperil the profits of the big drug producers in any serious way. The drugs were developed in response to markets in rich countries where the companies can continue to price them at levels that will ensure robust profits. This observation, however, tends to undermine the incentive-related argument for the TRIPS agreement. If the poor countries are really as marginal to the profit picture of IPR holders as these comments make them appear to be, then why should we believe that the TRIPS is important to their welfare? A second truth is that, the Doha Agreement notwithstanding, Big Pharma and other IPR holders will continue to assert their legal rights under the TRIPS agreement and will continue to leverage the power of their ties to official trade negotiators to win compliance with its provisions.

From the perspective of the LDCs the important question becomes, how might they arrange alternative institutional means for stimulating the R&D necessary for providing themselves with the lifesaving drugs and treatments? The problem of providing poor people in poor nations with expensive drug therapies is a difficult one that I do not believe is answerable by market solutions. Some have advocated that public–private partnerships are a way to combine the financial resources and technical-scientific capacities necessary to develop the needed treatments and therapies. An example that has received a great deal of press attention in recent years has been the Gates Foundation support for the effort to develop a vaccine to prevent malaria. The Gates Foundation announced in late 2005 its contribution of $258.3 million to be spent over five years on malaria research. This $258.3 million figure represents paradoxically both a lot of money and not really that much. It is a substantial portion of the annual $375 million that is spent on malaria research worldwide. It is a fraction (about a quarter) of the $1.5 billion spent in the wealthy countries on Viagra. Also, the bulk of the Gates donation was allocated to a major pharma transnational corporation, GlaxoSmithKline PLC, a company that sees its work in this area as a public relations effort more than a part of its real business.

Even if the Gates partnership with GlaxoSmithKline PLC does result in an affordable vaccine for malaria, for poor countries the fundamental problem is how to develop an independent capacity to develop R&D for health challenges that does not depend on the largesse of corporate donors. The WHO would seem potentially to have an important role to play in this effort. The WHO would need to realize a substantial infusion of resources, however, in order to carry out the research to develop treatments for tropical area diseases. The main advantage of the WHO, however, is that it would execute its research and development program in the global public interest and would require neither patent protection for its discoveries nor the rents derived from these protections.

A third area of noticeable hypocrisy is the way that First World interests have framed the question of IPRs in their relationships with the less developed countries of the world. This concerns the well-known fact that much of the raw materials, including germ-plasm, out of which new patentable commodities, including genetically modified organisms, are developed, are derived from the biologically diverse areas of the world, which are precisely the poor tropical and sub-tropical nations. First World innovators argue that this germplasm ought to be properly thought of as the 'common heritage of mankind' and they should have access to it in the interests of developing new commodities that will benefit the world's consumers. The Third World nations themselves, and particular sub-communities within these nations, often including communities of indigenous peoples, argue that they are the owners and caretakers of these biological resources, and that they reserve the right to their control and commercialization. That is, they have taken a page from the book of western capitalism and insisted on IPRs in these materials.

This conflict came to a head in the early 1990s when the claims of the TRIPS agreement confronted an opposing vision represented by the United Nations Convention on Biological Diversity (CBD). The TRIPS obligates its signatory nations to provide either patent protection or a *sui generis* system of law for plant breeders' rights as well as patent protection for microbiological and non-biological processes for plant and animal production. Working in conjunction with the Food and Agricultural Organization, the UN's CBD, on the other hand, seeks a global action plan to conserve and preserve plant genetic resources by providing local producers, especially those in Third World countries, with resources necessary to 'strengthen local capacity to produce, distribute and market farm-saved seed of crop varieties essential for food security, to help diversity and agricultural production systems through the increased use and commercialization of local and under-utilized crops' (FAO, 1993). Financing for this plan was to come from the signatory nations, particularly the developed countries. By the end of 1992, 156 nations had signed and ratified the CBD, with the United States being the most conspicuous exception.[6]

Finally, a fourth area of noticeable hypocrisy involves the singularly slippery concept of 'common heritage of mankind'. In June 2000, scientists working on the publicly funded Human Genome Project (HGP) announced the completion of a map of the human genome – a first approximation at our understanding of the complete listing of the genes in a typical human being. This important accomplishment of basic scientific research has important implications for health-related science and applications. Future study should reveal the functions of particular genes and gene sequences, thereby enabling scientists to develop diagnostic tests and new drugs and therapies to combat an array of diseases and genetically-based conditions.

Where there is the potential for tremendous breakthroughs in biomedical science and practice, there are, of course, also opportunities to reap equally tremendous profits and rents. In fact biotech companies have been taking out patents on genes and gene fragments and sequences for years prior to the HGP's completion of its 'Book of Life'. Human Genome Sciences of Rockville, Maryland, to take one example, already has patents on 103 human genes and has filings in process for another 7500. Celera Genomics, another Rockville-based corporation, has filed patent claims on 6400 gene sequences (Regalado, 2000). In some cases the patented genes can be linked to specific diseases such as arthritis or osteoporosis. In most cases, however, the patent holder has no such knowledge and has taken out patent rights in the hopes of identifying an important gene or sequence that will yield an important finding that will translate into an important drug, treatment or therapy. That is, biotech companies are literally *bio-prospecting* in anticipation of a profitable discovery.

Aside from the considerable legal and ethical issues surrounding private property rights in human life forms, or at least knowledge of human life forms, the privatization of the human genome raises troubling questions about the ability of researchers and medical care practitioners to conduct their work. The requirement to pay royalties and licensing fees to the holders of patented genetic information raises the costs of future research, diagnoses and treatments. The American Medical Association has recently become concerned enough that it is considering a moratorium on human gene patents reversing its previous support of the practice (Regalado, 2000, p. 53.) Even Big Pharma has objected to the trend towards gene patenting, arguing that it raises the cost of developing new drugs and therapies and that gene identification, along with their functions, is a matter of basic scientific discovery and for that reason does not fall under the category of patentable invention. Rather such discovery falls more appropriately under the 'common heritage of mankind' designation. It is obvious this characterization is appealing, depending on which side of the IPR enclosure one stands.

CONCLUSIONS

A convincing welfare case for a system of global harmonized intellectual property rights has not been made. And yet such a system now exists in the form of the TRIPS agreement. Answers to this inconsistency are to be found at the level of critical international relations and international political economy theory.[7] My own view of the matter (Richards, 2004) is that the TRIPS agreement is part of an emerging global regulatory – in fact, a global capitalist state. The fundamental purpose of this state system is to aid in the process of capital accumulation on a global scale. The primary agents responsible for the system's construction and articulation are the world's powerful TNCs. The usual conception of TNC power emphasizes their ability to bypass the regulatory control of the nation state and to maintain sovereignty unto themselves. This conception is a half truth. It is also true that transnational monopoly capitalism relies on state power to provide the institutional stability for its successful functioning. The defense of property rights, for example, is an essential task of state power, both at the national and international levels. The creation of the TRIPS within the established mechanism of the GATT/WTO renders this essential task operational and effective as it applies to IP.

Notwithstanding the fact of the TRIPS agreement, intellectual property remains contested ideological and political terrain. International organizations such as the World Health Organization and the Food and Agricultural Organization offer the potential as sites of resistance to the hegemony of transnational corporations and as sources of technical expertise. Third World leverage within the United Nations can work to advance agreements in the interests of more open sharing of information (United Nations University, 2006.) Non-governmental organizations also have an important role to play as advocates for the development of technologies that substitute for patent-protected commodities and processes. Especially important is for these organizations to support alternative technologies without buying into the established global rules to seek IP protection on their own innovations via patent protection.[8]

Finally, it should not be thought that the issue of IPRs is of concern only to residents of poor, developing countries. Consumers and workers in rich countries, including the United States, suffer from the same distortions introduced by monopoly control over price and quantity of patented goods and services. Technological progress is similarly delayed in rich countries when patents operate to block research and raise the cost of information and new knowledge. An important case involves the high cost of prescription drugs for US consumers as compared to their counterparts in Canada and Europe where generic versions of the same treatments are available at substantial savings. A number of US governors have reacted to the pressure that high drug costs impose on their budgets by permitting their states to import the lower-cost substitutes.[9]

NOTES

1. This is, of course, the key insight of Romer (1990) where limitless growth depends on the generation of externalities in knowledge. To the extent that spillovers are prevented by IPRs, these possibilities for endogenous growth are greatly reduced and the poor countries are consigned to a low-level steady state.
2. Clement (2003) discusses the economics profession's strong reaction for and against the claims staked out by Boldrin and Levine's arguments.
3. For a useful discussion of how corporations themselves manipulate the patent system to their clients' advantage, see Jaffe and Lerner (2004).
4. The problem of compulsory licensing is taken up in more detail below in the section on 'IPRs and first world hypocrisy'.
5. It is notable that only four countries belong to each of the two groups that Smith identifies as (positive) trade susceptible to increased patent strength. These are Bolivia, Romania, Tonga and Turkey, and constitute only 5.5 per cent of her sample.
6. The agreement was signed by the US in 1993 when the Clinton Administration took over, but it has not yet been ratified.
7. Useful, albeit partial, analyses are found in the works of Sell (1998), Matthews (2002), and May (2000).
8. An illustrative case involves the efforts of Indian NGOs ActionAid, Gene Campaign India and Consumers International to prevent the government of India from signing an agreement to commit the country to membership in the Union for the Protection of New Plant Varieties (UPOV). UPOV is an international organization dedicated to protecting property rights in new varieties of plants. According to the NGOs, UPOV membership will reduce or eliminate small farmers' rights to conserve, use, exchange or sell their seeds and may endanger small-scale agriculture overall (Capdevila, 2002). The benefits of membership are limited to the marketing of new varieties in other countries that are also UPOV members. These are primarily the rich countries and exclude other less developed countries that are important to India's agriculture.
9. A 2005 *New York Times* report (Ruethling, 2005) quotes Illinois governor Rod R. Blagojevich as noting that the I-SaveRx program begun in his state in 2004 has resulted in 10000 orders being placed in offshore markets on 78 common prescription drugs, with an average savings of 25 to 50 per cent.

REFERENCES

Anonymous (2005), 'Science and technology: Bayhing for blood or Doling out cash? Intellectual Property', *The Economist* 377, no. 8458, 24 December, p. 115.

AsiaNews.it. (2007), 'Bird flu: Indonesia will give WHO samples only if vaccines are cheap', **16**(14), 27 March, on-line: http://www.asianews.it/view4print.php?l=en&art=8843.

Boldrin, Michele and David K. Levine (2006), 'Globalization, intellectual property, and economic prosperity', *Spanish Economic Review*, **8**, 23–34.

Capdevila, Gustavo (2002), 'Agriculture: Seed patent regime detrimental to poor farmers', *Global Information Network*, 22 October, New York.

Clement, Douglas (2003), 'Creation myths', *Reason*, **34**(10), March, 30–38.

Deardorff, Alan (1992), 'Welfare effects of global patent protection', *Economica*, **59**(233), February, 35–51.

FAO (1993), 'The global plan of action for the conservation and sustainable utilization of plant genetic resources for food and agriculture', The Fourth International Technical Conference on Plant Genetic Resources, Leipzig, Germany, 17–23 June, http://www.fao.org/FOCUS/E/96/06/more/glopla-e.htm.

Ginarte, Juan Carlos and Walter G. Park (1997), 'Determinants of patent rights: A cross-national study', *Research Policy*, **26**, May, 283–301.

Helpman, Elhanan (1993), 'Innovation, imitation, and intellectual property rights', *Econometrica*, **61**(6), November, 1247–80.

Helpman, Elhanan and Paul Krugman (1985), *Market Structure and Foreign Trade*, Cambridge, MA: MIT Press.
Jaffe, Adam B. and Josh Lerner (2004), *Innovation and its Discontents: How our Broken Patent System is Endangering Innovation and Progress, and what to do about it*, Princeton: Princeton University Press.
Lee, Jeong-Yeon and Edwin Mansfield (1996), 'Intellectual property protection and US foreign direct investment', *Review of Economics and Statistics*, **78**(2) May, 181–6.
Maskus, Keith E. and Mohan Penubarti (1995), 'How trade-related are intellectual property rights?', *Journal of International Economics*, **39**(3–4), November, 227–48.
Matthews, Duncan (2002), *Globalising Intellectual Property Rights: The TRIPS Agreement*, London: Routledge.
May, Christopher (2000), *A Global Political Economy of Intellectual Property Rights: The New Enclosures?*, London: Routledge/RIPE studies in the global political economy.
Rapp, Richard T. and Richard P. Rozek (1990), 'Benefits and costs of intellectual property protection in developing countries', *Journal of World Trade*, **24**(5), October, 75–102.
Regalado, Antonio (2000), 'The great gene grab', *Technology Review*, **103**(5), September/October, 48–55.
Richards, Donald G. (2004), *Intellectual Property Rights and Global Capitalism: The Political Economy of the TRIPS Agreement*, New York: M.E. Sharpe.
Romer, Paul (1990), 'Endogenous technological change', *The Journal of Political Economy*, **98**(5), part 2(October), S71–S102.
Ruethling, Gretchen (2005), '5 drug-importing states add 2 countries as sources', *New York Times*, Section A, 19 July, p. 17.
Sell, Susan (1998), *Power and Ideas: North–South Politics of Intellectual Property and Antitrust*, Albany: State University of New York Press.
Smith, Pamela J. (1999), 'Are weak intellectual property rights a barrier to US exports?', *Journal of International Economics*, **48**(1), June, 151–77.
Subramanian, Arvind (1991), 'The international economics of intellectual property protection: A welfare-theoretic trade policy analysis', *World Development*, **19**(8), August, 945–56.
United Nations University (2006), 'Challenging intellectual property: Access to knowledge issues in open source and medicine', Research Symposium held at United Nations Headquarters, New York, April 13, www.merit.unu.edu/seminars/20040413_abstracts/report.php.
Wheeler, David and Ashoka Mody (1992), 'International investment location decisions', *Journal of International Economics*, **33**(1/2), August, 57–76.

Index